A Scholar's Path
晴山古道

An Anthology of
Classical Chinese Poems and Prose of
Chen Qing Shan

A Pioneer Writer of Malayan-Singapore Chinese Literature

A Scholar's Path
晴山古道

An Anthology of Classical Chinese Poems and Prose of
Chen Qing Shan

A Pioneer Writer of Malayan-Singapore Chinese Literature

English Translation and Appreciation by **Peter Chen** & **Michael Tan**
Reviewed by **Chan Chiu Ming**

NEW JERSEY · LONDON · SINGAPORE · BEIJING · SHANGHAI · HONG KONG · TAIPEI · CHENNAI

Published by

World Scientific Publishing Co. Pte. Ltd.
5 Toh Tuck Link, Singapore 596224
USA office: 27 Warren Street, Suite 401-402, Hackensack, NJ 07601
UK office: 57 Shelton Street, Covent Garden, London WC2H 9HE

British Library Cataloguing-in-Publication Data
A catalogue record for this book is available from the British Library.

A SCHOLAR'S PATH
An Anthology of Classical Chinese Poems and Prose of Chen Qing Shan
A Pioneer Writer of Malayan-Singapore Literature

Copyright © 2010 by World Scientific Publishing Co. Pte. Ltd.

All rights reserved. This book, or parts thereof, may not be reproduced in any form or by any means, electronic or mechanical, including photocopying, recording or any information storage and retrieval system now known or to be invented, without written permission from the Publisher.

For photocopying of material in this volume, please pay a copying fee through the Copyright Clearance Center, Inc., 222 Rosewood Drive, Danvers, MA 01923, USA. In this case permission to photocopy is not required from the publisher.

ISBN-13 978-981-4317-48-1 (pbk)
ISBN-10 981-4317-48-9 (pbk)

The front cover shows a bronze ding from the late Shang early Zhou Dynasty. Image courtesy of The National Palace Museum, Taiwan, Republic of China (國立故宮博物院).

Typeset by World Scientific Publishing Co. Pte. Ltd.

Printed by

Dedicated
to

Our Parents for their love and care
for the family

Father whose passion for poetry has enriched
our literary appreciation of fine poetry

Mother for her diligence and persistence
in collecting and preserving the poems

~~~~~~~~~~~~~~~~~~~~~~~

The Completion of this Book
marks

The fulfillment of Father's wish that his poems
are kept for his descendants as a family treasure

Contents

xiii ⊙ Preface I   **President S R Nathan**
                           Republic of Singapore

xv ⊙ Preface II   **Dr Ng Eng Hen**
                           Minister for Education and Second Minister for Defence
                           Republic of Singapore

xvii ⊙ Preface III   **Professor Wang Gungwu**
                           Chairman of the East Asian Institute,
                           National University of Singapore

xxi ⊙ Foreword   **Peter Chen • Michael Tan**

xxvii ⊙ Biography of Chen Qing Shan

xxxiii ⊙ Brief biographies of Editor Translators • Reviewer

Section 1 Familial Love 和鸣舐犊

3 ⊙ 1   The Messenger of Love 青鸟二首

9 ⊙ 2   Mid-Autumn Moon 中秋月

15 ⊙ 3   Mid-Autumn Song 中秋咏月有寄

19 ⊙ 4   Letter from Home 瑶缄二首

25 ⊙ 5   Listening to the Sermon 听经

33 ⊙ 6   Chanting the Scripture Random Thoughts 经堂

41 ⊙ 7 Returning Home 还家

49 ⊙ 8 A Solemn Vow 信誓

55 ⊙ 9 A Mooncake Poem for My Wife 中秋咏月饼寄内

69 ⊙ 10 Admonition to My Daughter Xuan 示璇女

75 ⊙ 11 Wedding Poem An Admonition to Mei Yu 嫁女辞示美瑜

85 ⊙ 12 Three Birthday Verses for My Wife 寿内三章

99 ⊙ 13 Response from Friends To My Birthday Poemfor My Wife
酬诸友见和寿内作

105 ⊙ 14 Buying Books 买书

109 ⊙ 15 Buying Books to Celebrate My Birthday, Ji-Hai Year
己亥初度买书自寿

_____ Section 2 Care and Concern 棠棣桃李

121 ⊙ 16 My Brother Guang He's 40th Birthday Invitation to
Dinner, A Poem in Greeting
光河弟四十初度招饮，为韵语祝之

129 ⊙ 17 Response to Guang Han's 60th Birthday Poem
光汉见示六十自寿诗，依韵和之

137 ⊙ 18 Another Two Verses for Elder Brother-in-law Guang
Han's 60th Birthday 再赠内兄光汉二首

145 ⊙ 19 New Farewell Poem to Wang Guang He
新别离词赠王光河

157 ⊙ 20 Colophon for Wang Guang He's 50th Birthday Snapshot
题王光河五十初度小影

161 ⊙ 21 Colophon on a Photograph of Two Sisters and their
Brother, viz., Jin Song, Yi Song and Guang He
义宋锦宋光河三姐弟合照题诗

169 ⊙ 22 Wedding Counsel for the Senior Normal Graduation Class of the Perak Girls' Middle School
广嫁女辞，赠霹雳女中高师毕业班同学

177 ⊙ 23 The Journey Ahead 有行

185 ⊙ 24 In Celebration of the Golden Wedding Jubilee of Elder Brother Ke Mo and Sister-in-law 可模兄嫂金婚志庆

195 ⊙ 25 To Younger Brother-in-law in Wuhu, a Poem in Rhyme with Guang Guo
寄君余内弟芜湖和光国韵

Section 3 Friendship 辅仁会友

211 ⊙ 26 Farewell to Rui Hua on Her Return to China
送瑞华姐回国

219 ⊙ 27 Farewell to Pastor Cai Xin De, a Poem in Unison with Yi Song
与义宋联吟，送别蔡信德牧师

227 ⊙ 28 To Elder Sister Shan Guang 赠善光姐

235 ⊙ 29 Farewell to Inspector of Schools Wang Fu Wen on His Promotion and Transfer to Kuala Lumpur
送王宓文视学升调吉隆坡

249 ⊙ 30 Congratulations to Guang Di on His New Home
贺光地新厦落成（晴山、光国联吟）

259 ⊙ 31 On Yuan Tang's "Wool Wedding Anniversary"
酬远堂羊毛婚纪念照题诗

273 ⊙ 32 Congratulations to President Bai Cheng Gen on being Honoured with the Appointment of Justice of Peace by His Highness the Sultan of Perak
白成根会长荣膺霹雳洲苏丹锡封太平局绅志喜

277 ⊙ 33 Thinking of Mei Ying on Malaya's Independence Day
马来亚独立，怀美英万隆

281 ⊙ 34 Solicitation of a Poem from Mr Bai Yang Feng of Taiping
向太平白仰峯先生索和

289 ⊙ 35 Despatched to Grand Master Xin Zai in Taipei for His Direction to Reveal the Missing Word in Poem
寄台北心在大师请示其诗阙文一字

295 ⊙ 36 A Poem in Rhyme with the Poem of Mr Ji Fen
季芬先生出示书怀一律，依原韵以酬

303 ⊙ 37 Colophon for a Snapshot on Behalf of Jing Bin
代静滨题小影

311 ⊙ 38 Colophon for the Portrait of Ms Jing Bin
题静滨女士玉照

319 ⊙ 39 Poem as Epilogue for Ms Zhang Ren Shi's Peony Album
题张纫诗女士牡丹诗画册后

325 ⊙ 40 For Zheng Zhu—A Seal Engraved 郑珠为刻印

331 ⊙ 41 To My Compatriot Yuan Tang 酬远堂侨鹤见赠

339 ⊙ 42 To Mr Bai Cheng Gen on his 60th Birthday
—Two Verses in Response
奉和白成根先生六十感怀二首

347 ⊙ 43 To Mr Bai Cheng Gen, Presentation of the Complete Works of Lu You as a Birthday Gift
既和成根先生六十感怀二首复奉放翁全集为寿赋卅六韵纪之

361 ⊙ 44 Presenting Three Verses to Professor Wang Shi Zhao
呈王世昭教授三绝并序

375 ⊙ 45 Visiting Professor Wang Shi Zhao's Lodging for Counsel on Poetry 诣王世昭教授旅寓问诗

381 ⊙ 46 For Professor Wang Shi Zao on His Departure to Penang
送王世昭教授赴槟

387 ⊙ 47 In Celebration of the "Tin Wedding" Anniversary of Mr Liang and Madam Peng
贺梁森元先生与彭士驎校长锡婚纪念

397 ⊙ 48 Another Six Verses to wish Mr Liang and Madam Peng *Bon Voyage* 再贺森元先生与士驎校长锡婚之庆

413 ⊙ 49 Presented to Mr Hong Lu Kuan for his 70th Birthday, a Double Celebration with His Wife
呈洪禄宽先生七秩双寿

_____ **Section 4 Reflections 感兴述怀**

423 ⊙ 50 The Fair Maiden Chen Yun Shan of Taichen
纪陈韵珊女士事

437 ⊙ 51 Portrait of General Wu 吴将军画像赋一首

449 ⊙ 52 No Title 佚题

461 ⊙ 53 A Song to Li Xiang Lan 咏李香兰

465 ⊙ 54 Postscript for Jiehui Anthology of Poems Sent to Xi Lang
题劫灰集后酬西浪

471 ⊙ 55 Reflections 感怀

477 ⊙ 56 On Passing by Lu Kuan's New House 过禄宽新居

489 ⊙ 57 Colophon for Mr Yi Jun Zuo's Calligraphy and Painting Exhibition Catalogue
题易君左先生诗书画个展特刊

497 ⊙ 58 To the Yunnan Garden Gathering of the Literati
闻云南园雅集有感，寄列座诸君子

507 ⊙ 59 Dragon Market—A Poem for Professor Wang Shi Zhao
龙市——呈王世昭教授

519 ⊙ 60 Thoughts While Chanting in Bed 吟榻述怀

529 ⊙ 61 Preface for Mr Huang Yun Shan's "Tian Nan Yin Cao"
为黄君愠山先生之《天南吟草》序

541 ⊙ 62 Preface for Guang Han's 60th Birthday Poems
《海屋唱酬集》序

561 ⊙ 63 My Seven Principles of Poetry 诗话七则

585 ⊙ Index of Allusions Used in the Poems

597 ⊙ Acknowledgements

Preface

President S R Nathan
Republic of Singapore

The publication of this book *A Scholar's Path* is a labour of love by Mr Peter Chen and his brother Michael—sons of the author, the late Chen Qing Shan, who died 50 years ago in 1960.

It is a compilation of 60 classical poems and 3 prose compositions written in classical Chinese, by the late Mr Chen over 35 years, from 1925 to the time of his death. *A Scholar's Path* reflects much of Mr Peter Chen's father's literary passion, his relationship with his family and friends, his philosophy of life, and not to mention his unattained ideals and ambitions. More importantly, they show his pure and irrepressible joy when indulging in Chinese poetry.

During his life, the late Mr Chen had witnessed and lived through the vicissitudes of the last days of the Qing dynasty, the early Republican era in China, and the Japanese Occupation in Singapore and Malaya. The poems in this book should therefore provide readers a glimpse of those eras past through the poet's eyes. Older readers will readily identify with the context within which these poems are set.

Published in both Chinese and English editions, it should cater for a wider readership. Younger Chinese Singaporeans, who may not be inclined to read anything written in Chinese, especially the Chinese classical poetry could find the Chinese edition rather intimidating. However, they have recourse to the English edition which explains in English the allusions and sayings found in the book and traces them back to their sources. This could help to open for them the doors to the treasure trove of Chinese language and literature.

For readers with a good command of Chinese, the Chinese edition contains a rendering of the poems in modern Chinese and is profusely annotated by Associate Professor Chan Chiu Ming of the National Institute of Education. Regardless of which edition, I am confident readers will find this an absorbing book, given the range of topics covered by its 63 chapters.

I share the hope of Mr Peter Chen and his brother that this publication in Chinese and English will be an important contribution towards the encouragement of the enjoyment of Chinese literature by our younger generation of all races brought up as they have been in a bilingual environment.

Preface II

Dr Ng Eng Hen
Minister for Education and Second Minister for Defence
Republic of Singapore

The publication of *A Scholar's Path* has come at an opportune time. The Ministry of Education is continuing its review to refine the learning and teaching of Mother Tongue Languages, for instance, for the learning and teaching of the Chinese Language, the objective is to help our students learn the language. The challenge is to enable our students to learn the Chinese Language in a fun way and to use it in daily life.

The collection of poems and prose written in classical Chinese by the late Mr Chen Qing Shan is a fascinating read. The works are a reflection of the sentiments and experiences he had at different points in his life—when he was separated from his family for an extended period of time, and when he was reunited with his family eventually, or when he was commemorating special events, like a birthday or a farewell. There are also poems that show his ardent affection for his wife.

Mr Chen's knowledge of and love for classical Chinese literature is manifested in his allusions to the classics throughout the collection. The background of each poem gives the reader a glimpse into the circumstances the author was experiencing. The additional elucidation on the use of references from classical Chinese literature allows readers to better understand the author's intentions and savour the essence of his emotions. For those of us who may not be well-versed in the Chinese language, the collection of poems comes with an English edition which explains the allusions and their sources, thus allowing more readers to enjoy the beauty of the Chinese language and literature.

I am sure *A Scholar's Path* will be a welcome addition to the local Chinese literature scene. I hope, too, that the book will be an encouragement to all learners of the Chinese Language to rediscover the joy of learning the language.

Preface III

Professor Wang Gungwu
Chairman of the East Asian Institute,
National University of Singapore

When Peter Chen told me that his father had published a poem to my father, I was both surprised and delighted. He had found the poem (Chapter 29 in this collection) in the 1 March 1952 issue of *Kin Kwok Daily News* (*Jianguo Ribao* 建国日报), the Chinese newspaper of Ipoh. I did not know that Chen Qing Shan and my father had been "literary friends (文友)" for some twenty years before that. Only when I saw the poem did I realise that there had been a deep relationship and that the poet understood my father pretty well.

Peter told me that he and his brother Michael were preparing a collection of his father's poems and plan to have them published, both in the original and in translation, in 2010 in memory of his passing 50 years ago. He wanted more information about my father so that he could describe the background to the poem more fully. It so happened that I had produced in 2002 a revised edition of a memorial volume of my father's writings to mark the 40th year of his death. This was 王宓文纪念集 *Wang Fo-wen jinianji* (Wang Fo-wen, 1903–1972: a memorial collection of poems, essays and calligraphy). That volume contained relevant information about my father's life in Ipoh from 1931 till 1952, and I gave Peter a copy. I really admired Peter for making great efforts to locate his father's poetry, following every connection he could find. In contrast, mine had been a much simpler task because my father had done an earlier collection of his pre-1945 poems. When he died, my mother and I found his later writings among his papers and put them all in the volume that was printed in 1972.

But I still had no idea how ambitious the Chen brothers were going to be with their collection. Only when he showed me what was done and asked me to write a preface for the work did I realise that he and Michael were not content merely to publish the poems with English translations. What they set out to produce was a comprehensive presentation of all aspects of the poems that would enable them to be widely appreciated. They were determined that these poems be read and, in order to do that, they went far beyond a translated collection. They invited Associate Professor Chan Chiu Ming of Singapore's National Institute of Education to help them research, render the classical verses into modern Chinese, and annotate every poem. This was to ensure that each of the poems would be fully understood even by those who knew little Chinese. The final work, both in Chinese and English translation, is so thorough that the work can serve as a valuable teaching text. It is one that can be used to capture the very mixed feelings of the Chinese sojourners (*huaqiao* 华侨) who came to British Malaya during the first half of the 20th century, especially those who had decided not to return to China after all.

The poems and a few prose writings are grouped in four sections. Each represents a set of emotions that most sojourners harboured and would have articulated if they could. Chen Qing Shan, like my father, belonged to a generation in China that was transiting from a civilisation in decline to a new nation in danger of being still born. That they were observing the trauma from afar in a foreign land that was itself undergoing transformation from colonial rule to independence made their condition doubly difficult to endure. They also shared a common experience as teachers of children of Chinese migrants dedicated to inculcating the desire to understand their origins in China. This was a delicate operation at the time, between 1930 and 1960, when local conditions were often conflict-laden if not hostile, and developments in China tumultuous if not despairing. Both had finally decided not to return to Mao Zedong's China. My father avoided political issues in his writings while Chen Qing Shan did express his dismay at what was happening to the values he found so precious in the culture he grew up with. Behind the joy in words and images in all his poems, that concern shines through in all four sections of the volume.

Nevertheless, deep sentiments rooted in the Chinese poetic tradition remain, the sense of family, the conventions of mutual caring, the wonder of friendship and the need for longer perspectives to think about the inner meaning of this life, are all there. With every word and phrase explained in both Chinese and English, these sentiments are made to reflect different aspects of the era's social adaptations, political mutations and cultural affirmations. Most are refracted through the eyes of one man and his relationships across the South China Sea.

When Peter and Michael decided to go so deeply into their father's heart and mind, they were going well beyond an act of filial piety. They were no less conscious of the state of Singapore society today and in the future. Can the people deal with the demands of modernity without forgetting what their fathers believed in? Should they be content to leave all things past in the untouched dusty pages of archives and historical collections? This volume of poems is the Chen brothers' answer. Without passing any kind of judgement, it uses extensive explications to outline the layers of change and response among those who lived through so much. It rejects the know-all certainty that successes today are forever. It affirms the capacity in each one of us to accept progress while remaining true to what is worth preserving. To be asked to write this preface has given me a chance to re-learn that simple truth. I thank Peter and Michael for the privilege and hope others who read the book will share my sense of fulfilment.

28 February 2010

Foreword

Peter Chen Min-liang (Singapore)
Michael Tan Min-hwa (USA)

> *"I shall place them in brocade-lined boxes and store them with fragrant scent for my descendants as a family treasure. They may not know how to read them but can look upon them as Zhou and Shang bronze ware of antiquity to be revered and treasured all the same."*
>
> **Chen Qing Shan (1957)**

A Gestation of Six Years

2010 is a good year for the publication of *A Scholar's Path* as it commemorates the 50th Anniversary of Father's demise on 6 June 1960.

A Scholar's Path, an anthology of Father's poems, was first conceived in late 2003, not long after the publication of our first book *Lychee Fragrance* in 2002. That book comprises a sample and cross section of Father's writings which we published bilingually in Chinese with its English translation.

Father's great passion was poetry. To attempt writing a book about his poetry is a project of an entirely different order of magnitude. We are not scholars, but we are both fully retired.

What we lack in scholarship might perhaps be made up by, what we thought we had, an abundant availability of "time". However, as we also have many other concurrent personal interests in life, it has taken us quite a while to complete this "assignment" we set ourselves.

We decided very early on, that every poem in the book should be complete with a Background, a verse Translation (in the English edition), a Paraphrase and an Appreciation. (In the Chinese edition, we would have Notes on the allusions used in the poems). This explains why this book has had a gestation period of six years!

We had advice from a number of people, including Associate Professor Chan Chiu Ming. Five years later, much of the work on the English edition and the rendering of the poems into modern Chinese were done, yet we had barely scratched the surface of the work for the Chinese edition. There were still many "gaps". We were a long way off from achieving our ambition to bring out concurrently an English and a Chinese edition of the book.

About a year ago, we sought more help from Assoc Prof Chan, without which the book would never have been completed. He took responsibility for the detailed research and the complete writing of the Chinese edition. Our contribution to the Chinese edition was in providing and authenticating the material for the Background.

As Assoc Prof Chan worked on the Chinese edition throughout the past one year, his scholarly work thus became a dynamic source of reference for the English edition. In several of the poems in the English edition, the interpretation of some lines was revised as a result. Moreover Assoc Prof Chan's interpretation and critique in the Appreciation section of each chapter of the Chinese edition provided fresh insight not previously available to us.

Source and Background of the Poems

After Father passed away, Mother carefully put together what she had kept of Father's poems. They were from a variety of sources: newspaper cuttings, Father's handwritten drafts and handwritten copies by others. It was only much later that we found some poems tucked away among the belongings of our fourth maternal uncle Wang Guang Guo, whose name features frequently in the Background of several chapters of this book. A couple of compositions published in the mid-1920s came from an old gentleman from Muar whom we had never even met. Finally we found a few more in the microfilm records of the Chinese Library of the National University of Singapore. But for the microfilm record, we would never have known of the existence of the 1952 poem in Chapter 29, *"Farewell to Inspector of Schools Wang Fu Wen on His Promotion and Transfer to Kuala Lumpur"*. Nor would we have known of the close "literary friendship" between Mr Wang Fu Wen and Father. (See Preface III by Professor Wang Gungwu).

No poem can be fully understood and interpreted without an adequate knowledge of the background and the circumstance of its writing. The poems were written over a period of 35 years from 1925 to 1960. Some of the circumstances of writing are within the personal experience of the two of us, but much is not. In the search for answers, we made many trips to Ipoh, Kampar, Taiping, Kuala Lumpur and even as far as Father's native Putian in Fujian. Alas, most of the people for whom the poems were written are no longer here. The most we could do was to speak to their children who are themselves already in their seventies, or look at what few photographs and documents they still possess.

We are fortunate to have the help of our two elder sisters Mei Xuan and Mei Yu. They each had a poem composed by Father, addressed to them (Chapters 10 and 11 respectively). They provided us background information about the two poems. Even more valuable, they narrated anecdotes about the family and our lives during a period of time when the two of us were too young to understand or even to remember.

Book Title and Cover

The book title *A Scholar's Path* is taken from the poem in Chapter 10, "*Admonition to My Daughter Xuan*".

The book's front cover is illustrated with the picture of a late Shang early Zhou *ding* cast in bronze, decorated with animal face motif (商末周初 獸面紋鬲鼎), reproduced with the kind permission of National Palace Museum, Taiwan, Republic of China. The choice is inspired by the closing lines of Paragraph 7 of Chapter 63 "My Seven Principles of Poetry", quoted at the beginning of the Foreword.

English Translation

The work of a translator is never easy; it is often a thankless task. A translation, especially of poetry, often satisfies no one. The translation of Chinese poetry into English is doubly more difficult. There are barriers of language and culture. It is almost an impossible task to have to convey the intended meaning, retain the imagery and maintain "readability" in English. Could we ever do justice to Father's classical Chinese poems by translating them into English, and worse, in verse form? We could lose all the beauty of the original "music", "imagery" and "culture"! Alternatively, we could have just done an English paraphrase of the poem and omitted the verse translation.

However, in the end, we took Professor Chan's advice, "A paraphrase is not a translation. A paraphrase is aimed mainly at the interpretation of the semantic meaning of the text. A translation, on the other hand, aims at the preservation of the 'poetry' of the poem. Poetry lies more in the 'images', which can be better translated, than the 'sound'." With the inclusion of an English translation in verse, we do hope to be able to draw out some measure of this "poetry".

No translation could ever capture all the qualities of the original poem. To make up for the deficiency of a translation, every chapter includes a Paraphrase and an Appreciation of the poem. What the reader misses in the translation, may be picked up in the Paraphrase. What is missed in the Paraphrase, is amplified in the Appreciation. Reading all three will, hopefully, help the reader to enjoy the "poetry" of the original poem. It will help even more those who read Assoc Prof Chan's detailed notes in every chapter (in the Chinese edition).

Spring 2010

Biography of Chen Qing Shan

by **Peter and Michael**

Father was born in 1894, the 25th Year of the Reign of Emperor Guangxu of the Qing Dynasty. His given name was Tian Fu (天福) which means "heavenly blessing". He was born to a late Qing scholar (*xiu cai* 秀才) Chen Jun Hou (陈俊侯) who lived in Putian city, Xinghua in Fujian Province (生于福建省兴化府莆田县城内). Grandfather Jun Hou was a learned scholar, well known locally as a strict schoolmaster and disciplinarian, but the parents were happy to send their children to his private school (*si shu* 私塾) located in his own house. Father was only four months old when his mother died. While his father had not remarried, his sister who was ten years his senior had to care for him.

Father was tutored in the traditional classics at home by his father. He used to tell us that when he was a boy, he had to pay homage to Confucius by *kowtowing* in front of a portrait of the sage before class began. If he forgot to perform that ritual, he would be punished. Grandfather had hoped that Father would study hard for ten years and then go on to pass the *xiu cai* and *jin shi* (进士) examinations and secure a position in the civil service. With this in mind, the education pursued by Father covered the four traditional branches of the curriculum comprising Classics, History, Philosophy, Poetry

(经史子集) that would establish for him a solid foundation later for his literary writings. Father was especially fond of poetry. Even as a teenager he and a group of young friends formed a poetry club called "Xiao Yu Poetry Club" (笑余诗社). They would get together after school to compose poems and play other words games. By the 30th Year of the Reign of Emperor Guangxu (1904), the old system of civil examinations was abolished in China and schools with new and more modern curricula were opened. Father entered one of such schools. After finishing in Tong De Primary School (通德) and the old-system Hanjiang Middle School (涵江), he apparently attended Normal teaching course in Fuzhou. He then taught the children of the Wang (王) family in a class organized by them in Jiangdou village (江兜) in Fuqing (福清). This was a family of scholarly background and some renown locally from where our mother Yi Song (义宋) came. From then on, Father spent most of the rest of his life as a teacher.

The Chen family's economic circumstances compelled Father to leave home for Malaya in May 1917. He taught variously in Telok Anson's Pei Hua 培华 Primary School (now Telok Intan), Kampar's Pei Yuan 培元 Primary School, Ipoh's Yu Cai 育才 Primary School. In June 1923, he returned to China and married Ms Wu Niao Mei (吴嬝妹), a teacher in Tong De Primary School. In December the same year, he and his wife returned to Malaya and he resumed teaching in Pei Yuan Primary School. Unfortunately his wife died during childbirth in Kampar. This was the saddest moment of his life as, writing later, he described this period as being "cheerless" (郁郁寡欢). It was not until 1925 that the Principal of Pei Yuan Primary School Wang Guang Han (王光汉) matched his younger sister Yi Song (义宋) to Father. Yi Song came to Malaya and they were married in Kampar in 1926. From about this time, Father often had his short stories and other prose writings frequently published in the newspapers. These works were compiled and later published in Putian by Li She (荔社) a few years later.

In 1932, Li Qing (砺青) High School in Putian needed an experienced Chinese Literature teacher. Several letters were written to urge Father to accept the position. It was difficult to decline such an earnest invitation and he finally returned to Putian. Although he taught in Li Qing for only about two years, his contributions were significant. Apart from editing the Li Qing Student News (砺青学报), he greatly encouraged the students to write and used his overseas connections to solicit contributions for the school's building fund. Father was earnest in his teaching and his students who achieved success after leaving school were many. One of them became a famous poet in the New China. He is the late Professor Peng Yan Jiao 彭燕郊 (former name was Chen De Ju 陈德矩). Professor Peng was Head of Literature in Hunan's Xiang Tang University (湖南湘潭大学文学系的系主任).

During the period when Father was teaching in Li Qing, he was not accustomed to witnessing the oppression on the people during the rule by warlords and local bullies. Irrational and unjust taxes were imposed on the local population. In the local weekly he edited, he wrote editorials that castigated the local bullying bureaucrats. According to Father's nephew Lin Zhao Lin (林兆麟 our cousin) who was also living in Putian, Father had a particularly sharp pen and he was one who "dared to anger and dared to speak" 敢怒又敢言. This aroused the support of the Putian population and at the same time angered the local bully who happened to be the local governor. Li Wan Chun (李万春). Some time after April 1934, a warrant for Father's arrest was issued. Forewarned of this, Father went into hiding. Governor Li then took Mother into custody as a hostage. At that time, elder sister Mei Yu (美瑜) was barely a few months old and still being suckled. Mother recalled that the baby Mei Yu had to be handed over to her through the small window of the lockup five six times a day to be breast fed.

Governor Li's warrant of arrest for Father stirred up the public anger of the education circle in the whole of Putian.

Classes in schools were boycotted as a sign of protest. Governor Li realized the serious consequences of his action and Mother was released and the arrest warrant against Father rescinded. According to our cousin Zhao Lin, an eye witness to these events, Governor Li realized that he had bitten off more than he could chew. As a gesture of apology, he invited Father to a dinner banquet. Fearing that this was only a ruse, Father never took up the invitation.

All these events compelled Father to leave Putian in 1934 and return once more to Nanyang to resume teaching in his former school Pei Yuan in Kampar. Not unexpectedly, he could only find enough money for his own passage to return by himself ahead of the family. His family could not join him until two years later. We can imagine how he must have felt to be separated from his family as evident in the poems written during this period of separation. It was only in 1936 that the whole family was together again in Malaya, except for one daughter left behind in China. Mother could only take along two of the three daughters: Mei Xuan 美璇 who was then about five years and Mei Yu 美瑜 two years old. The daughter left behind was Mei Yu 美育 who was three years old. With Father's entire family returning to Nanyang, Grandfather Jun Hou wanted to have one of his own "flesh and blood" to be near him in China. Mei Yu 美育 was a lively and attractive girl and was his favourite grandchild. After the family's return to Malaya in 1936, we were soon overtaken by the Japanese invasion of China, then Malaya. Even after the end of the Pacific War, the takeover by the Communists of mainland China was another event of even greater cataclysmic proportion. All thought and hope of ever returning to China was over. The finality of being unable to return to China had always weighed on the mind of Mother.

Malaya was occupied (1942–1945) by the Japanese army at the outbreak of the Pacific War. The occupation was to last three years eight months. Father had to go into hiding from the Japanese. He stayed in Kuala Lumpur most of the time and could only return in secret to Ipoh, at great personal risk, to see his family. How he felt on such a visit is described in one of his poems. This period of our life must have been the darkest and most difficult. Mother had to look after four children (one daughter was left behind in China). Mother had a sewing machine in half a shop front along Anderson Road and patched clothes for passersby as people were too poor to have any new clothes. This was what Mother did to eke out a living for the entire family.

After the surrender of the Japanese and the end of their occupation, Father returned from his hiding in Kuala Lumpur and was employed as the Secretary of the Perak Hokkien Association. He took on other odd secretarial and bookkeeping jobs to make ends meet. He had for a year or two, part-time teaching assignments in the weekend Normal Teachers Training Courses for Chinese schools. It was only during the last four years of his life that he started to teach regularly again, part time, at the Perak Girls' Middle School.

When we look back at Father's life, we can say that he grew up and lived in one of China's great moments of change in history. Born at the beginning of the Sino-Japanese War in Jiawu year (甲午1894), he would have lived through Emperor Guangxu's (光绪) abortive attempt at Reform (维新), the attack and occupation of Beijing by the Eight Power Allied Forces (八国联军), experienced the events of Dr Sun Yat-sen's revolution. In his youth, he would have known of the events of the "Northeast Flag Replacement" (东北易帜), the Mukden Incident of 1931 (which the Chinese often refer to as the "September 18" Incident), the "Xi-an Incident" (西安事变). He had personally lived through these momentous historical changes in China which must have had an impact on him. Hence there was a time in his youth when there reposed in him a patriotic fervour to want to do something for the country. He had once used his pen to fight against local injustice in his native Putian; he wrote in the local weekly "Pu Xian Report" (莆仙导报) and edited two others "Da Sheng Bao" (大声报) and "Hanjiang Bao" (涵江报). Unfortunately the local oppressive forces were prepared to drag his family into the fray and Father then gave up the fight. Father's regret at the unachieved ambitions of his youth are reflected in one of his last poems included in this book. He returned to his teaching part time, a vocation he seemed to enjoy, right up to the time of his death. He died of liver failure in the Ipoh General Hospital on 6 June 1960, aged 66.

Brief Biographies
• Editor Translators

Peter Chen Min-liang
born 1938 in Kampar, Malaya

The elder son of Chen Qing Shan, he received his education at the Anderson School in Ipoh. He was awarded a Colombo Plan scholarship and qualified as a Chartered Accountant in Australia. He joined Shell Companies in Singapore and retired in 1996 as their Chairman and Chief Executive. He entered politics after retirement from Shell. In 1997, he was elected Member of Parliament and was appointed Senior Minister of State for Education. In 2000, he was appointed Senior Minister of State for Trade and Industry. He retired from politics in November 2001 and is currently pursuing his own interests, writing and travelling.

Michael Tan Min-hua
born 1941 in Kampar, Malaya

The younger son of Chen Qing Shan, he was educated at the Yoke Choy High School in Ipoh. He qualified as a medical doctor in Japan and proceeded to the United States of America to qualify as a MD specialising in anesthesiology. He taught at the University of Rochester in New York State. He practised anesthesiology in Rochester until his retirement in 1998 and currently spends his time writing.

Brief Biography
- Reviewer

Chan Chiu Ming
Associate Professor, Asian Languages and Cultures
National Institute of Education
Nanyang Technological University

Chan Chiu Ming received his BA (Hons) in Chinese and Translation from the University of Hong Kong and his MA and PhD from the University of Wisconsin-Madison, USA, majoring in Chinese and with a minor in Comparative Literature. He had also obtained a Postgraduate Diploma of Teaching in Higher Education from the Nanyang Technological University. He is currently an Associate Professor at the Chinese Division, National Institute of Education, Nanyang Technological University. He was head of the Asian Languages and Cultures Academic Group of the National Institute of Education from July 2000 to June 2006. His research interests have been primarily in theories and practice of translation, use of translation in the teaching of the Chinese language, classical Chinese literature, the *Book of Changes* and philosophical Taoism. He has translated the *Book of Changes* (*I Ching*) and has taken part in the translation of the *Grand Scribes' Record* (*Shiji*), published by the Indiana University.

Section 1

Familial Love
和鸣舐犊

The love for his wife and family,
care and counsel for his daughters,
the joy experienced on receiving
a birthday gift from his son.

Chapter 1

qīng niǎo èr shǒu青鸟二首

其一

西飞青鸟去还来,
缄札瑶珰未忍开。
正似看花虽欲折,
不妨花外暂徘徊。

其二

开缄乍似解罗襦,
香泽微闻思有余。
秋在心头知几许,
讳将愁字不教书。

The Messenger of Love
(Two Verses)

Verse 1

My courier flies west; upon its return
Brings a beautiful letter I forbear to open.
To enjoy the flowers, pluck them I should,
But linger awhile to admire them I would.

Verse 2

Opening the letter's like undoing her silken blouse.
Just a whiff of fragrance, my many thoughts arouse.
Heavy does Autumn sit upon your Heart.
The word "Sorrow" from your letters depart.

Paraphrase

Verse 1

L1: My courier the Blue Bird flies away westwards, and returns
L2: With this beautiful letter from you. I refrain from opening it immediately,
L3: As I wish to prolong the joy and excitement of reading it, As in the enjoyment of flowers, rather than plucking the blooms immediately,

L4: I first pace around the flowers awhile longer to admire them.

Verse 2

L1: To open the letter is like undoing the silken blouse of a loved one.
L2: I am immediately met with a whiff of fragrance. It is more than enough to stir up my many thoughts and longings.
L3: Heavy do the sad thoughts of "Autumn" (秋) weigh upon your "Heart" (心).
L4: "Sorrow" (愁) is a word you have henceforth banished from all your letters.

Background

There are at least three distinct periods in Father's life when he was separated from his wife and family for any length of time.

Separation	Period	Family	Father
First	1931	Putian	Kampar, Malaya
Second	1934–1936	Putian	Kampar, Malaya
Third	1942–1945	Ipoh	Kuala Lumpur

This poem was composed probably during the "first separation" during the second half of 1931.

In 1931, Father was then teaching in Pei Yuan (培元) Primary School in Kampar, Malaya. With the onset of the Great Depression, schools were closed and he lost his job like thousands of others. Grandfather in China asked him to return. There was some family land at home and, if nothing else, they could at least live off the land and not starve. Fortunately, he secured a teaching post in Li Qing (砺青) Middle School in his native Putian. In the second half of 1931, he sent his wife and family of two sons and a daughter home to China

Qing Shan's wife Yi Song 义宋 (c.1920s). *"Heavy does Autumn sit upon your Heart. The word Sorrow from your letters depart."*

Qing Shan's two eldest sons standing on left and right respectively: Xi Dong 锡东 and Xi Geng 锡庚, and his daughter Mei Xuan 美璇 at the centre (carried by Qing Shan's stepmother), soon after Yi Song and the children arrived in China about mid-1931 while Qing Shan remained in Kampar, Malaya. (Both his sons died during the family's stay in China 1931–1936.)

ahead of himself. The sons were aged about five and four; the daughter was barely one year old. He had no money even for the family's passage. He had to take a loan from the Chairman of his school board, a wealthy tin miner in Kampar. Father stayed back for a few months to tutor the Chairman's children at home to repay the loan and to earn his own passage. He finally left Malaya in December 1931 and was reunited with his family in Putian in January 1932.

Appreciation

This poem of two verses was probably composed during the second half of 1931 when Qing Shan was separated from his wife and family—he in Malaya and his family in China. The circumstances for this separation are explained in the Background of the poem.

Verse 1 expresses how keenly the poet looks forward to receiving a letter from his wife. It uses the imagery of the legendary magical Blue Bird *qing niao* 青鸟 delivering the letter from his wife to him. He must have missed her so much that even a simple letter from her is described literally as "a document adorned with a beautiful jade pendant" (缄札瑶珰) as reflected in Line 2. It goes on to describe his anticipatory pleasure on opening and reading the contents of that precious document. The word *ren* 忍 (to bear) in the same line sums up the dilemma he is in. He is impatient to read the contents of the letter, yet at the same time, wants to prolong the anticipatory pleasure for as long as possible, comparing it with the pleasure of enjoying flowers. Even though the flowers in the garden would eventually have to be plucked, why not postpone this immediate gratification and pace around the plant and enjoy the flowers a little longer?

The first two lines of Verse 2 really bare the soul of the poet, bringing out the intensity of his feelings and longings. The otherwise simple act of opening a letter is compared with undoing the soft silken blouse of a lady. The poet is then filled with anticipatory excitement and pleasure and is greeted by a faint whiff of the womanly fragrance which is enough to arouse his many thoughts. Those not familiar with Chinese poetry may regard such an imagery as unacceptably sensuous and erotic. But it is not at all uncommon to find in Chinese classical poetry such "daring" imagery.

Reality finally sets in. It is only a letter. His loved one is not with him. Like "virtual reality", this pleasure exists only in his mind and the realisation of this only makes him feel all the more sad. This verse ends with a clever play on three Chinese words "Autumn" *qiu* 秋, "Heart" *xin* 心, and "Sorrow" *chou* 愁. The third line of Verse 2 asks rhetorically, in a literal translation, "How many 'Autumns' do sit upon your 'Heart'? 秋在心头知几许". The reader of Chinese will immediately recognise that the Chinese word for "Sorrow" is actually made up of the word "Autumn" sitting on top of the word "Heart". Playing word games or "riddles" such as this is a popular pastime among the Chinese. The final line ends the poem with the declaration, "'Sorrow' is a word you have henceforth banished from all your letters 讳将愁字不教书". Perhaps his wife thoughtfully does not wish to worry him unnecessarily.

Chapter 2

中秋月

tiān shàng tuán yuán hǎo
天 上 团 圆 好，

rén jiān yì bié yīn
人 间 忆 别 殷。

jìng fēng xiū yǔ zhào
镜 封 羞 与 照，

4 香 烬 不 教 焚。
xiāng jìn bù jiào fén

kǔ yì yún huán shī
苦 忆 云 鬟 湿，

yáo lián shuāng bìn fēn
遥 怜 霜 鬓 纷。

jīn xiāo yī lún yuè
今 宵 一 轮 月，

8 秋 思 两 平 分。

Mid-Autumn Moon

    A happy reunion high in Heaven above;
    Mankind recalls the parting pains below.
    Cannot bear to look in the mirror, my love;
4 Incense burned out, it'll be kindled no more.
    Painful my thoughts, your hair so soft and dewy;
    Afar I pine, dishevelled my frost white hair.
    The moon is full and round tonight, and yet
8 We are apart; our autumn thoughts each to bear.

Paraphrase

L1: There is a happy reunion in the sky above,
L2: Whereas we mankind below can only relive once more the deep and painful feelings of our parting.
L3: I put the mirror away, as I can hardly bear to look at myself, in my sad and sorry state.
L4: The incense which I have lit has already burned out and it will not be rekindled.
L5: It is with gnawing pains that I keep thinking of you.
L6: I think of your lovely bun of hair, soft as clouds and already moist with the early morning dew.
L7: Tonight, the beautiful moon is complete and round like a big wheel, but

L8: We are torn asunder, as two symmetrical halves each nursing our own sad autumnal thoughts.

Background

The three distinct periods when Father was separated from his wife and family are explained in Chapter 1.

Events leading to the Second Separation

This poem was composed probably during Father's "second separation" from the family during the two to three years from 1934 to 1936. During this period of separation, he would have had to spend at least two Mid-Autumns by himself. The poem is one of two "Mid-Autumn" poems composed during the period. He was then in his early forties.

Father had returned to his native Putian in China to teach Chinese language and literature in Li Qing (砺青) Middle School from the beginning of 1932. Soon after his return to China, he published a weekly paper *Da Sheng Bao* (大声报) which ran for only 30 issues from May 1932 until early 1933. Thereafter, he went on to edit another weekly paper *Hanjiang Bao* (涵江报) from March 1933. This paper was suspended in July the same year, after only four months of publication.

The suspension of *Hanjiang Bao* in July 1933 marked the beginning of a harrowing experience for Father. He had just turned 39. He was in his prime and full of the ideals of the "May Fourth" movement. Moved to anger, he dared to speak out against the corruption and injustice that he saw around him in the China of the 1930s. In the weekly papers that he published or edited, he wrote articles and editorials that exposed the prevailing corruption and rallied against the irrational and unjust taxes imposed locally. Offended by these articles, the Putian Governor eventually ordered Father to be arrested. This incident took place not long after April 1934.

Fortunately, Father was forewarned; he managed to escape and went into hiding. The Governor arrested Mother instead to hold as a hostage. Elder sister Mei Yu 美瑜 was only a few months old and had to be taken to the police lockup several times a day for Mother to breastfeed her. The schools in Putian went on strike over this incident. Mother was eventually released. The warrant for Father's arrest was rescinded. Realising the seriousness of the situation and as an expression of apology, the Governor invited Father to a banquet. Discretion was the better part of valour and the Governor's invitation was declined and Father left in secret and returned to Malaya, leaving his wife and children behind in Putian.

Father was thus separated from his family for a period of two to three years from 1934 to 1936 before they were eventually reunited in Malaya.

Appreciation

Like the Lunar New Year's eve, the Mid-Autumn Festival night is also a time for family reunion. The full moon on this night is a symbol of reunion. The Chinese text of the two opening lines have all the qualities of a couplet:

> "A happy reunion high in Heaven above; 天上团圆好
> Mankind recalls the parting pains below," 人间忆别殷

They contrast the happiness of a reunion in heaven above with the sorrow of separation endured by mankind on earth below. The comparison is quite "as a matter of fact", with no connotation of blame or rancour. This is perhaps a reflection of the traditional fatalism of the Chinese.

It is on such a night, when other families are busy enjoying the happy reunion with their loved ones, that Qing Shan's own state of separation becomes all the more poignant and painful. His unfortunate situation has reduced him to such a pathetic state emotionally and physically that he can no longer bear even to look at himself in the mirror, "Cannot bear to look in the mirror, my love 镜封羞与照". As the hours tick away in the poet's lonely night, the joss sticks on the altar are already reduced to ashes, but he is too distraught to re-light them, "Incense burned out, it'll be kindled no more 香烬不教焚".

The next pair of lines form yet another couplet that has complementary emotions:

"Painful my thoughts, your hair so soft and dewy;
苦忆雲鬟湿
Afar I pine, dishevelled my frost white hair."
遥怜霜鬓纷

The second part of each of the two lines contrasts her lovely bun of "hair so soft and dewy" with the poet's own dishevelled "frost white hair". Her hair is "dewy", moistened by the late night or early morning dew during the traditional practice of praying to the moon on such a night.

By the time we come to the last two lines of the poem, we begin to realize that this poem of eight lines is actually made up of four couplets, each pair of lines complementary and contrasting. The final two lines compare the complete and undivided union of two people (as symbolized by the full moon 一轮月, with the sorrowful autumnal thoughts 秋思 borne equally by two people 两平分. There is no rancour, only sorrow.

Chapter 3

中秋咏月有寄
zhōng qiū yǒng yuè yǒu jì

素娥如有约，
sù é rú yǒu yuē

佳节又逢秋。
jiā jié yòu féng qiū

漫道圆时好，
màn dào yuán shí hǎo

4 翻添分外愁。
fān tiān fēn wài chóu

青天长夜悔，
qīng tiān cháng yè huǐ

碧海一身浮。
bì hǎi yī shēn fú

千里清光共，
qiān lǐ qīng guāng gòng

8 知君正倚楼。
zhī jūn zhèng yǐ lóu

Mid-Autumn Song

    Like an annual appointment with Chang-E,
    It's the season of Mid-Autumn once more.
    They glibly say, "Full moon brings happiness".
4 Nay, it brings me exceptional sadness.
    Dark blue sky of regrets in this long night.
    Across the blue sea, a wanderer I've been.
    Thousand miles apart, we share this same light;
8 Pensive, across the balustrade you lean.

Paraphrase

L1: It is like an annual appointment with the Moon Fairy Chang-E.
L2: When the day comes, we realize that the Mid-Autumn season is with us once more.
L3: They glibly say that the time of a full moon is a happy one.
L4: On the contrary, it brings me exceptional melancholy.
L5: Beneath the dark blue sky on such a night as this, I regret
L6: Having wandered alone across the wide blue sea so far away from home.
L7: Even though we are thousands of miles apart, I am heartened to think that it is the same brilliant moonlight that we are both looking at.

L8: I know that you are at this very moment leaning pensively across the balustrade, watching the moon with me.

Background

This poem is the second of two "Mid-Autumn" poems composed by Father during his second period of separation from his family from 1934 to 1936. He had returned to his native Putian in 1932 to teach at a high school. The events leading to this "second separation" are more fully explained in the Background of Chapter 2.

Father was thus separated from his family for a period of two to three years from 1934 to 1936 before they were eventually reunited in Malaya.

Appreciation

This is Qing Shan's second "Mid-Autumn" away from his family in 1936. He is all by himself in Malaya and his family is left behind in Putian. It is the Mid-Autumn festival again. This is not a day he necessarily looks forward to. In the third and fourth lines of the poem, he tells us that contrary to what everyone so glibly says, this night is not a happy occasion for him. He is far away from his wife and children. In the Chinese text, Lines 5 and 6 form a well-matched couplet:

> "Dark blue sky of regrets in this long night, 青天长夜悔
> Across the blue sea, a wanderer I've been." 碧海一身浮

Qing Shan uses a well-known Chinese metaphor "blue sky, blue sea" 青天碧海 to denote the limitlessness or the far reaches of both time and space. As he muses the whole long night of Mid-Autumn, he feels a sense of regret for having sailed and wandered far away from home for so long.

The last two lines are perhaps the most touching in the poem:

"Thousand miles apart, we share this same light;
千里清光共
Pensive, across the balustrade you lean."
知君正倚楼

Qing Shan's wife Yi Song (c.1927). *"Thousand miles apart, we share this same light; Pensive, across the balustrade you lean."*

They touch on an experience many can identify with. When we are away from home in some distant land, even for short periods of time, we sometimes gaze up into the sky at night, looking at the moon and feeling all the more homesick. We imagine our wife or some loved one looking at the same moon and thinking of us, as we are of them.

Chapter 4

瑶缄二首

其一

油盐柴米话家常，
写入云笺字字香。
潦草数言知急就，
居然看作十三行。

其二

赓词不敢杂庄谐，
关禁方严怕误猜。
果是慧心防范密，
瑶缄未接已先开。

Letter from Home
(Two Verses)

Verse 1

> Oil, salt and rice, so common a chant.
> Yet every written word is so fragrant.
> Just a few words, scribbled in great hurry
> Are to me, a masterpiece in calligraphy.

Verse 2

> Your replies no longer dare to quip and jest.
> If misconstrued, will fail the Censor's test.
> You are cautious, our privacy achieved.
> Letters are opened before they are received.

Paraphrase

L1: Oil, salt, fuel and rice; these basic necessities in every home, may appear trivial and mundane.

L2: Yet when they are mentioned in letters (from home), every word is so fragrant.

L3: They may be no more than a few hurriedly scribbled words, but

L4: They are cherished by me as though they are a masterpiece in calligraphy ("thirteen lines", see Appreciation).

L5: Your replies no longer dare indulge in quips and jest,

L6: Lest they are misconstrued by the authorities as something worse.
L7: You are wise to be cautious so that we can protect our privacy (secrecy) in our correspondence,
L8: Because our letters are opened even before they are received by us.

Background

There are three distinct periods in Father's life when he was separated from his wife and family for an extended length of time.

The circumstance of these three periods of separation is more fully explained in the Background in Chapter 2. This poem was composed during the second separation from 1934 to 1936.

Father and Mother continued to correspond, he in Malaya and she in Putian with the children, but their correspondence would have been monitored by the local authorities in Putian. Mother (born 1897) was unusual for a woman of her time. She was literate and could write reasonably well, but her handwriting, although very legible, was not that of a scholar or calligrapher.

Appreciation

The poem comprises two verses. It is a nice mixture of sentimental expressions for his wife and a cheeky message for the prying eyes of the censors who intrude into their private correspondence.

The two opening lines evoke a familiar feeling among business travellers away for any length of time and are separated from the wife and family. In Qing Shan's situation, he is in Malaya earning a living while his wife and family are in

Qing Shan's family in Putian (c.1936) while he was in Kampar, Malaya. His elder sister is seated on the left, his wife Yi Song on the right. His five children then were (from left to right standing or seated): an adopted daughter Mei Lian 美莲, his own three daughters Mei Yu 美育, Mei Xuan 美璇, Mei Yu 美瑜, his son Xi Geng 锡庚 who died not long after the photo was taken. (Another older son had died earlier in China.)

China. This is in the days when letters are handwritten and sent by post. His wife's letters would normally deal with the most commonplace matters concerning everyday living. These are the usual letters asking for money to buy the essentials for the home. His reaction to these letters are however very different. Take the first two lines in Verse 1:

> Line 1: "Oil, salt and rice, so common a chant.
> 油盐柴米话家常
> Line 2: Yet every written word is so fragrant."
> 写入云笺字字香

"Oil, salt and rice" are normally a mundane topic. This is not how Qing Shan sees his wife's letters. The reality of the mundane in Line 1 is put in sharp contrast with the fancy of his imagination in Line 2. To fully appreciate the imagery of Line

2, we need to expand the original Chinese text into a "literal" translation which would read thus,

> Line 2: "Written on this cloud pattern water-marked stationery, every word is fragrant"

He imagines his wife's letters are written on expensive stationery "with a cloud pattern water mark" (云笺). Moreover every word smells fragrant to him (字字香). So much does he miss his wife that we can see him putting each page of the letter to his nose to inhale its fragrance, contemplating how every page has been touched by his wife.

Although the letters are in reality no more than scribbles hurriedly written by the wife in her busy domestic schedules, Qing Shan sees them differently. The next two lines:

> Line 3: "Just a few words, scribbled in great hurry
> 潦草数言知急就
> Line 4: Are to me, a masterpiece in calligraphy."
> 居然看作十三行

The English text "a masterpiece in calligraphy" is translated from the Chinese text 十三行 (literally "thirteen lines"). This is an allusion to a masterpiece in calligraphy *Luo Sheng Fu* 洛神赋 written by the great calligrapher and poet Wang Xizhi 王羲之 (303–361) of the Jin 晋 dynasty. By the time of the Southern Song 南宋 (1127–1279) only thirteen lines, comprising 250 words of the original work, were extant. The expression "thirteen lines" has thus become a metaphor for a beautiful piece of calligraphic work. In these two lines, Qing Shan heightens the emotion by again using the technique of sharp contrast between his wife's "few words scribbled in great hurry" with Wang Xizhi's "masterpiece in calligraphy".

After the effusive expression of his emotions in Verse 1, Qing Shan gets down to the practicalities of their correspondence in Verse 2. He notices that their correspondence, unlike their normally relaxed relationship between husband and wife, no longer indulges in the usual bantering. The change is due to the prying eyes of the censors.

Verse 2

> Line 1: "Your replies no longer dare to quip and jest.
> 庚词不敢杂庄谐
> Line 2: If misconstrued, will fail the Censor's test."
> 关禁方严怕误猜

Qing Shan has fled China to avoid arrest and he knows that the censors in China are watching the correspondence between him and his wife. He tells his wife that she is wise to be careful of what they write in order to preserve the privacy between them.

> Line 3: "You are cautious, our privacy achieved.
> 果是慧心防范密
> Line 4: Letters are opened before they are received."
> 瑶缄未接已先开

Qing Shan concludes the poem with these two lines, as a final act of thumbing his nose at the censors. It is as though he is saying to them, "Don't you think we know you're reading our letters?"

Chapter 5

听经
tīng jīng

几度听经向玉闺,
亲承洗礼接柔荑。
宿根虽浅心相照,
4 顽石无情首亦低。
结习未能除绮语,
他生深恐堕泥犁。
痴心亦作天堂想,
8 肯负双眉画不齐?

Listening to the Sermon

    In her chamber, her sermons I listen oft.
    Baptized by her hands, delicate and soft.
    Shallow my understanding, yet I respond.
4   Even the stubborn is stirred to reform.
    But bad habits linger, for long ingrained,
    I fear to be in the depths of Hell detained.
    Cherish I the hope to be with her in Heaven,
8   Answerable for her care up there even.

Paraphrase

L1: I have often listened to my wife's "sermons" in the bedroom.

L2: Having listened for so long to her "preaching", I am finally converted by her gentle persuasion. It is as though I am "baptized" by her soft and delicate hands.

L3: Although by nature my understanding of matters religious is shallow, my heart does respond positively to her teachings.

L4: I am like the normally dense and insensate rock that proverbially nods in understanding and acceptance of the teachings of an eloquent teacher.

L5: However, I am not rid yet of the bad habits long ingrained.

L6: I am most fearful of being cast into the depths of Hell in the next life.
L7: I dearly cherish the hope of joining her in Heaven.
L8: So that I may take care of her there.

Background

Summary

This poem was written probably in the late 1930s in Kampar (Malaya). It describes Father's conversion to Christianity but also shows up his skepticism of religion, due probably to his background of Confucianism. He once told us in passing that if you think about it, people embrace religion and do good deeds basically for selfish reasons; they want to go to Heaven!

Mother, on the other hand, was a practical but devout Christian. She went to church regularly but Father seldom attended church. As the poem suggests, Father was probably baptized on Mother's persuasion long after they were married. On the rare occasions that Father did attend church, we used to see him sitting in the pew with his eyes shut, more likely to be falling asleep rather than in some deep meditation.

Mother's Christian Background

As a child, Mother was adopted by the Guo 郭 family in Mianting 棉亭 (Fuqing 福清). The Guo family were staunch Christians and Mother went to an Anglican mission school there. She later worked as an assistant in the school's kindergarten. With this background, there is no doubt that she was baptized as a Christian at a very young age.

Clash and Fusion

It is possible that after she married Father, she may even have stopped attending church, especially during the years from

1932 to 1936 when the family returned to Putian for Father to take up a teaching position in Li Qing Middle School (1932–1934). The family lived initially with our paternal grandfather who was a traditional Confucianist. A woman occupied a very low position in the family hierarchy in a traditional Chinese household steeped in Confucianism. Grandfather ran a private school where the students had to show their reverence to Confucius every morning by kowtowing before his portrait. Even less welcome in such a household would be some new fangled foreign religion like Christianity. Life for someone like Mother who was educated in a Western Christian mission school must have been quite unbearable.

We know for certain that she returned to the church in the late 1930s in Kampar. After Peter was born in 1938 in Kampar, he was frequently ill. Mother had lost two older sons in China a few years earlier. Hence she was ever fearful of losing Peter. It was at this time that a staunch Christian, Madam Goh Soon Keat 吴纯洁, befriended her and she returned even more fervently to the church. Apart from praying for the sick child and the family, Madam Goh "adopted" Peter as her child, supposedly to distract and ward off the evil forces. Despite Madam Goh's Christian background, Chinese traditions never completely disappear. The Chinese have a way of fusing their traditions with new religions.

The Chinese Methodist Church in Lahat Road, Ipoh, where Qing Shan and his family worshipped from 1942 to the early 1950s.

Father, on the other hand, was brought up by his father who was a strict Confucianist, observing the tradition of ancestral worship and other similar practices and beliefs. But Father was also a pragmatic person. If being baptized as a Christian is the only way he can be with his wife in this world and the next, then he is willing to give it a try. This may be no different from the Chinese general attitude towards religion described often as "assimilative".

Appreciation

A short poem of only eight lines, it describes Qing Shan's own conversion to Christianity. On the other hand, it may also be just describing the experience of all those who embrace a religion in order to get married. In this poem, however, the situation is different. The "conversion" takes place after and not before the marriage. Prof Chan Chiu Ming makes an interesting observation about this poem. He says, "It portrays the loving relationship between husband and wife and in several places uses the terminology of both Christianity and Buddhism. A skillful piece of work indeed."

The poem is written in a playful but loving tone. Lines 1 and 2 describe how his wife has converted him to Christianity. Line 1 describes how in the privacy of their bedroom Qing Shan has so often heard his wife tell him about the teachings of her Christian faith. It is only in the evening, when all work is done that they have some quiet time together for such conversation. Line 2 moves quickly on to describe how he is persuaded by her "sermons" and is eventually baptized and received into the Christian faith.

A Literal Translation

We can take the enjoyment of this poem to the next level by an appreciation of the Christian and Buddhist terminology and imagery and metaphors used. To highlight the imagery used, the literal translation of some selected lines is given.

The English words underlined are the literal translation of the Chinese text shown in brackets. For example,

> Line 2: "Personally accepted the <u>sacrament of baptism</u> (*xǐ lǐ* 洗禮), administered by her <u>soft and delicate hands</u> (*róu yí* 柔荑)."

"Baptism" is of course a Christian terminology. The ritual or sacrament of baptism is traditionally performed by the pastor or priest by the sprinkling of water with his hand on the head of the convert. Interestingly, Qing Shan uses the metaphor *róu yí* 柔荑 to describe his wife's soft and delicate hands. The term *róu yí* is the name given to the soft new shoots of a type of grass. The metaphor was first used in the *Book of Poetry* 诗经 which contains a line "Hands like *róu yí* 手如柔荑" to describe a very beautiful noble lady.

The next two Lines 3 and 4 describe how Qing Shan who is normally not receptive to religious sermons is finally convinced by his wife's teaching. These two lines contain some terminology and notions from Buddhism.

> Line 3: "My <u>dormant roots</u> (*sù gēn* 宿根), <u>though shallow</u> (雖淺), <u>my heart does reflect on your teaching</u> (心相照)."

The term *sù gēn* literally means "dormant roots". It is the name given to the dormant roots of plants that grow once every two or more years. Even though the stem and leaves have perished, the roots remain "alive", and when Spring comes the plant thrives again. Buddhism believes in reincarnation and the same term *sù gēn* is used to denote the root of one's previous life carried into the present life. Here, Qing Shan uses the term to mean his "dormant roots" or "by his own nature".

Without further explanation, the literal meaning of Line 4 would sound rather strange:

Line 4: "The <u>obstinate rock</u> (*wán shí* 顽石), <u>insensate</u> (*wú qíng* 无情), too <u>bows its head</u> (*dian tou* 点头)."

This is a Buddhist expression that makes use of hyperbole or exaggeration to describe a monk *Zhú Dào Shēng* 竺道生 (335–424). It is said that he once preached to a group of stones, and his teaching of the Buddhist scriptures was so persuasive that even the insensate stones nodded their heads in understanding and agreement.

Similarly, other examples of Buddhist terminology are in:

Line 5 — *qǐ yǔ* 绮语 is used to describe the "bad habits" that have not been completely rid of. It literally means "damask-like or silken (beautiful) speech" and is one of ten taboos in Buddhism.

Line 6 — *ní lí* 泥犁 is the Chinese transliteration of the Sanskrit word niraya meaning "hell".

Line 7 — *tiān táng* 天堂 meaning "heaven" is used here in the Christianity sense. It is a real place and real experience where the people will live in the presence of God. It is different from the Buddhism concept which simply means liberation from suffering and the attainment of peace of mind, viz., nirvana.

There is an interesting allusion in Line 8. Qing Shan has said in Line 7 that he cherishes the hope to be with his wife in Heaven. Line 8 then gives the reason which has been somewhat simplified into "so that I may take care of her there." The literal meaning of:

Line 8: "I am willing to take the responsibility for (*kěn fù* 肯负) her pair of eyebrows not properly drawn (*shuāng méi huà bù qí* 双眉画不齐)."

This is a roundabout way of saying "I am willing to be answerable for her care". The allusion to the drawing of eyebrows is, firstly, a reference to a lady painting her eyebrows as part of the process of her make-up with the use of cosmetics. The allusion comes from the story of a court official called *Zhāng Chǎng* 张敞 who was very loving with his wife and who helps her with her make-up every morning before going to work. The expression *huà méi* 画眉 later became a metaphor to denote the affection between a man and his wife. For the story of Zhang Chang, please read the Appreciation in Chapter 24.

Chapter 6

经堂 jīng táng

其一

祷词礼赞本寻常,
dǎo cí lǐ zàn běn xún cháng

流出瓠犀分外香。
liú chū hù xī fèn wài xiāng

得傍裙边长俯首,
dé bàng qún biān cháng fǔ shǒu

人间原自有天堂。
rén jiān yuán zì yǒu tiān táng

其二

心祷喃喃语渐低,
xīn dǎo nán nán yǔ jiàn dī

暗中所愿俯蜷蛴。
àn zhōng suǒ yuàn fǔ qiú qí

郎心莫似天涯絮,
láng xīn mò sì tiān yá xù

一遇春风便不泥。
yī yù chūn fēng biàn bù ní

Chanting the Scripture Random Thoughts

Verse 1

    Sound of litany and hymns are but an ordinary thing;
    Poured out b'twixt her even white teeth, how alluring.
    If only I could forever sit and gaze at her,
4   That would be mankind's own heaven on earth.

Verse 2

    In a gradually softer tone, she drones on praying.
    Her fair slender neck bestirs my longing.
    My heart is not like the fluff of willow catkin,
4   Easily dispersed by the first gust of Spring breeze.

Verse 3

    All thoughts of other women are now forgone;
    The incense burner is where my heart's fixed upon.
    I shall care for her even in the privacy of our bedroom.
4   How could I not obey the Seventh Commandment?

其三

惹草沾花念已消，
一心只向博山烧。
画眉深浅闺中事，
戒律何嫌第七条？

The Chinese Methodist Church in Ipoh which still stands today at Jalan Yang Kalsom. This is the church where Qing Shan and his family worshipped during the years 1950-1960. His two daughters Mei Xuan 美璇 and Mei Yu 美瑜 were married in this church.

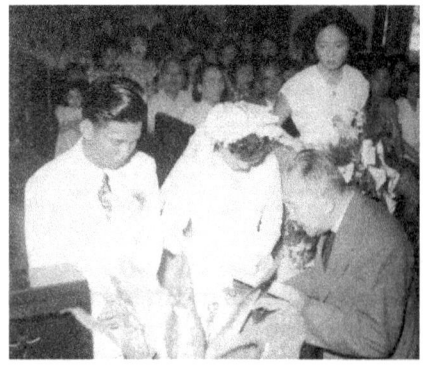

Qing Shan's eldest daughter Mei Xuan 美璇 was married to Khor Thian Sing 许天生 in the Chinese Methodist Church, Ipoh in September 1951, solemnized by Reverend Cai Xin De 蔡信德 (see Chapter 27).

Paraphrase

Verse 1

L1: Litany and hymns of praise are but ordinary things;
L2: But when poured out from between her even white teeth, makes them all the more beautiful.
L3: If only I could sit beside her, looking up at her forever more;
L4: That would be like mankind's own heaven on earth.

Verse 2

L1: She bows her head, droning in prayer in a gradually lower tone.
L2: Her fair slender neck bestirs my silent longing,
L3. My heart is not like the fluff of willow catkin.
L4. That is easily dispersed all over by the first gust of Spring breeze.

Verse 3

L1: All thoughts of other women are now extinguished.
L2: My heart is fixed solely on the incense burner, the centre of her devotion.
L3: I will care for her, even in the privacy of our bedroom.
L4: How could I not obey the Seventh Commandment.

Background

The poem was probably composed in the later part of the 1930s, before Father's conversion to Christianity. Father was brought up a Confucianist, whereas Mother, a devout Christian, was brought up by her adoptive parents who were Christians. Father eventually became a Christian (at least nominally) later in life, most likely at the behest of Mother. We have two other poems that have a church or religious connection in Chapter 5, "Listening to the Sermon 听经", and Chapter 27, "Farewell to Pastor Cai Xin De 送别蔡信德牧师".

For Mother's own Christian background, see Background to Chapter 5.

Appreciation

Qing Shan has a background of Confucianism and traditional Chinese beliefs, including Buddhism. Christianity is "new" and it is his wife who has brought it to him. The poem appears to have been written during the period when he is taken to church by his wife, probably in the late 1930s. As the title suggests, these are "random thoughts" while he is listening to a sermon. With allusions from the *Book of Poetry* 诗经 praising the beauty of a woman, it reads like a love song to his wife.

Verse 1 depicts a man madly and truly in love. The litany and hymns sung by his wife sound all the more beautiful because they "pour out" from between her orderly white teeth. Just to be beside her is like being in heaven on earth. Her beautiful teeth are simply called *hù xī* 瓠犀 as described in the *Book of Poetry*. The term *hù xī* is the name given to the pure white seeds of a type of gourd that grow inside the gourd in orderly rows.

The first two lines of Verse 2 is a continuation of this love song. It again uses allusions from the *Book of Poetry*. He listens to her chanting; as her voice grows gradually softer, he cannot help admiring her fair and slender neck. As in the *Book of Poetry*, the metaphor used for a woman's fair and slender neck is *qiū qí* 蝤蛴. Unattractive it may sound to us today, *qiū qí* is the larva of a type of beetle. Lines 3 and 4 of Verse 2 then declare his steadfast love for his wife, the woman with whom he is so much in love.

Line 3: "My heart is not like the fluff of willow catkin,
郎心莫似天涯絮
Line 4: Easily dispersed by the first gust of Spring breeze."
一遇春风便不泥

This is a very graphic figure of speech. The fluff of the willow catkin is normally dispersed all over by the wind, as nature's way to scatter the seeds of the plant. He declares his steadfast love for her by saying he is not like the willow catkin that is so easily dispersed (sown wildly) by the first gust of the Spring wind *chūn fēng* 春风. Apart from its literal meaning, the term "Spring wind (breeze)" also connotes "relationship with another woman".

There is an interesting story behind the metaphor of willow catkin. It can be better appreciated by looking at the literal meaning of the two lines:

Literal Meaning

Line 3: My heart (郎心) is not like (莫似) the far dispersed (天涯) fluff of the willow catkin (絮)
Line 4: That, once blown by a gust of the Spring wind (一遇春风), is not stained by mud (便不泥).

The fluff that lands on muddy ground will pick up some mud and be weighed down. The corollary is that, fluff that is not stained by mud will be easily dispersed by wind. In using a "double negative" in Lines 3 (莫似) and 4 (不泥), Qing Shan declares that his love is not like the willow catkin that is not stained by mud (不泥). His love for his wife is well anchored and steadfast. The idea of the "fluff of mud-stained willow catkin" (*zhàn ní xù* 沾泥絮) comes from two lines of a poem by the monk named Cān Liáo 参寥 who was a good friend of the Song poet Su Dongpo. The monk was also an accomplished poet. Su Dongpo once played a nasty prank on his friend. Curious as to what a celibate monk would write for a "lady of the night", he once arranged for a courtesan to approach the monk for a poem. This is what the monk wrote:

> This heart of "Zen" is now a fluff with mud stain;
> 禅心已作沾泥絮
> No more will it chase the wind without restrain.
> 不逐东风上下狂

We can see that Qing Shan has turned the original phrase "fluff with mud stain (沾泥絮)" into his own, by a double negative in his Lines 3 and 4: "not like…fluff (that) is not stained by mud".

Verse 3 gets a bit more intense. The intensity of love for his wife is seen not by what is said, but by what is not said.

> Line 1: "All thoughts of other women are now forgone.
>   惹草沾花念已消
> Line 2: The incense burner is where my heart's fixed upon."
>   一心只向博山烧

Line 1 of Verse 3 declares there shall be no more thoughts of other women except his wife. The literal meaning of Line 1, "*re hua zhan cao* 惹花沾草", is "to touch flowers and solicit grass". It is a metaphor for "promiscuity". The literal meaning of Line 2 is quite straightforward. It means "Wholeheartedly for you (一心) will I at the incense burner (向博山) light the incense to pray (烧)". The use of the terms "incense burner" and "light the incense" are more Buddhist practices which Qing Shan has not completely shaken off at this stage. This line uses the term *bó shān* 博山 for incense burner. It has connotations for the Chinese reader. The allusion comes from *Collection of Yuefu Poetry*《乐府诗集》收录《杨叛儿》. There are two lines in there which say:

A Scholar's Path

Boy: "The fragrant incense stick I'll gladly be. 欢作沉水香"
Girl: "Let the incense holder be just me.　　侬作博山炉"

In its connoted sense, the expression of love and unity between Qing Shan and his wife is a great deal more intense than is apparent.

Lines 3 and 4 of Verse 3 declare as a finality:

"I shall care for you even in the privacy of our bedroom.
画眉深浅闺中事
How could I not obey the Seventh Commandment?"
戒律何嫌第七条

For the story behind the allusion of *hua mei* 画眉, see Appreciation of Chapter 24.

The Seventh Commandment in the Bible is "Thou shalt not commit adultery."

Chapter 7

huán jiā
还家

　　zuó　yè　mèng　huán　jiā
　　昨　夜　梦　还　家，

　　huán　jiā　yí　réng　zuó
　　还　家　疑　仍　昨。

　　rù　shì　biàn　mó　suō
　　入　室　遍　摩　挲，

　　zhě　fān　yìng　fēi　cuò
4　者　番　应　非　错。

　　míng　jìng　wèi　kāi　lián
　　明　镜　未　开　奁，

　　tú　huà　zhì　gāo　gé
　　图　画　置　高　阁，

　　chǐ　sù　mò　yóu　nóng
　　尺　素　墨　犹　浓，

　　yàn　chí　shuǐ　wèi　hé
8　砚　池　水　未　涸。

Returning Home

    Came home in a dream, it seems so real.
    It's yesterday, yet it's not very clear.
    Into the house, I touch everything;
4 This time perhaps is the real thing.
    Unopened yet is her dressing mirror.
    Paintings pile atop the cupboard high.
    The paper's thick with ink, not dry;
8 The inkstone is still moist with ink.
    Eldest son hears dad arriving home.
    Leaps forward on his bamboo horse,
    With childish innocence, of course,
12 Begins to rummage my bag as never before.
    Tips and turns my trunk over,
    Like a ferocious tax collector.
    Younger son thinks a guest am I.
16 Startled he is, we lock eye to eye.
    Staring at me for a long while,
    He at last makes out who am I.
    Tuft of mud-stained weed he grabs,
20 Offering it as a present for his dad.
    Dust-stained still are my clothing.
    Can I refuse such an offering?
    Him, up I sweep, like a treasure!
24 This familial love, an unspoken pleasure.

大儿闻爷归,
竹马来如跃。
不解作温存,
12 搜检先囊橐。
倒箧复倾箱,
有如关吏恶。
小儿疑客至,
16 相顾初错愕。
良久细端相,
依稀似领略。
拾芥杂泥沙,
20 献爷博一噱。
征尘虽满襟,
此情不忍却。

抱儿置怀中,
24 暂享天伦乐。
老妻厨下来,
容颜近瘦削。
人前故矜持,
28 相见殊落寞。
邻姬舌悬河,
寒暄杂谐谑。
涕笑两皆非,
32 点头代唯诺。
明朝复远行,
天涯重飘泊。
回忆此时情,
36 苦杯盛甘酪。

    From the kitchen my wife comes hither.
    She appears to have grown thinner.
    Before all, she's prim and proper;
28 Looking indifferent as we meet each other.
    Old women around, they all prattle.
    Pointless small talk, all that tattle.
    I didn't know to sigh or to smile;
32 A nod now and again, just to be polite.
    A long journey tomorrow again!
    Wandering to the ends of the world.
    To recall this sweet memory is such a rub;
36 It's like honey filling a bitter cup.

Paraphrase

L1: Last night, I dreamt I returned home
L2: Now that I'm home, it's still not clear to me if it is a continuation of yesterday's dream.
L3: I enter the house and touch everything around to assure myself it's real.
L4: This time there should be no mistake.
L5: My wife's mirror at the dressing table has not yet been opened up (she's in no mood for it).
L6: The paintings are still there on the top of the cupboard;
L7: The ink is still fresh on the paper laid out,
L8: The inkstone is still moist with ink.
L9: My elder son hears the father arriving home;
L10: He leaps forward on his bamboo horse.
L11: With the guileless innocence of a child, he does not hug me.
L12: Instead, he begins to rummage my bag.
L13: He tips and turns my trunk over
L14: As though he is a ferocious tax collector.
L15: My younger boy thinks that it is a guest who has arrived.
L16: We look at each other and he is at first startled.

L17: After looking at me for a long time,
L18: He finally guesses more or less who I am.
L19: He grabs a tuft of mud-stained weed,
L20: Offering it as a present for his father.
L21: Though my clothes are still stained with the dust of the long journey,
L22: How can I not accept such affection shown by my little boy?
L23: I sweep him up to my bosom
L24: To savour for a moment the joy of familial love.
L25: My good wife comes in from the kitchen;
L26: She appears to have become thinner.
L27: In front of others (the neighbours), she appears unusually reserved.
L28: To see each other again (after this long separation), she seems indifferent to my arrival.
L29: The old women of the neighbourhood who have gathered round spoke in torrents,
L30: Asking about how things are and ceaselessly engaging in pointless prattle.
L31: I feel awkward, not knowing whether to sigh or to smile
L32: And can do no more than to nod now and again out of politeness.
L33: Alas, I will have to set off again the next morning on a long journey.
L34: Wandering to the ends of the world.
L35: To recall such sweet memory of home and then to have to part
L36: Is like drinking honey, filled though in a bitter cup.

Background

There were three periods of time when Father was separated from his wife and family for any length of time. The poem was composed during the third separation during the Japanese Occupation 1942 to 1945. As a Chinese school teacher, Father was like many educated members of the Chinese community whom the Japanese had targeted for elimination. During this period he was in hiding in Kuala Lumpur most of the time. His wife and family were living in a rented room above a shophouse in Anderson Road in Ipoh which was a distance of about 200 kilometres away from Kuala Lumpur.

He visited the family very occasionally and stayed only briefly. He worked in clerical jobs in Kuala Lumpur. Peter and Michael, as portrayed in the poem were only about six and three years old.

Appreciation

This is a poem of 36 lines, composed during the Japanese Occupation (1942-1945) when Qing Shan was in hiding in Kuala Lumpur while his family lived in Ipoh. He badly missed his wife and family and was only able to get home very occasionally.

The poem is a moving account of one of Qing Shan's rare trips home, but it is difficult, even for himself, to distinguish between what is reality and what is dream. It provides a vivid description of the scenes which can be divided into four parts:

1. The Scene at Home (Lines 1 to 8)

It begins with a description of his unexpected arrival home. It seems so real, yet he is not absolutely certain that it is. He touches everything in the house to reassure himself. His wife's dressing mirror has not been opened, the paintings are still piled on top of the high cupboard, ink on the paper has not dried; the inkstone is still moist with ink.

Qing Shan's family (c.1946) soon after the Japanese Occupation: two sons Peter 敏良 ("eldest son"), Michael 敏华 ("younger son"); two daughters Mei Xuan 美璇, Mei Yu 美瑜. His wife Yi Song 义宋 is seated, with Qing Shan standing behind her.

2. His Children (Lines 9 to 24)

Qing Shan is greeted by his eldest son of six, leaping forward on his toy horse of a single bamboo stem. He is old enough to recognize his father. In his childish innocence, instead of giving the father a hug, he rushes for his father's luggage to rummage it, turning it inside out like an overzealous tax collector.

His younger son, aged three, does not even recognize his father, thinking that he is a visiting guest. Startled at first, the child eventually shows some sign of recognition and grabs a fistful of mud-stained grass to offer as a present for his father.

3. His Wife and Neighbours (Lines 25 to 32)

Qing Shan's wife emerges from the kitchen to meet him. Alas, how thin she has become. In front of the neighbours who have begun to gather round, his wife is obliged to maintain her composure and an appearance of propriety. Under these circumstances, she even appears indifferent to his arrival. The old women from the neighbourhood are all there, talking incessantly in torrents (邻妪舌悬河). This is a picturesque description of these busybody neighbourhood women coming over to engage in pointless small talk. Out of politeness, he has to respond with the occasional nod to acknowledge their presence.

4. Familial Joy and Departure (Lines 33 to 36)

In four lines, this last part of the poem sums up its entire theme. His time at home is all too short. He will have to start on his journey again the next morning. How grateful he is to be able to find such familial joy even in adversity! The concluding two lines aptly express his feelings:

> "To recall this sweet memory is such a rub; 回忆此时情
> It's like honey filling a bitter cup." 苦杯盛甘酪

The word "honey" is used in place of the last two Chinese words *gān lào* 甘酪 because "honey" is a better known word in English. The literal meaning of the two Chinese words is "koumiss", a type of sweet fermented milk.

    The whole poem uses hardly any allusion and is so simple that even "the old woman from the neighbourhood" (*lín yù* 邻妪) would have understood — the hallmark of a good poem, as Qing Shan is fond of quoting the Tang poet Bai Juyi 白居易.

Chapter 8

信誓
xìn shì

一炷盟香带月焚，
yī zhù méng xiāng dài yuè fén

白头有约九天闻。
bái tóu yǒu yuē jiǔ tiān wén

尽教马帐成虚愿，
jìn jiào mǎ zhàng chéng xū yuàn

4　犹有牛衣誓不分。
yóu yǒu niú yī shì bù fēn

投笔且休夸定远，
tóu bǐ qiě xiū kuā dìng yuǎn

当炉也合伴文君。
dāng lú yě hé bàn wén jūn

会须共向临邛去，
huì xū gòng xiàng lín qióng qù

8　强似街头独卖文。
qiáng sì jiē tóu dú mài wén

A Solemn Vow

A joss stick is lit; before the moon we pledge
Never to part, though we may be grey with age.
My lifetime of teaching has come to nought.
4   Though poor, to be together is all we've sought.
My pen will seek the high office no more.
Just to be together, we'd rather be a wine vendor.
To hawk in our hometown where we're known
8   Is far better than to hawk my writings all alone.

Paraphrase

L1: A joss stick is lit to pray to the moon.
L2: Let Heaven hear our vow that we will be together till old age do us part.
L3: My lifetime of teaching has achieved nothing like that of the great teacher Ma Rong,
L4: But I do have you to share the hardship together and we vow never to part.
L5: I've ceased to harbour any grand ambition for achieving high office with my pen.
L6: Even as a wine vendor, we would rather be together, like Xiang Ru and Wen Jun.
L7: To hawk for a living in our own hometown where we are known would still be fine, so long as we are together.

L8: It's far better this way than for me to be hawking my literary works all alone.

Background

The poem was written probably during the few months immediately following the end of the Second World War. With this, the Japanese military occupation of Malaya and Singapore too came to an end. Father had come out of hiding (from the Japanese) in Kuala Lumpur. For the first time in the three to four years of the Occupation, Father could openly come home to Ipoh to be with his wife and family. There are several poems filled with his sentiments for the family or wife written during or soon after this period.

Mother, on the other hand, continued with what she had been doing during the entire Japanese Occupation from 1942 to 1945. She had a sewing machine parked in half of a shop front below where our family had rented a room to live. She made "our" living by sewing for people or mending their clothes. Our family income depended on what her takings were each day. With children then aged 14, 11, seven and four, this meager income was obviously not enough. Father had to start looking for a more permanent job in Ipoh when the War ended.

Appreciation

It is understandable why a constant refrain of this poem is about togetherness with his wife, about the poverty and hardship his wife has shared with him. During the Japanese Occupation from 1942 to 1945, his wife and family were left in Ipoh, virtually to fend for themselves while Qing Shan went into hiding from the Japanese. The first two lines of the poem start with a vow that he will never want to be parted from his wife again.

Line 1: "A joss stick is lit; before the moon we pledge
一炷盟香带月焚
Line 2: Never to part, though we may be grey with age."
白头有约九天闻

It is also retrospective, as he looks back at his entire working life up to that point. He is just past 50, an age which the Chinese term "The Age of Knowing" (what Heaven has decreed for one 知命). He has been a school teacher all his life and, until the Japanese Occupation, was still a school teacher. What has he achieved?

The next two lines express his disappointment with himself and renews his vow never to part with his wife.

Line 3: "My lifetime of teaching has come to nought.
尽教马帐成虚愿
Line 4: Though poor, to be together is all we've sought."
犹有牛衣誓不分

In Line 3, he laments his lack of achievement as a school teacher and there is nothing even to begin comparing with the great sage and teacher Ma Rong 马融 (76–166). Here Qing Shan uses the expression *ma zhang* 马帐 ("Ma Rong's screen") to describe "lifetime of teaching". It is said that the great teacher Ma Rong loved beauty and music. His lectures were attended by hundreds of students each time. He would have his male students sit in the front rows and lady musicians playing behind during his lectures. Separating them was a red screen of gauze material. Hence, the metaphor "Ma Rong's screen". In Line 4, Qing Shan says that even though they have to use "cattle blanket of straw" (*niú yī* 牛衣), he and his wife vow never to part. The metaphor "cattle blanket of straw" is used to express poverty. It is an allusion to the story of how Wang Zhang Shao 王章少, a poor scholar and his wife endured poverty together. The couple was so poor that they could not even afford a decent blanket and had to use the straw "blanket" that was used to keep the cattle warm. This story is from the *History of Han Dynasty* (*Han Shu* 汉书).

Having expressed the disappointment in his lack of achievement in life, Qing Shan goes on logically to declare in Lines 5 and 6 that he has given up any hope of achieving high office with his pen. He is content with being a street vendor if that is how he and his wife can stay together all the time.

> Line 5: "My pen will seek the high office no more.
> 投笔且休夸定远
> Line 6: Just to be together, we'd rather be a wine vendor."
> 当炉也合伴文君

To express this thought in Line 6, Qing Shan uses an allusion of a loving couple Sima Xiang Ru 司马相如 and his wife Zhuo Wen Jun 卓文君. The literal translation of Line 6 is, "Even as a wine seller (*dang lu* 当炉), I would want to be with Wen Jun." The story of this loving couple comes from *The Historian's Record* (*Shǐ Jì* 史记). Zhuo Wen Jun came from a rich family and Sima Xiang Ru was a poor scholar. She was in love with him and ran away with him against her parents' objections. The couple eventually sold their last possession and bought a wine shop to sell wine for a living. Whatever they did, the couple was happy just to be together.

The last two lines 7 and 8 continue with the allusion to this story. In essence, Qing Shan says that he will be willing to be a wine vendor even in their own hometown where they are known to their friends and family; for this is far better than to be separated from his dear wife and where he will be hawking his writings all by himself.

> Line 7: "To hawk in our hometown where we're known
> 会须共向临邛去
> Line 8: Is far better than to hawk my writings all alone."
> 强似街头独卖文

The Wen Jun allusion begun in Line 6 is continued in Line 7. The literal translation of Line 7 is, "We will proceed together to Lin Qiong 临邛." This is the name of the hometown of Wen Jun. To fill in a few other details of Zhuo Wen Jun, she was actually the widowed daughter of a wealthy household in Lin Qiong. She fell in love with the capable but poor scholar Sima Xiang Ru and the two eloped to Chengdu in Sichuan. Receiving no help from Wen Jun's wealthy family, the couple eventually returned to Wen Jun's hometown Lin Qiong. They sold all their belongings and bought a wine shop. Wen Jun, the daughter of a wealthy family, had to work as a waitress in the wine shop. This story became a metaphor denoting the steadfast love between a couple.

The poem is rich in the use of allusions from the classics. This shows Qing Shan's grasp and depth of knowledge of classical literature.

Chapter 9

中秋咏月饼寄内
<small>zhōng qiū yǒng yuè bǐng jì nèi</small>

年年中秋节，
<small>nián nián zhōng qiū jié</small>

月饼竞趋时，
<small>yuè bǐng jìng qū shí</small>

天上圆如镜，
<small>tiān shàng yuán rú jìng</small>

4　人间亦称之。
<small>rén jiān yì chēng zhī</small>

莲蓉与银月，
<small>lián róng yǔ yín yuè</small>

玉屑杂金丝，
<small>yù xiè zá jīn sī</small>

命名争纤巧，
<small>mìng míng zhēng xiān qiǎo</small>

8　花样斗新奇。
<small>huā yàng dòu xīn qí</small>

A Mooncake Poem for My Wife

Mid-Autumn is here with all its bustle;
Into the market, the mooncakes jostle.
The moon above, mirror-like round;
4   Mankind below, her praises resound.
Lotus paste, melon seeds and the best ham.
Tasty bits of many hues in them all cram.
They go with fanciful names in colours pretty,
8   Varieties are remarkable as they are many.
Ms Zhang next door from the east comes hither;
Auntie Li from the west hurries off thither.
Criss-crossing each other, presents in hand,
12 The servants complain not, a tireless band.
Sugar and flour, higher in price this year.
Shortage and hoarding, they become dear.
The moon rises, neither late nor early.
16 The mooncakes' arrival is somewhat tardy.
When they make their long awaited show,
They look like Xi-shi, without her glow,
Or very much like the "skinny" Fei-yan
20 Yet to regain the plumpness of Lady Yang.
The full moon will periodically appear.
Numerous are the morning stars above.
Other things are scarce and hence are dear.

东邻张氏姊，
西舍李家姨，
纷纷相馈赠，
12 婢媪不辞疲。
今年糖与面，
奇货居无遗，
出山月依旧，
16 上市饼偏迟。
偶然有所见，
亦似病西施，
尽同飞燕瘦，
20 无复玉环肥。

满月安可拟，
晨星未为稀，
物以罕而贵，
24 尝新自难期。
我闻昔人语，
画饼可充饥，
亦欲写一幅，
28 聊以慰相思。
无如绘事拙，
笔下仅有诗，
画饼虽不就，
32 咏饼或庶几。

24 I can't afford to taste the cakes, that's clear.
   I have always heard that the ancients say,
   To paint a cake can one's hunger allay.
   I too shall paint the picture of a cake
28 Merely for self consolation's sake.
   But I'm clumsy in my works of art.
   Only poems can my pen impart.
   Cake painting is not a skill I ever had.
32 A "cake" poem may not be too bad.
   I grind the inkstone and stretch the paper.
   Roll up my sleeves to be Master Baker.
   The poem's ready; I shall recite it now.
36 Its taste is sweet as maltose in my mouth.
   I shall seal it and post it straight to you,
   So that you too can its full flavour chew.
   Like "Jester" Shuo, I fear the meat won't keep!
40 But my good wife, please do not laugh at me.
   Holding the poem under the moon, I recite.
   To share its joy with our children tonight.
   Ah Xuan can read a great deal, really;
44 Perhaps she'll think her dad is too silly.
   Ah Yu has only just started school;
   She can but understand a little, true.
   Liang and Hua are too young to know;
48 Wherever I go, I have them in tow.
   Reunion with family, happiest of events.
   Unable to return, the traveller laments.
   Moist with fragrant dew, soft as clouds her hair
52 Bathed in moonlight, her jade-like arms so fair.
   I have now eaten all my poem's cake;
   No longer shall I frown for sorrow's sake.
   This Mid-Autumn in all our twenty years,
56 I know now the taste that brings such cheers.

磨墨复伸纸，
攘臂作饼师，
诗成自吟哦，
36 颇觉味如饴。
封缄付邮便，
与子快朵颐。
丹诚鉴臣朔，
40 细君且莫嗤。
持向月下诵，
分甘遍诸儿。
阿璇多识字，
44 倘或笑爷痴。

阿瑜初入学，
略解无与之，
良华皆幼稚，
48 绕膝亦依依。
团圆固可乐，
远人愁未归，
云鬟湿香雾，
52 玉臂映清辉。
啖罢诗中饼，
将毋蹙双眉，
廿载中秋月，
56 此味今始知。

Paraphrase

L1: As the annual Mid-Autumn festival approaches,
L2: The mooncake shops in town begin to jostle with one another fighting for a place in the market.
L3: The full moon in the sky above is round as a mirror;
L4: Mankind below all sing its praise.
L5: There are all kinds of mooncake, some filled with lotus paste, melon seeds,
L6: Sweetmeats such as ham and other tasty bits like sugared winter melon.
L7: They are packaged in many colourful ways and given all sorts of fanciful names.
L8: The mooncakes are as numerous in variety as they are remarkable.
L9: Ms Zhang from the east neighbourhood and
L10: Auntie Li from the west
L11: All hurry hither and thither to deliver the presents of mooncakes.
L12: The tireless band of household servants do not seem to complain of being overworked.
L13: The price of sugar and flour seems to have risen this year.
L14: Perhaps there is a shortage because someone is hoarding them.
L15: The moon rises from behind the hills, timely as it has always done, but
L16: The mooncakes appear to have come rather tardily on the market this year.
L17: At last, when they make their appearance,
L18: They look like the beautiful Xi-shi when she is suffering a bout of illness.
L19: They appear "skinny" as the slim and slender dancer Fei-yan, or
L20: They have yet to regain the fullness of the well-endowed Yang Guifei.
L21: The full moon will always appear from time to time and

L22: The myriads of morning stars will always be there.
L23: However, basic commodities can become scarce sometimes and their prices will inevitably rise on account of their scarcity.
L24: To be able to get a taste of this year's mooncakes, is too much for me to hope for.
L25: I hear the ancients say
L26: That you can allay your hunger by drawing a picture of a piece of cake and then "feast" your eyes on it.
L27: Let me too draw such a picture so that
L28: I can console myself a little.
L29: I'm unable to draw a decent picture of a cake;
L30: My pen can only write a poem.
L31: Although I'm not good at painting a cake,
L32: To recite a cake poem may not be too bad.
L33: Let me grind the inkstone and stretch out the paper.
L34: I then roll up my sleeves to take on the role of the Master Baker.
L35: When the poem is "done", I shall chant it myself.
L36: Oh, how wonderful its taste, sweet as maltose in my mouth.
L37: I can't wait to seal the poem in an envelope for the post.
L38: So that my wife too can savour its flavour.
L39: In my sincere anxiety to send you this delicious "morsel", you might think I'm behaving like the Han dynasty official, "the jester" Dongfang Shuo, who hurried off with the royal meat to his wife.
L40: But my good wife—please don't laugh at me.
L41: I can't wait to go out there and chant this poem under the moon.
L42: I have at first thought of sharing it with the children.
L43: Eldest daughter Ah Xuan can read a great deal,
L44: But what if she thinks her father is being silly.
L45: Number two daughter Ah Yu has just started school;
L46: She will understand but little.
L47: My two sons Liang and Hua are both still young.

L48: They will only stick to and follow me around.
L49: A family reunion at Mid-Autumn is normally a happy event,
L50: But sad is the traveller who is far away and cannot return home to his family.
L51: At home, the wife prays to the moon deep into the night till her hair, soft as clouds, is moist with the fragrant early morning dew.
L52: The jade-white complexion of her arms is reflected in the clear brilliant light of the moon.
L53: Having finished "eating" the mooncake of my poem,
L54: I will no longer furrow my brow in sorrow.
L55: In the Mid-Autumn festivals of the last 20 years,
L56: This is the first time I have tasted the sweet delights of the occasion.

Background

For Malaya and Singapore, the Second World War and the hated Japanese Occupation ended with Japan's surrender on 15 August 1945. Father had only just emerged from hiding and could then be with the family openly and without fear. He had been in "hiding" during the Japanese Occupation. The happier and lighter mood of this poem is in contrast with the poem in Chapter 7, "Returning Home 还家" written during the Occupation (1942–1945).

This poem was probably composed around the time of the Mid-Autumn Festival of 1945 (which fell on 20 September of that year). There was still a serious shortage of basic food commodities—and of money!

Our family was living in a rented room above a shophouse at 82 Anderson Road in Ipoh. In half of a shop front downstairs, Mother had her sewing machine, mending and sewing clothes for a living. Father had yet to find a job. There were four children to feed. They are all named in the poem: Ah Xuan 阿璇, Ah Yu 阿瑜, Liang 良, Hua 华 (Lines 43, 45 and 47). It was not until a month or two later that Father managed to secure a job as the paid Secretary of the Perak Hokkien Association 霹雳福建公会 at a salary of 60 dollars per month.

Qing Shan in 1946, soon after the Japanese Occupation. The family was too poor to be able to afford mooncakes.
"I too shall paint the picture of a cake, Merely for self consolation's sake." (Lines 27-28)

Qing Shan's wife Yi Song (1946). *"But my good wife, please do not laugh at me. Holding the poem under the moon, I recite."* (Lines 40-41)

Lotus seed paste-filled mooncakes that Qing Shan could not afford to buy.

"Lotus paste, melon seeds and the best ham. Tasty bits of many hues in them all cram." (Lines 5-6)

Appreciation

This is a light-hearted, humorous and also heartwarming poem about Qing Shan's first Mid-Autumn Festival after the dark days of the Japanese Occupation. The poem can be divided into five parts.

Part One

The first part comprising Lines 1 to 12 describes the usual festive scenes around the time of the Mid-Autumn Festival. The exotic fillings of the mooncakes are described in realistic details:

> Line 5: "Lotus paste, melon seeds, and the best ham.
> 莲蓉与银月
> Line 6: Tasty bits of many hues in them all cram."
> 玉屑杂金丝

For the more well-off families, there is the hustle and bustle in the shops and the busy time of buying and exchanging mooncakes as presents:

> Line 9: "Ms Zhang next door from the east comes hither; 东邻张氏姊
> Line 10: Auntie Li from the west hurries off thither.
> 西舍李家姨
> Line 11: Criss-crossing each other, presents in hand,
> 纷纷相馈赠
> Line 12: The servants complain not, a tireless band."
> 婢媪不辞疲

Part Two

The second part of the poem, Lines 13 to 24, describes the shortage of basic food commodities, resulting in few mooncakes coming late on the market. Qing Shan describes in a humorous way how the moon cakes fall far short of the usual quality:

> Line 17: "When they make their long awaited show,
> 偶然有所见
> Line 18: They look like Xi-shi, without her glow,
> 亦似病西施
> Line 19: Or very much like the "skinny" Fei-yan
> 尽同飞燕瘦

Line 20: Yet to regain the plumpness of Lady Yang."
无复玉环肥

Xi-shi 西施 and Yang Gui-fei 杨贵妃 (real name *Yáng Yù Huán* 杨玉环) are two of the four beauties of ancient China. The line on Xi-shi says literally that the "mooncakes look like when Xi-shi is ill" (亦似病西施). It is reputed that Xi-shi looks exceptionally beautiful during her bouts of illness that subject her to intense pain. The third historic figure in Qing Shan's gallery of beauties is a dancer called *Zhào Fēi Yàn* 赵飞燕 who is so slim, light and graceful that she is reputed to be able to dance on someone's palm!

Whatever the quality of the mooncakes, the reality is Qing Shan could not afford to buy them for his wife or family. He did not even have a job then.

Part Three

The third part of the poem, Lines 25 to 36, leads us to his "ingenious" solution. He resorts to what the Chinese describes as an act of self-consolation or make-believe, i.e., "painting the picture of a cake to allay one's hunger" (画饼充饥). Since he has no ability to paint, he does the next best thing by composing a poem about mooncakes. Hence his detailed description of all the delectable ingredients which go into the mooncakes.

Part Four

The fourth part, Lines 37 to 48, tells what happens when he has finished composing the poem. As he reads over the newly composed poem, he smacks his lips in satisfaction, "Its taste is sweet as maltose in my mouth 颇觉味如饴". He cannot wait to rush the poem to his wife and family but is a little afraid that his wife will laugh at him for being silly.

Line 37: "I shall seal it and post it straight to you,
        封缄付邮便
Line 38: So that you too can its full flavour chew.
        与子快朵颐
Line 39: Like 'Jester' Shuo, I fear the meat won't keep!
        丹诚鉴臣朔
Line 40: But my good wife, please do not laugh at me."
        细君且莫嗤

The reference to "Jester" Shuo fearing that "the meat won't keep" comes from an amusing story of a court minister called *Dōng Fāng Shuò* 东方朔. He lived in the Han dynasty during the reign of Han Wu Emperor 汉武帝. He was a clever man but given to jests. A custom in court during that time was the distribution of meat from the royal hunt. All the ministers of the court would assemble in front of the meat to await its distribution. The minister-in-charge would arrive to read out the Emperor's proclamation before the distribution can take place. On such an occasion one Summer, Jester Shuo stood among the other ministers to await the arrival of the minister-in-charge. The anxious group of ministers waited a long time and there was still no sign of him. Out of exasperation, Jester Shuo went forward, drew his sword and carved out for himself a big slab of meat. Tucking it under his robes, he left hurriedly home. This unbecoming behaviour was reported to the Emperor the next day and Shuo was summoned for an explanation. "Your Majesty," explained Shuo, "it was a very hot day. I was afraid the meat would go bad and decided to hurry home with it for my wife!" The Emperor was highly amused by his explanation and Jester Shuo was forgiven.

Qing Shan's use of the term *xì jūn* 细君 to mean "wife" is rather clever. It happens to be the name of Jester Shuo's wife and has since become a metaphor precisely for "wife". Moreover, the literal meaning of the two words 细君 is "little master (or mistress)" of the house!

Part Five

The fifth part, Lines 49 to 56, forms the conclusion of the poem. It starts with lines inspired by Du Fu's poem "Moonlight Night 月夜" which describes how his wife misses him. But in Qing Shan's poem, he turns it around to describe how he misses his wife.

As Prof Chan Chiu Ming pointed out, "It is common enough to find in classical poems themes in praise of the moon, of the eating of mooncakes and of husband and wife pining for each other. We see in this poem a completely fresh turn of these old themes by Qing Shan." As a consolation to himself who is unable to afford the "real" mooncakes, he has managed to use the composition and recitation of a mooncake poem as a substitute.

This final part of the poem appears to have three moods from "pensive", through "reflective" and then "joyous".

Mid-Autumn is normally a happy time for reunion with the family, but Qing Shan thinks of those who are still separated and are unable to return. He has not forgotten his own separation from his family and has himself only just come out of hiding.

> Line 50: "Unable to return, the traveller laments."
> 远人愁未归

Inspired by lines from Du Fu's poem, he reflects on how he has missed his wife:

> Line 51: "Moist with fragrant dew, soft as clouds her hair 云鬟湿香雾
> Line 52: Bathed in moonlight, her jade-like arms so fair." 玉臂映清辉

Then, comes the joy. He has finished writing and reciting his mooncake poem. He imagines he has eaten his fill of the imaginary mooncake.

Line 53: "I have now eaten all my poem's cake;
　　　　 啖罢诗中饼
Line 54: No longer shall I frown for sorrow's sake.
　　　　 将毋蹙双眉
Line 55: This Mid-Autumn in all our twenty years,
　　　　 廿载中秋月
Line 56: I know now the taste that brings such cheers."
　　　　 此味今始知

So happy is he that it is only now that he begins to know the "full flavour" 此味 of Mid-Autumn. This is the best Mid-Autumn he has experienced in his 20 years of marriage. Qing Shan's joy is not surprising, after three years and eight months of suffering under the Japanese Occupation!

Chapter 10

shì xuán nǚ
示璇女

zǎo bèi rú guàn wù dào jīn
早被儒冠误到今，

bǎi wú yī jiù dàn cháng yín
百无一就但长吟。

xiū cóng yé nòng shēng huā bǐ
休从爷弄生花笔，

qiě xué niáng chuān qǐ qiǎo zhēn
且学娘穿乞巧针。

Admonition to My Daughter Xuan

Long have I suffered pursuing a scholar's path.
Good in nothing but the classics is not enough.
Do not follow your father, wielding a fancy pen.
From your mother's sewing, learn all you can.

Paraphrase

L1: I have long suffered the consequences of a scholar's cap (pursuing a scholar's career in life),
L2: Without even one accomplishment in a hundred, except to recite the classics all day.
L3: Cease following your father's footsteps in wielding a pen writing fancy words.
L4: Instead, learn from your mother the finer points of threading (sewing).

Background

After the Second World War ended in 1945, elder sister Mei Xuan, who was then 15, resumed her schooling which had been interrupted by the war. She finished primary school at the end of 1947. She was encouraged to learn sewing in Mother's tailoring school rather than to go on to high school.

The teaching staff of Yi Song's tailoring school in Ipoh (May 1949), with Mei Xuan, standing third from left. *"From your mother's sewing, learn all you can."* Upon graduation from the tailoring school, Mei Xuan became an instructor in the school.

Mei Xuan (centre) with her fellow tutors at Mother's tailoring school.

Mei Xuan as a school girl in Perak Girls' Primary School in Ipoh.

Mei Xuan in school uniform at the age of 16.

Father's own experience during the Japanese Occupation (1942–1945) created a disillusionment with his own lack of ability for business or a vocational skill. During the Occupation, being a scholar was more of a liability than an asset. The Japanese initially looked upon writers and the intelligentsia as their enemies who might have been involved in anti-Japanese activities prior to the invasion and who had supported the war against the Japanese in China. In a wartime economy under enemy occupation, people like scholars and teachers could only undertake lowly paid administrative and clerical work. Those who could wheel and deal or trade in the black market and those who had vocational skills did much better. Mother was able to eke out a living with a sewing machine in the front of the shophouse where we lived, waiting for passerby customers who wanted their shirts or pants mended.

Mother had a tailoring school in Kampar in 1940–1941. The family had moved to Ipoh at the beginning of the war. After the war ended, Mother found a partner (one of her pre-war tailoring students) who had the capital and re-started her tailoring school in Ipoh on 15 July 1947.

After her primary school education, Mei Xuan took up tailoring in Mother's school. Upon graduation from the tailoring school, she became an instructor, continuing on until a couple of years later when she married and started a family.

Appreciation

This short poem of four lines was composed for Qing Shan's eldest daughter Mei Xuan in 1947–1948. It reflects the poet's frustration and disillusionment with his own position while giving sound practical advice for the situation soon after the Japanese Occupation.

The poem uses very simple words and is easy to read. In Line 1, the Chinese text uses the expression *rú guān* 儒冠 (scholar's cap) as a metaphor for "pursuing a scholar's path".

The poet is being self-deprecatory here. The sentiment of frustration similar to that expressed in this poem is found in these two lines of Du Fu's poem:

> The idle rich do not starve, inept they are. 纨绔不饿死
> The scholar struggles in vain, how bizarre! 儒冠多误身

In Line 2, Qing Shan describes himself as being "Without even one accomplishment in a hundred, except to recite the classics all day 百无一就但长吟". By using the words *chang yin* 长吟 "reciting (the classics) all day long", he evokes the very caricature of a scholar who can be talented but yet "hungry".

In Line 3, he advises his daughter not to follow in his footsteps as a scholar who is typecast as wielding a pen producing only fancy words that cannot earn enough for a decent living. The Chinese text contains a rich and colourful expression "wield a fancy pen" 弄生花笔, i.e., wield a pen that produces beautiful words. The original expression with a positive meaning has been turned on its head by Qing Shan. The original expression *shēng huā miào bǐ* 生花妙笔 means "a gifted pen". This is from a story about the Tang poet Li Bai 李白. When he was young he dreamt that flowers were blossoming out of the tip of his pen and this was supposed to foretell his literary talent that was to come.

The final word of advice comes in Line 4, "From your mother's sewing, learn all you can." The plain English text "your mother's sewing" is actually a translation of the Chinese text "*chuān qǐ qiǎo zhēn* 穿乞巧针" (literally "to thread the needle"). The custom of "threading the needle" or *qǐ qiǎo* 乞巧 is very ancient. It is said that when the legendary Cowherd and the Weaving Girl meet every year on the 7th day of the 7th month, the women folks would perform the custom of threading a needle, presumably in the hope that they would become as skillful as the Weaving Girl. A distinctive feature of Qing Shan's poetry is its rich lode of classical allusions that have become part of the Chinese language and therefore are familiar to the average Chinese reader.

The construction of Lines 3 and 4 is beautifully done. This is better appreciated in Chinese and a literal translation. This pair of lines has the characteristics of a well-constructed couplet, with every phrase in Line 3 matching and complementing the corresponding expression in Line 4 in their respective parts of speech and position in the line (e.g., "Stop follow" matches with "But learn (from)". The imagery in one line contrasts with that of the other (e.g., "fancy pen" contrasts with "needle").

休从	爷弄	生花笔
Stop follow	father wield	fancy pen
且学	娘穿	乞巧针
But learn (from)	mother to thread	needle

For elder sister Mei Xuan, these two lines will be her "quotable quote" that rolls easily off the tongue, an important attribute of a good poem. Indeed Mei Xuan has this poem written out by a calligrapher in Xiamen. It is now displayed in the living room of her house.

Chapter 11

嫁女辞示美瑜
jià nǔ cí shì měi yú

阿婆将嫁女，
ā pó jiāng jià nǔ

施巾复结褵，
shī jīn fù jié lí

婿家虽咫尺，
xù jiā suī zhǐ chǐ

4 惜别亦依依，
xī bié yì yī yī

唤女且暂驻，
huàn nǔ qiě zàn zhù

殷勤为致辞，
yīn qín wèi zhì cí

行当为人妇，
xíng dāng wéi rén fù

8 可念在家时。
kě niàn zài jiā shí

Wedding Poem
An Admonition to Mei Yu

    Mother is sending her daughter off;
    Hurriedly she adjusts the bridal veil.
    Although son-in-law's home is just close by,
4   It's for mother a reluctant goodbye.
    Pause for a moment before you depart,
    Your mother has a few words to impart.
    In your new role as daughter-in-law,
8   Remember the lessons from which to draw.
    You had only mother to love before;
    You have now your husband to care for.
    It's good to have love between husband and wife,
12 But don't over-depend on him all your life.
    Although we come from a poor family
    We do not seek either wealth or glory.
    If my daughter is not a lady of leisure
16 That'll be our honour of great measure.
    You're born with a pair of hands and a brain,
    How could you and a man be not the same?
    There's no gender difference in the workplace,
20 Inferiority complex you should all erase.
    She who shuns hard work to seek an easy day
    Will fail in all she does, due to a life of play.
    A girl who puts to good use her youthful years,
24 With her husband will spend their golden years.

宿昔只怜母，
怜婿今过之，
恩爱固应尔，
12 倚赖殊不宜。
吾家素贫贱，
富贵非所期，
但令无游女，
16 便足耀门楣。
汝生具手脑，
何异一男儿，
事业无性别，
20 慎勿长自卑。

恶劳而好逸，
业乃荒于嬉，
盛年自珍惜，
24 偕老方可期。
眄彼笼中鸟，
终日但画眉，
笼上丝作系，
28 笼外金为篱，
琼浆调玉粒，
不愁渴与饥，
所嗟负双翼，
32 临风不能飞。

       Just look at the bird that's kept in a cage.
       It does nothing but preens herself all day.
       Above the cage hangs the fine silk thread;
28   Around the cage the gold rails barricade.
       Provided with nothing but the best of food,
       Never for hunger or thirst will it brood.
       It's like a fledgling without any wing
32   That can't fly even in a gust of wind.

Paraphrase

L1:   Mother is about to send off her daughter in marriage;
L2:   She is busy making last-minute adjustments to the bridal veil.
L3:   Although the son-in-law's home is just close by
L4:   It is nevertheless a reluctant goodbye for mother.
L5:   She asks the daughter to pause for a moment
L6:   For mother to impart a few earnest words of counsel.
L7:   In your new role as a daughter-in-law
L8:   You must remember what you've been taught in our home.
L9:   In the past, you have only your mother to love
L10: Now, you will have your husband to care for.
L11: It is right that there should be mutual love between husband and wife
L12: But it is inappropriate for you to be over-dependent on your husband.
L13: Although we are from a poor family,
L14: We do not seek great wealth and honour.
L15: We only want our daughter not to become an idle lady of leisure
L16: That would be sufficient to reflect positively on our family.
L17: You have a pair of hands and the brains to go with them,
L18: How could you be any different from a man?
L19: In the working place in society there is no distinction between genders,

L20: Do not therefore bear any feeling of inferiority.
L21: A person who shuns hard work and seeks only a life of leisure
L22: Will ultimately fail in work due to a whole life of play.
L23: A girl should value and make good use of her youth,
L24: Only then would she and her husband enjoy their golden years together.
L25: Take a look at the bird kept in a cage.
L26: It does nothing else but preens itself all day.
L27: Its cage is hung by silken threads above;
L28: It is barricaded in by gilded rails all round.
L29: Provided with nothing but the best of food,
L30: It never has to worry about hunger or thirst.
L31: Alas, it is now like a fledgling, but without its wings,
L32: Unable to take off and fly, even in a gust of wind.

Background

Summary

This poem was written for elder sister Mei Yu 美瑜 for her wedding on 14 December 1957.

Ten years earlier, Father had written a short poem for our eldest sister Mei Xuan 美璇, viz., the poem in Chapter 10, "Admonition to My Daughter Xuan 示璇女", counselling her to learn sewing from Mother instead of continuing with her high school education.

Although schooled in the classics, Father had very modern views on the role of women in society. The "old" thinking had been a woman's place is in the home; this is where a virtuous woman belongs. Father's recurring theme in his poems to his daughters and to his graduating classes of girls in his school was very clear: "Acquire a skill, do not be over-dependent on your husband, do not aspire to be a lady of leisure."

Mei Yu was already 23 in 1957 and had been teaching for three years. An unmarried girl at 23 was considered rather "advanced" in age in those days. Madam Peng 彭, the Principal of the school where Father was teaching part time, "matchmade" Mei Yu with Jun Yuan 均元. He was a relative of Madam Peng and already 32 and still a bachelor. Jun Yuan lived only twenty houses away down the same road in Leong Sin Nam Street in Ipoh. His family, though not fabulously wealthy, was well-off. Jun Yuan worked in his father's business.

Mei Yu continued working after her marriage and retired as a Chinese school teacher in 1990 (aged 55). She and Jun Yuan have two children, and two grandchildren. On 14 December 2007, they celebrated their golden wedding anniversary in Singapore.

Wedding Trousseau

After their marriage, Mei Yu and Jun Yuan rented a room to live in. This one room was their entire matrimonial home. Father insisted that Mei Yu put up on the wall in their room all her certificates and diplomas: primary school and junior high school graduation certificates, teacher training diploma, tailoring and embroidery school certificates.

When their "matchmaker" Madam Peng came to visit their room, she was highly amused by this display of certificates and diplomas on the wall. She did not think these vocational skills and primary school diplomas were anything worthy of display. She could hardly conceal her amusement and poor Mei Yu was rather embarrassed by Madam Peng's involuntary sniggering.

Madam Peng was from a well-to-do family and came originally from Hunan province. She was a college graduate and was now married into a wealthy tin miner family in Ipoh. She became the Principal of the girls' school at a relatively young age of 31. Academically well-qualified and from a well-to-do background, it was not surprising that she should be amused by the display of Mei Yu's diplomas including one as basic as an embroidery certificate!

Qing Shan's third daughter Mei Yu and her husband Jun Yuan (Kuan Nyean) on their Wedding Day (December 1957). *"Although son-in-law's home is just close by, It's for mother a reluctant goodbye"*. Jun Yuan lived only twenty houses away down the same road.

Mei Yu's wedding poem in Qing Shan's own calligraphy.
Qing Shan in his later years, did not like to use a brush pen too much, except for very special occasions.

It was only by repeatedly reading Father's poem that Mei Yu eventually realized the depth of the message behind this seemingly strange display of certificates and diplomas on her bedroom wall. They were a representation of the vocational skills and education Mei Yu had acquired. She would be well equipped to start off in life as a worthy partner with her husband. The qualifications were not much by today's standard, but were acquired within the means of the family. They had stood her in good stead throughout her long working career. Is her trousseau not worth more than "silver and gold"?

Recipe for a successful marriage

Father had also reasoned that when a woman has some skills of her own, this would more likely result in a more equal husband-and-wife partnership, thereby contributing to a durable marriage.

Appreciation

The poem is written as counsel by a mother to her daughter as she is sending her off on her wedding day. The language is simple, the imagery and metaphors used are easily understood.

Action

Each line of only five words, the rhythm is brisk, making the poem very much alive and filled with action.

> Line 1: "Mother is sending her daughter off; 阿婆将嫁女
> Line 2: Hurriedly she adjusts the bridal veil." 施巾复结褵

We can imagine the mother fussing over the bridal dress and hurriedly making last-minute adjustments to the veil as the bridal car arrives.

Line 5: "Pause for a moment before you depart,
唤女且暂驻
Line 6: Your mother has a few words to impart."
殷勤为致辞

Although the daughter's new home is only a short distance away, mother is still reluctant to say goodbye. Right up to the very last, mother still holds onto her to whisper final words of counsel to her.

Counsel

The daughter is reminded of the husband she now has to care for, but it is important she is not over-dependent on him. She should have a set of skills herself. Rather ahead of the times, Mother tells her there is no difference between a daughter and a son and she should not harbour any sense of inferiority complex. A more balanced relationship between husband and wife will also make for a more enduring marriage. If mother's daughter has not become a lady of leisure, that will be a positive reflection on the honour of the family.

Bird in a Gilded Cage

In Lines 25 to 32, Qing Shan uses, in an interesting way, the parable of the bird in the gilded cage. This is really the punch line of the poem. He compares a lady who opts for a life of leisure to a bird in a gilded cage.

Line 25: "Just look at the bird that's kept in a cage.
晒彼笼中鸟
Line 26: It does nothing but preens herself all day.
终日但画眉
Line 27: Above the cage hangs the fine silk thread;
笼上丝作系

Line 28: Around the cage the gold rails barricade."
   笼外金为篱

It is a meaningless existence. She trades her freedom and individuality for the life of luxury in a gilded cage.

Line 29: "Provided with nothing but the best of food,
   琼浆调玉粒
Line 30: Never for hunger or thirst will it brood.
   不愁渴与饥
Line 31: It's like a fledgling without any wing
   所嗟负双翼
Line 32: That can't fly even in a gust of wind."
   临风不能飞

So used to a life of luxury is she that in due course, she becomes "useless" and unable to help herself should the need arise. She is like a fledgling who has never used her wings and never developed. When the time comes, she has become permanently disabled.

Chapter 12

寿内三章

内人王义宋女士主持霹雳妇女裁剪训练所十年，今岁六一初度，及门诸女棣欲以文字付铅椠为寿，征诗及余，率成三首，并先发稿于所知吟侣，以就正焉。

其一

卅年心跡两相亲，
嫁得黔娄信夙因。
举案籲天欣有託，
立锥无地不愁贫。

Three Birthday Verses for My Wife

My wife Wang Yi Song has directed the Perak Women's Tailoring Centre for ten years. She is sixty-one this year and her many students wish to compile a publication to commemorate her birthday. They approach me for a poem and I hurriedly compose herein three verses to send out to my poetry friends for their comment and advice.

Verse 1

    For thirty years our hearts are one, such is our love.
    It's predestination you're married to a poor "Qian Lou".
    You thank Heaven we have mutual support in each other.
4   We own not an inch of ground, but you despair not ever.
    It's good to have the ruddy looks of youth, they often say.
    Only now do I know how precious it is to age till grey.
    Many start the journey of marriage, but fail to run the course.
8   The fallen are mostly young, their journey ending in divorce.

Verse 2

    Ten years of labour, how the tailoring venture has grown.
    Pretty materials, clothes adorned with orchids are sewn.
    The art of sewing is passed on to many ladies indeed;

等闲争说朱颜好,

此日方知白发珍!

多少蘼芜山下过,

相逢尽是少年人。

其二

十载辛勤创业难,

苊荷制就又纫兰。

广将衣钵传妆阁,

独领裙钗主艺坛。

垂老双眉从未敛,

片时十指不曾安。

养生自信无他巧,

体但常劳心但宽。

4   The training of women in sewing, by yourself you lead,
    Right up to your old age, never a single frown you've shown.
    Busy always, your ten fingers never pause for a moment.
    In preserving health, you know there is no special recipe
8   But to keep the body busy and the spirit relaxed and happy.

Verse 3

   The greying hair on our pair of temple each, making four,
   Is perhaps a consolatory blessing of Longevity after all.
   Celebration of a sixtieth birthday is nothing extraordinary.
4 Your repute among tailoring schools is a source of pride,
   Your students rush to display for you all they know.
   My literary work is nothing over which to crow.
   Long though have I wielded this pen of mine for a living,
8 It's no match for your Bingzhou scissors for tailoring.

Paraphrase

Verse 1

L1: Throughout our thirty years together, we have remained loving to each other.
L2: That you're married to someone poor as Qian Lou (黔娄) like me, I believe is due to the predestination in our previous lives.
L3: Like Meng Guang, you thank Heaven for the blessing of mutual love and respect we have.
L4: Although we have not even a square inch of ground (enough space to even hang an awl), you never despair of poverty.
L5: Everyone places so much importance on the good looks of youth.
L6: Only on this day, do I realize how precious it is for two people to be able to grow old together.

其三

四鬓斑斑见二毛,
天教将寿慰牢骚。
六旬相庆浑闲事,
一技成名且自豪。
桃李不言争献艳,
文章何价枉鸣高,
频年苦抱毛锥子,
未抵并州一剪刀。

L7: There are so many out there who have failed to complete this journey of married life together.
L8: We meet these fallen along the way, but alas! They are all still so young. (allusion to abandoned or divorced wives)

Verse 2

L1: Ten years of hard and diligent pursuit to build up the enterprise (tailoring school).
L2: Beautiful material (water chestnut and lotus leaves) is cut and sewn into clothes decorated with orchids.
L3: The art (of tailoring) is thus passed on to the young ladies;
L4: On your own, you led in the training of women in the skills of tailoring.
L5: Right up to your senior years you have never frowned.
L6: Busy all the time, never a moment do your ten fingers even pause.
L7: In the art of preserving your health, you know there is no special recipe,
L8: Other than to be constantly occupied in body, and to be relaxed and happy in spirit.

Verse 3

L1: As for the two of us—the hair on our pair of temple each (making a total of four) are now grey.
L2: Perhaps this is a consolatory blessing by Heaven in giving us this longevity so that we would not grouch in life.
L3: The celebration of a sixtieth birthday is in reality a very ordinary event.
L4: To be renowned in the field (of training women in the skills of tailoring) is truly something one can be proud of.
L5: It goes without saying there are now multitudes of your students and they all want to display the skill they have acquired from you.

L6: How could my literary composition, compared with your accomplishments, be worth any more than a vain attempt to crow.
L7: Many long years have I practised wielding that pen of mine for a living,
L8: Yet it is still no match for your pair of (tailoring) scissors from Bingzhou.

Background

Summary

This is the poem "seeded" by Father to invite his friends to send in their poems for the celebration of Mother's 61st birthday (actually 60th by Western reckoning).

The poem was composed by Father in 1957 for the double celebration of Mother's 60th birthday and the 10th anniversary of the tailoring school she founded. Behind this poem is the story of a couple who married each other relatively late in life. They and their family lived not in abject poverty, but a rather hard life nevertheless. Both had suffered personal tragedies (see "Two Personal Tragedies" in this Background) before they married each other in 1926. They suffered further tragedies in the family during a brief sojourn back home in China in the 1930s when their two sons died (their firstborns). They survived the trials and hardships of the Japanese Occupation 1942–1945. It was only in the last few years of their life together, at the time this poem was written, did they achieve a modicum of material comfort for the first time.

A magazine for this double commemoration was published in 1957. This poem was among the several poems sent in by eighteen of Father's poetry friends. The poems were placed at the end of the publication in a section titled "Poetry Forum" (吟坛). Father also wrote a delightful epilogue for this section (see Chapter 63, "My Seven Principles of Poetry 诗话七则").

Tailoring School

The school, Perak Women's Tailoring Centre, was a very important part of our family life after the Second World War. In October 1945, Father was employed as Secretary to the Perak Hokkien Association at a salary of 60 dollars per month. The income was hardly sufficient for our family of four children in Malaya and a daughter in China, all still in school.

The tailoring school was founded by Mother and officially opened on 14 July 1947 at No.79 Anderson Road, Ipoh. It was the brainchild of Father who was also the person behind the scene. It was in the middle of a row of double-storey linked townhouses originally designed as private residences. The best years of the school was during the Korean War (1950–1953) when the price of natural rubber was at its height. Many of the school's students came from the rural area of Malaya and were the direct beneficiaries of the economic boom of the early 1950s.

The school became immensely successful and well-known throughout Malaya and Singapore. Students came from all over the country. The more enterprising students would upon graduation return to their home states to open schools of their own. As the founder and principal of their alma mater, Mother was invited all over Malaya and Singapore as guest lecturer and conducted the graduation examinations for the schools established by her students.

The tailoring school in Ipoh was in fact a "successor" to the tailoring school Mother set up in Kampar in 1940–1941. It had to close upon the Japanese invasion of Malaya in late 1941. Although Father gave no credit to himself, it was his brainchild and he singlehandedly did all the administrative work.

Two Personal Tragedies

Father first came to Malaya in 1917 and returned to Putian 莆田 briefly in 1923 for six months to get married at the behest of his father. He and his wife returned to Malaya at the end of 1923 and Father resumed teaching in Kampar 金宝. Tragically in the following year, his wife died at childbirth together with the child. Father was thus widowed and a broken man; he later wrote, "I was gloomy and depressed...There are people who when beset by sorrow are still able to drink. I regret I am not one of them" (Chapter 61).

Mother, whose family name is Wang 王, was adopted by the Guo 郭 family from a neighbouring village and who were good family friends of the Wangs. She was well loved by the Guo family and when she was about 16 (c.1913) she was betrothed to the son of a wealthy and prominent family. To her horror, Mother only discovered on the wedding night that the groom was in fact mentally handicapped. Both the Guo family and Mother had been cruelly deceived by some dishonest matchmaker.

The New Matchmaker

Mother then returned to her natural parents in the Wang family, beyond the reach of the groom's family. Her own father died in 1922 and the groom's family persisted in demanding Mother's return. Meanwhile in 1923, Mother's elder brother Wang Guang Han 王光汉 became the principal of Pei Yuan 培元 School in Kampar where Father was teaching. In 1924, Father was about 30 and had just lost his wife. Mother was by then about 27 years old and considered very advanced in age for a girl of that time. Father would have seen Mother in the Wang household in China when she was still in her teens, because prior to leaving China for Malaya in 1917, Father had been a tutor to Mother's younger brother Wang Guang Guo 王光国. Her elder brother Guang Han thought Qing Shan was a good match for her younger sister Yi Song 义宋. Mother came to Kampar, and her first marriage in China was legally annulled by the court in Malaya. The long saga of Mother's first marriage that had taken place in a faraway village in Fuqing 福清 some ten years earlier and her flight from her first "husband", was finally brought to an end. Father and Mother were married in Kampar in 1926.

Appreciation

This poem was composed in 1957 for a "double celebration" —the 60th Birthday of Qing Shan's wife and the 10th Anniversary of the tailoring school she founded. This poem was sent out to eighteen of his poetry friends who responded with their poems, matching the rhyming scheme set by this poem.

Verse 1

This verse praises his wife Yi Song as a virtuous, loyal and loving wife who went through all the hardship with him without complaining. They were married in 1926; by 1957 they would have been married for 31 years. In Line 1, the reference to "thirty years" is therefore an approximation.

Line 2 which refers to his wife being married to a poor "Qian Lou" 黔娄 makes two points. Qian Lou lived during the Spring Autumn Period (770–476 BC). First, it describes Qing Shan's own poverty and second, it praises Yi Song as a virtuous and capable wife. Qian Lou was and chose to live as a poor scholar recluse. He rejected offers of high official and ministerial positions to live in poverty while writing extensively on the principles of *Dao*. His wife came from a rich and noble family and chose to marry and live with Qian Lou in poverty. His wife *Shī Liáng Dì* 施良娣 was an intelligent and well-schooled lady. Her reputation was enhanced by a repartee between her and one of Confucius' disciples *Céng Zi* 曾子. When Qian Lou died, Ceng Zi came to pay his respects and was considering what posthumous name should be given to Qian Lou. The wife suggested the name *Kāng* "康" which means "wellbeing and happy". As Qian Lou had lived in abject poverty all his life,

Yi Song's tailoring school opened in Ipoh on 14 July 1947 at 79 Anderson Road. It was known as "Perak Women's Tailoring Instruction Centre". The photo was taken at the school's celebration of "Double Ten" (双十节) on 10 October of that year. Yi Song is seated fourth from the left in the photo.

Qing Shan (right) and his wife Yi Song (c. mid-1950s)

Qing Shan and Yi Song in Qing Shan's office in the Perak Hokkien Association (霹雳福建公会) in Ipoh (c.1958).

the posthumous name *Kāng* did not seem very appropriate to Ceng Zi, nor could he understand the reason for her suggestion. Qian Lou's wife explained, "My husband enjoyed the barest in life, felt completely at ease in his humblest of position, never felt uneasy with poverty, never sought riches. He sought benevolence and was so rewarded; he sought righteousness and was so rewarded. He was filled with wellbeing and happiness, how could it not be appropriate?" Ceng Zi was so moved by her answer that he exclaimed, "Only a remarkable man could have such a remarkable wife!" The expression "Qian Lou's wife" 黔娄妻 then became a metaphor for a wise and capable wife.

Lines 5 and 6 compare the value others put on youth with Qing Shan's own realization of the preciousness of being able to live happily together into their twilight years as husband and wife. The last two lines 7 and 8 make the observation that today, many marriages end in divorce which is especially prevalent among the younger set. Qing Shan probably has in mind the lady Lu Jing Bin 卢静滨 then in her thirties who was in the midst of divorce proceedings. He later composed two poems of consolation for her (Chapters 37 and 38).

The literal meaning of the two Lines 7 to 8:

Line 7: "So many mi-wu pickers, at foot of hill have come by; 多少蘼芜山下过
Line 8: Those we meet are all young people." 相逢尽是少年人

The expression "mi-wu" 蘼芜 comes from an old ballad about a wife who was asked to leave her husband. After their "divorce", they met each other on the way to and from picking this herb called mi-wu. The expression "mi-wu" has come to mean "divorce". The ballad is told in the Appreciation of Chapter 38.

Verse 2

The second verse praises his wife for her accomplishments and virtues. The "ten years" in Line 1 refers to the 10th Anniversary of the tailoring school. Line 2 says "Pretty material, into clothes adorned with orchids, are sewn" 芰荷制就又纫兰. The "pretty material" in the line is from the two words *ji he* "芰荷" meaning the leaves of water chestnut and the lotus. They were traditionally used for the clothing worn by learned men of high principles who declined official positions and chose to live as recluse. This is described in Qu Yuan's "Li Sao" (离骚): "Chestnut and lotus leaves for clothes, to which are adorned with lotus flowers" 制芰荷以为衣兮，集芙蓉以为裳. The use of this allusion connotes a person of high principles. Qing Shan chooses his words aptly to refer to his wife's vocation of tailoring and her virtue.

The rest of the verse shows Qing Shan's appreciation of his wife's hard work in passing on her tailoring skills to others, without any complaint. He attributes her good health to her ability to keep busy and at the same time to remain relaxed, and to keep her spirits high.

Verse 3

This Verse concludes the poem with the reference to the 60th birthday celebration. Lines 1 and 2 start off with an unusual way of referring to their advanced age and is followed up by the rationale that longevity is a consolation to compensate us for growing old.

> Line 1: "The greying hair on our pair of temple each, making four, 四鬓斑斑见二毛
> Line 2: Is perhaps a consolatory blessing of Longevity after all." 天教将寿慰牢骚

The mathematics of Line 1 is obvious. Line 2 appears to be quite a reverse of the saying, "Those whom the gods love die young." Qing Shan's logic here seems to be saying "Those whom Heaven loves die old!" Lines 3 and 4 play down the importance of even a 60th birthday, compared with the celebration of the success of his wife's tailoring school which has been successful for the last ten years.

In Line 5, "Your students" is expressed by the phrase *táo lǐ bù yán* 桃李不言 which means "the peach and plums do not speak…". It comes from a proverb that says, "The peaches and plum do not speak, yet a path will naturally come into being beneath the tree" (桃李不言，下自成蹊). In other words, if the fruits are sweet, people will find out by reputation and will naturally go to the tree to pluck the fruits, thus forming a "beaten path" leading to the tree. With these four words Qing Shan conveys two messages: (i) his wife's tailoring school is renowned throughout Malaya and Singapore, (ii) the school's graduates are themselves successful with their own schools attracting students. By comparison, Qing Shan says in Line 6 that his literary compositions are not anything when compared with his wife's accomplishments.

Lines 7 to 8 compare his pen, the tool of his "trade" with the mighty Bingzhou (tailoring) scissors used by his wife. Bingzhou is located in Taiyuan, Shanxi (山西太原) and has been famous for the manufacture of cutting instruments since ancient times.

> Line 7: "Long though have I wielded this pen of mine for a living, 频年苦抱毛锥子
> Line 8: It's no match for your Bingzhou scissors for tailoring." 未抵并州一剪刀

Qing Shan says humbly that despite all his learning, he has to bow down to his wife's very practical vocation. This same thought is reflected in his poem with advice to his eldest daughter Mei Xuan (Chapter 10).

Chapter 13

酬诸友见和寿内作
chóu zhū yǒu jiàn hè shòu nèi zuò

其一

同甘藜藿愧称觞，
tóng gān lí huò kuì chēng shāng

乞得诗瓢献孟光。
qǐ dé shī piáo xiàn mèng guāng

不信抛砖真引玉，
bù xìn pāo zhuān zhēn yǐn yù

果然益寿有奇方。
guǒ rán yì shòu yǒu qí fāng

其二

老妻绣谱钞佳句，
lǎo qī xiù pǔ chāo jiā jù

幼妇新辞满和章。
yòu fù xīn cí mǎn hè zhāng

友谊家珍足千载，
yǒu yì jiā zhēn zú qiān zǎi

殷勤付与子孙藏。
yīn qín fù yǔ zǐ sūn cáng

Response from Friends To My Birthday Poem for My Wife

Verse 1

    Ashamed that she'd rejoice with such coarse fare,
    I ask my friends for fine poems, with her to share.
    I cast a tile and am rewarded with a jade—incredible!
4   Birthday poems for longevity, such a wondrous formula.

Verse 2

    My wife is pleased, copying every verse like embroidery.
    The pages are soon filled with beautiful poetry.
    They express our friendship, a family treasure to hold.
4   I shall earnestly tell my children to cherish them like gold.

Paraphrase

Verse 1

L1: I am embarrassed, when you so willingly share with me such coarse fare in celebration of your birthday.
L2: Hence I invite my esteemed friends for some good poems to present you, my good wife.

L3: I had not believed that even as I cast a tile (my poor composition), I would succeed in attracting a piece of jade (excellent poems from friends).

L4: A compilation of these birthday poems can indeed be a remarkable formula for longevity.

Verse 2

L1: My wife, being exceedingly pleased, copied them down carefully as though they were delicate pieces of embroidery.

L2: Filling up pages with the many beautiful and remarkable poems of response.

L3: These poems express their friendship for us and will be preserved as our family treasure forever more.

L4: I will earnestly tell my children and grandchildren to keep them for all time.

Background

The double celebration of Mother's 60th birthday and the 10th Anniversary of her tailoring school was held in 1957. Father had sent to his poetry friends a poem composed for the occasion, inviting them to respond with a poem with the same rhyming scheme. The "seed" poem which Father sent out is the poem in Chapter 12.

The poem in this Chapter was written after his friends had sent in their response poems. It is like an epilogue, giving an account to Mother of the whole exercise, and at the same time telling his friends, in Chapter 63, how he would treasure their compositions.

It is interesting to read in Father's own words in Chapter 63 his criteria for the invitation: *"As for my humble composition of three verses for my wife, although I sent out several stenciled copies to my close friends, I did not do so out of desperation, sending them out to all and sundry. I had my own criteria for drawing the* boundary. Firstly, avoid sending them to those who are not friends I have known for a long time. Secondly, avoid sending them to those who have no interest in classical poetry, even if they are longstanding friends. Thirdly, avoid sending them to those prolific writers who write 'on demand' whenever and whoever asks of them. Working on this "Three Avoids", I myself avoid being a nuisance to others and do not impose an awkward obligation on them. As for compositions undertaken out of obligation, they are no gift to the world and fall short of being worthy to pass on to our children and grandchildren.

These are not what I am looking for. Now that I have seen the actual responses of all and they are indeed what I had wished, it is even more apparent that the strict conditions that had been set are not without benefit."

↑ Yi Song (left) and Qing Shan carrying Mei Yu and Mei Xuan respectively. The two girls were two and four years old then. The photo was taken in Kampar soon after their return from China in 1936.

← Qing Shan and Yi Song with their two daughters Mei Xuan (standing) and Mei Yu (seated). The photo was taken in Kampar in the first half of 1938.

(Chinese text to be read from right to left.) The two poems in Chapters 12 and 13 as they first appeared (1957) in Mother's tailoring school magazine for the double commemoration of the school's 10th Anniversary and Mother's 61st birthday.

Qing Shan and his family in August 1957.
Back row from left to right: Jun Yuan (Mei Yu's fiancé), Michael, Peter, Thian Sing (Mei Xuan's husband).
Seated from left to right: Mei Yu, Mother, Father, Mei Xuan.
Front row: Mei Xuan's two sons.

Appreciation

Verse 1

In Lines 1 to 2, Qing Shan expresses embarrassment that his wife should so willingly celebrate her birthday with just the coarse fare that he can offer in the form of his birthday poem for her. To make up for it, he has asked his friends to compose some fine poems to present to her, whom he refers to as a "Meng Guang" 孟光. The name is often used by Qing Shan as a personification of a loving and respectful wife. The allusion is explained in the Appreciation in Chapter 47. In the next two lines, he says he could hardly believe his luck when he sees the quality of his friends' response. He uses the proverb "to cast a tile in order to receive a jade" (抛砖引玉) to describe what his "humble" poem has brought in. Perhaps fine birthday poems are the right formula for longevity.

Verse 2

Verse 2 is most likely targeted at his poetry friends who have sent in their poems. Lines 1 to 2 describe how his wife would so lovingly copy each verse into her book as though she was working on a fine piece of embroidery. Soon her pages are filled with these excellent compositions. The next two lines are perhaps the most important point of the message, meant not just for his friends but also for his own children. He says that these poems are sincere expressions of friendship and he would exhort his children to keep and treasure them for all time.

Chapter 14

mǎi shū买书

mǎi shū rú xīn qǔ
买书如新娶，

yī yè jǐ mó suō
一夜几摩挲。

zuò duì yán rú yù
坐对颜如玉，

hún wàng bìn yǐ pó
浑忘鬓已皤。

Buying Books

A new book is like a newlywed,
Tender caresses till night has fled.
Gazing upon her lustrous look of jade,
Oblivious that my hair has greyed.

Paraphrase

L1: The joy of buying a new book is like the joy of a newlywed.
L2: To lovingly turn the pages is like the tender caresses throughout the night.
L3: Sitting face to face, gazing upon her lustrous look of jade,
L4: The hours and years would pass timelessly by, oblivious that the head of hair, that was once jet-black, has faded into grey.

Background

This short poem of only four lines was written in June 1959 at the same time as the poem in Chapter 15 "Buying Books to Celebrate My Birthday, Ji-Hai Year 己亥初度买书自寿". On Father's 65th birthday, Peter had sent him a birthday gift of five Australian pounds. Father used the gift to buy two sets of books, *Collected Works of Hu Shi*《胡适文存》and *Analects of Chinese Literature*《中国文学史论集》. So delighted was he with

Collected Works of Hu Shi 《胡适文存》, first of two sets of books bought in May 1959 by Qing Shan for his birthday on 12 June in that year, with the birthday gift of money from his son Peter (敏良), studying in Australia.

Inscribed in the book is Qing Shan's delightful poem on the joy of "Buying Books", in the calligraphy of his younger brother-in-law Guang Guo (光国).

the books that he composed this short poem and asked Uncle Guang Guo (Mother's fourth younger brother) to write it in his calligraphy on the inside cover of the first volume of Hu Shi's works. The calligraphy is beautifully written. These sets of books are still in our possession. Father died a year later on 6 June 1960 at the age of 66. We are happy he derived so much joy from his books. Even a birthday gift of just a small sum of money could bring so much happiness.

Appreciation

Although consisting of only four lines, the poem is easy to read and understand. It is said that a good poem, like a good tune, will always have one or two lines that are so "catchy" that no one can miss them and which will be easy to remember. They are what we might call "quotable quotes".

All four lines of this poem are in fact "quotable quotes". We two brothers are extremely fond of buying books ourselves and sometimes visit bookshops together. As we rush out of the bookshop and impatiently make our way home to read them, we would find ourselves instinctively quoting to each other the first two lines, "A new book is like a newlywed, Tender caresses till night has fled". Similarly if we see a starry-eyed couple lost in each other's gaze, you will find us quoting the last two lines of the poem, "Gazing upon her lustrous look of jade, Oblivious that my hair has greyed". There is fun indeed in poetry.

There is passion too in poetry. The analogy between the excitement of a new book and a newlywed may cause some eyebrows to be raised among the more prudish of readers. For the less prudish, this is a rather clever and even pleasurable analogy. Not everyone would think any less of Tao Yuanming 陶渊明 (317–420) when he wrote his love poem "Ode to A Fantasy of Love 闲情赋" in which he fantasized how he longed to be close to his love. Two pairs of the more sensual lines from Tao Yuanming's poem are quoted as an illustration:

愿在衣而为领	I'd love to be the collar of her dress,
承华首之余芳	To breathe in the lingering fragrance in her tress…
愿在裳而为带	I'd love to be the sash encircling her gown,
束窈窕之纤身	To tightly clasp her dainty waist around…

Chapter 15

己亥初度买书自寿
jǐ hài chū dù mǎi shū zì shòu

吾生欲忘年，
wú shēng yù wàng nián

平居厌序齿。
píng jū yàn xù chǐ

昨日闻妇言，
zuó rì wén fù yán

4　六十逾半纪。
liù shí yú bàn jì

妇言不足听，
fù yán bù zú tīng

自寿聊尔尔。
zì shòu liáo ěr ěr

大儿就外傅，
dà ér jiù wài fù

8　寄书从万里。
jì shū cóng wàn lǐ

殷勤劝加餐，
yīn qín quàn jiā cān

复媵券一纸。
fù yìng quàn yī zhǐ

Buying Books to Celebrate My Birthday, Ji-Hai Year

    I've never liked to recall my age, much less
    To compare our years with friends we meet.
    Yet my wife reminds me yesterday
4 That six and sixty I soon will be.
    A woman's word is not worthy of heed,
    Even so, there's no harm to celebrate.
    My eldest son, studying abroad
8 Sends me a letter from afar.
    On food I should indulge, he says.
    With loving thoughts he sends me a cheque,
    Being money saved from his scholarship
12 For me to buy my favourite dish.
    Roast meat, delicious dates,
    Neither of these I particularly crave.
    Regrettably I'm without official rank,
16 But eating meat dulls one's wit, they say.
    Do as you wish, so cries the wife,
    Off to town to buy whatever you like.
    What I desire are many indeed,
20 But what I love most are books.
    Home I come with a bagful of books,
    Their flavour is just superb.
    Words, like food can our hunger satiate,
24 More sumptuous than any exotic dish.

云是膏火资，
12 节以奉甘旨。
脍炙与羊枣，
而翁皆不喜。
自愧无远谋，
16 肉食更可鄙。
妇曰从所好，
任君持入市。
所好虽云多，
20 大欲在书史。
换得一囊归，
其味无穷已。
煮字可疗饥，
24 况兹尽肥美。

小儿欲分甘，
未敢便染指。
举案遗细君，
28 但亦一笑耳。
所好各不同，
安能强妻子！
含笑复咀华，
32 置诸腹笥里。
适性以养生，
此中有玄理。
富贵非所期，
36 帝乡难响迩。
愿以书为城，
吾将老于是。

      Young son clamours to taste the fare,
      But hesitates to dip his finger in.
      I offer to share these with my wife.
28 With a faint smile, she declines.
      Everyone has his own delight.
      How can I impose this on my wife?
      I devour and savour every word,
32 Digesting and storing all within.
      Lead your life as what your heart inclines;
      This philosophy embodies a mystic truth.
      Gold and silver are not my desire,
36 A celestial abode is beyond my reach.
      Surround me with a wall of books;
      In my old age, content I thus shall be.

Paraphrase

(By Chen Qing Shan)

On the occasion of my birthday this year, I composed a classical poem "Buying Books to Celebrate My Birthday". It has a total of 19 [pairs of] lines. As it is written in the classical form, all my children would not be able to understand it. Hence my wife insisted that I paraphrase it for them. Actually it is not that easy to do, but under the circumstances, I have no alternative but to paraphrase its meaning line by line as follows:

L1: I really wish to forget my age.
L2: It is especially annoying that whenever friends meet, they invariably discuss one another's age and try to sort out who is older and who is younger.
L3: Yesterday my wife again raised the subject with me.
L4: She said that I will be sixty-six years old this year. Her intention is to plan a birthday celebration for me.
L5: One should take no heed of a woman's word which is not always reliable. I really cannot believe that I am that old.

L6: However, there is no harm in a birthday celebration involving only immediate family members and having a meal together.
L7: Coincidentally, my elder son who is studying abroad
L8: Sent me a letter from afar. Naturally, it was also in connection with the same subject.
L9: Apart from the usual words of felicitations for my birthday,
L10: The letter also included a remittance draft.
L11: He has managed to save a portion of his scholarship money
L12: To send me this small remittance. His intention is for me to buy some of my favourite food to celebrate my birthday.
L13: These are naturally his very kind thoughts. I recall that Confucius had a disciple by the name of Zengcan who treated his father with the utmost filial love and respect. He frequently bought dates and shredded roast meat for his father, because these were his father's favourite food.
L14: However as I have no particular craving for either of these, why waste money on such delicacies?
L15: I normally like meat, but there is a Chinese saying, "The meat eaters, they are the stupid ones". The original intention of this saying is to mock those bureaucrat officials who only knew how to indulge in eating meat (but are otherwise quite useless).
L16: I have never been a bureaucrat official and therefore deserve no such ridicule and hence have no intention to indulge in meat.
L17: What shall I do? My wife then said, "Since the money is meant for you,
L18: You might as well just go into town and buy whatever you fancy."
L19: I like many things: smoking, going to the movies, listening to singing. It is not just one thing,
L20: But my favourite is still reading. It is books then that I will use the remittance to buy.
L21: Indeed, after cashing the remittance, the cash was exchanged for a big bag of purchases.

L22: Naturally, it is a bagful of books; but my enjoyment of these are not any less, and in fact even greater than the best of delicacies.

L23: The ancients used to describe the occupation of those who make a living by writing as "cooking words". Indeed writing is like cooking by using words as the ingredients; when it is done, it can satiate our hunger, i.e., our craving for food.

L24: We can thus expect even more from books, because every word has been prepared and transformed—put another way "cooked"—by some ancient writer, making the meal all the more delicious and sumptuous.

L25: My second son watching by the side naturally wanted to partake in all these;

L26: But he has yet to learn to enjoy classical literary works, which are probably indigestible for him. In the end, he could only stand by to watch.

L27: I too wished to share these delicious fare—my new books—with my wife; she could at least have some variety and a change of taste.

L28: But she politely declined the invitation with a smile.

L29: I can hardly blame her. Everyone has a different taste and preference.

L30: We should not impose our own preference even on someone as close as our own wife. And so I let it be.

L31: Since no one else wishes to share these with me, I will enjoy them by myself, slowly chewing and savouring every bit of it, ingesting every nutrient into my stomach.

L32: The ancients say that when you read a great deal, your stomach will be filled with knowledge and your stomach becomes like a trunk filled with books which can be called *fu-si* 腹笥 literary meaning "stomach trunk" (which has become a metaphor for a book trunk). Naturally, it is my hope that such knowledge reposes in my *fu-si* forever, never to be lost.

L33: To nurture the life one leads, there is no rigid prescription for any particular nutrient. The important thing is to follow one's own inclination and character and longevity will follow.

L34: I subscribe to this age old philosophy of the ancient philosophers.

L35: I have neither sought nor clamoured for riches and honours. It is also beyond me to try to emulate the immortals.

L36: As the poet Tao Yuanming wrote: "Riches and honours are not my wish, Nor a celestial abode my desire." I too subscribe to this philosophy;

L37: For my mere desire is to buy more books to wall myself within.

L38: And therein shall I abide to live out my old age.

Recorded by Qing Shan, 23 June 1959.

Background

According to the lunar calendar, Father was born on the seventh day of the fifth month of 1894. This corresponds with the Gregorian Calendar 10 June of that year. In 1959, the year this poem was composed, Father's birthday would have been on 12 June.

This is the only poem for which he wrote a paraphrase; it was dated by him on 23 June 1959. Peter left Ipoh in late January 1958 to study in Australia on a scholarship. He said goodbye to his family and friends at the Ipoh Railway Station. Naturally Father was among those present that day.

Father was 66 in 1959 (by Chinese reckoning). His birthday that year was not anything special. It was special only because it was the first time Peter had enough money to send him a present. This was the first present Father had ever received from his son. One can imagine the pride and joy he felt.

Qing Shan saying farewell to his eldest son Peter (敏良) at the Ipoh Railway Station (January 1958). Peter was going abroad to study in Australia. Qing Shan is (seated) third from the right with Peter (seated) next to him.

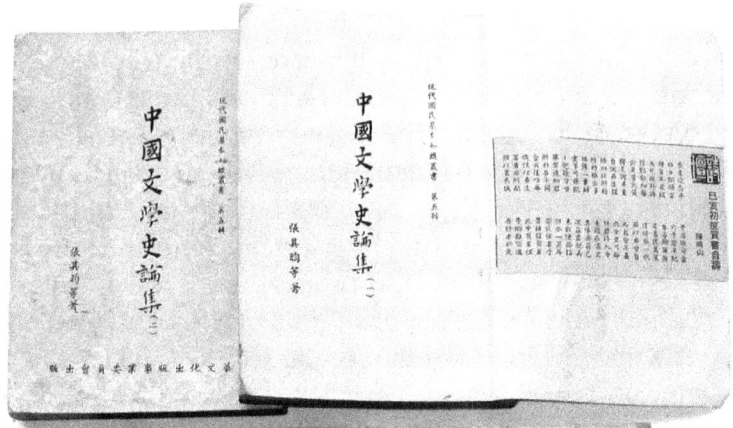

Analects of Chinese Literature (《中国文学史论集》), second of two sets of books bought by Qing Shan in May 1959 for his birthday on 12 June of that year, with the birthday gift of money from his son Peter (敏良), studying in Australia. Pasted in the book, is a newspaper cutting of his poem "Buying Books to Celebrate My Birthday, Ji-Hai Year 己亥初度买书自寿".

Father had great love for classical poetry. His only regret was that none of his children and grandchildren were likely ever to understand his poems and those written by his friends for Mother on her 60th birthday celebrated two years earlier in 1957. This sentiment was expressed by him in his epilogue for the collection of Mother's 60th birthday poems (see Chapter 63).

It must be for this simple reason that he took the trouble to paraphrase this particular poem in modern Chinese.

Appreciation

This is probably one of the happiest poems Qing Shan has composed. First and foremost, his eldest son for the first time is able to send the father a present of money. This is an expression of filial piety which deeply moves him. Secondly, he has decided to spend the money on books as he loves reading above everything else. Qing Shan has likened the happiness of buying a new book to the joy of one's wedding night (Chapter 14).

This poem has a total of 38 lines and can be divided into three sections (line references here are for the whole poem]. The first section comprising the first six lines (1 to 6) introduces the subject of "birthdays". The second section's twenty-six lines (7 to 32) provides the background, the leading events, and his feelings upon his "going to town" to buy the books. It forms the kernel of the poem. The third section comprising the last six lines (33 to 38) of the poem states explicitly that he loves books and provides the reasons for buying books.

The first eight lines of the second section (Lines 7 to 14) describe how his eldest son, Peter, has eked out his scholarship money to send a gift (of five Australian pounds) for his father to buy something that he likes to eat. Qing Shan sees in the gift a concrete expression of filial piety and reverence for the parents. Among the Chinese, having children who show such respect and care is the greatest reward for all their hardship and sacrifice in bringing up children. Qing Shan is greatly moved and can hardly hide his joy and pride as he tells everyone:

Line 7: "My eldest son, studying abroad 大儿就外傅
Line 8: Sends me a letter from afar. 寄书从万里
Line 9: On food I should indulge, he says. 殷勤劝加餐
Line 10: With loving thoughts he sends me a cheque
复媵券一纸
Line 11: Being money saved from his scholarship
云是膏火资
Line 12: For me to buy my favourite dish.节以奉甘旨
Line 13: Roast meat, delicious dates, 脍炙与羊枣
Line 14: Neither of these I particularly crave."
而翁皆不喜

Line 11 uses an interesting metaphor "*gāo huǒ zī*" 膏火资; the term *gāo huǒ* 膏火 literally means "animal fat for lighting". It now means a stipend for poor students during the Qing dynasty and *zi* 资 just means "money". Line 12's *gān zhǐ* 甘旨 means sweet delicacies; it is now a personification of filial care of one's parents. Line 13 uses another allusion "*kuài zhì* and *yáng zǎo*" 脍炙与羊枣; it means "shredded roast meat and sheep dates". Its personification of reverence for one's parents is elaborately explained by Qing Shan in his own paraphrase of this line.

As Qing Shan's interest is not in exotic food but in books, he decides to go to town and buy himself two bagfuls of books. They are even more "delicious" than any delicacies! His own description of this is found in his paraphrase of the two lines of the poem:

Line 23: "Words, like food can our hunger satiate,
煮字可疗饥
Line 24: More sumptuous than any exotic dish."
况兹尽肥美

The literal meaning of Line 23 is "Words can be cooked to satisfy our hunger". This is Qing Shan's own version of the original line by Song dynasty's *Huáng Gēng* 黄庚 who wrote the following in self-deprecation:

> My addiction to books has become incurable;
> 耽书自笑已成癖
> "Cooking" words has never been able to "cure" hunger.
> 煮字元来不疗饥

The hallmark of Qing Shan's poems is his ability to turn an expression round to suit his purpose, giving an otherwise hackneyed phrase a fresh new meaning.

There are places in the poem where he mentions his wife too:

> Line 17: "Do as you wish, so cries my wife," 妇曰从所好
> Line 27: "I offer to share these with my wife." 举案遗细君

Qing Shan uses the expression *ju an* 举案 to describe his inviting his wife to share in his newly acquired books. It is an expression connoting great respect and comes from the story of Liang Hong and Meng Guang (refer Appreciation in Chapter 47).

A filial son and a loving wife! This poem simply exudes his irrepressible joy.

Section 2

Care and Concern
棠棣桃李

The care and concern for his relatives,
counsel for his students.

Chapter 16

guāng hé dì sì shí chū dù zhāo yǐn
光河弟四十初度招饮，
wéi yùn yǔ zhù zhī
为韵语祝之。

zhuó jiǔ hé bì jīn pǒ luó
酌酒何必金叵罗，

jǐn yī wèi bì shèng bì luó
锦衣未必胜薜萝。

dàn shǐ miào táng mǐ gàn gē
但使庙堂弭干戈，

huán yǔ shēng píng hǎi bú bō
4 环宇升平海不波。

hán bǔ yì zú yǎng tiān hé
含哺亦足养天和，

yuàn yǐ cǐ zhù wú dì hé
愿以此祝吾弟河。

sān nián bā yuè wàn jié guò
三年八月万劫过，

bào rì yì nán nài rǔ hé
8 暴日亦难奈汝何。

My Brother Guang He's 40th Birthday Invitation to Dinner
A Poem in Greeting

    A celebratory drink does not need a golden cup;
    Silken finery is no better than a rustic garment.
    But let the Powers that be put the weapons down.
4   The world's at peace, the sea unruffled and calm.
    Food in our mouth too, can cultivate our vigour.
    My brother He, let me greet you with this poem.
    Three years eight months of plunder are now over.
8   You and all have endured the cruel days of terror;
    The days ahead should now impede you no further.
    May your every year this day be free from troubles.
    I join you, your wife and children to sing and dine.
12 Ten years your senior, grey this hair of mine.
    Lend me your wine cup, that I may have a ruddy look.
    Wine revives the Old, but what about the Young?
    A good scholar is no match for a good merchant.
16 In a stupor, let not the years slip into a distant.

Paraphrase

L1: Even for a celebratory drink, why do we need to be so opulent as to use a gold wine cup.

qián tú qǐ fù yú kǎn kē
前途岂复虞轗轲，

nián nián cǐ rì bǐ wú é
年年此日俾无讹。

jí ěr fù zǐ yàn qiě gē
及尔妇子宴且歌，

12 wǒ zhǎng shí líng fā yǐ pó
我长十龄发已皤。

jiè rǔ jiǔ bēi yán yóu tuó
借汝酒杯颜犹酡，

lǎo dāng yì zhuàng shǎo zé nuó
老当益壮少则那？

qiáng shì bú rú shàn jiǎ duō
强仕不如善贾多，

16 zuì zhōng suì yuè mò cuō tuó
醉中岁月莫蹉跎。

L2: Wearing the best finery for such an occasion is not necessarily better than wearing a simple ordinary garment [like that worn by a wise old rustic recluse].
L3: Let the Powers that be [the Imperial Court] put away all the weapons of war.
L4: The whole world is now at peace and the sea is tranquil.
L5: [Unlike the time of the Japanese Occupation, we no longer suffer from hunger, and] "Food in our mouth" too, can cultivate the natural vigour of our mind.
L6: In this simple fashion, let me greet you my good brother Guang He.
L7: The plunders of this tragic disaster of three years and eight months are now all a thing of the past.
L8: Those cruel days were truly terrible for all and you like everybody else too had to endure them.
L9: But in the brighter days that lie ahead, we will not have to worry again about achieving our aspiration as nothing any longer stands in our way.
L10: May this day of every year, your birthday, be free from all tribulations.
L11: Let me join you, your wife and children to dine and to sing.
L12: I am only ten years your senior but my hair has already gone all grey.
L13: I borrow your wine cup to drink a little, so that my complexion will have the ruddiness of youth.
L14: Wine makes the old hale and hearty, but what effect has it on the young?
L15: Even a learned scholar, however brilliant he is, cannot be regarded as successful as a good businessman—not by a long shot.
L16: But in your happy state of success, don't let the years and months slip by you unknowingly.

Background

Malaya and Singapore were under Japanese military rule from

1942 until the Japanese surrender in August 1945. The population was subject to three years and eight months of cruelty and privations, commonly referred to as the "Occupation" among the English-speaking Chinese. Among the man-in-the-street Chinese, it is often referred to as *riben shiqi* 日本时期, the "Japanese period".

We have not seen any of Father's poems, except for the poem in Chapter 7, "Returning Home", that we can positively identify as having been written during the Occupation. To write anything at all, or to be identified as a scholar could be "life-threatening" because scholars and intellectuals were seen by the Japanese as anti-Japanese and what they write would be viewed with suspicion.

But as soon as the Occupation ended, it was like being liberated from some concentration camp. While the "military" put away their guns, the scholars and writers were out in force with their pens. We begin to see their literary works and poems published, including some that would have been secretly written during the Occupation.

One can be reasonably sure that an undated writing that uses the expression "three years eight months" would have been written within months or a year after the Japanese Occupation ended in August 1945. This poem is easier to date because the title says that it is composed for our fifth uncle Guang He's 40th birthday. We know that Mother was born in 1897 and ten years older than Guang He. Uncle Guang He would have been 40 years old in 1947. However, the Chinese always regard themselves as one year old on the day they are born. There is some logic in this if one takes into account the period of gestation. Hence according to the Chinese way of reckoning age, Guang He was 40 in 1946 (not 1947). The poem was therefore composed in 1946, a year or less after the Occupation ended in August 1945.

Uncle Guang He was the youngest of Mother's six surviving siblings. After our maternal grandmother died, grandfather took another wife. The stepmother treated Guang He badly and Mother would stand up for him to protect him. Hence, a very strong and affectionate bond was formed between Mother and Guang He. We owe much to Uncle Guang He for our survival through the privations during the Japanese Occupation. Although without much formal education, Guang He was a good businessman. He was financially much better off than us during the Japanese Occupation. To be street-smart and to be able to "wheel and deal" had a higher economic value than being a teacher or poet. Guang He would bring us food when we were hungry and gave us or loan us money when we needed it.

He was a businessman of principles. We never forget what Mother used to tell us of the important distinction between a loan and a gift. Uncle Guang He would make a very clear distinction between the two. On giving our family financial assistance during the Japanese Occupation, he would say to Mother, "This is a gift to you—there's no need for you to repay." When lending us money, he would say, "This a loan—which you must repay." (Two other poems in Chapters 19 and 20 were also composed for Uncle Guang He.)

Appreciation

The poem is written from the perspective of Qing Shan's wife who is the elder sister of Guang He. It is written as Singapore and Malaya emerge from the dark shadows of the Japanese military occupation which ended with the Japanese surrender in August 1945. It has been a terrible three years eight months of privations and all kinds of hardship for the civilian population. Times are better in 1946. There is food on the table, but it is not as though the country has overnight become a land flowing with milk and honey.

The poem's first two lines therefore seem a little odd and incongruous, "A celebratory drink does not need a golden cup; Silken finery is no better than a rustic garment." What belies this incongruity is Qing Shan's self-ridicule of his own

Yi Song 义宋 and her younger brother Guang He 光河, photo taken in Ipoh (1947). Yi Song was then fifty and Guang He, forty years old. It was two years after the privations suffered under the Japanese Occupation (1942-1945). *"Food in our mouth too, can cultivate our vigour. My brother He, let me greet you with this poem."*

unfortunate lot. He certainly has neither a "golden cup" nor anything that can be called "finery". He is like a starving man, gnawed by the pangs of hunger, consoling himself that he must not overeat as it would be bad for his health.

In Line 3, "But let the Powers that be put the weapons down" is translated from the more colourful Chinese text *dàn shǐ miào táng mǐ gàn gē* 但使庙堂弭干戈. It literally means "Let the Imperial Court put away the shields and spears". In Line 4, "The world's at peace, the sea ruffled and calm"—it must have been quite a relief for Qing Shan to write this, having himself just lived through and survived the Japanese invasion and Occupation.

The privations of the Occupation have left an indelible mark on Qing Shan as can be seen in Line 5 where he writes "Food in our mouth too, can cultivate our vigour 含哺亦足养天和".

These seemingly simple words use two ideas that originate 1,500 years apart. The first two words *hán bǔ* 含哺 ("to hold food in one's mouth") come from the philosopher Zhuangzi 庄子. He had used the expression in a passage to describe a time when people were in a state of happy naturalness—"joyously had food in their mouths and wandering about leisurely with their bellies full" *hán bǔ ér xī, gǔ fù ér yóu* 含哺而熙, 鼓腹而游. The phrase "含哺" is carefully chosen by Qing Shan as a sharp reminder of the Japanese Occupation when people often had to go hungry.

The second part of Line 5 "...too can cultivate our vigour 亦足养天和" is an idea from a Su Dongpo 苏东坡 poem. Su Dongpo had said, "An open mind can cultivate our vigour (of mind) *xū huái yǎng tian hé* 虚怀养天和". However, for one who has experienced hunger during the Japanese Occupation, it is "food" that becomes more relevant than Su Dongpo's "open mind"!

This is a good illustration of Qing Shan's ease in his use of the classics, vividly drawing colourful analogies and applying them to the poem. The otherwise familiar expressions are often given a new twist and spirit.

Several lines of the poem are reflective of the Qing Shan's own recent experience of war and the Japanese Occupation. It is from Line 10 onwards that the poem deals with the subject of Guang He's birthday celebration. Beyond Line 10, the poem is mostly standard fare for a birthday poem, for example, Line 13's, "Lend me your wine cup; that I may have a ruddy look" is so typical that it would almost not be a birthday poem without it.

Line 15 praises Guang He for being a successful businessman. Qing Shan says with a hint of irony in the line "A good scholar is no match for a good merchant", as proven during the Japanese Occupation when all the literary brilliance of someone like him did not count for anything.

As this poem is from an elder sister to a younger brother, it has to close with some encouragement and a word of advice. Line 16 says, "In a stupor [your happy success], let not the years slip [away] into a distant." In other words, don't let success get into your head and even as you celebrate, continue to work hard because time will just pass you by before you realize it.

Chapter 17

光汉见示六十自寿诗,依韵和之

其一

翩翩裙屐忆当年,
垂老情怀尚跃然。
但使童心长不改,
尽教岁月暗中迁。

其二

客中两地浑相忘,
选胜征歌未算狂。
典尽锦衣余一杖,
夜行何必定还乡?

Response to Guang Han's 60th Birthday Poem

Verse 1

    Our youthful halcyon days we recall.
    Old as we are, but our hearts still leap.
    Let our youthful hearts forever beat;
4   Let the years flow, and bother us not.

Verse 2

    "Home" or "foreign", we now can't tell apart.
    It's not a wild excess to chant your songs.
    To go home with none but a staff in hand,
4   Why bother to head for the native land?

Paraphrase

Verse 1

L1: We recall the halcyon days, the carefree days of our youth.
L2: While we have grown older, our hearts still leap with sprightly steps.
L3: Let us preserve our youthful hearts always.
L4: We can let Time take its own course without bothering us.

Verse 2

L1: In our sojourn overseas, we no longer know the difference between what is "home" and what is "foreign".
L2: To travel and sing your verses can hardly be said to be wild excesses.
L3: You head for home in retirement with no possessions but your staff in hand.
L4: If it is to go home inconspicuously into retirement without great wealth, why bother to head for the native land?

Background

The poem was written in late 1949 or in 1950. Wang Guang Han 王光汉 was the elder brother of Mother, in other words, Father's brother-in-law. Uncle Guang Han (born 1890) was four years older than Father and their relationship was closer than would ordinarily be between brothers-in-law. Guang Han's role in matchmaking his younger sister Yi Song (Mother) to Father in 1925 has already been explained in the Background to Chapter 12. Moreover, Father was a teacher in the school in Kampar throughout the period when Uncle Guang Han was its principal from 1923 to 1940. Both had received a traditional education in the classics in China and were fond of poetry.

The poem in this Chapter is one of two that Father wrote in response to Uncle Guang Han's 60th Birthday Poems (六十自寿). The other poem is in Chapter 18. Besides these two poems, Father also wrote the Preface to the collection of birthday poems published by Guang Han in celebration of his 60th birthday (Chapter 62).

Prior to his leaving China for Malaya in 1917, Father had been a tutor to Guang Han's younger brother Guang Guo 光国 in their native village of Jiangdou 江兜 in Fuqing 福清. Guang Han himself left China only two years earlier in 1915. With a relationship between them that dated from their youth in

Yi Song's elder brother Guang Han's 光汉 60th birthday poem in his own calligraphy, dated 18 December 1949, that accompanied an invitation to his friends to respond in poem. His final two lines read: "*Worried am I over the raging war at home, Home is now retirement in foreign land* 只为故乡烽火急，杖乡犹是杖他乡".

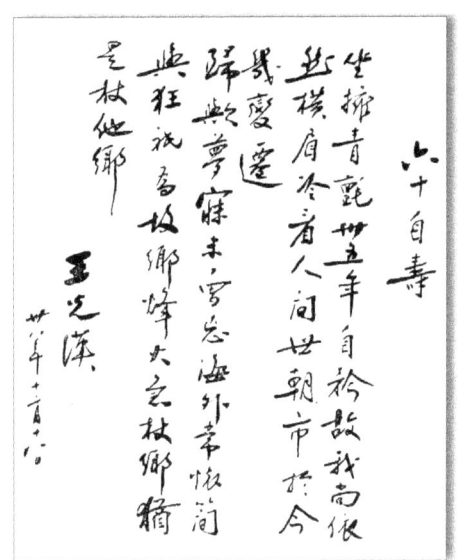

Guang Han and his wife (December 1950), their portrait in the publication of the poems sent in by his friends for his 60th birthday. Qing Shan's response to the final two lines of Guang Han's "invitation" poem was: "*To go home with none but a staff in hand, Why bother to head for the native land?* 典尽锦衣余一杖，夜行何必定还乡？"

China and later in Nanyang, it is natural that Father's poem should begin with a reminiscence of their youth.

For more details of Wang Guang Han's family details, refer to Chapter 62, the preface to *"Hai Wu Collection of Birthday Poems"* 《海屋唱酬集》序.

Appreciation

This poem is a response to Guang Han's poem dated 18 December 1949 for his 60th birthday. To better appreciate Qing Shan's response, one has to set it side by side with Guang Han's

王光汉《六十自寿》 Wang Guang Han's own 60th Birthday Poem	陈晴山之和诗 Chen Qing Shan's Poem in response
I treasure the memories of 35 years ago　　坐拥青毡卅五年，	Our youthful halcyon days we recall.　　翩翩裙屐忆当年，
I have not changed since the time of old.　　自矜故我尚依然。	Old as we are, but our hearts still leap.　　垂老情怀尚跃然。
The fame and fortune in this world, I watch askance.　　横眉冷看人间世，	Let our youthful hearts forever beat.　　但使童心长不改，
How drastically has the world advanced.　　朝市于今几变迁。	Let the years flow, and bother us not.　　尽教岁月暗中迁。
Even in my dreams I think of going home.　　归欤梦寐未曾忘，	"Home" or "foreign", we now can't tell apart.　　客中两地浑相忘，
A wild and simple life I often yearn to roam.　　海外常怀简与狂。	It's not a wild excess to chant your songs.　　选胜征歌未算狂。
Worried am I over the raging war at home,　　只为故乡烽火急，	To go home with none but a staff in hand,　　典尽锦衣余一杖，
Home is now retirement in foreign land.　　杖乡犹是杖他乡。	Why bother to head for the "native land"?　　夜行何必定还乡？

poem. As Prof Chan Chiu Ming has said of such an exercise, "It is difficult enough to comply with the rhyming scheme in terms of tone and rhyme in the right places, it is doubly difficult to respond to the subject matter at the same time." In the English translation of the poem, it is not possible to enjoy the response in rhyme and tone of Qing Shan's poem, but Qing Shan's masterly use of allusions in his response and its appropriateness is evident. The bilingual reader is invited to read the Appreciation (赏析) of the Chinese version of the book.

Appropriateness of Response

Some examples of this can be highlighted:

Verse 1, Line 2: When Guang Han says he has not changed and that he is still himself, Qing Shan's response is, "Oh yes, we both have changed in that we are much older. However, our hearts (spirit) still leap with sprightly steps (remain just as sprightly)."

Verse 1, Line 4: When Guang Han says how drastically has the world advanced (changed over time), Qing Shan's response is "Let the years flow (pass by), and bother us not (don't let it bother us)."

Verse 2, Line 1: When Guang Han says even in his dreams, he thinks of going home (to his native land in China). Qing Shan responds, "[We have sojourned for so long in this foreign land, that] we have forgotten the distinction between these two places ("native land" at home in China and "foreign land" where we sojourn)."

Verse 2, Lines 3 and 4 are perhaps the most pointed. Guang Han says he is worried about the war that has been raging at home and hence he is now resigned to staying on in this "foreign land" in retirement (the Communists took over the whole of mainland China officially on 1 October 1949 after a protracted civil war). Qing Shan pointedly gives another rationale in his two lines:

Line 3: "To go home [to the native land in China] with none but a staff in hand [without having amassed a great fortune and therefore unnoticed]." 典尽锦衣余一杖

Line 4: "[If it is to go home inconspicuously without great wealth,] Why bother to head for the native land [in China]?" 夜行何必定还乡？

The remarkable thing about classical Chinese poetry is its ability to convey so much in just those fourteen words. The two lines are drawn from a story about Xiangyu, the King of Chu (楚霸王项羽) as recorded in *Shi Ji* (史记•项羽本纪传). After conquering Xianyang 咸阳, he killed the Qin 秦 royal household and burned down the palaces. His advisers urged him to stay put in Xianyang, hold it as a fort and set up the capital. Xiangyu looked around and saw that everything had been burned to destruction; besides, he was feeling homesick and greatly wanted to return east. He seized the valuables and took the women and was determined to return to his own state of Chu. His response to his advisers was, "Not to return home with all the riches is like wearing all your silken finery to travel in the night. Who can see all the glitter and glory? 富贵不归故乡，如衣锦夜行，谁知之者？"

The literal translation of Verse 2, Lines 3 and 4:

典尽锦衣余一杖 "Pawned all your finery, leaving only your walking staff (stick)."

夜行何必定还乡 "If it is to travel by night [dressed in your silken finery and no one can see you], why bother to head for the "native land" [in China. You might as well stay put in Malaya]."

In Line 3, Qing Shan, of course, does not mean that Guang Han literally pawns all his belongings. It is just another way of saying that as a teacher, Guang Han, has not accumulated a fortune to justify returning home to China in a blaze of glory. Line 4 does not mean that Guang Han is a nocturnal traveller. Qing Shan's message to Guang Han is based on a simile used by Xiangyu who said "Not to return home with all the riches [which Guang Han had none in any case] is like wearing all your silken finery 衣锦 [to travel] in the night 夜行 [when no one will notice your display of wealth]." Qing Shan gives Xiangyu's original saying a new twist. Qing Shan is saying here to Guang Han in effect, "Since you have no great wealth to display to your folks back home, you might as well be travelling by night when no one will notice you anyway. That being the case, why bother to go back to your native land for your retirement since you have no great wealth to display."

The corollary of what Xiangyu said is now expressed in the modern day expression, "To return home (to the native land) wearing your silken finery" (衣锦还乡). It is the traditional ambition of every Chinese who goes away to seek his fortune to return home in glory.

Chapter 18

再赠内兄光汉二首

光汉内兄自吉隆坡来，出示六十自寿诗，既依韵和之，意有未尽，辄成二律。光汉精于医，然不轻试；从事侨教卅余年，其两郎亦执教鞭，可称一门师范。令妹王义宋女士，现长霹雳妇女裁剪训练所，以刀尺授徒，方致力于职业教育，故并及之。"槟榔"句用刘穆之事，穷愁犹昔，借以自嘲耳。

其一

文章寿世笔如椽，

肘后况兼探秘篇。

Another Two Verses for Elder Brother-in-law Guang Han's 60th Birthday

My elder brother-in-law Guang Han from Kuala Lumpur composed a poem to celebrate his 60th birthday. I have responded with a poem in the same rhyming scheme. Not having said everything I wanted to say, I now compose another two verses. Guang Han is skilled as a physician, but uses his medical skill only selectively. He has been in education for more than thirty years overseas and his two sons too are teachers. It can be said that they are a family of educators. His younger sister Wang Yi Song is now the Principal of Perak Women's Tailoring Training Centre teaching the art of tailoring, devoting her efforts to vocational education. Hence she is mentioned in the tribute. The reference to "betel nuts" is from the anecdote about Liu Mu Zhi 刘穆之; I borrow the allusion in self-deprecation.

Verse 1

    Vibrant, inspiring in literary works are you.
    A good physician and skilled in prescription too.
    Trained as a teacher before you teach others,
4   You teach your children and worthy scholars.

术未活人先活己，
4 学曾传子更传贤。
直看舞彩为儿戏，
未免称觞累俗缘。
事业千秋正无限，
8 何须花甲记流年。

其二

相逢客里太郎当，
挈妇将雏进一觞。
且向盘中吟苜蓿，
4 休从饭后笑槟榔。
君家旧物青毡在，
天下英才玉尺量。
却被左芬争一席，
8 别寻蹊径树门墙。

We see from you, filial are your children.
   Accept their filial piety, as is the custom.
   Your teaching will be felt for unending years.
8 Why at sixty, do you measure the bygone years?

Verse 2

   Among your guests, there is a poor church mouse.
   My family come, raise we our cup in your house.
   With no present, an unpolished poem is all I bring.
4 Please do not mock it as indigestible a thing.
   Your family of teachers is a heritage of treasure.
   The talents are outstanding by any measure.
   Younger sister has earned a place at the family table,
8 For she too has found a different road to be a teacher.

Paraphrase

Verse 1

L1: Vibrant your calligraphy, inspiring are your literary compositions.
L2: Besides your physician's skills, you are also knowledgeable in medical prescriptions.
L3: You are yourself well-trained (as a teacher), before you begin to educate others.
L4: You have passed your learning to your own children and to many other worthy young scholars.
L5: With you, we can see that your children are filial as Lao Lai Zi.
L6: As is customary, you should accept your children's celebration of your birthday.
L7: Your teaching as an educator will be felt in the unending years to come.
L8: Why should you at sixty need to measure the years that have passed?

Verse 2

L1: Among your fellow sojourners away from home, you have a guest who is poor as a church mouse.
L2: I bring my wife and children to greet you and join in the celebration,
L3: Regrettably I am just able to put onto the "platter" (your collection of poems) my unpolished composition [implicitly] as our present for you.
L4: Please do not laugh at it as being so coarse that the proverbial betel nuts are needed to aid in its digestion.
L5: You and your family, all scholars and educators, are indeed a treasured heritage.
L6: The talent of everyone is outstanding by any measure.
L7: Your younger sister too has found a place at your family table of talents.
L8: She has found a different avenue (tailoring) as a teacher (of vocational skills).

Background

The poem was written in late 1949 or in 1950 as a sequel to the poem in Chapter 17 for Wang Guang Han 王光汉 who was Mother's elder brother. For fuller details of the background, please refer to the Background in Chapter 17 and the Preface in Chapter 62.

There are, however, a few anecdotes and family stories that are worth mentioning as additional background to this poem. Uncle Guang Han's calligraphy was greatly admired, especially in the writing of large "characters" for signboards of business or other public buildings. We once saw him in action. A huge sheet of paper was laid out on the floor. He would position himself over the paper, legs astride and knees half bent in a *kung fu* posture, and holding the huge brush about one third of the length of a broom, he would begin to write. There is a standing joke, only within the family, about Uncle Guang

Han's calligraphy. Many of the businesses, whose signboards were written by him, failed to prosper.

It is not well-known that Uncle Guang Han was a skilled physician in traditional Chinese medicine. His father Wang Dan Ru 王淡如 and his uncle Wang Xue Dan 王学丹 (Dan Ru's elder brother) were both well-known painters in their prefecture. Xue Dan was also a skilled physician and a *kung fu* master, the two skills often going together. It is quite possible that Guang Han had acquired his physician's skill from his uncle or under his influence.

Uncle Guang Han's younger sister Yi Song 义宋 was, of course, our mother. In 1939, Father had encouraged her to attend tailoring school in Kuala Lumpur. After graduation, she returned to Kampar and opened a tailoring school. It had to close when the Japanese invaded Malaya at the end of 1941. After the war, the school was reopened in Ipoh in 1947. At the time this poem was written, Mother's tailoring school had already been operating successfully for about two to three years.

Appreciation

The purpose of this poem is very clearly explained in the preface by Qing Shan himself. His first poem (in Chapter 17) was written in response to the 60th birthday poem of his brother-in-law Guang Han. A poem "in response" (依韵和之) has to conform to the rhyming scheme set out in Guang Han's "seed poem". There is a lot more Qing Shan wants to say than is possible in a poem "in response".

In this poem, Qing Shan explains in a rather long preface some of the lesser known facts about Guang Han and his family, for example, he is a skilled physician in traditional Chinese medicine. Qing Shan also takes the opportunity to pay tribute to Guang Han's younger sister Wang Yi Song who—as it turns out—is also Qing Shan's wife! The tribute is well-deserved, as justified by Qing Shan in the preface. She is after all the

Principal of her own tailoring school which has become well-known throughout Malaya and Singapore. A rather unusual thing about the preface is Qing Shan taking the trouble to explain an allusion which he intends to use in the poem. It is from the story of Liu Mu Zhi and the proverbial betel nut. We can only surmise that Qing Shan wants to make sure that the allusion is intended to mock himself in self-deprecation of his own poverty—in case it is misunderstood.

This poem is free from the rules of having to rhyme with Guang Han's original poem, but the subject matter is, nevertheless, in consonance therewith.

Verse 1 praises the calligraphy and literary compositions of Guang Han. He is well-known for his calligraphy, especially the large characters for signboards and business names. Guang Han's two sons are both teachers and the family is praised as educators. Verse 1 closes with two lines which contrast against each other:

Line 7: "Your teaching will be felt for unending years.
事业千秋正无限
Line 8: Why at sixty, do you measure the bygone years?"
何须花甲记流年

Since the effect of your work as a teacher will be felt for unending years (i.e., infinitely), why at the age of sixty (花甲) should you bother to measure the years that have gone by?

Verse 2, Lines 1 to 4 are Qing Shan's self-deprecation. He tells Guang Han that among his guests who sojourn with him in this corner of the earth, there is someone, viz., himself, who is down and out and poor as a church mouse. He has brought his family to the celebration party without a present, as he is too poor to afford one. However, he does bring along an "unpolished" poem. He compares his poem with the very coarse horse feed (alfalfa grass, *mu xu* 苜蓿). He pleads with his host not to laugh at him for bringing something so indigestible that it would require the aid of the proverbial betel nut to help digest it (休从饭后笑槟榔). The allusion is from the story about a scholar Liu Mu Zhi 刘穆之. He was extremely poor and took every opportunity to go to his wife's wealthy family to have a free meal. Betel nut was believed to be an aid to digestion. After a full meal, the diners would chew betel nuts. It became a habit for Liu Mu Zhi to turn up at every meal time to the annoyance of his brothers-in-law. One day, after a meal at his in-laws' home, Mu Zhi aped the habit of the others and asked for betel nut. His brothers-in-law decided to teach him a lesson and told him, "Mu Zhi, betel nuts are to help digestion. Since your stomach is always empty, why do you need betel nut?" The whole town knew of this incident and Mu Zhi vowed never to go there again. Qing Shan takes the precaution to explain in the preface to the poem that the allusion is used in the poem to mock himself.

The rest of Verse 2 continues to praise Guang Han's family, with the last two lines a tribute to Guang Han's younger sister Yi Song—Qing Shan's wife. Line 7 compares Yi Song with Zuo Fen 左芬 (of Jin dynasty). Zuo Fen was a talented and famous scholar. She was the younger sister of Zuo Si 左思 who wrote the famous poem *San Du Fu* 三都赋. As Guang Han and his two sons are all teachers, Qing Shan praises Yi Song as having earned a place at the family table of talented educators. Yi Song too is an educator by a different route. She is the Principal of her own tailoring school and has taught hundreds of girls in acquiring a vocational skill either to sew for the family or to make a living.

Chapter 19

xīn bié lí cí zèng wáng guāng hé
新别离词赠王光河

guāng hé nèi dì jiāng jiù shāng jí lóng pō　yī yī yǒu xī bié yì
光河内弟将就商吉隆坡，依依有惜别意，
gù fǎn qí cí yǐ shì zhī
故反其词以释之。

zì gǔ shāng lí bié
自古伤离别，

lí bié yì hé shāng
离别亦何伤？

rén shēng yǒu jù sàn
人生有聚散，

hún rú xì yī chǎng
4 浑如戏一场。

gē tái yǔ wǔ xiè
歌台与舞榭，

zuó xiāo fāng dǎ yàng
昨宵方打烊；

jīn yè huá dēng shàng
今夜华灯上，

xiān yuè yòu piāo yáng
8 仙乐又飘扬。

New Farewell Poem to Wang Guang He

Guang He, my younger brother-in-law, is about to move to Kuala Lumpur in pursuit of his business interest. In expression of my deep regret at his leaving, I forward this composition.

    Parting is such sad sorrow since time of old.
    But why should our parting too be so?
    To meet and then to part is our lot in life;
4 What's real and what's not, it's hard to say.
    Life is also like a singing, dancing stage:
    Only the night before, the curtains fall;
    Tonight, the lights are all ablaze once more,
8 Enchanting music once more fills the air.
    In life we meet and then again to part,
    Our parting may not be that long either.
    Floating duckweeds disperse and gather;
12 To part or to meet is not a "forever".
    Why shouldn't it be so for you and me?
    We've wandered long, away from home.
    Though you'll only be a hundred miles away,
16 We will both still be away from home
    We've been together twelve years or more,
    This short parting we shouldn't mind at all.
    It's like the three meals we eat a day:
20 If every meal is for a gourmet,

人生聚必散，
散亦不复长。
浮萍吹忽聚，
12 离合讵有常？
何况吾与子，
去国久栖遑。
此去百英里，
16 一样是他乡。
相处漫逾纪，
小别固无妨。
譬如三餐饭，
20 日夕餍膏粱。
偶然夹藜藿，
转觉菜根香。

又如鸡林贾，
24 满载白与黄。
有时思风雅，
亦复重词章。
时间有昼夜，
28 气候有炎凉。
相形虽成绌，
相得乃益彰。
纵谓别离苦，
32 此味亦应尝。
雪州风月好，
买醉任千觞。
首都多名卉，
36 看花不厌狂。

An occasional dish of the very coarse food
Will taste like a feast of fragrant herbal root.
Again it's like the clever Merchant of Jilin,
24 With his cartload of silver and gold jingling.
Even he sometimes has the cultural urge too,
Dabbling in the arts by writing a poem or two.
Time too has its changes, day and night;
28 Weather can be hot and can be cold.
A comparison may show one inferior to the other;
A combination will in fact enhance each other.
Though it's said that, "Parting is such bitter sorrow."
32 Yet we have need to sometimes taste it to know.
Enjoy the beautiful scenery of Selangor State,
Get the wine and drink a thousand cheers!
Its Capital is renowned for its abounding flowers.
36 You won't tire of flowers, enjoy them all you want.
Move on, away you go and don't look around.
Start your journey at the first light of dawn.
Embarrassed am I, with no precious gift for you,
40 I call my sons to sing the farewell Weiyang Song.

Autumn of Jiawu Year, 1954
15th day of the 7th Month
Qing Shan in Ipoh

Paraphrase

L1: Parting has always been a sad occasion
L2: In reality, why should it be so?
L3: Life is full of partings and meetings up again.
L4: It is like a play and difficult to tell what's real and what's not.
L5: It's also like a performing stage;
L6: Only the night before, the curtains fall and the stage closes.
L7: Tonight the lights are again all ablaze,
L8: And enchanting music fills the air once more.

行行莫四顾,
前路趁晨光。
愧乏琼瑶赠,
40 呼儿唱渭阳。

　　　　　　一九五四甲午之秋七月既望
　　　　　　陈晴山于怡保

L9: In life just as there are meetings, there are also partings.
L10: We will not be parted for long; we will meet again soon.
L11: Floating duckweeds are dispersed by the wind, but they soon come together again.
L12: To meet and part are normal; how could life be always the same?
L13: Everyone knows this inevitability, why should you and I be the exception?
L14: We left home a long time ago and have since been dashing around making a living.
L15: Where you are going is only a hundred miles away.
L16: And we are both still in a foreign land.
L17: We have lived together in the same town for over twelve years.
L18: We should not mind this short parting.
L19: If, for example, we eat three meals a day
L20: And every meal is a feast, day in day out;
L21: An occasional meal with coarse bramble
L22: Will taste like a delectable dish of fragrant herbal root.
L23: Again, even the clever Merchant of Jilin,
L24: Though he is immensely rich with silver and gold,
L25: Will have the occasional urge to take on a little culture,
L26: By even penning a verse or two.
L27: Each twenty-four-hour period is divided into day and night;
L28: A year has hot and cold seasons.
L29: When the two are contrasted, one may pale by comparison.
L30: Put together they complement each other and become even better.
L31: Although it's said "Parting is such sad sorrow"
L32: Yet we need to taste it sometimes.
L33: Where you're going, enjoy the breeze and moon (scenery) of Selangor.
L34: To dispel your sorrow, get the wine and drink a thousand cheers.
L35: Where you will live, the Capital is renowned for it flowers.
L36: You can enjoy the flowers as much as you like.
L37: Go, get on your way and don't look around any further.

L38: Start your journey at the first light of day.
L39: I'm embarrassed not to have any precious gift for you
L40: I can only call my sons to say farewell by singing the Weiyang Song.

Background

Summary

This poem was written in 1954 to say farewell to Uncle Guang He who was moving from Ipoh to Kuala Lumpur. Guang He was the younger brother of Mother and was therefore Father's younger brother-in-law.

Our two families had lived in Ipoh since the Japanese invasion in 1941–1942. Guang He was in the motor spare parts business in Ipoh and in 1954 he decided to move to Kuala Lumpur to further his business interest.

Mother was ten years older than her younger brother Guang He, but there was a very strong and special bond of kinship between the two. Guang He being a businessman was better off than our family, especially during the Japanese Occupation. The warmth that existed between our family and Uncle Guang He is apparent in the poem.

Uncle Guang He

Apart from an elder brother and elder sister, our mother (Wang Yi Song 王义宋) had four younger brothers. Guang He 光河 was the youngest among them and was also one whom she loved and looked after most. They spent their childhood in the ancestral home at Jiangdou 江兜 village in the county of Fuqing (Fujian province). When our maternal grandmother passed away, grandfather remarried. The stepmother did not treat Guang He kindly and Mother always had to stand up for him.

He never forgot what Mother did for him and would repay her kindness later in life. During the Japanese Occupation in Malaya, Uncle Guang He provided our family with shelter and often with food.

Uncle Guang He never liked to study when he was young, but he was astute in business. In Ipoh (Malaya), he went into partnership with his compatriots from his native county to set up a motor spare parts business which flourished. Two of the four brothers of the Wang family (our first and fourth uncles) became teachers and were both accomplished calligraphers and poets. But Guang He went on to become a successful well-to-do businessman.

Despite his lack of formal learning, he nevertheless inherited his father's artistic talent and wrote well with the brush pen. Guang He also dabbled in composing poems. In the art of poetry, he was looked down somewhat by fourth uncle Guang

Family of Guang He, younger brother of Mother (photo taken in Ipoh c.1949). Guang He and his family moved from Ipoh to Kuala Lumpur in 1954.
"Parting is such sad sorrow since time of old. But why should our parting too be so?"

Guo, but our father, Qing Shan, was a lot more sympathetic towards his younger brother-in-law's attempt at poetry. This is reflected in the lines of the poem which observed that even the clever Merchant of Jilin sometimes has the cultural urge to dabble at composing a poem or two.

In 1954, Guang He decided to move his family to Kuala Lumpur to further his business interest and he had to part from his elder sister (our mother) and his elder brother-in-law (our father) who had all lived in the same town Ipoh for several years. The two families had to "regretfully part" which was why Father wrote this poem of farewell. It was first published in the supplement of the local paper *Jianguo Daily* 建国日报.

Appreciation

This poem falls into the category of "farewell poems", yet it is not quite the same as the usual sorrowful and tearful compositions. Although it expresses the sentiments of a sorrowful parting, it is not overdone. On the contrary, in many places the poem encourages and exhorts the younger brother-in-law to go forward in life. This is the most distinctive point about the poem.

The poem is full of antithetically balanced pairs of lines which make very interesting reading. For example:

    Line 1: "Parting is such sad sorrow since time of old.
               自古伤离别
    Line 2: But why should our parting too be so?"
               离别亦何伤

    Line 6: "Only the night before, the curtains fall;
               昨宵方打烊
    Line 7: Tonight the lights are all ablaze once more,"
               今夜华灯上

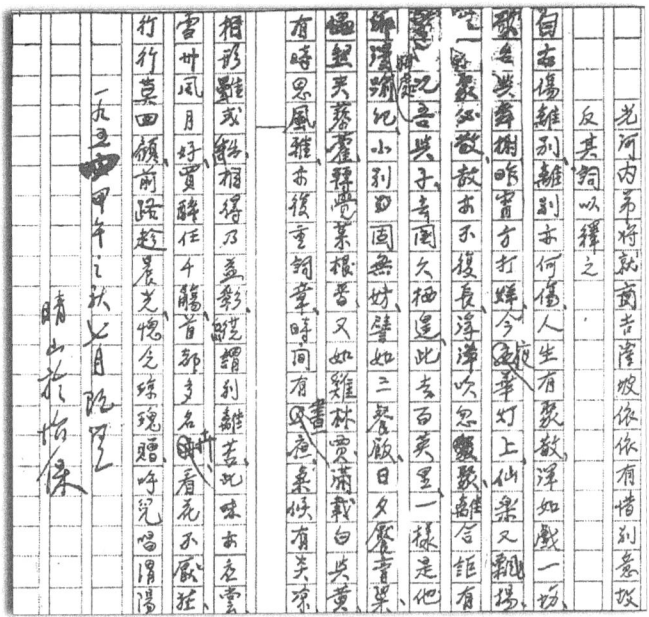

Qing Shan's 1954 handwritten draft of farewell poem to his younger brother-in-law, Guang He 光河, who was moving from Ipoh to Kuala Lumpur with his family.

Hong Ngek Restaurant in Kuala Lumpur which served Putian or Xinghua (Hinghwa) cuisine throughout the 1950s and was a favourite restaurant of the local Hinghwa community (picture was taken in 2002). The literal meaning of its name in Chinese, Feng Yue 风月, is "breeze and moon", a figure of speech for "beautiful scenery"—a metaphor used in Line 33 of the poem.

Line 9: "In life, we meet and then again to part,
         人生聚必散
Line 10: Our parting may not be that long either."
         散亦不复长

As the lines alternately flip and turn, sing and respond in counterpoint fashion, the use of antithetical statements enlivens the poem for the reader.

The language used is simple and unadorned and yet able to bring out the deeply felt sentiments. Qing Shan loves the poems of Bai Juyi and is fond of following the dictum of the poet who said, "There is no such thing as the correct sound (in composition). Whatever that pleases the ear, that then is the right sound 天下无正声，悦耳即为娱". Qing Shan once wrote, "The poems of Bai Juyi can be understood by even the old lady of the village 香山之诗，老妪都解，此真诗人也". The composition of this farewell poem fits such a description. Every word is plain and simple, but every phrase exudes the deeply felt sentiments held within.

Farewell poems are mostly sad and melancholic. For example,

Li Bai's [Farewell to Uncle Yun, the Imperial Librarian at Xie Tiao's Pavilion in Xuanzhou 宣州谢朓楼饯别校书叔云]:
"Raise your wine cup to dispel your sorrow; sorrow begets sorrow" 举杯消愁愁更愁

Wang Wei's [Wei City Farewell 渭城曲]:
"I urge you Sir, let another wine cup flow;
劝君更尽一杯酒
West of the Southern Pass you'll meet no one you know."
西出阳关无故人

Du Fu's [A Farewell Gift 赠别]:
"The candle with its wick bears the parting pain,
蜡烛有心还惜别
For thee, its tears will flow till morning comes again."
替人垂泪到天明

But this farewell poem of Qing Shan has a certain liveliness of spirit. It exhorts Guang He not to be overly sad because of the parting, but to go forward in life. For example,

Line 35: "Its Capital is renowned for its abounding flowers.
首都多名卉
Line 36: You won't tire of flowers, enjoy them all you want.
看花不厌狂
Line 37: Move on, away you go and don't look around.
行行莫四顾
Line 38: Start your journey at the first light of dawn."
前路趁晨光

The last Line 40, "I call my sons to sing the farewell Weiyang song 呼儿唱渭阳" is an example of Qing Shan's clever application of classical allusions. Guang He is the uncle to his two sons. When Qing Shan summons them to come forward, he paints a scene of nephews bidding farewell to their uncle. With this simple line, Qing Shan has transported a 2,000-year-old allusion into the poem. The allusion is from the story of Duke Kang of Qin (秦康公) who bid farewell to his uncle by accompanying the uncle on the journey as far as the bank of the Wei River. The reference to "Weiyang" now personifies "farewell", in addition to personifying the close relationship between nephew and uncle.

Chapter 20

题王光河五十初度小影

guò xì jū guāng guò yǎn yān
过隙驹光过眼烟，

wú shēng zhī mìng biàn chāo rán
吾生知命便超然。

zhù yán yǒu shù píng hóng yǐng
驻颜有术凭鸿影，

liú qǔ tā shí zì gù lián
留取他时自顾怜。

Colophon for Wang Guang He's 50th Birthday Snapshot

Worldly things will pass, fleeting like a foal.
At fifty, I know my future and goal.
This snapshot will keep the image of mine,
For to ponder on, at some future time.

Paraphrase

L1: All worldly things, like Time will flit by as quickly as a foal galloping past when viewed through a crack (白驹过隙) and disappear before our eyes like a puff of smoke (过眼烟).

L2: I have reached fifty, the "Age of Knowing one's Destiny" and have hence become philosophical about life.

L3: I can perhaps rely on this one snapshot, the magical art that preserves forever my youthful looks.

L4: Putting it safely away, I shall take a look at it in future in order to console myself when age finally catches up and Youth is all but gone.

Background

(For a background of Guang He, please see the Background section of Chapter 19.)

This poem was composed in 1956 when Guang He was actually 49. However, by the Chinese method of counting age, Guang He was 50 years old in 1956.

In March the same year, Mother visited Kuala Lumpur and got together with Guang He, and her elder sister Jin Song 锦宋. The three siblings from the oldest to the youngest were born ten years apart. This event was commemorated in the poem in Chapter 21. There are two other poems composed in relation to Guang He, in Chapters 16 and 19.

Guang He loved to drink. He died prematurely in 1958 due probably to alcohol-related illness.

Appreciation

The poem was composed in 1956. It is written as though the words were from Guang He himself, reflecting his life so far at the age of fifty. While the subject may sound serious, the tone of the poem is light-hearted and fairly reflects the character of Guang He. He was a jovial and generous person and got on well with everyone.

Line 1 is expressed fully in the paraphrase. To describe how fleetingly time passes, it uses the imagery of someone viewing a galloping horse through a narrow crack. To describe how transient worldly things are, it uses the imagery of the horse disappearing before our very eyes like a puff of smoke.

Although the title tells us it is for Guang He's 50th birthday, Line 2 does not use the word "fifty". Instead, it uses the term *zhī mìng* 知命 which means "the age of knowing one's destiny", a term used for age 50. (see full quote from Confucius in Chapter 49 Appreciation) At this age, a man is supposed to know what he is destined to achieve and has set his goals or may even have achieved some if not all of them. He is philosophical about life and should have no regrets.

Lines 3 and 4 express the light-hearted spirit of the poem. Line 3 refers to the snapshot of Guang He as some sort of magical art that can preserve the image of him forever with his youthful looks. Line 4 gives the reason for wanting to keep the photograph so that at some future time when he is no longer young, he can always look at it to console himself how young he once looked.

Chapter 21

义宋锦宋光河三姐弟合照题诗

六十初度,偕锦宋姐、光河弟合照书怀。余三人者,序齿各以十差,而碌碌浮生,则有同感。

五十无闻愧后生,
六旬七秩亦虚声。
寿筵未敢邀俦侣,
4 春酒惟应共弟兄。
桃实分为三处种,
棣华愿见一家荣。
老来手足情何限,
8 忍向天涯各旅程。

　　　　义宋

丙申三月初十日于怡保

Colophon on a Photograph of Two Sisters and their Brother, viz., Jin Song, Yi Song and Guang He

On my 60th Birthday, a photograph was taken with elder sister Jin Song and younger brother Guang He, as a memento. The three of us are ten years apart in age; although we are all busy in our own lives, we nevertheless share a strong empathy with one another.

    A "nobody" at fifty, ashamed to stand before those younger.
    Neither are the sixty and seventy any more remarkable,
    Inviting friends to our dinner, we would hardly dare;
4   To make merry among siblings, is a private affair.
    Planted in three places apart, the seeds from one peach tree.
    We siblings wish each other's family every prosperity.
    Growing older, siblings' bond are even more precious.
8   Painful it is to meet and in separate ways, to disperse.

        Composed by Qing Shan on behalf of Yi Song
        10th Day of the 3rd Month, 1956

Paraphrase

L1: Still a "nobody" at fifty, one might feel embarrassed in front of the younger generation that are born after me.
L2: On the other hand, to be sixty or seventy is also nothing remarkable.
L3: For our birthday dinner, we have not invited any of our friends.
L4: This dinner should really be celebrated by us three siblings on our own.
L5: The seeds of a single peach tree are planted in three different places.
L6: We siblings all wish to see each of our families well and prospering.
L7: As we grow older, the love and bond between siblings become immeasurably even more precious.
L8: It is really regrettable that (after this birthday gathering), we will all have to go our separate ways once again.

Background

Summary

This poem was composed by Father on behalf of Mother (Yi Song 义宋). It was inscribed in calligraphy by our fourth uncle (Guang Guo 光国), below a photograph of three persons. They are: our fifth uncle (Guang He 光河), our first aunt Jin Song (锦宋) and Mother.

The colophon as inscribed in Uncle Guang Guo's calligraphy was abbreviated from Father's original composition (perhaps to fit into the available space). On the back of a printed copy of this photo is the full version of the colophon in Father's own handwriting. It gives a more comprehensive background, as follows:

"At my 60th Birthday in Bing-shen year (丙申 1956), my siblings from Kuala Lumpur, elder sister Jin Song and younger brother Guang He and I got together to ask about our families and how we have been getting on lately. The three of us are ten years apart in age; although we are all busy in our own lives, we nevertheless share a strong empathy with one another. As I again think of my third younger brother who has long sojourned in Wu Hu (芜湖), I feel extremely disappointed (due to his absence). When I read Bai Juyi's line about 'sharing the same thought of home this night' (一夜乡心), I am overcome by sadness for a long time. Determined to put aside my sorrow, I raise the cup to commemorate the birthdays (of the siblings here) and have this photograph taken together to capture the event, with a poem composed by Qing Shan. Herewith the record.

Yi Song
10th day 3rd month 1956"

Bai Juyi's Poem

In the comprehensive colophon written by Father on the back of the photograph, the Bai Juyi poem was mentioned. It stirred up such sad thoughts about Mother's third brother Guang Po 光坡 living in faraway Wu Hu in Anhui province. The poem was composed by Bai Juyi in 799. He was born in Henan province and in his poems, he referred to Henan as his "native home". The poem is titled "Feelings upon gazing at the moon" 望月有感. It has a long preamble that describes the turmoil of war and uprisings in the Henan 河南 region that brought about mass starvation. As a result, his siblings were dispersed far apart to look for their own livelihood. As he gazed at the moon one evening, he was bestirred and overcome by his thoughts of the other siblings from whom he was separated. He composed the poem and sent it to each of them. Following are the closing two lines of Bai Juyi's poem that similarly provoked the sad thoughts in Father and Mother about Guang Po in China:

Gazing at the same moon on high; our tears begin to flow.　共看明月应垂泪
All think of home this night, in five distant places below.　一夜乡心五处同

It is especially sad because at the time of Father's poem in 1956, Guang Po was living in very poor circumstances in China. His children were still at school. In order to keep them in school, he finally had to resort to selling the family's precious cotton wadding (quilt), which was the only asset left that was of any value. He carried it on a bamboo pole and went out into the street hawking it. A poor household had no heating and the winter temperatures in Wu Hu could fall to freezing point.

Mother's Siblings

There were altogether eight children on the side of Mother's family, but only six survived to adulthood. The children are:

By order of seniority

1 Jin Song	锦宋	(1887–1976)	daughter
2 Guang Han	光汉	(1890–1956)	son
3 Yi Song	义宋	(1897–1979)	daughter
4 Guang Dou	光斗	dates unknown	son (died young)
5 Guang Po	光坡	(1900–1971)	son
6 Guang Guo	光国	(1905–1971)	son
7 Guang He	光河	(1907–1958)	son
8 Guang Fu	光复	dates unknown	son (died young)

The three siblings in the photograph of the poem were born in 1887, 1897 and 1907. Guang Po at the time of the poem (1956) was in Wu Hu, Anhui province in China where he had worked and lived since the mid-1930s.

The three siblings from left to right: Guang He 光河, Jin Song 锦宋, Yi Song 义宋 celebrating their fiftieth, seventieth and sixtieth birthday respectively, in Kuala Lumpur (1956). Qing Shan's poem with an abridged colophon appears below the photo in Guang Guo's (光国) calligraphy. *"A 'nobody' at fifty, ashamed to stand before those younger. Neither are the sixty and seventy any more remarkable."*

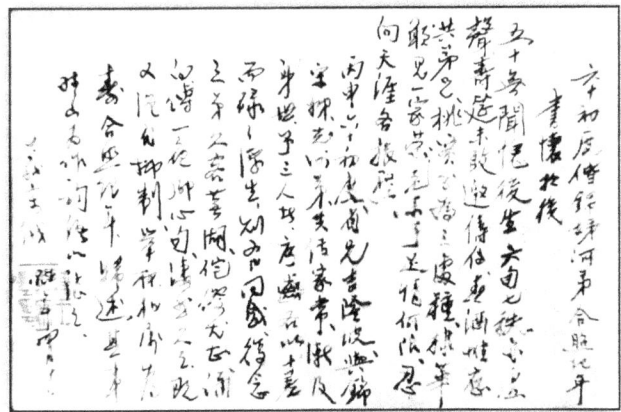

An extended version of the colophon is written on the back of the photograph expressing great sadness at the thought of the absence of another sibling Guang Po 光坡 who was then in China (in 1956).

21 Colophon on a Photograph of Two Sisters and their Brother

Other Related Poems

- Chapter 16 光河弟四十初度招饮，为韵语祝之
  My Brother Guang He's 40th Birthday Invitation to Dinner, A Poem in Greeting
- Chapter 19 新別離詞贈王光河
  New Farewell Poem to Wang Guang He
- Chapter 20 題王光河五十初度小影
  Colophon for Guang He's 50th Birthday Snapshot
- Chapter 25 寄君余内弟芜湖和光国韵
  To Younger Brother-in-law in Wu Hu, A Poem in Rhyme with Guang Guo

Appreciation

This is a relatively short and simple poem for the get-together of three siblings for the 60th birthday of Qing Shan's wife, Yi Song. The special significance of the event is the fact that the three of them are all ten years apart in age. Guang He is fifty, Yi Song, sixty and Jin Song, seventy. (Their ages are calculated by the Chinese method of reckoning. By the Western method, the three would be 49, 59 and 69). What is even more important is that they are all very closely bonded to one another.

Though simple in is its language, the poem still uses allusions, but only those that can be understood even in a literal sense. A good example is Line 1, "A 'nobody' at fifty, ashamed to stand before those younger" (五十无聞愧后生). It has the literal meaning: "At fifty 五十, I'm still not heard of 无聞 (i.e., I have not made a name for myself); I'm therefore ashamed (i.e., embarrassed 愧) to stand before those that are born after me 后生 (i.e., the generation after me). This is a quote widely known from the Confucian Analects: "*A youth is to be regarded with respect* (后生可畏). *How do we know that his future will not be equal to our present? If he reaches the age of forty or fifty, and has not made himself heard of, then indeed he will not be worth being regarded with respect.* 后生可畏,焉知来者之不如今也？四十、五十而无闻焉,斯亦不足畏也已。" Typically, Qing Shan turns the original quote round. Since Guang He is already fifty and still has not achieved fame, "he will not be worth being regarded with respect" and is hence embarrassed to stand before the younger generation.

In the typically cheeky style of Qing Shan, Line 2 then says in effect, "Your two elder sisters are already sixty and seventy and they too haven't achieved anything more remarkable than you either!" Line 3 then makes the excuse, "In that case, we wouldn't dare invite any of our friends to celebrate with us as we wouldn't want to embarrass ourselves any further." Moreover, "The celebration with the 'Spring' wine (春酒) should be a private affair among us siblings only" (Line 4). The poem is written in the third month of the lunar calendar and is, hence, in the middle of the Spring season.

Line 5 uses the metaphor and analogy of a peach tree whose seeds are dispersed and planted in three different places. "Peach seeds" (桃实) is a metaphor for brothers and sisters. Guang He and Jin Song are in Kuala Lumpur and Yi Song is in Ipoh. We cannot be sure if the "third" place is a subconscious reference to the third brother Guang Po who is in Wu Hu, China. Guang Po is not one of the three in the photograph nor mentioned in the colophon written below the photograph with the poem. But he is never far from the thoughts of Qing Shan and Yi Song, as explained in the Background.

The concluding two lines say how as we age, the relationship and bond between the siblings become even more precious. How painful it will be that after this birthday gathering, the three siblings will disperse and go their separate ways once again. The poem begins in a light-hearted way but ends in a serious tone with regret for yet another parting.

Chapter 22

广嫁女辞，赠霹雳女中高师毕业班同学

向作嫁女辞，朋辈许为达，因广其意，更作二首示诸同学，为临别之赠。

其一

嫁女复嫁女，

相对两无语。

待汝为母时，

方识母心苦。

Wedding Counsel for the Senior Normal Graduation Class of the Perak Girls' Middle School

I once composed a poem "Counsel for My Daughter on Her Wedding". My friends praised it as having attained a high standard. In response to their request, I now compose two new verses for the entire group of graduating students to bid them farewell.

Verse 1

    Another daughter is soon to be married.
    Mother faces daughter without a word.
    "Only when you're mother would you know"
4   "A mother's toil and suffering untold."
    To whom should a mother speak her pain?
    Thus has Nature endowed a mother's bane.
    The mighty eagles for their young they care;
8   Wild tigers suckle their cubs in the lair.
    Animals in the wild care for their offspring new
    How could mother abandon you?

母苦向谁言？
天性所赋予。
鸷鸟尚将雏，
8 於菟亦哺乳。
顾瞻下一代，
弃置岂由汝。

其二

日日治嫁妆，
阿娘为汝忙。
无如十指拙，
4 两载不盈箱。
去去且莫怨，
门前路正长。
人生贵自立，
8 何用多忧伤？
多少蓬门女，
未识绮罗香，
一别仅三日，
12 衣锦还故乡。

Verse 2

    Mother prepares the trousseau day by day.
    Busily for you she works without delay,
    Her fingers no longer nimble as they were.
4 Two years pass; the trousseau trunk's no fuller.
    As you leave, resent not your mother's wanting.
    The journey ahead is both long and daunting.
    To stand on your own two feet is vital in life.
8 No cause for worry when troubles are rife.
    The girls who come from a poor household
    Have never seen a dress of silk and gold.
    Those with a firm resolve will soon return
12 To their own home with finery resplendent.

Paraphrase

Verse 1

L1: A daughter was just married off last year and now another daughter is about to be married.
L2: Sad beyond words, mother and daughter sit silently facing each other.
L3: Only when you become a mother yourself,
L4: Will you realize the toil and suffering of a mother.
L5: To whom can a mother speak her pain?
L6: This is what Nature has endowed a mother with.
L7: Even the mighty eagle cares for her young;
L8: So too the ferocious tiger suckles her cubs.
L9: They too care for their next generation,
L10: How could mother abandon and not care for you?

Verse 2

L1: Mother daily prepares your wedding trousseau.
L2: Busily she goes about her task for you without a pause,
L3: But her fingers are no longer as nimble as they used to be.
L4: After two years of preparation, she has yet to fill the trousseau trunk.
L5: As you are about to leave home, try to overlook your mother's shortcoming.
L6: The journey ahead, is a long one.
L7: The most important thing in life is to be able to stand on your own two feet.
L8: You don't need to be unnecessarily worried or sad.
L9: Untold number of girls from poor households too
L10: Have never ever experienced the luxury of a silken dress.
L11: Yet in a brief period of just three days (just a short time)
L12: You will return home bedecked in all the finery (independent, with full self-respect).

Background

Summary

In 1957, after an absence from teaching for 16 years, Father was invited to teach in the newly established Senior Middle Classes in the Perak Girls' Middle School, in addition to the ongoing two-year Senior Normal Diploma Course in the school. Father only took classes in the mornings as he was still working as the paid Secretary of the Perak Hokkien Association.

This poem was composed in 1957 for the graduating class of the Senior Normal Diploma Course of this girls' school. There was no graduation magazine for this two-year course and the poem would no doubt have been published in the local paper.

Father had only shortly before this, written the poem in Chapter 11, "Wedding Poem, An Admonition to Mei Yu 嫁女词示美瑜". This was widely acclaimed as the poem's preface indicates. He must have found it a convenient way to bid farewell to his graduating students with a serious piece of advice and encouragement. An "omnibus" farewell message may also have obviated the necessity of signing tens of autograph books for the departing students, as was a popular practice in those days.

Long-time Career as Teacher

Father started life as a teacher. Even before he first came to Malaya in 1917, he had been a tutor for the Wang family of Jiangdou village in Fuqing. Our fourth uncle Guang Guo, as a teenager, was taught by Father.

When Father came to Malaya, he started teaching in various towns in Perak (the longest tenure being Kampar) until the Japanese invasion of Malaya and Singapore in December 1941. His teaching career up to then had included a spell of two years, 1932 and 1933, in a high school in Putian. After the war, he secured a job as the paid Secretary of the Perak Hokkien Association in Ipoh in October 1945. It was only in the early 1950s, for a couple of years, that he taught weekend classes conducted for the Normal Training courses for Chinese school teachers. Except for this, he had not taught in schools since 1941. It was in early 1957 that he was invited to teach again by Madam Peng Shi Lin, Principal of the Perak Girls' Middle School in Ipoh. An account of this can be read in the Background in Chapter 48.

Appreciation

This poem of two verses was composed in December 1957 for the graduating class of teachers of the Perak Girls' Middle

School in Ipoh. Qing Shan had earlier composed a similar poem counselling his own daughter and must have found it equally appropriate to address this poem to the entire cohort of his graduating students.

The first verse uses the analogy of a teacher as the mother to her daughters who are about to leave home, just as these students are about to leave school to become teachers themselves. Hence, Lines 3 and 4 virtually remind the students that only when they become teachers themselves would they really know how their teachers have toiled for them. The higher purpose of this verse is to encourage them to discharge their role as teachers to the utmost of their ability. It is, as pointed out in the rest of the verse, the natural order of things that one generation has to care for the next. Likewise, they as teachers must care for their next generation of students.

Lines 1 to 4 of Verse 2 are words of humility and apology by the teacher (mother) saying the two years of preparation for their wedding (graduation), the trousseau trunk (their learning) is still not adequately filled. It is a self-effacing metaphor for saying and apologising that as their teacher, he has not adequately prepared them for their role. Lines 5 to 8 advise them on the importance of being able to stand on their own two feet and with that ability, they can confront any situation without worry. Lines 9 to 12 are more like what Qing Shan, a poor school teacher, has counselled his own daughter personally in an earlier poem:

Line 9: "The girls who come from poor household
多少蓬门女
Line 10: Have never seen a dress of silk and gold.
未识绮罗香
Line 11: Those with a firm resolve will soon return
一别仅三日
Line 12: To their own home with finery resplendent."
衣锦还故乡

The poem is written using simple language free from complicated allusions from the classics and can hence be easily understood by the students. Moreover, the use of the analogy of a teacher as the mother of the graduating class gives it that much more a personal touch.

Chapter 23

有行
yǒu xíng

海阔天寥廓，
hǎi kuò tiān liáo kuò

休嗟行路难。
xiū jiē xíng lù nán

有风皆可御，
yǒu fēng jiē kě yù

4 无浪不奇观。
wú làng bú qí guān

恨每因金屋，
hèn měi yīn jīn wū

愁多倚画栏。
chóu duō yǐ huà lán

驱车过胜母，
qū jū guò shèng mǔ

8 慎勿望长安。
shèn wù wàng cháng ān

The Journey Ahead

    How vast the ocean, how boundless the sky!
    Though arduous the road, you should not sigh.
    There will be storms, but shelter there will be.
4 An ocean without waves is a dull scene to see.
    Women of yore oft regret a life in gilded cage,
    Sad and lonely, leaning across the balustrade.
    Go forward! Surpass your mother's generation.
8 Seek not easy comfort, despite the temptation.

Paraphrase

L1: The road ahead is vast as the ocean and boundless as the sky.
L2: Yet do not be discouraged by the long and difficult journey.
L3: If you should meet with a storm, you can always take shelter and pause for rest.
L4: After all, a calm sea without the billowing waves is hardly a worthy scene to behold.
L5: Women of former times who live in a gilded cage, often regret
L6: Such a woeful and lonely existence, idly leaning across the balustrade.
L7: Go forward and you will surpass your mothers' generation.
L8: Never look for a whole life of easy luxury.

Background

Summary

The poem was composed in 1959. It was published in the 1959 graduation magazine 毕业特刊 of the Perak Girls' Middle School 霹雳女子中学 in Ipoh. It is a special issue because it is a combined publication for the first cohort of the Senior Middle Three graduates 高中第一届 and the 22nd cohort of the Junior Middle Three graduates 初中第廿二届.

Father started teaching in the school when the first Senior Middle class was started there in 1957. He was invited by the then Principal Madam Peng Shi Lin to teach part-time in the school as he was already holding a full-time job as Secretary of the Perak Hokkien Association. He taught Chinese Literature and Language (国文) in the classes in the Junior Middle Three, Senior Middle One and the two-year course known as the Senior Normal Teachers Training course 高师. The poem is a message of encouragement to the graduates.

Well Respected

He was well respected by the Principal, his teaching colleagues and students alike. The following excerpt, taken from an article written in 2002 by Principal Madam Peng Shi Lin very vividly describes Father and the esteem with which he was held:

> "Qing Shan was a gaunt and kindly-looking old gentleman; he spoke politely but his eyes shone brilliantly with a stern and commanding countenance. I explained the purpose of my visit [in 1956, to invite Qing Shan to the position of teacher of Chinese literature and language 华文教员]. After listening to me, he very humbly said, 'My learning is insufficient. I may not be able to measure up to the position." I told him, "The President of the Hokkien Association 福建公会 Mr Bai Cheng Gen 白成根 has

The Senior Middle Three Graduating Class (1959) of the Perak Girls' Middle School 霹雳女子中学 in Ipoh. Qing Shan, Chinese Literature teacher of the class, is seated seventh from the left. Qing Shan's poem "The Journey Ahead" (有行) composed for this class appeared in its graduation magazine.

highly recommended you. I am sure you will be able to. I have known of your deep and wide learning and have seen many of your poems published in the newspapers.' Mr Chen then agreed to consider the invitation."

" …In 1957 the Perak Girls' Middle High School re-opened the Senior Middle classes. Mr Chen and I each assumed responsibility for one Chinese literature class. Mr Chen was an extremely conscientious teacher. His lectures and explanations in Chinese literature were absolutely clear. He spared no effort in his marking of the written essays of the students. Not only are specific sentences corrected, a general critique is also given at the end of the whole composition. His work was well admired by his colleagues and greatly admired by the students…"

23 The Journey Ahead

Schools Ranking

By 1960, Father was responsible for Chinese literature and language for two classes of Junior Middle Three and one class of Senior Middle One. Madam Peng herself took the Senior Middle Three class.

At that time, the highest level of Chinese high school education in Malaya was the more prestigious Senior Middle Three. That Father was teaching the "lower" levels of Junior Middle and Senior Middle One classes was not at all surprising. These were the important foundation classes to provide the students with a sound basis for those who aspire to enter Nantah (Nanyang University 南洋大学) in Singapore or to go overseas, for example to Taiwan. Moreover, the Senior Middle Three examinations were Pan-Malayan public examinations conducted by the government. The results were published throughout the country in the newspapers and the schools' reputation is often judged by these results.

The Subject of Guo Wen 国文

English schools in Malaya at the time had two distinct subjects: English Literature and English Language. Chinese schools had only one equivalent subject known as Guo Wen 国文 which literally means "National Literature". The "readers" or textbooks used are prescribed texts comprising compositions from Chinese literature ranging from classics to modern writings. The "subject" comprises two elements: (i) understanding and appreciation of the prescribed text (i.e., literature), and (ii) the language component focusing on "use" of the language. The latter consists of essay writing and understanding of grammar. The essays can be on any subject, but the student may be expected to apply the techniques, language and expressions learned from the prescribed text and other writings he is encouraged to read. The term "Chinese Literature and Language" is thus used here to describe the subject Guo Wen 国文.

Source of this Poem

This poem was given to us by Madam Lin Ai Yu 林爱毓 who was in the Senior Middle Three graduating class of 1959. Ai Yu is the wife of Wang Han Zhong 王涵中, son of our maternal uncle Wang Guang Guo 王光国 whose name is mentioned frequently in the Background of many of the Chapters in this book.

Appreciation

The poem, appeared in the 1959 combined graduation magazine of the Junior 初中 and Senior Middle 高中 Three classes of the Perak Girls' Middle School in Ipoh. The title of the poem *yǒu xíng* 有行 is rather unusual. Taken at its face value, it means "The Journey Ahead" or it can also mean a daughter's wedding 嫁女, i.e., the wedding of one's daughter when she is about to leave home. The latter meaning comes from the *Book of Poetry* 诗经 which contains these lines: "The daughter is about to start on her journey (get married). She will soon leave her parents and brothers to go afar (女子有行，远父母兄弟)".

In the same graduation magazine, Qing Shan had also written an accompanying message titled "Your Capital and Prospects" 出路与资本. The message to the girls is that they are equipped with a certain amount of "capital" in their twelve years of education received. This may not be sufficient to take them on a journey round the world, but enough to ensure their journey will not end in a kitchen! They should embark on a career for themselves when they step out of school into the world. It is like starting on a long and arduous journey.

This advice is echoed in this poem. The theme is extended in this poem of eight lines which exhorts the girls not to take the easy option of merely getting married in order to aspire to a life of ease and idleness.

The first four lines of the poem set the scene. They use the metaphors of the "vast ocean" and "boundless sky" to paint a picture of the long journey ahead. The arduousness of the journey is described as "storms" the traveller will encounter. As though making a virtue out of inevitable hardship, Line 4 provides the consolation, "An ocean without waves is a dull scene to see 无浪不奇观".

The second half is really the meat of the poem. The literal meaning of Line 5 is "Regrets there often will be if a woman aspires to live in a gilded cage 恨每因金屋". The Chinese text does not point to "a woman", but uses the phrase "gilded mansion" 金屋. It is a code word that immediately conjures up the image of a woman being "kept" in luxurious surroundings, living a life of ease. The allusion comes from "The Story of Hanwu Emperor" 汉武故事. When the emperor was still a young man, his paternal aunt 姑母 once asked him if he liked his elder cousin sister "Ah Jiao" 阿娇 (i.e., his aunt's own daughter), he replied, "If only I could have Ah Jiao as my wife, I would keep her (safely and for myself) in a golden mansion 若得阿娇作妇，当作金屋贮之也". Line 6 spells out the consequences. Women of former times had no formal education. Implicitly referring to these women who would be economically dependent on their husbands, the line warns that they would spend their lives, beset by worries, "leaning across the balustrade 倚画栏". This is a common expression in Chinese poetry. It describes a woman living a lonely life, often with nothing to do except to spend her time waiting and looking forward to the return of her absent husband.

Lines 7 and 8 sum up the admonition to the girls. Taken at its more literal meaning, Line 7 says, "Drive on in your carriage along the journey and you will surpass mother 驱车过胜母". In one sense, it means if you start on this new journey in the next phase of your life, you will surpass the position of women in your mother's generation. Qing Shan chooses his phrases deliberately. The phrase "sheng mu 胜母" means "surpass mother". It too has a metaphorical meaning. The allusion comes from *The Historian's Record* 史记 (written in the Han dynasty) which tells the story of Zeng Zi 曾子 (505–436 BC), a disciple of Confucius. Zeng Zi came upon a place and he asked his disciples for its name. When they told him the name was "Sheng Mu 胜母", Zeng Zi refused to enter it. The explanation for his curious behaviour was given by Sima Zhen 司马贞 of Tang dynasty: "Zeng Zi refused to enter because its name is not in accordance with our ancient value (of filial piety) 曾子不入，盖以名不顺故也". In other words, a place with a name like "Surpass Mother" can only be disrespectful to parents and a totally unprincipled place. With this interpretation, Qing Shan is also giving the advice that in the pursuit of their careers, "avoid doing anything which is unprincipled (过胜母)". Qing Shan is a master at puns. His poems can often be read in one way or the other, or both.

The final Line 8 exhorts the girls not to aspire to "Chang An 长安". Unlike the English language, there is normally no indication in Chinese whether the two words "chang an 长安" is a place name (proper noun) or two ordinary words. The words can refer to "Chang'an" the capital of ancient China for ten centuries or the two ordinary words "chang an" meaning "perpetual peace". The historic capital Chang'an was a place where opulent palaces of emperors and mansions of the wealthy were located. Either way, it is understood by Chinese readers to mean a life free from worry or a carefree life of luxury.

Chapter 24

可模兄嫂金婚志庆
kě mó xiōng sǎo jīn hūn zhì qìng

主眷方隆日，
zhǔ juàn fāng lóng rì

春光大好时。
chūn guāng dà hǎo shí

华筵呈彩舞，
huá yán chéng cǎi wǔ

4 银烛照金禧。
yín zhú zhào jīn xǐ

箧发催妆稿，
qiè fā cuī zhuāng gǎo

奁搜却扇诗。
lián sōu què shàn shī

可曾翻旧谱，
kě céng fān jiù pǔ

8 重与画双眉？
chóng yǔ huà shuāng méi

In Celebration of the Golden Wedding Jubilee of Elder Brother Ke Mo and Sister-in-law

    Abundantly has the Lord blessed you.
    A day of Spring with its brightest hue,
    Banquet and colourful dances we see;
4   Silver candles light your Golden Jubilee.
    The old poem to hasten the bride you find,
    In the trunk too are verses for her bridal fan.
    Browsing the betrothal documents together,
8   You recall and relive your love once more.

Parahrase

L1: The Lord has blessed you and your household with prosperity.
L2: The brilliance of Spring shines magnificently upon this day.
L3: At the grand banquet, there are dances and lavish entertainment for you.
L4: The silver candles light up the celebration of your Golden Jubilee.

L5: Rummaging through the old trunk, you find the poem that was sent to hasten the new bride to get ready for the wedding.
L6: You also manage to find the verse composed on the bridal fan.
L7: Together, you look over the old betrothal documents,
L8: You recall and relive the tender love between you once again.

Background

Summary

The poem was composed in 1960 for the Reverend Canon Guok Koh Muo (郭可模 *Guo Ke Mo*) of Singapore and his wife, on the occasion of their Golden Wedding Jubilee. Reverend Guok was the founding vicar of the (Anglican) parish of the Church of the True Light, founder of the Singapore Bible College and an Honorary Canon of St Andrew's Cathedral in Singapore. Reverend Guok was not only a diligent worker for the church but was also a successful businessman who gave generously for God's work.

As a child of five, Mother was adopted by one of the families in the Guo (郭) clan of Mianting (棉亭) village in Fuqing (福清). She grew up there and was very close to many members of the Guo clan throughout her life.

Reverend Guok Koh Muo

Reverend Guok, also known as Guo Zi Qin 郭子钦, was born on

Reverend (Canon) Guok Koh Muo. *"Abundantly has the Lord blessed you. A day of Spring with its brightest hue."*

Reverend and Mrs Guok with family celebrating Reverend Guok's 70th birthday and their golden wedding anniversary at home (1959). Reverend Guok was from the Guo (郭) clan into which Mother was adopted as a child.
"Banquet and colourful dances we see; Silver candles light your Golden Jubilee."

Reverend Guok and his wife, Madam Chen Tian Song 陈添宋.
"Browsing the betrothal documents together, You recall and relive your love once more."

24 In Celebration of the Golden Wedding Jubilee of Elder Brother

12 March 1891 in Mianting village in the prefecture of Fuqing in Fujian province. He was six years older than Mother. He was a devout Christian from an early age, and an intelligent child with great love for the classics and a prodigious memory. Family tradition has it that at the age of six, he was instrumental in persuading his grandfather to convert to Christianity.

He married Chen Tian Song 陈添宋 a bride of his parents' choice, in the year 1910 when he was only 19 years old. With new family responsibility, he had to start making a greater contribution to the family finance and hence left home in the following year to come to Singapore. He took on clerical jobs and doubled as a news reporter as well. But he always found time to evangelise for his faith and became an unpaid catechist for the Hinghwa-speaking congregation of St Peter's Church then in Stamford Road on the site of the "National Library" (since demolished to make way for the Singapore Management University).

Reverend Guok was a remarkable man. His education in China comprised a firm foundation in the Chinese classics in a traditional village school followed by three years in the Heling Anglo Chinese School in Fuzhou 福州 and two years in the Xinghua School of East-West Philosophy. He was bilingual in Chinese-English, a scholar and calligrapher. Despite his background in learning, he became successful in business and still found time for his zealous work in evangelism and work among the poor throughout his life. Many of the parishioners of the church he founded were poor rickshaw pullers of the Hinghwa (Xinghua 兴化) dialect group living in the Jalan Besar area in Singapore. He gave generously to both the church and charity in Singapore and to his Fuqing natives.

How does the Guo family of Mianting, Fuqing relate to our family? It is a long story and the connection is through our mother who, too, came from Fuqing, from a village called Jiangdou (江兜) about 5 kilometers away. Our maternal grandfather Wang Dan Ru 王淡如 was a good friend of the Guo's in the neighbouring village. The village of Mianting was predominantly of the surname Guo and Jiangdou was predominantly Wang 王. The Guo "clan" of Mianting were descended from the Guo line that comprised six branches (representing the original six male siblings). Reverend Guok's family was descended from the first branch. His father was a scholar; although of modest means, he was nevertheless a civic leader in the village and was well respected.

Mother was Adopted by a Family of the Guo Clan

Wang Dan Ru was a very good friend of a Mr Guo from one of the six branches of the Guo clan (not Reverend Guok's branch). This Mr Guo and his wife had no children. When Mother was born (in 1897), Dan Ru already had a son and a daughter; Mother was his third child. It was a common practice among relatives and good friends to take a child from another family for adoption. For those without children or had few children, it was believed that the adopted child will bring more children or better still, male offspring. Mother was a very attractive

Reverend Guok celebrated his 60th birthday in 1949. The group photo was taken on 11 April 1949 at the Chinese YMCA in Singapore. A copy of the photo signed at the back was given to Mother and Father. See next photo.

child with fair complexion. When Mrs Guo (whose maiden name was Liu 刘) saw what a lovely child Mother was, the family asked to adopt her. Mother was then five years old (1902). Her adoptive mother Mrs Guo, then in her late twenties, was still without child. Not long after Mother was adopted, her adoptive mother gave birth to three children.

Love and Warm Relationship with Her Guo Relatives

Throughout Mother's life, she continued to maintain close and warm contact with members of the Guo clan in China, Singapore and Indonesia. To some of the other needy members of the Guo family in China, she often sent gifts and money. They were part of her family during the ten formative years of her life from the age of five to about 16. They had become her family for life.

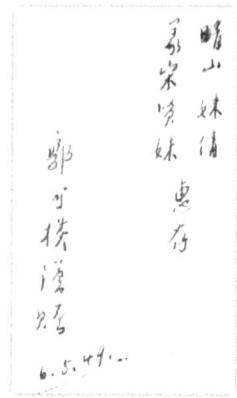

The back of the photo taken at Reverend Guok's 60th birthday of 1949, addressed to Mother and Father, signed and dated by Reverend Guok on 6 May 1949.

Reverend Guok Koh Muo, being six years senior to Mother, was like an elder brother to her. That the poem was addressed to "Elder Brother Ke Mo" is, hence, more than an ordinary term of respect and politeness.

Appreciation

The poem is a warm message of congratulation to Ke Mo and his wife for their golden wedding jubilee. The reader will know from the Background that "Ke Mo" is Reverend Guok Koh Muo (Guo Ke Mo) and his wife Chen Tian Song. It is addressed to "Elder Brother Ke Mo". Although we do not now know how the poem is actually "signed", it is likely to be in the name of both Qing Shan and his wife. Qing Shan was three years younger than Reverend Guok and Mother was six years younger. Mother was like a younger sister to Reverend Guok as she was adopted by a family from the Guo clan in Mianting 棉亭, Fuqing 福清.

The first two lines of the poem are the usual words of praise and congratulation, but they are, in fact, a good reflection of the Christian background and prosperity of Reverend Guok and his family in Singapore. Line 1, for example, uses a recognizably Christian greeting "Abundantly has the Lord blessed you 主眷方隆日".

The next two lines describe the scene of celebration and festivities of the occasion. Line 3 "Banquet and colourful dances we see" actually says a great deal more than the literal meaning of the Chinese text. It uses the imagery of "banquet" (*huá yàn* 华筵) and "colourful dances" (*cǎi wǔ* 彩舞). The phrase "colourful dances" suggests that the children of Reverend Guok have arranged the celebratory banquet for their parents, as an act of filial piety. The connection between "colourful dances" and filial piety comes from "The 24 Acts of Filial Piety" (二十四孝). It is the story of how Laizi 莱子, even at the age of 70, still dressed up in colourful costumes to dance and clown about for the amusement of his even more aged parents of over 100 years old. Readers with a background of Chinese literary culture will, in the context, immediately recognize this phrase *cǎi wǔ* (colourful dances) as alluding to an act of filial piety.

Line 4's "Silver candles light your Golden Jubilee" uses the word "Silver" 银 to complement the word "Gold" 金. "Silver" is often used as an adjective for candle (银烛) in Chinese poetry, probably because of the bright light it emits. It is an excellent choice of word here to complement the occasion of "Golden Wedding Jubilee".

The second half of the poem, Lines 5 to 8, begins to be more nostalgic. The lines describe an old loving couple rummaging through the dusty trunk of documents and other memorabilia. Excitedly, they find the traditional poem (*cuī zhuāng gǎo* 催粧稿) that had been composed to hurry the bride to quickly finish dressing up and be ready for the sedan chair. They find, too, the traditional poem recited by the groom during the wedding ceremony. This traditional poem is known as "declining fan poem" (*què shàn shī* 却扇诗), so called because it invites the bride to "decline" or "lower" the fan she has hitherto been holding up to "hide" her face from view. The bride upon arriving and getting down from the sedan chair would have been shielding her face with a fan (equivalent to a veil today). At the wedding ceremony, the groom would invite the bride to decline her fan so that everyone can now see her face, supposedly for the first time. This was a prevalent custom during the Tang dynasty. Qing Shan has effectively used it to paint a vivid picture of the couple's wedding day like a flashback in the mind of this couple now celebrating their golden anniversary.

The closing two lines describe the "discovery" of yet another piece of memorabilia from the couple's wedding. Line 7 identifies this memorabilia as their betrothal documents called *pǔ* 谱 (refers to 合婚谱), viz., cards containing the couple's name, date and time of birth that were exchanged between the two families. These "biodata" cards were once used by the respective families to cast the horoscope of the prospective bride and groom to ensure their compatibility. They, in actual practice, served as a symbol of betrothal or "engagement".

We can imagine the loving couple looking at this piece of memorabilia with nostalgia as they fondly recall that day 50 years earlier. The final Line 8 of the poem says how they remember and still relive the love between them. Here, Qing Shan demonstrates his mastery in the use of allusions by employing another picturesque metaphor in Line 8. A literal translation of the line will say: "Once again will I draw her pair of eyebrows 重与画双眉". The allusion has become a metaphor to depict a loving relationship between husband and wife. It is from the story of Zhang Chang 张敞, a court official in the Han dynasty. Zhang and his wife were so loving that he would help draw (or paint) the eyebrows for his wife during her daily make-up. Word about his odd behaviour soon got around; his colleagues thought that this was rather unbecoming of a scholar court official. They reported the matter to the emperor who summoned Zhang for an explanation. Zhang replied, "Sire, I have heard that whatever takes place in the bedroom between man and wife is strictly a private matter between them. Besides, there are more 'unbecoming' bedroom pleasures than drawing the eyebrows for one's wife that other people indulge in." Behind this sharp reply was a stern rebuke for his sanctimonious colleagues who themselves indulged in far more "illicit" pleasures of concubines and courtesans.

Chapter 25

寄君余内弟芜湖和光国韵
<small>jì jūn yú nèi dì wú hú hè guāng guó yùn</small>

其一

天涯劳燕倦犹飞，
<small>tiān yá láo yàn juàn yóu fēi</small>

生计年来百事非。
<small>shēng jì nián lái bǎi shì fēi</small>

差幸养生传妙术，
<small>chà xìng yǎng shēng chuán miào shù</small>

饱尝忧患自忘饥。
<small>bǎo cháng yōu huàn zì wàng jī</small>

其二

锦江春色水东流，
<small>jǐn jiāng chūn sè shuǐ dōng liú</small>

领略当年悔未周。
<small>lǐng luè dāng nián huǐ wèi zhōu</small>

多少蹉跎将寿补，
<small>duō shǎo cuō tuó jiāng shòu bǔ</small>

一生不向老低头。
<small>yī shēng bù xiàng lǎo dī tóu</small>

To Younger Brother-in-law in Wuhu
A Poem in Rhyme with Guang Guo

Verse 1

    Like two weary swallows, keep flying we must;
    To earn a living, with nothing going our way.
    Take heart—you've a recipe to live life better.
4   A worry-filled stomach inures you to hunger.

Verse 2

    The River Lu flows east, beautiful as ever.
    Regret though, I did not then enjoy the view better.
    Those misspent years we should now replace.
4   We fear not to confront Old Age in the face.

Paraphrase

Verse 1

L1: Afar and thousands of miles apart, we're like two parting swallows each going its own way. We are weary, but we still have to continue flying (working).

L2: We struggle to earn a living all year round and yet a hundred and one things are not going our way.

L3: But we should not be depressed. Fortunately, we still have the recipe for the art of living on which we can rely.

L4: We have tasted so much difficulties and are now inured by it, as though we are so full with hardship that we forget our stomach is empty with hunger.

Verse 2

L1: The River Lu is beautiful as ever; its waters continue to flow eastwards.

L2: I regret now that I had not taken more time to fully enjoy its beauty.

L3: How many misspent years have we wasted that we should now make up for with the rest of our life?

L4: We should make the best use of our life, never to be intimidated by anything or Old Age.

Background

Summary

This poem was probably Qing Shan's last poem, according to a note written by our uncle Guang Guo 光国 (Mother's younger brother). The poem was written shortly before Father was admitted into the Ipoh General Hospital in late May 1960, where he died on 6 June. The poem was written for Uncle Guang Po 光坡 in Wuhu 芜湖, Anhui 安徽 in China. Guang Po was the elder brother of Guang Guo and was, therefore, also Father's brother-in-law.

Uncle Guang Guo had written a poem for the 60th Birthday of his elder brother Guang Po. Father's poem is in response to and in rhyme with the Guang Guo poem (which will be featured in the Appreciation). Guang Guo made a record of his own poems meticulously written out in his beautiful calligraphy in a book. As Father's poem was a response in rhyme to his own poem, he included Father's poem in his own record of poems with the following note:

> *"This is Qing Shan's last poem. Soon after it was sent off [to his brother-in-law], Qing Shan became ill and was admitted to the Ipoh General Hospital. After that, Qing Shan did not write anything while on the sickbed. Hence I attach his poem here [to my own poem] to be used later as a reference."*

Father had always been very close to his brothers-in-law; he was eleven years and seven years older than Guang Guo and Guang Po respectively. He had in fact been the tutor to Guang Guo in the home of the Wang family in Jiangdou 江兜 village. Father would also have known Guang Po in Malaya during his stay in the country from 1917 to 1928, except for a brief period when his father died in China in 1922.

Guang Po had spent part of his youth in Malaya during Father's early days in the country. He was planning to return to Malaya in 1936. He never made that trip as he was offered a job in Wuhu. He spent the rest of his life there, brought up his family and eventually died on 2 November 1971 at the age of 70.

The Story of Wang Guang Po

Separation

Guang Po (born 1900) was the third son among Mother's siblings. He was in Malaya for two periods, 1913–1915 and 1917–1928, except for a brief period 1922–23.

Father came to Malaya in 1917. In 1931, Father and his family went back to China for a few years and then returned to Malaya in the mid-1930s. That was the last time Father saw Guang Po.

Guang Po, too, had wanted to return to Malaya in 1936 and had, in fact, bought a steamer ticket. Just then his brother

Guang Guo, wrote him a letter to say that his former university-mate, a Dr Huang Pu Ren had gone to Wuhu as Director of a hospital. Dr Huang had just bought Wuhu's first motor vehicle and wanted a fellow "clansmen" (同乡) as his driver. Guang Po could have the job of driver if he wanted it. Wuhu is in Anhui province, hundreds of miles northeast of Putian. He immediately took up the offer of the job in Wuhu and eventually got married and raised his family there.

Hard Life

Through the war years and the Revolution in China (pre-1949), Guang Po had had to work hard under the most difficult circumstances to support his family of four children. He had been driver to doctors, the county governor, Director of the Chinese Red Cross and had sold cigarettes by the roadside after the Revolution of 1949.

Throughout the period when his two daughters were all still in school, his elder sister Yi Song (our mother) and younger brother Guang Guo sent him money to help. At the end of each month, he could not even come up with the children's monthly bill of 7.50 yuan per head for food in school. He had just about sold everything in the house that had any value at all. The school was about to stop feeding his children in school; he finally had to resort to selling the family's precious cotton wadding which he carried on a bamboo pole and went out into the street hawking it. Even those who sympathized with him could not understand him, asking, "You are already under such difficult circumstance; one can understand you nurturing your son, but why do you still want to educate your two daughters? They could at least go out and earn one yuan a day in jobs like washing cars or packing charcoal." (One yuan a day could then feed the whole family). He would reply adamantly, "Whether sons or daughters, my children must be educated. Those who choose not to receive an education will

Yi Song's younger brother, Guang Po, and his family (c.1946) in Wuhu 芜湖 where he had lived since 1935, leading a very hard life to bring up his family.
"Like two weary swallows, keep flying we must; To earn a living, with nothing going our way."

Four years after Qing Shan passed away, Yi Song and her elder sister Jing Song were able to return to Putian in 1964. Their younger brother, Guang Po, travelled several hundred miles from the north in Wuhu to see his two elder sisters whom he had not seen for 30 years. Photo taken in Putian on 11 July 1964.

end up no better than pigs. When my children finish school, it does not matter what they become, be it postmen or nurse, these are all jobs allotted to us by society. Even if I have to pawn my last pair of trousers to support them through school, I would still do it."

He would often tell his children, "In life, I have two fears: one is 'having insufficient money', the other is 'having too much money'. When he was short of money, whether one yuan or two, or even 30 to 40 cents, he would borrow from others. He always kept his word and repaid the loan on time. When he had some money to spare, he too would often lend to others. He had with him always a well-battered cigarette case in which he had only a piece of paper. On one side of the paper was written "I owe others …" and on the obverse side, "Others owe me …"

At the time the poem was written in 1960, he was working as a storekeeper in a fuel depot and later as its receptionist. He continued to work until he fell ill and died in the Anhui University Hospital on 2 November 1971 at the age of 70. When he died, he had only about 20 yuan on him, which was about his current month's salary.

Misspent Youth

Wang Guang Po was hardworking and caring for his family. Among the four (surviving) boys of the Wang family, he had the most cheerful outlook in life and had an irrepressible sense of humour. Everyone in the Wang family, from children to adults, loved Guang Po, known affectionately as "Uncle Gao-liang" 高粱舅, because of his fondness for *gao-liang* wine. He could also be cavalier in a perhaps "misspent" youth. Father wrote fondly of Guang Po in a 1946 story with the following description:

> "(he was) vibrant as Spring (春), lively as running waters (水), frivolous as a doggerel (小诗), spontaneous and broadbrush as a xie-yi painting ('写意), irreverent as the 'Outlaws of the

Marshes' (緑林豪士)... He had many vices, such as women, opium and mahjong."

Cheerful and Optimistic

Guang Po had a cheerful and optimistic outlook on life. He had a spontaneous, irreverent attitude and a sense of humour, even when confronted by serious circumstances. This creates an aura of him as someone always youthful, even seemingly naïve and exuding optimism. There are many anecdotes in his and our family that show this side of him.

Once his infant child died at birth and the poor little thing was buried in the back garden. One day, he heard his wife wailing in the garden and he came over to ask her what the matter was. His wife told him that the dogs had been digging at the grave and dug up the body. He consoled the wife, telling her, "Don't be sad. Next time, I will make sure the grave is a lot deeper!"

The 1950s and 1960s were financially most difficult for his family. In 1952, his wife was hospitalized for a serious illness. His salary at that time was only about 30 yuan per month, while he had "five mouths to feed" and the burden of his children's schooling. After two months in the hospital, the hospital bill piled up to 200 yuan which was an astronomical sum to him. The hospital hurried him to discharge the wife, lest the bill would get even higher. Guang Po obviously did not have the money to pay and he persuaded the hospital to accept an I.O.U. Against the place on the I.O.U. where a surety was expected to sign, he nonchalantly signed it himself with his name "Wang Guang Po". This was unheard of! How could anyone be acceptable as his own surety and the poor hospital administration was between "tears and cheer" (啼笑皆非) but it had no choice but to discharge his wife.

Poor as he was, he was cheerful and able to share his fun and joy in life with his children. In the early 1960s, he was then wearing a 26-yuan "Zhongshan" brand Chinese wristwatch.

Whenever Radio Beijing's time signal came on, he would point proudly to his watch to say, "Look, how accurate my watch is. Even Radio Beijing has to set the time by my watch." The children would burst out laughing and he too would join in the laughter.

Appreciation

A Word from Elder Brother Qing Shan

A brief description of the nature of this poem is given in the Summary of the Background section. Qing Shan's poem is composed "in response to and in rhyme with" (和韵) a poem Guang Guo has written for Guang Po. The Chinese text of Guang Guo's poem is quoted below and will be followed later with a translation in English in the next section "Literal Translation of Poem":

寿君余兄六十时在芜湖

鹭江犹记惜分飞，
北上当年计已非。
酌酒天南聊献寿，
一杯难疗一家饥。

大好年光似水流，
自怜花甲亦将周。
纵教明月圆时有，
相对何堪两白头？

Qing Shan is older than Guang Po, hence he says in the title of his poem "...to my younger brother-in-law...余内弟". Guang Guo, on the other hand, is younger than Guang Po, hence he addresses him as "…my elder brother…余兄". As the title of Guang Guo's poem suggests, it was to commemorate the 60th birthday of Guang Po who was then living in Wu Hu "寿君余兄六十时在芜湖".

Both the poems of Guang Guo and Qing Shan are reflective and rather unconventional for a birthday poem. They are not poems of "congratulation" nor "celebration". As can be seen in the Background, there is nothing great to celebrate in Guang Po's life, at least not in material terms. Apart from just the title, there is a striking difference in tone between the "response" poem by Qing Shan and the "original" poem by Guang Guo.

Qing Shan's poem is a lot more encouraging. He is like the elder brother giving encouragement to the younger Guang Po. He has a great fondness for him and empathises a great deal with him. Qing Shan's expressions used are also more subtle and richer in classical allusions. In the latter respect, he is like the master showing his skill to his even younger student Guang Guo, for Guang Guo had indeed been his student in China.

Literal Translation of Poem

It is not possible to demonstrate in a translation how Qing Shan responds in rhyme to Guang Guo's poem for Guang Po. It is possible, however, to show Qing Shan's response in the content and imagery of his poem. To facilitate this comparison, the technique of a literal translation is used in the following, preserving at the same time the text and syntax of the original two poems in Chinese.

Verse 1

Line 1:

<u>Guang Guo</u>: *At River Lu, we recall (鹭江犹记) and regret flying separately (惜分飞) (parted ways).* The line is quite as a matter of fact.

Qing Shan: *Far away (天涯), the poor swallow is tired (燕倦) but still needs to keep flying (犹飞)*. Qing Shan shows great empathy by taking up the analogy of birds, introduced by Guang Guo.

[Note: River Lu is actually not a river but the very narrow stretch of water between Xiamen (厦门) and the island Gulang Yu (鼓浪屿). Xiamen is a port and was the embarkation point for many Chinese migrants going to South-east Asia.]

Line 2:

Guang Guo: *The year you went north from Putian to Wuhu (北上当年) is so long ago that it is no longer in our memory (计已非)*. Strangely though, it was Guang Guo who had introduced the Wuhu job to Guang Po. This line refers to Guang Po's change of mind about returning to Malaya in that fateful year of 1936.

Qing Shan: *To make a living throughout the year (生计年来), a hundred things do not turn out right (百事非)*. Qing Shan does not dwell on Guang Po's biggest mistake of his life in not returning to Malaya in 1936. Instead he picks up the word "year 年" from Guang Guo and uses it in another sense. He shows understanding of Guang Po's current circumstance by saying that even as Guang Po tries hard to earn a living throughout the year, not everything turns out right as expressed in the three words *bai shi fei* 百事非. The three words are taken from a poem by the talented Manchurian scholar official, *Nà lán xìng dé* 纳兰性德 (1655–1685). That source poem reads:

"*And only now does one realise that past error, pitiful and confused is the heart. Red tears stealthily flow; the eyes are filled with the joy of Spring but a hundred things do not turn out right.*"（而今才道当时错，心绪凄迷。红泪偷垂；满眼春风百事非。）

Qing Shan hints at that mistake of 1936, but does not say it. Only those who know this particular poem of *Nà lán xìng dé* will know the inherent message.

Line 3:

<u>Guang Guo</u>: *Let me drink to you from the far south (酌酒天南) at least a toast on your birthday (聊献寿)*. The use of "at least" or "just" (聊) harbours a sense of "consolation". This is after Guang Guo has reminded Guang Po in the previous line of his mistake of 1936.

<u>Qing Shan</u>: *Fortunately (差幸), a recipe for living (养生) must have passed down to you this remarkable art (传妙术)*. Qing Shan is more encouraging. He praises Guang Po for his resilience which must have come from some formula for living which he possesses.

Line 4:

<u>Guang Guo</u>: *With a single cup of wine (一杯), it's difficult to satiate (难疗) one entire family's hunger (一家饥)!* This is a rather depressing line for a "birthday toast" to Guang Po.

<u>Qing Shan</u>: *When our stomachs are filled with worries (饱尝忧患), we will naturally be unaware that we are hungry (自忘饥)*. Qing Shan lightens this depressing reality with a touch of humour. In other words, when the stomach is "full" with worries, it will no longer be "empty" and we can't feel "hungry" on a full stomach! Qing Shan's previous line has praised Guang Po's remarkable "recipe for living". He now tells us how Guang Po would shrug off his problems. This is more in the character of Guang Po who is cheerful, positive and irreverent even in the face of adversity.

Verse 1, especially Line 4, should not be seen as just an example of a poet's hyperbolic description of Guang Po's plight.

A reading of "The Story of Wang Guang Po" in the Background section of this chapter should convince one otherwise.

Verse 2

Line 1:

<u>Guang Guo</u>: *Most of the years have passed by (大好年光), as the rivers flow (似水流)*. This is a scene setter and echoes his reference to River Lu in Verse 1. It denotes the passage of time and the years.

<u>Qing Shan</u>: *The scenic sight of this beautiful river, (锦江春色), its waters eastward flow (水东流)*. Qing Shan's line is reminiscent of a line in the poem *yú měi rén* 虞美人 by the Southern Tang 南唐 Emperor Li Hou Zhu 李后主 who was then no more than a regional ruler, subservient to the powerful Song dynasty in the north. Emperor Li's poem has a touch of melancholy for the loss of the greater part of the Tang empire and nostalgia for his predecessors' glorious past. A line in his poem reads: *"The river, its beautiful waters eastward flow 一江春水向东流"*. With the inclusion of just these five words "river, Spring, waters eastward flow" (江、春、水东流), Qing Shan has managed to add a new dimension to his own poem; he is, in fact, alluding to Guang Po being in Wuhu, located far north from his native Putian in the south. Guang Po misses his native Putian. China is such a vast country; poor Guang Po might as well have been in some distant foreign country separated by oceans.

Line 2:

<u>Guang Guo</u>: *Regret that I myself will (自怜) the "cycle of sixty" (花甲) also about to complete (亦将周)*. It means "I too am about to reach the age of 60". Guang Guo himself is two years short of 60 years old at the time of writing. The

Chinese number their years with a system of a 60-year cycle. A complete cycle of 60 years is called a *huā jiǎ* 花甲. Guang Guo uses the word *zhōu* 周 as a verb, meaning "to complete" or "to bring it to a close". The word has another meaning and we shall see how Qing Shan uses it differently.

<u>Qing Shan</u>: *I realise that (领略) at the time (当年) I regretfully did not thoroughly appreciate the beauty of the scenery (悔未周)*. He uses the same word *zhōu* 周 as an adjective, meaning "thorough". Having acknowledged in his own previous line how beautiful the river is, he expresses regret in not having enjoyed the scenery more thoroughly.

Lines 3 and 4 (the concluding lines):

<u>Guang Guo</u>: (Line 3) *Even though (纵教) another full month (reunion) there will be again (明月圆时有)*, (Line 4) *Facing each other (相对), could we bear to see (何堪) two white heads (两白头 old men)?"* Guang Guo becomes more reflective, probably as he himself will soon be 60.

<u>Qing Shan</u>: (Line 3) *The many misspent years (多少蹉跎), we should now make good with the remaining years (将寿补)*. (Line 4) *In this life of ours (一生), we should confront Old Age in the face (不向老低头)*. Qing Shan is less pessimistic and more encouraging.

Section 3
Friendship
辅仁会友

Wide range of thoughts, concern, congratulations for his friends and humorous jousts with them.

Chapter 26

送瑞华姐回国
sòng ruì huá jiě huí guó

天南地北隔烽烟，
tiān nán dì běi gé fēng yān

辜负双眉笔久悬。
gū fù shuāng méi bǐ jiǔ xuán

露布可曾忘起草？
lù bù kě céng wàng qǐ cǎo

4 寒衣谁复为装棉？
hán yī shuí fù wéi zhuāng mián

缅怀故国云千里，
miǎn huái gù guó yún qiān lǐ

奏记粧楼日一笺。
zòu jì zhuāng lóu rì yī jiān

此去枕边凭细语，
cǐ qù zhěn biān píng xì yǔ

8 不劳青鸟作邮传。
bù láo qīng niǎo zuò yóu chuán

Farewell to Rui Hua on Her Return to China

    A divide between you, are the flames of war;
    Your eyebrows, he could no longer draw.
    Have they told him we've won the fight?
4   Who will line his jacket for a winter night?
    You long for the old country so far away,
    A letter from him is on your table every day.
    It will from thence be pillow talk instead.
8   And no more will the courier be called.

Paraphrase

L1: Separating you (and your husband) are the flames of war; he in the North and you in the South, far apart as between Heaven and Earth.

L2: There is no longer the daily routine of drawing your eyebrows; the eyebrow pencil has long been put away.

L3: Victory against the enemy has been announced by the High Command, but has anyone told him yet?

L4: Who is there now to reline his winter jacket once again?

L5: You think of the old country thousands of miles away.

L6: He thinks of you and a letter arrives daily from him at your dressing table.

L7: Once you return, he will be with you in person to softly whisper into your ears in the privacy of your bedroom (pillow talk).

L8: No longer is there a need to call in the courier and trouble him with your mail.

Background

Summary

Rui Hua and her daughter and son lived in the same house as our family in Ipoh throughout the Japanese military occupation from 1942 to 1945. There were other families too in the house. Rui Hua and her two children were good family friends of ours. The poem was written for Rui Hua on her departure from Ipoh for mainland China to reunite with her husband not long after the Japanese surrender in August 1945. Her daughter *Ruò Xiá* 若霞, whom we all called Ah Xia, would have been about 13 in 1943. She was at most a year or two older than our elder sister Mei Xuan. Her brother *Ruò Léi* 若雷 would have been about eight or nine years old and much older than Peter and Michael who were then only five and two years old.

Rui Hua's husband was in the Chinese army fighting the Japanese before the Second World War. Her husband had sent her and the family to Malaya thinking that it would be safer for them. When the Japanese invaded and occupied Malaya and Singapore, Rui Hua and the family were trapped and stranded in the country.

As soon as the Japanese surrendered, Rui Hua's husband sent for her and the children to return to China. As children, we were very sad to lose our playmates of the past four years. In the immediate post-war years, people who returned to China for schooling were the envy of those left behind. We too felt left behind. But for Rui Hua's family, it was a time for reunion. That was the last we heard of Rui Hua, and our childhood playmates, Ah Xia and Ah Lei. We wonder how they fared through the ten turbulent years of China's Cultural Revolution from 1966 to 1976.

Public Lover No.1

Ah Xia had a sweet and impish face and sported a girlish fringe of hair just above the eyebrows. She was friendly and gregarious. She had a tanned complexion because she was something of a tomboy. We remember her as always active, skillful in climbing trees and often going about barefooted. Despite her tomboyish looks and behaviour, she was overall an attractive girl and there was always someone with whom she was in love. We used to call her "Public Lover No.1" *dà zhòng qíng rén* 大众情人. We remember Ah Xia falling head over heels in love with a boy living next door. We lived in a row of two-storey shophouses along Anderson Road in Ipoh. Ah Xia's family lived on the second storey in the front room facing the street. Ah Xia was madly in love with the "boy (literally) next door" who also lived in the front room next door, cheek by jowl with Ah Xia's room. To the amusement of us all, the two were sometimes seen communicating with each other by passing messages back and forth ingeniously placed on badminton rackets. The long handles of the badminton rackets enabled a greater reach!

On Opposite Sides of the War

How did Rui Hua come to be thrown into the same house as we were during the three dark years and eight months of the Japanese Occupation? Rui Hua's husband was actually the brother of the chief tenant of the house. He was a military officer fighting the war against the Japanese in China and had sent Rui Hua and the two children over to Malaya to be with his sister. But the Pacific War broke out and the Japanese invaded Malaya in December 1941. What was thought to be a safe haven from the war, became the cauldron in occupied land.

Rui Hua was not the only relative of the chief tenant staying with us. The chief tenant had another brother (whom we shall call) GB who lived in the same house with his wife, a son about five years old and an adopted daughter of about 12. GB worked for the Japanese in occupied Malaya, quite unlike his brother who was fighting the Japanese in China. The two brothers were in effect on opposite sides of the war!

The Japanese Cap

We were not sure what exactly was GB's work, but he was always dressed in white shirt and khaki shorts or trousers. The most unforgettable part of his dress code was his cloth cap, similar to the baseball cap we see today. This was the headgear commonly worn by the Japanese soldiers in Malaya.

GB was a bully and a particularly nasty man. He was known to have gone to the local market wearing his distinctively Japanese "uniform" swaggering about and kicking down the market stalls, sending the stallholders scurrying away in fear and panic. Our family and other tenants in the house too lived in constant fear of him and had to endure all the abuse and bullying. This is in contrast to our warm relationship with the family of GB's sister-in-law, Rui Hua, for whom the poem was composed. Everyone in our family remembers at least one nasty experience with GB or his wife.

We lived on the second floor of a two-storey shophouse. Our kitchen was at the back of the house on the second floor overlooking the open courtyard below. The only bathroom in the house was in this courtyard. When the tap was turned on in the bathroom below, the communal kitchen on the second floor would be deprived of water as there was insufficient pressure for the water to reach the second floor. One day, elder sister Mei Yu was in the kitchen preparing to cook our evening meal. The kitchen tap suddenly dried up. She was halfway through washing her pot of rice. She looked out of the kitchen window and could hear the tap running in the bathroom below. Someone was obviously having a bath in the bathroom. The water pressure was never sufficient to supply the bathroom and kitchen concurrently. This was not an unexpected phenomenon. When this happened, it was also an accepted practice in the house for the person in the kitchen upstairs to holler to the person in the bathroom, "Person downstairs, turn the tap off please". The person in the bathroom would normally respond by turning off the tap for a few minutes to enable the user in the kitchen on the second floor to get on with the cooking. When Mei Yu had no response from the bathroom below, she thought perhaps she was not heard. She then took a small piece of charcoal and threw it down at the zinc roof of the bathroom below to attract some attention. Mei Yu waited, hoping the water would soon resume gushing out of the kitchen tap. She got more than she bargained for. The next thing she knew, it was GB who came rushing into the kitchen like a wild man, still half-drenched, wearing only his towel coming up to Mei Yu to give her a big tight slap on the face. Mei Yu was only nine years old. This is an incident which Mei Yu has never forgotten to this day.

Eldest sister Mei Xuan, then about 12 years old, had her fair share of being bullied by GB's wife in the use of the communal kitchen. Even Mother was bullied to the point of tears by GB or his wife. As children, Mei Xuan and Mei Yu could never understand why we always had to yield to such bullying and asked Father why we had to fear this man GB. Father patiently explained to the two girls, "It is not him that we fear. We only fear his Japanese cap!" This was the simplest explanation possible. Everyone lived in fear during the Japanese Occupation, especially of someone who worked for the Japanese authorities of the military occupation. A wrong word said could result in one being reported as an anti-Japanese element with dire consequences. GB's Japanese cap was a lot more than just a cap. It was the symbol of authority and power. During the occupation, the Japanese occupiers had the power of life and death. There was every reason to fear the Japanese cap!

GB was not the worst of those who worked for the Japanese. At least he did not kill or cause the death of anyone, as far as we knew. He was just a nasty big bully, although it was enough to make life "hell" for us. When the Japanese surrendered and the Occupation ended in August 1945, retribution was swift for the many other collaborators who had committed deeds most foul.

Appreciation

The poem was written in early 1946, soon after the Japanese surrender and communication between Malaya and mainland China was restored. It is a farewell poem for our family friend and co-tenant Rui Hua who had, by a twist of fate, been separated from her husband during World War II.

A Japanese army cap worn during Second World War. *"It is not him that we fear. We only fear his Japanese cap!"*

In the eight short lines of the poem, Qing Shan takes us from the battlefront scenes of the "flames of war" to Rui Hua being reunited once more with her husband, whispering tenderly to each other in the privacy of their own company. The translation of "flames of war" comes from the original Chinese text 烽烟 *fēng yān* which can refer to beacon fires used as a means of communication in the defences along the northern frontiers of China in ancient times. In just two words, the poet has painted a picture of the turbulence and tension of the times.

The three years, eight months of separation that they endured has taken its toll on their normal lives. Rui Hua and her husband could no longer be together to enjoy the love and intimacy between husband and wife. The imagery used to describe this situation is "Neglecting to draw your eyebrows, and the eyebrow pencil has long been put away" 辜负双眉笔久悬 *gū fù shuāng méi bǐ jiǔ xuán*. It could mean Rui Hua no longer grooms herself, now that her husband is not with her. Actually it means more than its literal sense. The use of the metaphor "draw eyebrows" usually alludes to the story of Zhang Chang of the Han dynasty who was so loving to his wife that he would help draw her eyebrows during her daily make-up. It has become a personification of the love and intimacy between husband and wife (see Appreciation of poem in Chapter 24 for the story of Zhang Chang). The battle has been won, but perhaps no one has told him the news.

Although husband and wife are not in communication with each other, it does not stop her pining for her old country and continuing to worry about his personal welfare: "Who will reline his jacket for a winter night?" He too continues to send her a letter daily.

When at last peace finally returns, he sends for her. Rui Hua looks so much forward to being reunited once more with her husband, and being able to whisper tenderly into each other's ears: "It will from hence be pillow talk instead." The postman is finally dismissed with the last line: "And no more will the courier be called." (The metaphor used for "courier" is *qing niao* 青鸟, the magical legendary magical Blue Bird as used in Chapter 1.)

Chapter 27

与义宋联吟，送别蔡信德牧师
_{yǔ yì sòng lián yín sòng bié cài xìn dé mù shī}

惆怅亡羊觅旧途，
追随讲席四年余。（晴山）
听经每为停针线，
4 望道常愁困簿书。（义宋）
甚欲及门同问字，
未容投辖暂留车。（晴山）
离筵唱彻骊歌后，
8 方悔平时领略疏。（义宋）

Farewell to Pastor Cai Xin De
A Poem in Unison with Yi Song

    Like a distressed lost sheep seeking the old path,
    I have followed your sermons for four years or more.
                                  (Qing Shan)
    Absorbed in your teachings, I pause in my sewing.
4   Yearns he to seek "The Way", yet needs make a living.
                                      (Yi Song)
    I too seek a better understanding from you.
    We pleaded for you to stay, but it's no use. (Qing Shan)
    It's only when we've said our final farewell,
8   Meagre is our insight, this we know too well. (Yi Song)

Paraphrase

L1-2: Like a disconsolate strayed sheep which has lost its way, I've followed your sermons for four years or more. *(Qing Shan)*

L3-4: So absorbed am I with your sermon that I forget momentarily to carry on with my sewing. He too yearns to devote more time to seek (your teaching of) "The Way", but he is burdened by the daily need to earn a living. *(Yi Song)*

L5-6: I too wish to become your disciple to seek a better understanding of your teaching. We try to stop you from leaving, but to no avail. *(Qing Shan)*

L7-8: It's only after we've said our farewell that we realize how scanty our understanding of your teaching has been. *(Yi Song)*

Background

Summary

The poem was composed as a farewell message to our family pastor Reverend Cai Xin De 蔡信德 in 1947. Mother was a devout Christian from a young age, but Father attended church with the family only occasionally. Mother probably gave him more than a nudge in getting him baptized, as seen in the poem in Chapter 5. Father's church attendance, albeit occasional, explains why he was close enough to Reverend Cai to be part of the farewell poem to him.

Reverend Cai Xin De

Reverend Cai grew up in a Christian family in Fujian. After graduation from theological college, he preached, worked in schools and was engaged in youth work. He was also principal of a school. He came to Malaya as an itinerant preacher with the Methodist Church before the Japanese invasion and occupation of Malaya (1941–1945). With the outbreak of war, he was unable to return to China and stayed on. He was assigned to the Ipoh Chinese Methodist Church as the Acting Pastor throughout the whole three years eight months of the Japanese Occupation.

In October 1946, he was appointed Pastor-in-Charge of the Ipoh Chinese Methodist Church located then in Lahat Road. He was re-assigned and left our church in Ipoh in 1947 to return to China.

Family Church and Pastor

We attended the Chinese Methodist Church in Ipoh from early 1942 and that was how our family came to know Reverend Cai. As children, we attended Sunday School and were all baptized by Reverend Cai who was a popular figure in church. After he left our church in 1947 for China, he returned to Malaya in the 1950s and 1960s. Elder sister Mei Xuan and her husband-to-be were members of the church choir. Their wedding in 1951 was solemnized by Reverend Cai in our church.

"Praise the Lord!"

Reverend Cai spoke and preached in Hokkien (Fujian or Minnan dialect 闽南话). As Ipoh was a Cantonese and Hakka-speaking area, his sermons had to be translated in church, sentence by sentence. This inevitably made for a long church service. Reverend Cai preached very forcefully in his clear and piercing voice. Our best memory of Reverend Cai was the frequent punctuation of his sermons with the words *"Gam-sia Zu, O-lo Zu* 感谢主，阿咾主". In the Minnan dialect, this means "Thanks be to God and Praise the Lord". We did not quite know then what they meant.

Appreciation

This poem is not in the usual form. The format of this poem is called "joint-recital 联吟" or "joint-lines 联句" and is usually composed impromptu. It conforms to the rules of classical poetry in its structure of meter and versification ("prosody"). Poems of this type during the Tang dynasty conform to the rules of the regulated verse. There are many variations of this format, some complex and some simple.

Appointment of Reverend Cai Xin De as Pastor-in-charge of the Ipoh Chinese Methodist Church on 16 October 1946.

Portrait of Reverend Cai, who had long been a spiritual guide and friend of the Chen family and was highly respected by Qing Shan.

This poem is in its simpler form "participated" by two persons, viz., Qing Shan and his wife Yi Song. There are four pairs of lines (couplets) with the first couplet by Qing Shan

(Lines 1-2), the second couplet is by Yi Song (Lines 3-4), then Qing Shan rejoins the poem at Lines 5-6 and Yi Song concludes with Lines 7-8.

The application of the rules of prosody can only be fully appreciated in the original Chinese text of the poem. Another feature of a "joint-recital" is for a couplet to "echo" and develop further a subject introduced in the preceding couplet. The English versification of this poem has been done in a way to illustrate this point—only with some degree of success.

Qing Shan's Line 1 uses the metaphor of "lost sheep" 亡羊 drawn from a parable in the Bible (Luke 15, verses 3-7). The Christian faith believes that all men have sinned and they can only be saved if they repent their sins by believing in Jesus Christ. The "lost sheep" in the parable collectively refers to those who have yet to repent and believe. Qing Shan has yet to accept the Christian faith and has been following the "sermons" of Reverend Cai for more than four years (Line 2).

The next couplet by Yi Song's immediately picks up the idea of the biblical "lost sheep" and develops its Christian association. Her Line 3 says she is so absorbed in "listening to the teachings" 听经 of Reverend Cai that she pauses in the middle of her sewing and momentarily forgets to carry on with her needlework. In Line 4, Yi Song speaks on behalf of Qing Shan saying, "Yearns he to seek 'The Way', yet needs to make a living". The original Chinese text of Line 4 is "望道常愁困簿书". Its literal meaning is "Although I wish to seek 'The Way' (望道), I often have to worry about and am burdened by (常愁困) 'documents' (簿书)". The term *bù shū* 簿书 in classical poetry means "official documents and records" that keep account of property, income and expenditure. It is used here as a metaphor for "to earn a living" and is always associated with a man. Hence, Line 4 refers to Qing Shan.

There is a Christian connection in Line 4's "To seek 'The Way' (望道)". In the Bible, John 14, verse 6 says, "Jesus answered, I am the way and the truth and the life. No one comes to the Father except through me." Qing Shan chooses the phrase *wàng dào* 望道 for Yi Song's couplet because it has both biblical and Chinese cultural connection. The same word *dào* 道 is also the name given to the philosophy or religion of Daoism (道教).

The second half of the poem uses mainly allusions from Chinese classics. It starts with Lines 5-6 by Qing Shan. In the same vein of Yi Song's Line 4 "To seek 'The Way' (望道)", Line 5 says "I too seek a better understanding from you". To enjoy the allusion of this line, we need to look at the original Chinese text which uses the phrase *jí mén wèn zì* 及门问字. Its literal meaning is "arrive at the door to seek the meaning of a word". It is derived from the proverb "bring wine to seek the meaning of a word" *dài jiǔ wèn zì* 戴酒问字. The proverb comes from the story of the Han dynasty scholar, philosopher, linguist *Yáng Xióng* 杨雄 (53–18 BC). He was poor but loved wine and had few visitors. He had this remarkable gift of knowing every word there was in the language, including the most unusual and obscure. There would be the occasional visitors who had just such a need to identify the meaning of an unusual word. They would arrive at his door with a gift of wine to ask for his help with the problematic word.

Line 6 pleads with Reverend Cai not to leave. The literal meaning of the line: "To no avail (未容), I throw away (投) the linchpin of your carriage wheels (辖) to temporarily (暂) detain your carriage (留车)". The allusion is from the *History of Han dynasty's* story of *Chén Zūn* 陈遵. Chen was an official and loved to wine and dine, and to host huge dinner parties. After his promotion, due to his meritorious service in the suppression of some local bandits, even more people visited him in his mansion. After all the guests had arrived, he would ask his servants to lock the gates, remove the linchpins from the wheels of their carriages and throw the pins into the well. This was to prevent his visitors from leaving! This is a really drastic measure. The mouthful of an expression in English "Throw linchpins away to detain the carriage" is succinctly said in four words in Chinese *tóu xiá liú jū* 投辖留车. It is used to describe the earnestness of a host wanting his guest to stay on, for ex-

Farewell to Reverend Cai Xin De in 1947 on his first return to China after serving as Pastor-in-charge of the Ipoh Chinese Methodist Church. Qing Shan is seated fourth from the right.

ample, at his party. [The usual form of the metaphor is *tóu xiá liú bīn* 投辖留宾 "Throw linchpins away to detain the guests".]

Yi Song picks up the thread of "a party" implied in Qing Shan's Line 6 with her own Line 7 (literal translation): "Departing from the party (离筵) after singing the "Black Stallion Song" (唱彻骊歌后). The term *lí gē* 骊歌 used in the poem is abbreviated from 骊驹歌 or "Black Stallion Song" in full. It is an ancient poem by that name and was alluded to in the Story of Wang Shi 王式 as a farewell song. Line 7 says "It is only after we've said our farewell that …" (continued in Line 8), "We realize how scanty our understanding of your teaching has been."

It is a delightful poem to read with two parties "singing" their verses alternately. As befitting the occasion of a farewell poem for Reverend Cai, it uses biblical and Christian terminology and concepts in the first half. As a classical poem, it also uses interesting allusions from the Chinese classics.

Chapter 28

赠善光姐
zèng shàn guāng jiě

廿载天涯岁月淹，
niàn zǎi tiān yá suì yuè yān

辛劳忧患两相兼。
xīn láo yōu huàn liǎng xiāng jiān

尽抛笔砚亲刀尺，
jìn pāo bǐ yàn qīn dāo chǐ

4 又订经书志米盐。
yòu dìng jīng shū zhì mǐ yán

膝下都因儿女累，
xī xià dōu yīn ér nǚ lèi

鬓边渐见雪霜添。
bìn biān jiàn jiàn xuě shuāng tiān

昔年姐妹惟君健，
xī nián jiě mèi wéi jūn jiàn

8 几度停针起远瞻。
jǐ dù tíng zhēn qǐ yuǎn zhān

To Elder Sister Shan Guang

    Twenty years abroad, now a distant past.
    Into toil and worry have I been cast,
    Discarding the pen for scissors instead.
4   Books have I compiled, for our daily bread.
    It is our children, for whom we toil.
    White as snow our hair, in this mortal coil.
    But you have always been healthy as new.
8   I often pause in my sewing to think of you.

Paraphrase

L1: For twenty long years, in this far corner of the earth, I have remained.
L2: Toil and hardship, my twin companions are always with me.
L3: Abandoning the pen and inkstone (teaching), I take up the scissors and ruler (tailoring).
L4: I've compiled a few manuals on tailoring for our "rice and salt" (daily living)
L5: It is for our children that we toil.
L6: Our sideburn (hair) is gradually becoming whiter, as snow and frost
L7: Between we two sisters from since bygone days, you are still hearty and healthy.

L8: How often have I paused in the midst of my needle work to think of you from afar.

Background

Summary

Lin Shan Guang 林善光 was a childhood friend of Mother in Fuqing. They once worked together as teaching assistants 幼稚园助理 in the same kindergarten run by the Anglican mission in Fuqing 福清馨英女学校. Shan Guang was a few years older than Mother who was born in 1897. Hence, we all referred to her as Shan Guang *jie* 姐 (meaning elder sister), following the way Mother addressed her.

Mother and Shan Guang parted ways when Mother left China in 1926 to come to Malaya to get married to Father. Shan Guang herself subsequently left China and arrived in Sitiawan 实兆远 in Malaya. She became a midwife and was well known to all the residents in the area. She and Mother had lost contact and were not aware of each other's presence in the same country. It was through chance in late 1941 that they came to know about each other. Mother was then in Kampar 金宝 and Shan Guang in Sitiawan, separated by no more than 50 kilometres. However, they never had a chance to meet as shortly after this, the Japanese invaded Malaya in December 1941.

Contact between these two childhood friends was not re-established until after Second World War ended in August 1945. This poem, dated February 1947 was composed by Father on behalf of Mother and presented to her childhood friend Lin Shan Guang after a separation of about 20 years.

Lin Shan Guang

We actually know very little about Shan Guang except what Mother told us about her, viz., she was a few years older than

Mother, they were good friends and they both worked in the same Anglican mission kindergarten in Fuqing.

Shan Guang subsequently came to Malaya and practised as a midwife in Sitiawan. A midwife would have a fair amount of basic medical knowledge. In those days, especially in a remote place like Sitiawan, she would be expected to play the role of a village doctor, attending to other medical needs of the people in the village. She worked for several years in the Methodist Mission Clinic in Sitiawan. Even till today, she is remembered by the more senior people from Sitiawan as "Xian-goon Jia". This was her name pronounced in the Fuzhou dialect meaning "Shan Guang elder sister". People now aged 60 to 70 even told us that they were "delivered" at birth by "Xian-goon Jia".

Shan Guang never married but adopted and brought up a son, whom we knew as Ah Hui, and a daughter. Subsequent to Ah Hui and her sister, she is known to have adopted other children. Shan Guang died in Sitiawan on 5 December 1984. On her gravestone are recorded the names of a total of seven adopted children and four grandchildren.

A Chance "Discovery"

There is an interesting anecdote about how Mother and Shan Guang first found out about each other's presence in Malaya in 1941. After Mother opened a tailoring school in Kampar in 1940, she had a student from Sitiawan who returned there. In late 1941, this student invited Mother to conduct classes in Sitiawan which was about 50 kilometres from Kampar. Mother had her hands full with her children: Mei Xuan was ten, Mei Yu was seven, Peter was three and Michael was barely nine months old. Mother could not go and instead despatched a trusted staff, Ms Feng De Zhen 冯德贞, who took elder sister Mei Xuan 美璇 along with her. While in Sitiawan, Mei Xuan needed medical attention for a sore on her leg and she was taken by De Zhen to a lady Chinese "physician". The physician looked at Mei Xuan and told De Zhen how much Mei Xuan

The second cohort of graduating students of Mother's tailoring school in Kampar. In this photo taken on 30 March 1940, the staff are in the front row, including Mother's trusted staff (first from the left) Ms Feng De Zhen. (See "A Chance 'Discovery'" in the Background section of this chapter.)

The tombstone of Lin Shan Guang who died on 5 December 1984. Recorded on the tombstone are the names of her eight adopted children and four grandchildren.

230 A Scholar's Path

reminded her of a good friend of hers. When names were disclosed, the physician turned out to be none other than Shan Guang *jie*, and De Zhen identified Mei Xuan as the daughter of her good friend, our mother.

Mother's 1941 tailoring class venture in Sitiawan did not last long. De Zhen fell ill and had to return to Kampar. Then came the Japanese invasion of Malaya in December 1941, and our entire lives were turned completely upside down. We eventually moved to Ipoh.

Reunion After 20 Years

After Mother and Shan Guang had learned about each other's presence in Malaya in late 1941, they never had a chance to meet because of the Japanese invasion of Malaya. It was only after the war that they re-established contact with each other in early 1947. Mother re-opened her tailoring school at 79 Anderson Road in Ipoh on 15 July 1947. Shortly after that date, Mother was invited by Shan Guang to come to Sitiawan to conduct a "crash" course on tailoring for her and her friends there. Her friends were all working and could not come to Ipoh to attend Mother's tailoring school.

Sitiawan was (and still is) a Fuzhou 福州 dialect speaking area. Shan Guang and Mother both grew up in Fuqing 福清. The Fuzhou and Fuqing dialects are similar. Mother was a perfect fit to conduct the tailoring classes.

Mother took Michael (who was then six years old) along to Sitiawan. The distance was 50 kilometres and they went by car hired for the trip. The condition of the road was poor. Mother and son, not being used to riding in a motor vehicle, threw out along most of the way. They finally arrived in Shan Guang's house in Kampong Koh in Sitiawan. It was a very rural environment. This was the house where Mother would live and teach for the duration of the tailoring course. The house was a wooden structure with a roof of galvanised metal sheets. The house was very clean and the floor was cement-paved. There was a well situated in a separate structure which served as a bathroom. Michael was not allowed to be by himself near the well for fear he would fall in. He was bathed by Mother or sometimes by Shan Guang's son Ah Hui who was much older than Michael.

Young Michael once wandered into the nearby rubber plantation to play and became lost. It was getting dark and panic set in and he started to cry. Just then, he saw a light in the distance—it was light from a kerosene lamp. Ah Hui had come looking for him. How happy and relieved they both were.

Michael's seven to ten days stay in Shan Guang's house were the happiest days of his childhood. He had soft-boiled eggs and kaya with bread every morning for breakfast. These were the ultimate of luxury during and soon after the Japanese Occupation. Shan Guang had a dog with yellow fur and Michael used to play with the dog under the large table while Mother taught her students how to cut a dress with patterns laid out on the table top.

Mother too was happy with the stay in Sitiawan as she was handsomely rewarded for her effort, thanks to her good friend Shan Guang *jie*.

Appreciation

As indicated by its title, the poem is written for presentation by Qing Shan's wife, Yi Song, to her childhood friend, Shan Guang *jie*. The poem is written in a straightforward language without the use of any literary allusion.

The two good friends have not seen each other for 20 years. In the first four lines of the poem, Yi Song gives an account of herself. She has had to work hard during the last 20 years. In that time, she has given up teaching (in a kindergarten) and taken up tailoring for a living and even compiled some tailoring manuals.

Knowing that Shan Guang had adopted two children to care for, Yi Song in a moment of weariness, expresses a common lament of parents in Lines 5-6: "It is our children, for whom we toil. White as snow our hair, in this mortal coil."

In Line 7, Yi Song praises Shan Guang; for despite toiling as a parent, she still looks the healthier of the two. Line 8 is perhaps the most picturesque scene of the whole poem. It is also a touching description of how Yi Song thinks of the old friend she had not seen for 20 years. Even while she works, she would often stop her needle to pause awhile in thought, wondering where her old friend is.

Chapter 29

sòng wáng fú wén shì xué shēng diào jí lóng pō
送王宓文视学升调吉隆坡

rén shēng yù hé qǐ sù yīn
人生遇合岂宿因？

dì běi tiān nán hū bǐ lín
地北天南忽比邻。

lùn jiāo yǐ yù èr shí zǎi
论交已愈二十载，

píng jū bù jiàn yún ní zài
4 平居不见云泥在。

hū chuán kǎo jì bào shēng qiān
忽传考绩报升迁，

huàn qíng bié yì liǎng máng rán
宦情别意两茫然。

xiān shēng yú zhōng wú suǒ dòng
先生于中无所动，

lín qí dàn suǒ shī yī piān
8 临歧但索诗一篇。

Farewell to Inspector of Schools Wang Fu Wen on His Promotion and Transfer to Kuala Lumpur

    Could two persons be predestined to be friends?
    From north and south, we're suddenly neighbours.
    We've known each other more than twenty years.
4   A lofty rank and lowly position are never barriers.
    I suddenly hear you're soon moving on promotion;
    I'm upset we'll part but happy at your elevation.
    You're completely composed without a start.
8   All you asked of me is a poem before we part.
    I know you're tired to hear words that flatter.
    To say I'm sad sounds foolish and sentimental.
    Material for poetry's aplenty; the choice's my plight.
12 I raise my pen, but still know not what to write.
    How about your upright character and skills literary?
    You will modestly refute these as not extraordinary.
    I hardly dare write a single word of praise.
16 Perhaps I can all your strengths to raise.
    If I commend you on your role in Education,
    You'd say you're just performing your function.
    "To crow about one's job, is like a chef-butcher
20 Or carpenter bragging his skills," you'd proffer.

先生厌听恭维语，

伤离又恐大儿女。

诗料尽多选择难，

12 笔下不知何所取。

取其道德与文章，

先生自视却寻常。

我亦一辞不敢赞，

16 本无所短恶乎长。

取其作人与造士，

先生谓此分内事。

庖人治庖若论功，

20 梓匠轮舆宁有异？

If I praise your propriety, prudence and integrity,
You'd say the standard for yourself is not lofty.
You can be naturally happy without much money;
24 A meager salary still provides for the daily necessity.
An official position will fill most with self-importance;
You're not like that despite your rank in officialdom.
"A scholar" to describe you would be a fitting term.
28 You will say you're merely an impractical bookworm.
Whatever genuine praise I express, you would deny,
Like someone restraining my hand, even if I try.
You might be happier if I point out your shortcoming.
32 I try to nitpick and attempt to look for something.
Yet no defect in the proverbial jade can I discover.
It's hard to be your critic and I'm loathe to flatter.
Not allowed to praise, yet I've nothing bad to say!
36 What's there left to say that comes from my heart?
I can only wish you a future of health and happiness,
That you can be a model for all future scholars.
You've always said you're but an ordinary person.
40 How could we train all men to be ordinary like you,
Ordinarily prudent in words and earnest in practice?
If we could, we would have a perfect, peaceful world.

Paraphrase

L1: Could the meeting of two persons who can get along well really be predestined?
L2: Coming from the opposite ends of the world, you from the north and I from the south, we suddenly found ourselves as neighbours.
L3: You and I have known each other for more than twenty years.
L4: In our relationship, I have never felt the wide gap between your lofty rank and my lowly position.
L5: I now suddenly learn of your promotion and transfer.

持躬谨饬洁以廉，
自云律己非特严。
安贫乐道性则尔，
薄俸况足供米盐。
世人作官居侈气，
先生作官浑不似。
倘以学者称先生，
但云本是书呆子。
我所欲言皆曰否，
执笔如有人掣肘。
告以有过喜可知，
亦曾吹毛索其疵。

L6: I'm disconcerted at the thought that we will soon have to part, necessitated by the continuing progress in your official career.
L7: But you yourself are completely composed and unruffled.
L8: Just before we part, all you ask of me is a poem.
L9: I know that you are tired of hearing flattering words,
L10: And I'm afraid that to express my sad feelings on our parting will make me look like a sentimental fool.
L11: There is abundant material for poetry, but what to pick is a difficult task.
L12: I raise my pen, but I am still uncertain of what I should write.
L13: Should I write about your principled character and your literary skills?
L14: You would (in your normal modest way) consider these as not so extraordinary (as to be singled out for mention).
L15: Besides, I hardly dare write a single word of praise (which would be tantamount to gilding the lily).
L16: As you do not have any weakness to speak of; perhaps I can talk about your strengths.
L17: If I commend your contributions in bringing up (the next generation of) our intelligentsia and in encouraging the fulfillment of the potential of everyone,
L18: You will say that you are only doing your part of the responsibility,
L19: If an educator behaves like the proverbial chef-butcher who in fulfilling his duties in the kitchen, starts to brag about his skills and contributions,
L20: He would be no different from a common carpenter-carriage maker who boasts about his skills.
L21: If I were to praise your propriety and prudence in the strict observance of personal integrity,
L22: You would say the standard you set for yourself was not particularly stringent.
L23: Given your disposition, you can easily be happy without the need for a great deal of money.

白璧之瑕求不得，
强作诤友耻投机。
道善不可道恶无，
尊前何以致区区。
但愿道履长康泰，
雅范常为士模楷。
先生自谓庸人耳，
安得人人庸如此？
庸言之谨庸德行，
天下从兹太平矣！

L24: Moreover, even a meager monthly salary is enough to provide for the basic necessities of everyday living, you'll say.
L25: Most people, on attaining an official position of importance, would swank and be filled with pomp and self-importance,
L26: But you are never like this even in your official position.
L27: If I called you a scholar,
L28: You would modestly refer to yourself as an impractical bookworm.
L29: Whatever (genuine words of praise and respect) I want to express, you will deny.
L30: As I hold my pen to write, there is as though an invisible hand restraining me.
L31: In that case you might be happier if I pointed out any shortcomings.
L32: Therefore, I have tried to nitpick and attempt to find something negative to say,
L33: But I am unable to find any defect in the proverbial jade (shortcoming) to talk about.
L34: It is really taxing for me to play the role of a forthright critic, and I am loathe to resort to flattery.
L35: I'm not permitted to speak of your merits, and yet I cannot find any shortcoming to admonish you for;
L36: Then what is there left for me to say to you that I can sincerely express from my heart?
L37: All I can say is to wish you the very best for a long and healthy, happy future.
L38: And that your noble example will become a model for the scholars.
L39: You've always maintained that you're but an ordinary person.
L40: How can we transform all men to be "ordinary" in the way you are?
L41: Come the day when all men become "ordinary" like

you: prudent in their words and earnest in the practice of ordinary virtues in their everyday life,
L42: The world will from thence be a world of peace.

Background

The poem was composed in 1952 for Mr Wang Fu Wen (Wang Fo-wen 王宓文 1903–1972). Mr Wang was then the Inspector of Chinese Schools in the state of Perak, still under the British colonial administration in Malaya. The poem was published in Ipoh's local Chinese newspaper *Kin Kwok Daily News* (*Jian Guo Ri Bao* 建国日报) on 1 March 1952. Mr Wang was about to be transferred from Ipoh to Kuala Lumpur on promotion to become Chief Inspector of Chinese Schools for the then Federation of Malaya.

Mr Wang came from a scholarly family in Taizhou in Jiangsu province (江苏泰州). He did not attend regular school when young but was tutored at home in the traditional classical texts and the selected writings of notable writers. He started his formal education in the post-May Fourth era and was taught Mathematics and English. He loved literature and also wanted to excel in the English language. Hence, he studied English Literature, reasoning that being bilingual in English and Chinese, he could become a language teacher. He had not realized then that the combination established the foundation for his career in education in British colonial Malaya.

After his graduation from what was to become National Nanjing University, he was recruited as a teacher to serve in Nanyang. He came to Nanyang in 1925 and taught variously in Singapore's Chinese High School, Kuala Lumpur's Zunkong High School (尊孔), Malacca's Peifeng High School (培风). He then went to Surabaya (泗水) in Java as high school principal, but returned eventually to Singapore-Malaya when the economy took a bad turn in the Dutch East Indies.

Wang Fu Wen and his wife (c.1941).
"How could we train all men to be ordinary like you, Ordinarily prudent in words and earnest in practice?"

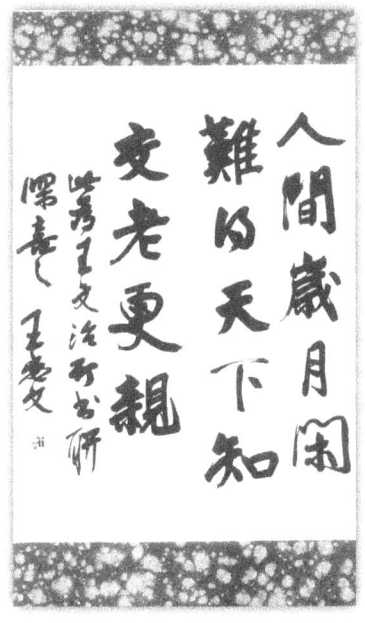

A birthday scroll in the distinctive calligraphy of Mr Wang Fu Wen, given to his friend. Text of the scroll: "In this world, a moment of leisure is difficult to get; In friendship, the older the friendship, the more intimate." 人间岁月闲难得；天下知交老更亲。Mr Wang was always a friend and a gentleman, as Qing Shan said of him, *"We've known each other for twenty years. A lofty rank and lowly position are never barriers."*

29 Farewell to Inspector of Schools Wang Fu Wen

He was recruited to the position of Assistant Inspector of Chinese Schools in the state of Perak in 1931. This would have been the first time when Father, then 37 years old and a teacher, first met Mr Wang who was 28 years old. They both lived in the Ipoh area and their friendship was to continue for 20 years until Mr Wang left Ipoh in 1952 on promotion. Mr Wang was the very model of the classical scholar-gentleman, learned and modest, courteous without being officious, treating all kindly and with respect.

Appreciation

The poem of 42 lines could be seen as comprising three sections. In Section 1, Qing Shan gives a short account about their friendship. Section 2 is the main body of the poem which Qing Shan uses to heap all the praises which he says Wang Fu Wen, being a modest man would deny. Section 3 concludes the poem with the greatest possible compliment in the form of a mock repartee with him.

Section 1 (Lines 1–8)

The first two lines ask, almost incredulously whether it is true that Qing Shan and Mr Wang are predestined to meet as friends in Nanyang, far away from their own native homes in China. They are nine years apart in age, Qing Shan is from the southern province of Fujian and Mr Wang from Jiangsu, further north. That they can become good friends and enjoy a rapport with each other must be due to their common love of the classics and Mr Wang's scholar-gentleman demeanor and personality. Qing Shan was but a teacher in a Chinese school and Mr Wang holds the lofty rank of Inspector of Schools in the State Education Department under the British colonial administration. The gap between their respective ranks is enormous, a difference described in the Chinese text of Line 4 as between "the clouds 云 above and the mud 泥 below". But Line 4 praises Mr Wang: "A lofty rank and lowly position are never barriers (to our friendship)".

On hearing of the impending departure of Mr Wang from Ipoh, Qing Shan is genuinely upset at the prospect of losing a good friend. At the same time, he is glad that Mr Wang is moving ahead in his career. One would expect Mr Wang to be excited about his promotion and the prospect of having to move to another town, but he is completely composed and unflappable. All he asks from Qing Shan is a farewell poem!

Section 2 (Lines 9–34)

This section is the beginning of Qing Shan's feigned agony of not knowing what to write in his farewell poem. Lines 11–14:

Line 11: "Material for poetry's aplenty; the choice's my plight.　诗料尽多选择难
Line 12: I raise my pen, but still know not what to write.　笔下不知何所取
Line 13: How about your upright character and skills literary?　取其道德与文章
Line 14: You will modestly refute these as not extraordinary."　先生自视却寻常

Qing Shan goes on with this "game", but in the process lists Mr Wang's qualities one by one. The words of praise are genuinely felt. All who know Wang Fu Wen will have no doubt how well deserved the praises are. The enjoyment of this poem is the skill and style with which the genuine admiration for Mr Wang is presented. It also brings out Mr Wang's character as a true gentleman. The next six lines 15 to 20 are an illustration:

Line 15: "I hardly dare write a single word of praise.
　　　　我亦一辞不敢赞
Line 16: Perhaps I can all your strengths to raise.
　　　　本无所短恶乎长

Line 17: If I commend you on your role in Education,
取其作人与造士
Line 18: You'd say you're just performing your function.
先生谓此分内事
Line 19: 'To crow about one's job, is like a chef-butcher
庖人治庖若论功
Line 20: Or carpenter bragging his skills,' you'd proffer."
梓匠轮舆宁有异

Mr Wang has been an educator all his life, as teacher, principal and inspector of schools. The reference to "chef-butcher" and "carpenter" bragging about their skills are two interesting allusions. In the context of Lines 19 and 20, the characters of "chef-butcher" (庖人) and "carpenter-carriage maker" (梓匠轮舆) are used to personify one who is skilled in a technique but does not necessarily know the higher principles behind it. An educator or teacher, in the widest sense, teaches the principles, the "why" instead of merely the "how". For Mr Wang to accept praises for his responsibility as an educator, he would be no different from a technician who boasts about his technical skills, even though he does not have a full understanding of the principles involved.

The reference to the chef-butcher is from Zhuangzi's "Essentials for Keeping a Good Health" 《庄子·养生主》. Zhuangzi tells the story of a skilful chef-butcher in the service of the King giving a demonstration of how he could deftly dismember a whole carcass of beef. Wielding his razor-sharp butcher's knife, he went on rhythmically with the task and within a short time the whole task was done. The King marvelled at his skill and the chef-butcher explained with visible pride how he had developed his uncanny skill.

The allusion to the carpenter-carriage maker is from Mencius' "Jin Xin" 《孟子·尽心》 in which Mencius said, "A carpenter-carriage maker may give a man the compass and square, but cannot make him skilful in the use of them 梓匠轮舆能与人规矩，不能使人巧".

Both the chef-butcher and carpenter-carriage maker can boast of their skills, but neither can be compared with the educator who transforms men as education does.

Since Qing Shan is not allowed to praise Mr Wang, he changes tack and asks whether "You might be happier if I pointed out your shortcomings." He tries to nitpick but can find no defect in the "proverbial jade".

Section 3 (Lines 35–42)

Qing Shan's sense of "frustration" is finally expressed in this last Section, beginning with Lines 35 and 36:

> Line 35: "Not allowed to praise, yet I've nothing bad to say! 道善不可道恶无
> Line 36: What's there left to say that comes from my heart?" 尊前何以致区区

Despite the injunction against him praising Mr Wang, Qing Shan is not about to give up. He holds Mr Wang out as a model for all future scholars and expects him to again downplay himself. Qing Shan, however, gives himself the last word in the final four lines of the poem. He says of Mr Wang in Lines 39–42:

> Line 39: "You've always said you're but an ordinary person. 先生自谓庸人耳
> Line 40: How could we train all men to be ordinary like you, 安得人人庸如此
> Line 41: Ordinarily prudent in words and earnest in practice? 庸言之谨庸德行
> Line 42: If we could, we would have a perfect, peaceful world." 天下从兹太平矣

Chapter 30

贺光地新厦落成
（晴山、光国联吟）

湖海元龙豪气赊，（晴）

半生踪迹寄天涯。（国）

卜居何处非吾土？

4　聚族于斯便是家。（晴）

不为妇言疏麴蘖，

每兴乡思话桑麻。（国）

故山醉里依稀见，

8　岭上寒梅正著花。（晴）

Congratulations to Guang Di on His New Home
Jointly by Qing Shan and Guang Guo

    Bold and indomitable your heroic spirit spreads. (Qing)
    Half your life, in this far corner you've made a mark. (Guo)
    Your chosen home becomes your new found land;
4   Where your clan gathers, there you your home will park.
                                                   (Qing)
    Don't let the wife tell you to go slow with the wine.
    To reminisce without restraint is a joy untold.   (Guo)
    In a mild stupor, in your native land you dimly see
8   On the hilltop, the winter plum its petals unfold. (Qing)

Paraphrase

(Qing Shan)
L1: Bold and indomitable, your heroic spirit like that of Chen Yuan Long has spread far and wide.

(Guang Guo)
L2: You have spent half of your life in this far corner of the earth away from your native land, but you have also made your mark here.

L3: You're not fastidious; wherever you choose to live, that will be your new "native" land.

(Qing Shan)
L4: Nonetheless, wherever your fellow clansmen gather, such a place will be like home to you.
L5: However well-meaning she is, don't let your wife tell you to restrain yourself with the wine tonight;

(Guang Guo)
L6: For there is no greater joy than to reminisce with your fellow clansmen without restraint.
L7: In a mild stupor, through the dimness of your vision, you can just about see the old village

(Qing Shan)
L8: With the winter plum on the hilltop now in bloom.

Background

Summary

This is one of four poems that we re-discovered from a pile of manuscripts that our cousin sister Xia Xian 霞仙 handed over to us in February 2005. The manuscripts belonged to her father, our fourth uncle Wang Guang Guo 王光国. Father died in 1960 at the age of 66 and Uncle Guang Guo died in 1971, coincidentally also aged 66. The close relationship between Father and Guang Guo can be seen in the Background to the poem in Chapter 60, suffice to say that they were good "poetry friends", despite their age difference of 11 years.

The manuscript of this poem is in Guang Guo's handwriting. It is a "joint" poem between Father and Guang Guo, with the author's name clearly marked at the end of each line or pair of lines to indicate authorship.

The poem was written in 1954 to congratulate Wang Guang Di 王光地 on the occasion of his moving into a "new" house. Guang Di was a distant cousin of our mother Wang Yi Song 王义宋. The Wang clan have lived in Jiangdou in Fuqing for a few hundred years. Guang Di came to Nanyang at the age of 12 and made his fortune through hard work and became a wealthy businessman in Ipoh.

The "New" House

The "new" house of the poem was not exactly new, but was a large double-storey pre-World War II bungalow of brick (first storey) and of timber (second storey). It is located along Lahat Road in Ipoh, next-door to the Anglo Chinese School in Ipoh.

Guang Di and his extended family moved into the house in 1954 from a shophouse in Hale Street. Guang Di passed away in 1969, but the family continued to live there for another 10 years until the late 1970s when his children built their own houses and gradually moved out to live on their own. As part of the distribution of the estate, the house was given to his eldest child and daughter. It was later torn down and the land is now being rented out to a motor servicing and car polishing company.

Wang Guang Di, the Man

Wang Guang Di (1900–1969) was born in the village of Xia Po 下坡 in Fuqing. He was actually a native of Jiangdou 江兜, the same village and of the same surname as our mother. His family and ours were descended from the same ancestor, if we trace back far enough.

His so-called "middle" name "Guang" 光 given to him is the same as that given to all Mother's brothers (i.e., our maternal uncles). There is a prescribed order, with the male descendants of each generation using a word taken from a poem or couplet. When all the words in the poem are "exhausted", the next generation will start this cycle of names all over again. Hence, the middle name of anyone from Jiangdou with the surname Wang indicates which generation he belongs to.

How did he come to be born in Xia Po, a village not far from Jiangdou? His eldest son Xian Zhi 先智 took great delight in telling us the story. Guang Di's father was a poor barrel maker in Jiangdou, but was taken in as a son-in-law by a rich family (surname Zheng 郑) in Xia Po. Guang Di was the youngest of four children. When he was about three years old, his mother died and his father returned to his native Jiangdou to resume his former occupation as a barrel maker. Here in Jiangdou, the family returned to their former poor circumstance and young Guang Di at the age of eight had to work as an oyster (or mussel) picker. The village of Jiangdou is on the coast of Fuqing and at low tide, the water recedes several hundred metres exposing large areas of the seabed with all sorts of shellfish ready for picking.

Guang Di came to Nanyang (Singapore) at the age of 12 and worked as an apprentice in the mechanical workshop of his elder brother by the name of Wang Zheng Tong. In 1920, at the age of 20, he returned to Jiangdou to marry his young bride, Huang Fu Jin 黄富金, who was then 18.

He brought his wife to Singapore and had to eke out a living with the wife supplementing the family income by sewing shirts for sale. As she had never been taught tailoring and cutting, she was resourceful enough to unpick one of her husband's shirts, lay the "dismembered" shirt out as a template in order to "produce" the new shirts for sale.

Portrait of Wang Guang Di's wife Huang Fu Jin 黄富金.

Guang Di left Singapore when he was still in his twenties and came to Ipoh to work as a foreman in a mechanical workshop. In time, he owned his own workshop in Hale Street (now known as Jalan Tun Sambanthan). He expanded his business

Yi Song's distant relative, Wang Guang Di's "new house", purchased in 1954, was a large double-storey pre-Second World War bungalow in Lahat Road, Ipoh. His extended family continued to live there for several years after he passed away in 1969.

Portrait of Wang Guang Di.

by dealing in motor spare parts in 1935–1936 and the family lived above the shophouse where business was conducted.

When the Japanese invaded Malaya in December 1941, his business ceased. During the Japanese Occupation, he applied his inventive mind to either inventing or making all sorts of devices such as a motor-driven machine for spinning ropes; attaching a side carriage to a bicycle and combining them into a three-wheeled "trishaw" for goods or passengers: making or improving combination padlocks, etc.

Wang Guang Di's eldest son Xian Zhi 先智 and wife are at the left and right of the photo. Guang Di's daughter Rui Zhen 瑞珍 is in the centre. Xian Zhi, an Australian-trained engineer, is now running the business that Guang Di started.

After the Japanese Occupation, Guang Di together with others went into the passenger transport business by providing bus services between Ipoh and the surrounding towns of Parit, Bruas, Tronoh, Tangjong Tualang. His company is known as Pu Tong or General Transport, a company that still operates today. He continued to develop and expand his business in the motor workshop and spare parts business and became a wealthy business person. He also acquired real estates in and around Ipoh, including his "new" house which is the subject of this poem and one or two industrial buildings that still bear his name today.

His eldest son Wang Xian Zhi, an Australian-trained mechanical engineer, today manages the business that Wang Guang Di had started some half a century before.

Appreciation

A poem written by two people is known as *lian-shi* (joint poem). This is one of only two poems in this book which are in the form of a joint poem. The other one in Chapter 27, comprises alternating lines by Qing Shan and his wife. This poem for Guang Di's new house is truly a joint poem in that it is clearly authored by two persons. The two poets, Qing Shan and Guang Guo, have a close rapport with each other and are a good match in the art of poetry. Each poet seems to know what the other has in mind and is able to pick up the theme from where the other left off. This rapport will be more apparent as we read through the poem.

Qing Shan opens with the first line, "Bold and indomitable your heroic spirit spreads 湖海元龙豪气赊". It is a lot more colourful in the original Chinese which literally says "The mighty dragon of the lake and sea, its heroic spirit (spreading) far and wide". The line immediately impresses upon the Chinese reader, a scene in which a mighty dragon roams far and wide unchallenged, breathing out its bold and indomitable spirit. The more literary among the readers will know that this is an allusion to a historical person by the name of Chen Deng 陈登 from "The Three Kingdom". Chen, known for his bravery and gallantry, had an alternative name Chen Yuan Long 陈元龙 meaning "mighty (i.e., 'big') dragon". Since "Chinese" dragons are supposed to have their residence in the lake and sea, he was therefore known as 湖海士 "the gallant one of the lake and sea". The first line praises Guang Di for his bold spirit when, at the tender age of 12, he dared to venture so far from home by coming to Nanyang (Singapore) to earn a living as a mechanical workshop apprentice. In contrast, Qing Shan came to Nanyang (Malaya) as an adult and became a teacher at the age of 24.

The cue from the first line is immediately picked up by Guang Guo in his second line, "Half your life, in this far corner you leave your mark 半生踪迹寄天涯". It notes that Guang

Di, having spent half of his lifetime in this far corner of the earth, has at least successfully left his mark behind. He has a large extended family, successful business enterprises and real estate in Malaya.

The third line, also by Guang Guo changes tack a little: "Your chosen home becomes your new-found land 卜居何处非吾土". It makes the point rather rhetorically by saying "Wherever you have chosen to live as your home, is there such a place that you can regard as not your [native] land?" In other words, wherever you have chosen to settle down, that then is your "native land".

Qing Shan qualifies this point in his fourth line, "Where your clan gathers, there you your home will park 聚族於斯便是家". What Guang Guo says in the third line may well be true, but what really makes the difference to you is where your "clansmen", the people and friends from your native village, gather. Whichever place they come together to live, that too is your chosen home and where you will "feel at home". For obvious reasons, this is very true of that time and even today to some extent. Migrants tend to converge in places in a new country where people from their home regions are most numerous.

In the fifth line, Qing Shan says tongue-in-cheek, "Don't let the wife tell you to go slow with the wine 不为妇言疏麴蘖". Perhaps it was not really "tongue-in-cheek"; Guang Di loved to drink and it would not be surprising that his wife would, from time to time, try to restrain him for good reason. However, on the occasion when he meets with his clansmen, Guang Di could be given a bit more licence to indulge.

Guang Guo picks up that "drinking" point in his sixth line, "To reminisce without restraint is a joy untold 每兴乡思话桑麻", which he will later develop in his seventh line. Guang Guo appears to attempt to soften Qing Shan's "ill-advised" suggestion that Guang Di should be allowed to drink a bit more when he is with his clansmen. It is such a joyous occasion when he has a chance to chatter nostalgically with them and reminisce about old times "back home".

Guang Guo develops the points about "drinking" and "nostalgia for the old country" further in his seventh line, "In a mild stupor, in your native land you dimly see 故山醉里依稀见". The mixture of much wine and nostalgia may even cause you to have visions of the familiar scenes back home.

Qing Shan, in the eighth and last line, provides the scene back home that Guang Guo has held out tantalizingly in his seventh line. The last line of this poem paints the scene "On the hill top, the winter plum its petals unfold 岭上寒梅正著花". The scene which you might just be able to see is indeed the winter plum sitting on the familiar old hilltop—it is in bloom! Such a scene is a very fond image used by Chinese poets.

Chapter 31

酬远堂羊毛婚纪念照题诗

远堂以羊毛结婚纪念照题赠内诗邮示,又赠予夫妇一律;略傚其体以酬之。

其一

欧化东渐遍九州,
纵非名士亦风流。
七年之病悲黄脸,
几个相随到白头?
垂老方知伉俪笃,
平生不识别离愁。
羊毛出在羊身上,
多福由来只自求。

On Yuan Tang's "Wool Wedding Anniversary"

On his "wool wedding anniversary", Yuan Tang composed a poem for his wife. I too mailed him and his wife a *lǜ-shī* poem more or less in the same format as his, in their honour.

Verse 1

    West to East, the wind pervades our land.
    It's easy to be Bohemian for any man.
    For many, divorces follow the "seven-year itch";
4   To grow old together is beyond their reach.
    How stable a marriage, in old age we'd know.
    You have never had a day of parting sorrow.
    Sheep's wool grows on the body of a sheep;
8   Your blessings come, they are what you seek.

Verse 2

    We've said all that can be said in the past forty years.
    The old country has had her upheavals and tears.
    The famed men of ancient times, are they still here?
4   Friendship of humble folks are still held dear.
    Our childhood of yesteryears seems like yesterday.
    Our numerous children form two long queues today.

其二

四十年来话短长,
故园北望几沧桑。
风云一世今安在?
4 贫贱之交尚不忘。
回忆童年如昨日,
相看儿辈各成行。
当君花烛辉煌夜,
8 我向天南正放洋。

一九五六年七月卅日晴 山

While the candles shone on your wedding night,
8　I was at sea heading south, no more in sight.

Qing Shan
30 July 1956

Paraphrase

Verse 1

L1: The culture of Europe has gradually pervaded the East, over our entire land.
L2: One no longer has to be a famous talented scholar in order to be "Bohemian".
L3: The "seven-year itch" has regrettably afflicted us, with its attendant evil of divorces (abandoned wives).
L4: How many couples today stay and grow old together?
L5: It's only when we reach old age together that we realize how enduring a husband-and-wife relationship can be.
L6: In all your life you have never experienced the pain of parting from each other.
L7: Sheep's wool grows only on a sheep's body;
L8: Your blessing of good fortune comes only because you worked on it.

Verse 2

L1: In our forty years of friendship, what can be said has all been said.
L2: The old country up north has experienced much change and upheavals.
L3: Where are they today who were once powerful enough to have "rebuked the wind and the clouds"?
L4: The friendship between humble ordinary folks like us are never forgotten.
L5: I recall our boyhood days as though they were just yesterday.

L6: Now, just look at your children and mine; they are numerous enough to form their own queue.
L7: While you were celebrating your wedding night,
L8: I had already put to sea heading south.

Background

Summary

The poem was composed in 1956 in response to a poem that accompanied a photograph given to Father by his childhood friend Lin Yuan Tang 林远堂. It was a photo of Yuan Tang's family taken on his 40th wedding anniversary referred to as "wool" anniversary, an influence of the Western practice.

Yuan Tang (born 1895) was one year younger than Father. They were childhood friends in Putian 莆田 from a very young age. When Yuan Tang got married in 1917, it was Father who helped him with all the preparations for the wedding. Unfortunately, Father had to leave for Nanyang before the wedding.

After Father left for Nanyang, he and Yuan Tang met again only twice during his two stays in China in 1923 and 1932–1933. Father and Yuan Tang never saw each other again after that, but continued their close friendship through the exchange of letters and poems. Dated 30 July 1956, this poem is one of such exchanges.

Father passed away in 1960 at the age of 66 and Yuan Tang lived to 80. The warm and enduring friendship of two individuals who grew up together a hundred years ago has now been passed on to our generation. Peter and Michael are in regular contact with Yuan Tang's son Qi Xian 启贤 who retired as a teacher in China.

Two Young Poetry Friends

In Yuan Tang's autobiography, he told a number of interesting stories about the years when he and Father were growing

Yuan Tang 远堂 celebrated his "wool" wedding anniversary in 1956. This photo was taken in Putian in the Spring of 1963 of Yuan Tang (then aged 68) and his family. Seated (right to left) are Yuan Tang and his wife. *"Sheep's wool grows on the body of a sheep; Your blessings come, they are what you seek."*

The painting of Yuan Tang (in his late seventies) and his wife. *"How stable a marriage, in old age we'd know. You have never had a day of parting sorrow."*

up together in Putian. Apart from an elder sister, Father had no other siblings in the family. He and Yuan Tang were like sworn brothers 义兄弟.

As teenagers, the two of them bought their first *qin* 琴 (stringed musical instrument) at the same time and visited each other's house to make music. Yuan Tang, Father and one other friend Pin Tuo 频陀 formed a poetry club and often got together to play and compete in word games with poems and couplets. A crowd would gather around them to watch and break into applause from time to time. In his autobiography, Yuan Tang recalled nostalgically the happy memories of their verbal games and lamented that all these came to an end when they finally had to part and went their own way to work or for further studies. Father left Putian and went to Fuqing 福清 to set up a private school sponsored by Wang Dan Ru 王淡如 (Mother's father).

A Broken Candle

Yuan Tang admired Father greatly and narrated this account. They once visited the home of Yuan Tang's uncle in Hanjiang 涵江 (Putian). The uncle had only one child, a son. It so happened that it was his family's turn that year to host the annual religious festival in the community. A huge candle was specially made, all ready to welcome the gods. The uncle's little boy, who knew nothing of these things, inadvertently caused the candle to break into two near its base. The uncle saw this as a bad omen but could not make himself openly express his extreme displeasure, for fear of bringing more bad luck. The poor man could only go about murmuring uneasily and grumbling under his breath. Father immediately sensed what was really troubling the man. He calmly went forward, removed the base of the candle that had broken off and placed the rest of the whole candle back on the candlestick. Naturally, there was absolutely no trace of the damage. The candle was whole again and good as new, with no trace of a breakage. Yuan Tang's uncle praised Father highly, saying scholars were really smart after all and accorded him the warmest welcome in the house.

Yuan Tang's Wedding

On the 29th day of the third month of 1917 (19 May 1917), Yuan Tang married Ms You De Xin. Yuan Tang wrote in his autobiography, "Qing Shan had, in fact, helped me make the arrangements for my wedding. Having completed all the preparations, he could not stay on because he had to leave for Nanyang." Father himself remembered this date all his life. Forty years later, he was to write, "I remember vividly the day of Yuan Tang's wedding, I was already in a boat sailing on the high seas. These forty years have just gone past in a flash. As I think of his wedding anniversary today—alas, all the memories of yesteryears come flooding back to me." Father was leaving his native land in China for the first time in his life, stepping into a new world that was unknown to him.

Qing Shan's Lunch

Even after his arrival in Malaya, Father continued to write to Yuan Tang about his life in the new country. Yuan Tang narrated in his autobiography, "Although Qing Shan was far away overseas, he wrote frequently. His letters came like little notebooks, reporting on his life out there. When he first arrived in Ipoh 怡保 (in Malaya) and before he managed to secure employment, money was very tight. His meal would consist only of some salted vegetable. One day, he was caught in the rain and had no choice but to spend an extra four cents to take a rickshaw home. In his diary, he recorded: 'salted vegetables, two cents; transport, four cents'." It was typical of Father not to lose his sense of humour even in adversity.

Despite all the years and distance that separated them, Father and Yuan Tang maintained regular contact with each other by post. The last time they saw each other was during the period 1932 to 1933 when Father returned to teach in Putian. Father died in 1960 at the age of 66 and Yuan Tang passed away at the age of 80 in 1975.

The letter of consolation dated 27 July 1960 written by Yuan Tang to Mother, with an elegiac poem for Father who passed away on 6 June that year. It also recalls a poem that Yuan Tang had sent Father "the year before", urging him to return to China to see him and Qing Shan's elder sister then living in China. (Refer to Chapter 41.)

Appreciation

This is one of three compositions in the book that can be read in conjunction with Chapter 63, "My Seven Principles of Poetry" 诗话七则. Chapter 63 is very special because in it, Qing Shan personally narrates in great detail the circumstances of the three poems and the lively exchanges between him and his friends.

The colophon of this poem to his lifelong friend Yuan Tang explains the reason for his writing this poem. It is in response to Yuan Tang's own poem to his wife celebrating his "wool" wedding anniversary. Yuan Tang's poem for his wife recalls nostalgically how in their 40 years, despite the adversity and hardship, they have had a wonderful life together. He praises his wife for successfully raising their children. Qing Shan, in writing subsequently about Yuan Tang's poem, says how much he is touched by the love between them—in Qing Shan's own words, "the deep affection between husband and wife surfaces itself even on paper 伉儷之情，活現紙上".

It is a rare treat to be able to hear from the poet himself the circumstance of his composition. The following is what Qing Shan says about Yuan Tang's poem and his own poem in response:

"[Yuan Tang's] poem [to his wife] reads, 'On our reckoning, we have been husband and wife for 40 years. The time to commemorate our wedding anniversary has come around once again. You praise me as an honest and sincere person, but I am not truly worthy. An exemplary mother you truly are, and there can be no doubt of that. Of our children you have brought up, nine out of ten are accomplished, often topping their class in school. Although we live a spartan life of adversity, yet our life together is sweet. Indeed, let us drink once more to that and be joyful.' [Qing Shan's comments] The tender feelings between husband and wife come to life even on paper. I once composed for him [Yuan Tang] two verses of a seven-word regulated poem. The first verse [of this poem] reads, "...[reference to the poem in this Chapter 31]". The expression 'seven-year disease' is originally 'seven-year itch', but I found it too crude and hence changed it. The reference to 'sheep's wool' arises because Yuan Tang was born in Yi Mo 乙未 year which is the year of the sheep. It is a pun on his year of birth and a common colloquial expression. To use such a pun in a poem just about makes it a doggerel. The second verse [of this poem] reads, "... [see paraphrase of

this poem] ". I remember vividly the day of Yuan Tang's wedding, I was already in a boat sailing on the high seas. These forty years have just gone past in a flash. I think of his wedding anniversary today—alas, all the memories of yesteryears come flooding back to me."

Qing Shan's poem has two verses. The first is in praise of the enduring love between Yuan Tang and his wife and how all their happiness together had not been merely fortuitous. It is the result of their seeking and working on it together.

The poem is especially rich in the metaphors and colours of the Chinese language. It is "convenient" to read the English translation of the poem in its versified form or a normal paraphrase, but some of the colours could be missed. We would like to enhance the reader's enjoyment of this poem by expanding beyond the two translation formats mentioned, for some of the lines. The following is a literal translation for the selected lines:

Verse 1

<u>Line 1</u>: "From West (Europe's culture 欧化) to East (东), pervades (gradually sweeps across 渐遍) our land ('nine states' 九州, a reference to ancient China)."
<u>Paraphrase</u>: The culture of Europe has gradually pervaded the East over our entire land.

<u>Line 2</u>: "Even if (zòng 纵) one is not (fēi 非) a famous personality (míng shì 名士), one can still be (yì 亦) Bohemian (fēng liú 风流)."
<u>Paraphrase</u>: One no longer has to be a famous talented scholar in order to be "Bohemian".

It used to be thought that only among the very talented can we find people who are eccentric and non-conformist enough to be "Bohemian" in their way of life. Qing Shan is saying here that under the influence of Western culture, it has become commonplace—even the very ordinary person can be a "Bohemian".

<u>Line 3</u>: "Seven-year sickness (七年之病) sadly afflicts (悲) the poor old wife (黄脸婆)."
<u>Paraphrase</u>: "The 'seven-year itch' has afflicted us, with its attendant evil of divorces."

Qing Shan uses the metaphor "seven-year itch" which, out of decorum, he changes to "seven-year disease". He obviously knows this expression comes from the West. The metaphor became more in vogue after the 1955 movie of the same name starring Marilyn Monroe. The English expression "poor old wife" is translated from the Chinese colloquialism *huáng liǎn pó* 黄脸婆 which literally means "yellow-faced woman". It refers to the old wife being relegated to doing all the housework and thus becomes old and unattractive, compounding the cause for the husband to turn his attention elsewhere.

<u>Line 7</u>: "Sheep's wool (羊毛) comes forth (出在) on a sheep's body (羊身上)."
<u>Paraphrase</u>: "Sheep's wool grows only on a sheep's body."

This line is best loved by Qing Shan and his friend Yuan Tang. It is a play on words arising from a commonplace but popular Chinese saying, *"Sheep's wool grows only on the body of a sheep"*. The Chinese saying means that Yuan Tang's blessing of 40 years together with his wife has not been just a matter of luck, but a consequence of something else. Line 8 then provides the reason, viz., their happiness comes only because they seek it and work on it. If that is all there is to Line 7, there would be nothing remarkable about the line. The clever thing about the line is that Yuan Tang was born in the "year of the sheep" and this was also Yuan Tang's 40th wedding anniversary, otherwise known as 'wool' anniversary. We know that Yuan Tang loved this line about the "sheep's wool" because he wrote about it in his autobiography in 1974.

Verse 2

<u>Line 2</u>: "The old country (故园), [as I] look north (北望), innumerable upheavals (几沧桑)."

<u>Paraphrase</u>: "The old country up north has experienced much change and upheavals."

Relative to Nanyang where Qing Shan is, China is in the north. Since they last met in 1932–1933, the "old country" has been through a period of warlordism and finally came through the communist revolution in 1949. The Chinese expression *cāng sāng* 沧桑 is used to describe the "upheavals". It is a compression of the expression *cāng hǎi sāng tián* 沧海桑田 which literally means "the sea is transformed into a mulberry field". It describes the swift and complete turn in world affairs.

Lines 3 and 4 together form a couplet contrasting the transience of fame with the durability of friendship between two common persons. The Chinese text of the poem is shown as a couplet below:

"The famed men of ancient times, are they still here?
风云一世今安在
Friendship of humble folks are still held dear."
贫贱之交尚不忘

Line 3's first expression of the two words *fēng yún* 风云 with the literal meaning "wind and clouds" is interesting. The expression is associated with the story of Zhou Yu 周瑜 who defeated Cao Cao 曹操 at the Battle of Red Cliff 赤壁. At this battle, Zhou Yu set Cao Cao's naval fleet on fire and made use of the sudden gust of east wind to engulf the whole fleet thus defeating him. The typical scene in the mind of the Chinese reader is the heroic Zhou Yu standing majestically commanding and rebuking the wind and the clouds to do his bidding. This line in the poem echoes the typical sentiments which Chinese poets often express. For example, the opening lines of Su Dongpo's 苏东坡 famous *ci* (poem 词) 《念奴娇·赤壁

怀古》 says, "The mighty river flows east, its rolling waters take along with it every trace of even the heroes of the time in every age 大江东去，浪淘尽，千古风流人物". Su Dongpo used these lines to set the scene for the theme of his *ci* which likens the nature of human life to a dream, transient and ephemeral. Qing Shan uses the imagery of the heroic personalities who were the heroes only of the time and then asks, "Are they still here today?"

Qing Shan then responds with Line 4, "Friendship of humble folks are still held dear (not forgotten) 贫贱之交尚不忘." In other words, the high and mighty (described in Line 3) are routinely swept away by the passage of time, but not so the friendship between two humble individuals.

Line 5 and Line 6 bring back a flood of memories to Qing Shan. It was as though only yesterday that he and Yuan Tang were playing their poetry and word games, but today they look back at their own families with some satisfaction.

The last two Lines 7 and 8 of Verse 2 are perhaps the most poignant of the whole poem. Like all good friends, Qing Shan has helped Yuan Tang prepare for his wedding. But come the actual day, Qing Shan is not there any more. We can imagine how sad Yuan Tang must be in the middle of the festivities to see the hand of Qing Shan in all the preparations, but not the man.

"While the candles shone on your wedding night,
当君花烛辉煌夜
I was at sea heading south, no more in sight."
我向天南正放洋

On Yuan Tang's wedding night 40 years before, Qing Shan was in some old ship sailing south towards Singapore on his first trip away from his native home in China. We can also imagine how Qing Shan must have felt, crowded below deck, with his mind still full of the pleasant memories of his carefree days of youth and of Yuan Tang's wedding night.

Chapter 32

白成根会长荣膺霹雳州苏丹
锡封太平局绅志喜

乡邦推硕彦，
闺阁仰贤名。
但作苍生雨，
4 应教碧海晴。
感时人望治，
有志事终成。
翊赞凭长策，
8 垂绅致太平。

霹雳福建公会妇女组同人敬贺

Congratulations to President Bai Cheng Gen on being Honoured with the Appointment of Justice of Peace by His Highness the Sultan of Perak

There is among our compatriots, a man of great learning.
His high repute, the Women's Group have long been hearing.
As the rain moistens the earth, he brings prosperity,
4   Enabling us to live in peace and tranquility.
With political change the people look for peace indeed.
Driven by ideals to serve, such a man will surely succeed.
Helping the State to govern, a man with strategies.
8   A bearer of peace to the people, a Justice of Peace.

> Respectful Congratulations from Women's Wing
> Perak Hokkien Association

Paraphrase

L1: There has arisen from among our compatriots overseas, a person of great learning.

L2: The women's group (in the Perak Hokkien Association) too have heard of his reputation.

L3: Such a person is able to bring prosperity among the people, just as the rain moistens the earth,
L4: And allows them to live in peace and tranquility.
L5: In time of (political) change, the people anxiously look for peace in the land.
L6: One who is driven by ideals in the service of the people will ultimately succeed.
L7: A person with good strategies will help in governing the people;
L8: A Justice of Peace will bring peace to them.

Background

Bai Cheng Gen was the President of the Perak Hokkien Association (霹雳福建公会) in Ipoh. Qing Shan was employed as the Secretary of the Association from 1945 to 1960. Bai was a successful rubber merchant and a prominent leader of the Chinese community in Ipoh. He loved poetry and loved to compose them. He hence belonged to Father's cohort of poetry friends.

The portrait of Bai Cheng Gen 白成根 (Dato Peh Seng Koon, DPMP, JP).

The Association had a Women's Wing and its Head was Bai's wife. The then Deputy Head was our mother Wang Yi Song.

The relationship between Father and Bai Cheng Gen was more like members of an informal poetry group or friends rather than that of "boss" and subordinate. Father respects Bai as his "boss" and Bai has high and courteous respect for Father's literary accomplishment. Bai would often ask Father for advice on his own compositions.

There are two other poems written for Bai Cheng Gen in this collection:

    Chapter 42 To Mr Bai Cheng Gen on his 60th Birthday
    Chapter 43 Presentation of the Complete Works of Lu You as a Birthday Gift.

The two poems are a great deal more personal and of considerable length.

Justice of Peace

By the 1950s in the then Malaya, the honour and rank of Justice of Peace was conferred by the Sultans of the component States. The more formal powers and duties of a lower rank magistrate have largely been replaced by legally qualified magistrates. Nevertheless, the title, abbreviated to the initials "JP" after one's name still enjoys a very high status in the local community, with certain legal powers such as solemnization of marriages and the attestation of certain legal and other documents. In practice, a JP as a community leader still occasionally plays the role of "keeping the peace" when called upon by disputing parties to settle their differences. The rank of "JP" no doubt lends credibility to such a role.

Appreciation

This is a poem composed in 1956 by Qing Shan on behalf of the Women's Wing of the Perak Hokkien Association in Ipoh. The occasion is the conferment of the title of "Justice of Peace" on Mr Bai Cheng Gen, President of the Association.

Given its nature of a congratulatory message written on behalf of an organization like the Women's Wing, it is less personal than is typical of Qing Shan's poems. Nevertheless, it is well structured in form and the expressions used are very appropriate for the purpose.

The central theme of the poem is the word "Peace", taken from the title of Justice of Peace. Bai is praised as a man of learning and implicit wisdom. The Women's Wing of the Association too respects his high reputation as a wise leader.

The use of several phrases: "As the rain moistens the earth" (苍生雨), "live in peace and tranquility"(碧海晴), "the people look for peace" (人望治), "assume the rank of (垂绅) Justice of Peace" (致太平) cumulatively denotes bringing peace to the community.

Chapter 33

马来亚独立日，怀美英万隆

海国暾初出，
东方散绮霞。
新尝平等果，
4 争看自由花。
英印犹同室，
华巫共一家。
如何闺阁侣，
8 长是在天涯？

Thinking of Mei Ying on Malaya's Independence Day

    Brightly shines the morning sun on the country,
    The eastern sky is splashed with glorious beauty.
    To first taste the fruit of Equality,
4   We clamour to see the bloom of Liberty,
    As British and Indians share the same space,
    Chinese, Malays are united as one family.
    Why are two ladies who are bosom friends,
8   Separated for so long in these far-off lands?

Paraphrase

L1: In the new country bordered by the sea, the morning sun has just risen at the horizon.
L2: The rose-tinted clouds are splashed brilliantly across the eastern skies.
L3: Looking forward to the first taste of the fruits of Equality,
L4: Clamouring to see the bloom of Liberty,
L5: Whether British or Indian, they now share the same space.
L6: Chinese and Malay are united as one big family.
L7: Why are two ladies who are childhood friends,
L8: Separated for so long in these far-off lands?

Background

Mother was adopted at the age of five by the Guo 郭 clan of Mianting 棉亭, Fuqing 福清. The circumstance is more fully explained in the Background in Chapter 24, a poem for the celebration of Reverend Guok Koh Muo's Golden Wedding Jubilee.

Mother lived with her adoptive family in the Guo clan until she was 16. Throughout her life, she continued to maintain close and warm contact with members of the Guo clan in China, Singapore and Indonesia. They had become her family for life.

The "Mei Ying" 美英 of this poem was Mother's childhood friend from the Guo clan. We believe her family migrated to Indonesia, but Mother was in contact with her from time to time. The poem was composed, as the title suggests, around 31 August 1957 when Malaya, a former British protectorate, became independent.

Appreciation

The poem was most likely composed at the behest of Qing Shan's wife, Yi Song, around 31 August 1957, as indicated by the title "On Malaya's Independence Day". The "Mei Ying" 美英 in the title of the poem is Yi Song's childhood friend.

The name used in the title in Chinese is somewhat problematic. It reads "Mei Ying Wan Long 美英万隆". We know who Mei Ying is, who or what is "Wan Long"? Since Mei Ying lives in Indonesia, is Wan Long the Indonesian city, Bandung, where she lives? But that is not the usual way in Chinese to indicate that Mei Ying comes from Bandung. The usual way is to reverse the order with the place name coming first: "Wan Long Mei Ying" 万隆美英. Or is "Wan Long" the name of another person, for example, Mei Ying's husband? That interpretation would also not sit too well when we come to Line 7 of the poem which contains the phrase *guī gé lǚ* 闺阁侣 meaning a "lady's childhood friend". This would suggest that the poem is addressed to Mei Ying alone. In view of doubt as to what "Bandung" refers to, the word is omitted from the English translation of the title.

The poem does not use any classical allusion and is in fairly straightforward language. Even the imagery used can be easily understood. Line 1 uses the imagery of a "morning sun (just risen)" 暾初出 to signify the start of a new era of Independence. Line 2 paints a picture of a beautiful sunrise: "The eastern sky is splashed with glorious beauty" 东方散绮霞. The imagery signifies the dawn of a wonderful future. The English translation "glorious beauty" is an inherently inadequate expression of the original Chinese *qǐ xiá* 绮霞 which literally means "beautiful rose-tinted clouds". Unfortunately, there is no equivalent word in English for the rose-tinted clouds (霞) that we sometimes see at sunrise or sunset.

Lines 3 and 4 use metaphors like the "first taste of the fruit of Equality" and "see the bloom of Liberty" to signify the achievement of Independence and all that it brings. In a straightforward manner, Lines 5 and 6 express the hope that all ethnic races being now one family can co-exist together.

The personal touch comes in the last two lines of the poem. Lines 7 and 8 ask why two ladies (Yi Song and Mei Ying) who have been childhood friends, should have for so long lived far apart in their respective corner of the world.

Chapter 34

向太平白仰峰先生索和
xiàng tài píng bái yǎng fēng xiān shēng suǒ hè

闻君慷慨乐输将，

安得吟囊似义囊？

雁使北来频问讯，

4 鷄林何日复通商？

居奇莫遣骚坛寂，

有美休教韫椟藏。

诗市岂同胶市看，

8 欲求善价始装箱。

Solicitation of a Poem from Mr Bai Yang Feng of Taiping

A generous donation I hear is your great pleasure.
Why not a donation from your literary treasure?
I ask the postal courier coming from the north,
4   "When will the poetry market reopen thenceforth?"
Poems are not commercial merchandise to hoard.
Beautiful things should not be hidden for greater reward.
How could Poetry and the Rubber market be the same,
8   Waiting for a price rise before they're boxed its aim?

Paraphrase

L1: I hear you're generous and happy to donate your wealth to charity.
L2: How could I loosen the "purse string" of your literary hoard?
L3: I often ask the postal courier coming from the north,
L4: "When will the 'poetry market' be open again?"
L5: Don't let the hoarding of poetry be the cause of the current doldrums in the market.
L6: Beautiful things should not be locked up (but shared with others)
L7: How could the "poetry market" be looked upon in the same way as the "rubber market",

L8: To await a higher price before the merchandise is boxed and released for sale?

Background

Summary

When Mother celebrated her 60th birthday in 1957, it was concurrently the 10th anniversary of the founding of her tailoring school in Ipoh. For this double commemoration, Father composed a poem of three verses and sent out to his poetry friends, inviting them to respond with their compositions (see poem in Chapter 12).

Mr Bai Yang Feng, a rubber merchant of Taiping 太平, was one of several poetry friends Father invited to respond. Mr Bai was rather tardy in his response and Father wrote this poem hoping to provoke him into action.

The story behind this particular poem for Mr Bai is told by Father himself, thus:

> "After I sent out the draft of my poem, friends from far and near all began to respond except for Mr Bai Yang Feng of Taiping. At first, I thought one of my criteria of 'Three Avoids' had gone awry. I then playfully wrote a [this] poem to provoke him [into action]…
>
> Yang Feng is a well-known personality in the Perak rubber trade and is generous with his wealth in giving to charity. Hence my poem to him. Not long after this, I was rewarded with the receipt of a poem from him in response to my birthday poem for my wife. In addition, he wrote a poem in response to the poem I had sent him.
>
> I am embarrassed to offer my poem even as a 'donation'.
> Your urgent importunities spur me into undoing my bag.
> If only I had known the pen to be my 'true love'!
> I now regret having turned away from pen to trade.

*A great love begets a great loss;
The greater your possession the greater the loss.
Three meals a day is all we need to live,
Why bother whether it's a thousand or ten thousand boxes we have."*

[Extract from Chapter 63, "My Seven Principles of Poetry"]

Mr Bai Yang Feng 白仰峰, a rubber merchant of Taiping, was one of Qing Shan's poetry friends.
"How could Poetry and the Rubber market be the same, Waiting for a price rise before they're boxed its aim?"

Bai Yang Feng

Bai Yang Feng came from Anxi, Fujian (福建安溪) as a young man. Like many educated immigrants from southern China, he started life working for Tan Kah Kee's business (陈嘉庚). He later settled down in Taiping in the state of Perak where he started to trade in rubber under the name Yang Feng Company (仰峰公司) at No. 164 Main Road.

After the Marco Polo Bridge Incident (卢沟桥事变) in China on 7 July 1937, Tan Kah Kee in Singapore organized a Pan Malayan-Singapore Committee to raise funds among the overseas Chinese for China's war against the Japanese. Yang Feng as the President of the Taiping Rubber Dealers' Association organized and led the Taiping branch of the Committee. The Malayan Communist Party too organized their own boycott of Japanese goods with public demonstrations against the merchants and importers of Japanese merchandise. Yang Feng, as the local Chinese community leader, had to come out to speak and disperse the demonstrators. The British colonial government therefore suspected him to be a Communist Party member and he was deported to China in 1939, leaving his family behind in Taiping. He did not return to Malaya until the Japanese surrender in 1945. He passed away in Beijing in 1969 while on a visit to see his daughter who was living there.

Bai Yang Feng and Bai Cheng Gen (see Background in Chapter 42) were paternal cousins. They and Hon Lu Kuan (see Background in Chapter 49) were the few successful businessmen who were, at the same time, good poets—a very rare breed indeed. They were once described as "scholar-merchants" (儒商).

Appreciation

There are two poems in this book that we may call "interactive" in the modern sense of the word. They are written deliberately to provoke a response from the "target". They are written tongue-in-cheek and therefore entertaining. The other such poem is the one written for Zhuang Xin Zai 莊心在 of Taipei and it brought out an equally entertaining response from Xin Zai in Chapter 35.

After Qing Shan has sent out his own poem with an invitation to his friends to respond with their poems, replies begin to come in. Eventually everyone has responded, except this Mr Bai Yang Feng of Taiping. He is a well-to-do rubber merchant in Taiping, about 50 miles north of Ipoh where Qing Shan lives. He is also an accomplished poet and a good friend. There is no excuse for him not to respond! Qing Shan decides to have a bit of fun and writes him this provocative poem to tease him out.

Line 1 first praises him for his generosity in giving his monetary wealth to charity, "A generous donation I hear is your great pleasure 闻君慷慨乐输将".

Line 2 follows up swiftly with a jab at him, "Why not a donation from your literary treasure? 安得吟囊似义囊". In other words, why are you not equally generous with your hoard of literary compositions as you are with your wealth?

In Line 3, Qing Shan begins to feel anxious and keeps a lookout in the post for a response from Yang Feng. The postman coming in from the north is frequently asked the same question, "I ask the postal courier coming from the north 雁使北来频问讯". What that question is gets revealed in the next line. On Line 3, there are two interesting points. The first is the use of the term *yan shi* (雁使, literally meaning "wild goose emissary") to mean postal courier or postman. The word *yan* (雁) is used in combination with other words as metaphors connected with "couriers" or "letters", for example, *yan shi* (雁使 a metaphor for "postman"), *yan shu* (雁书 for "letter"). The association of wild goose with the "post" can be found in the story of Su Wu (苏武, died 60BC) as recorded in *Han Shu* (*Annals of the Han Dynasty* 汉书). Su Wu had been sent by the Han Emperor as an emissary to the Huns (匈奴) in the north. He was detained by the Huns and made to shepherd sheep for many years in the wilderness. Repeated attempts by the Han Emperor to secure his release were rebuffed with the lie that he had died. Finally, the Han court countered this lie with their own lie reporting that Su Wu had sent the emperor a letter attached to the leg of a wild goose. This finally secured Su Wu's release and return to the Han Court.

The second reference to the postal courier "coming from the north" is obvious since the Huns were located in the northern borders of the Han kingdom. And so is Taiping, where Yang Feng lives, 50 miles north of Ipoh where Qing Shan lives. The analogy of "the postal courier from the north" is therefore a very apt one.

Line 4 poses the question referred to in Line 3, "When will the poetry market reopen thenceforth? 鷄林何日复通商". The literal meaning of the line in Chinese is "When will the Chicken Forest (*ji lin* 鷄林) open up again for trade". "Chicken Forest" is an old Chinese name for Korea, but what has Korea got to do with the "poetry market"? Even in ancient times, the poems of the Tang poet Bai Juyi (白居易) were so highly treasured that a Korean merchant, with a keen eye for business, was able to sell them to his country's Ministers for one gold piece each. There was literally a "poetry market"! Qing

Shan is, of course, pulling Yang Feng's leg here, comparing him with the astute Korean merchant trading in poems. Since Yang Feng has not sent in his poem, perhaps there has been an interruption in the "poetry market".

Line 5 continues with the analogy "Poems are not commercial merchandise to hoard 居奇莫遣骚坛寂"). It is said literally in a rather more colourful and different way in the original Chinese text, "When you hoard your poems in the hope of an even bigger profit later and do not release them now, the 'market' for literary works would be such a quiet and desolate place". This line is rich in allusions. The goods (i.e., poems) that Yang Feng is accused of "hoarding" in the hope of an even bigger profit later is expressed in the "shorthand" of just two words *ju qi* (居奇). It comes from the expression "remarkable merchandise that are worth storing up" (*qi huo ke ju* 奇货可居). The expression comes from the story of Lü Buwei (吕不韦) during the Warring States period (453–221 BC) as recorded in *The Historian's Record* (*shi ji* 史记). Lü was an astute and farsighted merchant who saw the potential in a prince, Ying Yi Ren (嬴异人) of the state of Qin 秦. The prince was, at that time, held as a hostage in the state of Zhao (赵). Lü Buwei saw in the prince a really worthwhile investment and began to invest money and influence to secure his release and return him to Qin. Lü, at that time, had a beautiful concubine who was already a couple of months pregnant with his child. He allowed this concubine to be given to the prince Ying Yi Ren as his wife and passed off the child, that was subsequently born, as the natural son of Yi Ren's. Ying Yi Ren eventually returned to Qin, later ascended the throne of Qin and Lü was appointed Prime Minister. Ying Yi Ren ruled for three years, died and was succeeded by his then thirteen-year-old "son", Ying Zheng, who became the First Emperor (Qin Shi Huang 秦始皇)! Lü was indeed a merchant of great foresight.

Line 6 says that such beautiful things as poetry are not something to be hidden so that they could later be sold for a higher profit. "Beautiful things should not be hidden for greater reward 有美休教韫椟藏."

Line 7 goes on to make fun of the rubber merchant poet Yang Feng, "How could Poetry and the Rubber market be [looked upon in] the same [way] 诗市岂同胶市看".

Line 8 administers the coup de grace, "Waiting for a price rise before they're boxed, its aim 欲求善价始装箱".

Yang Feng must be a very busy man, but is finally provoked into action. He sends in a birthday poem for Mother but also writes a reply in the form of a poem as an answer to Qing Shan's cheeky "attack". He makes the usual protestations about how unworthy his poems are and that he has not written for a long time. Yang Feng is actually a very learned man as can be seen from his answer to the mock "accusation" that he is being miserly with his poems. He answers Qing Shan by saying why should anyone be miserly with anything at all. He uses an allusion from Laozi's proposition, "Great love, great loss and the greater the possession the greater the loss". He then concludes philosophically that all we can consume is three meals a day. Ultimately, what difference does it make how much our worldly possessions amount to. Qing Shan must have thoroughly enjoyed this exchange with Yang Feng as can be seen from the exuberance with which he writes.

For Bai Yang Feng's equally clever reply, see Chapter 63, "My Seven Principles of Poetry 诗话七则".

Chapter 35

寄台北心在大师请示
其诗阙文一字

诗城坐拥久称王,
乍降纶音喜欲狂。
衮职偶然差一着,
顿教补阙拾遗忙。

Despatched to Grand Master Xin Zai in Taipei
For His Direction to Reveal the Missing Word in Poem

In the City of Poets, long has ruled the King.
Joyously we hear the royal edict announcing
The King's inadvertent error of omission.
Busily engaged we are on this royal commission.

Paraphrase

L1: In the "City of Poets", you have long sat as King.
L2: We're wild with joy to be unexpectedly given a royal command.
L3: The King has indeed inadvertently left out a word.
L4: We are set about busily looking for the missing word in this royal omission."

Background

Summary

This is very much a "fun" poem extracted from an epilogue which Father wrote in 1957 for a compilation of poems sent in by his friends to celebrate Mother's 60th birthday. It is one of three poems that Father had picked for mention in that epilogue, giving a full account of its composition (see Chapter 63, "My Seven Principles of Poetry 诗话七则").

When Zhuang Xin Zai 庄心在 of Taiwan sent in his poem for Mother, he inadvertently left out a word from one of the lines. Father and his small cohort of poetry friends tried to work out what the missing word was. Father then wrote this poem in jest and sent it to Xin Zai to check if they had got it right. Xin Zai had spent some years hitherto in Penang as the chief editorial writer of the Penang paper, *Guanghua Ribao* (光华日报).

Full Account (an extract from Chapter 63)

"Xin Zai from Taipei sent a poem of eight lines. The 'couplet' (comprising the third to sixth lines) within the poem appears to have the final word missing from line: 'Past disciples are everywhere, the Teacher is X' (盈门桃李儒家X). Each one of us among Lu Kuan (禄宽), Cheng Gen (成根), Guang Guo (光国) and Ting You (亭又), chose a replacement word for the missing one; it was like trying to solve a word riddle. We sent our 'replacement' words by airmail to Xin Zai in Taipei with an accompanying poem,

> In the City of Poets, long has ruled the King.
> Joyously we hear the royal edict announcing
> The King's inadvertent error of omission.
> Busily engaged we are on this royal commission.

Not long after, I received a reply to say the missing word is the word 'Happiness' (乐), taken from Meng Zi's principle of 'Three Happiness'. This was not among any of the words we had chosen as replacement. We now know that when there is a missing or defective word in ancient texts, it is not without reason. Xin Zai's reply came with a poem with rhymes matching the poem sent to him:

> In former days, the uncrowned King of Penang was I.
> A wild excess of youth in poetry and wine, I cannot deny.
> A lower intake of wine, lowers the quality of poetry.
> Troubling you all to patch up my work, I am sorry.
>
> (旧日槟城无冕王，一时诗酒少年狂，
> 而今酒少诗才拙，却累诸家补缀忙)

During Xin Zai's sojourn in Nanyang, he had been the chief editorial writer of the Penang newspaper Guanghua Ribao which explains why he had written thus."

Appreciation

An elaborate account of the composition of this poem is given in the Background. Qing Shan and his small cohort of poetry friends take it on as a challenge and obviously have great fun trying to speculate what the missing word is. He then sends their guesses to Xin Zai with a poem teasing him. Prior to returning to Taipei, Xin Zai had been the chief editorial writer of a major newspaper in Penang, well respected in the literary circle of Penang which was known by its sobriquet "City of Poets".

Qing Shan refers to Xin Zai as the (literary) "King" in Penang; and refers to his own cohort of poetry friends as "court officials" who become wild with joy when this "royal command" came unexpectedly, commissioning them to look for the missing word. The Chinese expression he uses for "royal command" (*lún yīn* 纶音) is interesting and colourful. The two words literally mean "silken voice", referring not to the velvety voice of the King but to his edicts and commands traditionally written on silk.

Continuing with his teasing of Xin Zai as the King who has inadvertently committed an error of omission by leaving out a word, Qing Shan uses the expression *gǔn zhí* 衮职 to mean the "King". It is another expression rich in literary connotation. The first word 衮 literally means "royal robe" and 职 means "office" or "post" and two words together *gǔn zhí* 衮职 means either an official post in the King's court or the King himself. The expression comes from the *Book of Poetry* 诗经 which tells the story of the upright and capable Premier Shan Fu (山甫) who was a close and trusted confidante of the King. He was the only one honest and courageous enough to point out any of the King's error or omission: "The King commits an error, only Shan Fu dares help him correct it" (衮职有阙，维仲山甫补之). The use of this allusion also connotes the close relationship between Qing Shan and his friend Xin Zai, a relationship that allows one to point out a mistake of the other.

Xin Zai's reply is equally clever. He refers to himself as the "uncrowned" King since it is only Qing Shan who "crowns" him with the title. Xin Zai then explains that with his current diminished intake of wine, the quality of his poems has similarly been diminished. Hence his error of omission. He closes his poem with a mock apology to Qing Shan's cohort of self-appointed "court officials": "I apologise for having troubled you gentlemen to patch up my work."

Qing Shan's repertoire of compositions covers a wide spectrum, ranging from the very sorrowful poem lamenting the death of his first wife (Chapter 52) to this almost frivolous "fun" poem teasing his friend. It shows his joy and love for poetry, as well as his versatility.

Chapter 36

季芬先生出示书怀一律，依原韵以酬。

百岁光阴任两梭，
闲情逸兴老来多，
生花犹自饶江笔，
4 反日何须借鲁戈。
诗思久沉心未已，
吟笺屡易墨重磨，
骚坛对叠输君健，
8 且当书函再乞和。

A Poem in Rhyme with the Poem of Mr Ji Fen

    Swift and unyielding the years pass by.
    Ease and leisure now fill your life.
    Time and talent will sharpen your skill;
4   Need not hold back Time, even if you will.
    My inspiration to write is all but gone;
    Try and fail as I did, however long.
    In matching of rhymes, I bow down to you.
8   Your acceptance I seek with this note in lieu.

Paraphrase

L1: Even a hundred years fly by, inexorably as the rising and setting of the sun and moon, swiftly as the movement of the shuttle of a weaving loom.

L2: In old age, there is more time to enjoy a life of ease and leisure.

L3: With the passage of time the quality of your compositions will naturally be taken to even greater heights, due to your abundant talent.

L4: There is no need to turn the clock back by "borrowing the halberd of General Lu to summon back the sun".

L5: My poetic inspiration has long recessed into the back of my mind and has yet to surface.

L6: The draft has been chopped and changed many times. I have ground and reground the inkstone repeatedly (yet I still cannot produce a decent poem).

L7: In the matching of rhymes in poetry, I must bow to your superiority.

L8: With this, I write to seek your acceptance of my capitulation.

Background

Summary

As the title suggests, this is Father's response in rhyme to a poem by Mr Yang Ji Fen 杨季芬. Mr Yang was a poet and a teacher in Yoke Choy High School (育才中学), the premier Chinese high school in Ipoh attended by Michael. Father and Mr Yang appear to be "poetry friends" who sometimes "joust" with each other in poetry. We were not aware of their friendship, other than on one occasion when Michael was asked if he was the son of Chen Qing Shan.

In 1957, Mr Yang was one of eighteen friends whom Father invited to compose a birthday poem to celebrate Mother's 60th birthday. Mr Yang responded with four poems! Father was quite selective in whom he invited to write and Mr Yang must have been someone he respected as a poet. Other than his poems for Mother's birthday, we unfortunately do not know of any other poems of Mr Yang.

Mr Yang was already 72 years old in 1957. He was hence nine years older than Father who was 63 at that time. Unfortunately, we do not have Mr Yang's original poem (to which this poem is a response). It is reasonable to believe that this poem is written around 1957.

Mr Yang Ji Fen

According to the recollections of Michael, Mr Yang was his Chinese language teacher when he was in Junior Middle II (初中二) in Yoke Choy High School in Ipoh. Mr Yang taught him for only one year in 1956. When Michael first entered the school in 1955, Mr Yang was already in the school.

Mr Yang had taught in a Chinese school in Indonesia, prior to his arrival in Yoke Choy High School. He was brought in by the then Principal Mr Cai Ren Ping (蔡任平) because there was an acute shortage of Chinese language teachers in Malaya at that time. It was a booming economy in the tin and rubber industry town of Ipoh during the 1950s.

Mr Yang Ji Fen 杨季芬, an old teacher of Yoke Choy High School (育才中学), a premier Chinese school in Ipoh. Mr Yang was one of Qing Shan's poetry friends and they sometimes "joust" with each other in poetry. *"In matching of rhymes, I bow down to you. Your acceptance I seek with this note in lieu."*

Chinese schools were expanding rapidly. However, it was also the height of the Communist insurrection and the "Emergency" rule had been imposed by the then British colonial government in 1948. The entry of teachers from mainland China was prohibited. Most of the teachers recruited were local, but a few came from other sources, like Mr Yang Ji Fen from Indonesia and a chemistry teacher Miss Bai Gui Ying (白桂英) from Taiwan.

Presumably because these teachers were single, they were provided with living quarters in the rear building of the school. During Michael's badminton games in the school in the early evenings, he recalls seeing an old man walking slowly by with a cooking pot in his hand. It was Mr Yang and he must have been going to cook his dinner because he lived alone.

The Subject Guo Wen (国文)

Mr Yang taught the subject "Guo Wen" which in the context means "Chinese Language". Yet it is not really either—in the sense as we know it today. The subject included a wide spectrum of Chinese literature from the classics to the modern, comprising prose, poems, novels and essays which are all part of the Confucian concept of education.

The literal meaning of "Guo Wen" (国文) is "national literature". At that time, Malaya had not acquired full independence and the Chinese Malayans still thought of "Chinese" as the "national language". Today, we would probably call the subject "Hua Wen" (华文) meaning "Chinese Literature".

Nickname

Just like students everywhere, students in Ipoh give nicknames to their teachers. It was interesting to know that Father, teaching in Perak Girls' Middle School (霹雳女子中学), and Yang Ji Fen in Yoke Choy High School shared the same nickname given by their students: Lao Fu Zhi (老夫子)! Even though it is primarily intended to tease and poke fun, the term Lao Fu Zhi actually has a connotation of great respect. According to the dictionary, the word was originally used to address a teacher but later was used in a humorous sense to describe an old teacher, usually a scholar, who is interested in nothing surrounding him other than classical poems.

As far as we know this fits the character of the older Yang Ji Fen: a teacher, an old man, and a scholar in the classical Chinese sense. It partially describes only one side of Father who had rather modern ideas of the role of women and displayed managerial ability in organizing Mother's tailoring school before and after the Second World War (see Background in Chapter 12 under the sub-heading, "Tailoring School").

Appreciation

This short poem of eight lines contains a number of figures of speech, allusions or their "transformations". Qing Shan is obviously composing it for a "poetry friend". It is written with a rhyming scheme to respond to a poem composed by Mr Yang. Unfortunately, we do not have Mr Yang's original poem. Even without it, we can see a cheeky streak in Qing Shan's poem. It is not a poem of great or serious subject matter. For want of a better word, we could call it a "fun" poem.

At the time of writing, Mr Yang was already 72 years old. The first two lines, while recognizing his literary talent, teases him. The line says there is no need to be concerned about old age because he will have more time to enjoy his leisure. Although Time passes by quickly and inexorably, his literary skills would also increase through the passage of time because of his innate literary talent.

The speed and the unyielding passage of time is expressed in the first line in a rather clever way. There is a Chinese proverb *rì yuè rú suō* 日月如梭. Its literal meaning is "The sun and the moon are like the shuttles of the weaving loom". It compares the sun and moon with the two shuttles that are thrown alternately over the loom in the process of weaving. The movement is fast and relentless. The proverb is used to personify the speed and the unyielding passage of time. The line does not use the proverb in the normal way. Instead of referring to "the sun and the moon" as in the original proverb, it says so obliquely by using the term "the two shuttles of the loom" (两梭). It is a "transformation" of the normal figure of speech. The literal translation of the Line 1 would read thus:

> "A hundred years of Time (百年光阴) move uninterrupted like (任) the twin shuttles of the weaving loom (两梭)".

Line 3 gives Mr Yang the assurance why, even at the age of 72, he should not be overly concerned about his age. If only we could have seen Mr Yang's poem which has prompted this line, it would be all the more interesting! It says that with the passage of time, the quality of his compositions will naturally be taken to even greater heights, due to the abundant talent he possesses. Here, Qing Shan combines two allusions to convey this rather long message in just seven words. First let us look at the literal meaning of the actual words used and explanation of the two allusions will follow.

> Sprouting flowers (生花) can still spring forth (犹自) abundantly from Mr Jiang's pen (饶江笔).

The first allusion "Sprouting flowers" comes from the story of the Tang poet Li Bai 李白. When he was a young boy, he dreamt that the pen he was using sprouted flowers at one end. This was taken as a foretelling of his literary talent. The phrase *shēng huā miào bǐ* 生花妙笔 is now used to praise a fine composition.

The second allusion "Mr Jiang's pen" comes from the story of a Mr Jiang Yan 江淹 who lived during the Southern dynasty. When he was still young, he dreamt that someone presented him with a multi-coloured pen which enabled him to produce remarkable literary work. This is the origin of the phrase "Jiang Yan's pen" *jiāng yān bǐ* 江淹笔 which is now used to describe a remarkable literary talent.

The Chinese language is so rich in its culture and history that with just a couple of words, used like a code or shorthand, it can express so much.

Having assured Mr Yang in Line 3 that his literary work will become even better with the passage of time, Qing Shan's Line 4 tells him there is no need to resort to holding back time. Here, Qing Shan uses another "modified" allusion. Let us examine the line's literal meaning in order to enjoy the allusion:

> To reverse the sun (反日) why need borrow (何须借) General Lu's halberd (鲁戈)?

In English, the syntax might be "Why need borrow General Lu's halberd to reverse the sun?" The word "sun" (日) in Chinese can also mean "day", i.e., "time" in this context. In other words, "Why is there a need to hold back 'time'?"

The allusion comes from a story in a collection of writings compiled by the King of Huai Nan and others (*huái nán zi* 淮南子) during the Western Han dynasty. It is the story of General Lu 鲁 who was in the thick of battle and on the verge of victory. But the sun was about to set. General Lu was not about to let nightfall rob him of his victory. He waved his halberd at the sun and thundering at the top of his voice ordered "the sun to step back from the horizon (反日)." Time was "stopped" and the daylight thereby extended to enable the battle to continue.

The second half of the poem (Lines 4–8) provide the reason or excuse why Qing Shan is not a match for his senior Mr Yang. It implies that Mr Yang is older and hence a better poet. The poem ends with a playful act of capitulation to Mr Yang.

Chapter 37

代静滨题小影

人海茫茫寄此身，
大千世界一微尘。
浮生自古原如梦，
4 往事何曾敢认真。
秋水春山仍故我，
新愁旧恨了无痕。
相看不厌知谁所，
8 顾影还怜镜里人。

Colophon for a Snapshot on Behalf of Jing Bin

    In the limitless sea of life, sojourn we must.
    In this universe, we're but a speck of dust.
    Our life has always been transient as a dream.
4 Take not the past to heart; it's just a gleam.
    My eyes and eyebrows, they're the same old me.
    Sorrows new or old, wiped out without trace to see.
    We gaze at each other, but who is whom really?
8 For her reflected within, I feel a great empathy.

Paraphrase

L1: In the limitless sea of humanity in which we sojourn,
L2: In this boundless world of our existence, we are but one tiny speck of dust.
L3: Since time immemorial, this mortal life of ours has always been brief and transient as a dream.
L4: How could I take the past too much to heart; all that have passed are no more than just a transient gleam.
L5: Like my eyes and eyebrows, I am still the same person.
L6: Whether current or past, all sorrow and grief are wiped away without a trace.
L7: Looking at the person in the snapshot, wondering who the person really is.

L8: Irrespective of who she is, I feel a great empathy with her.

Background

Summary

This is one of two poems composed for a lady by the name of Lu Jing Bin 卢静滨, written not long before early 1958. Jing Bin approached Father one day and asked if he could write something of her life in a poem for her. Father did not promise her immediately, but said, "Let me see if I could (我可试试看吧)". The poem was eventually composed "on behalf of" Jing Bin and dated "New Year Day, 1958" (一九五八年元旦). The poem is "signed" with the words "Colophon by Jing Bin on her own behalf" (静宾自题), as would be the custom since it was composed on her behalf. The other poem in Chapter 38 was composed at about the same date. Jing Bin was 37 years old at the time when these two poems were written.

It was fashionable in those days to inscribe words on the back of photographs and snapshots to be kept or given to someone. The words are to commemorate some event, relationship or just a farewell message or a message of encouragement. Jing Bing liked the two poems so much that she had the text printed on the front just below her two portraits.

Jing Bin first came to Mother's tailoring school in the latter part of 1948 to learn tailoring. She was then 27. After her graduation from the school, she stayed on as an instructor and even briefly became a business partner in the school. In October 1949, she went to Kuala Lumpur to open her own tailoring school. She continued to maintain close touch with our family and had by then become a family friend.

Jing Bin was married and widowed in her early twenties during the Japanese Occupation (1942–1945). She had a daughter by her first husband; he was taken away by the Japanese and was never heard of again. The daughter was brought up by her mother-in-law. This was not a happy episode in her life.

After she left to open her own school in Kuala Lumpur, she met someone, fell in love and married. She eventually returned to Ipoh to live. She had children by her second husband but marital problems arose. It was during this unsettled period of her life that Father and Mother tried to console her.

Lu Jing Bin

Jing Bin came originally from Kampar, a tin mining town just 35 kilometers south of Ipoh. Jing Bin was already a young lady of about 20 at the beginning of the Japanese Occupation in early 1942. She married into a family in Grik (now Gerik) in the upper part of the state of Perak in Malaysia. Gerik was a hotbed of anti-Japanese activities throughout the Japanese Occupation and Jing Bin's husband was taken away by the Japanese and was never heard of again. She had a daughter by her husband. This was the first tragic episode of her life. She herself went into hiding from the Japanese as she had been a member of a choir organization that had raised funds for the anti-Japanese efforts in China.

Lu Jing Bin 卢静滨 (then aged 37) reflecting on her own life in the poem by Qing Shan, inscribed on her photograph. "*We gaze at each other, but who is whom really? For her reflected within, I feel a great empathy.*"

After the war ended in August 1945, she took a job as a business manager for a local newspaper in Penang, *Xian Dai Ri Bao* (*Modern Daily News* 现代日报). This was an anti-colonial paper which was subsequently closed down by the British colonial government.

She had always been interested in children and she started to sew for a girls' home run by The Salvation Army. She had no tailoring training and used to take and make measurements with a piece of gunny string. In 1948, she decided to take up sewing lessons, after reading news or advertisements of Mother's tailoring school in Ipoh. A careful manager of money, she had saved enough money to enroll for the course as a "boarding" student in the school.

She came to Mother's tailoring school in the latter part of 1948 in Ipoh and graduated in the school's 9th Batch in March 1949. She was an attractive lady with sharp features. She was intelligent, streetwise and independent. In May 1949, Mother invited her into partnership to start a branch of the tailoring school to cater to students who could only attend classes in the evening. In October that year, Mother had to reluctantly let her leave for Kuala Lumpur to start her own tailoring school there.

By then, Jing Bin had become a close family friend and was on very good terms with elder sister Mei Xuan who also taught in Mother's school. She got along well with both Mother and Father. She was one of Mother's favourite graduates of the school and was able to appreciate Father's classical poems.

Father was aware of Jing Bin's background and the tragic loss of her first husband during the Japanese Occupation. By the time she left us for Kuala Lumpur, our parents had become a confidant of sorts to her, and she would sometimes come to Father for advice. This particular poem was written at the request of Jing Bin herself, intended originally for inscription on the back of her snapshot.

There is a sequel to Jing Bin's story. This will be told in the Background of the next poem in Chapter 38, also composed for her.

The Search for Lu Jing Bin

Soon after we decided to work on the book, we started the legwork of tracking down the people who may know something of the background of the poems. We spoke extensively to elder sister Mei Xuan who worked with Jing Bin in Mother's tailoring school. We spoke to Jiang Bao Qin 江宝琴, one of Jing Bin's business partners in her Kuala Lumpur tailoring school in 1949. Bao Qin provided us with many photographs, but did not know where Jing Bin was. We met by chance another of Jing Bin's business partners Chen Hui Xuan 陈惠璇 in faraway Vancouver. They all remembered Jing Bin very well, but no one seemed to know where she was.

Out of desperation, we inserted articles in the Singapore Chinese newspaper *Lianhe Zaobao* and Kuala Lumpur's *Sin Chew Jit Poh*. All these drew a blank. It was again by chance that we

The newspaper article inserted in *Lianhe Zaobao* in Singapore on 9 March 2004 in search of Jing Bin. We had lost track of her and made many fruitless enquiries of her whereabouts since we started working on this book. It was not until 2008, by pure chance, that we discovered that she has been living in Ipoh all these years.

Jing Bin in 2008. Now in her eighties, she is a devout Christian, living happily with her daughter in Ipoh.

found out that Jing Bin had been living in Ipoh all along. We finally met her again in 2008—after 50 years!

Appreciation

The poem is written "on behalf of Jing Bin". It is as though written by her as she looks at her own image in the snapshot in front of her. It is a poem of reflection and consolation, as she looks back on the ups and downs of the past 37 years of her life.

The opening two lines express a common and traditional philosophy of life at times of adversity. We are all only sojourners in this vast ocean of humanity. In the boundlessness of the universe, we are insignificant as a speck of dust. The two lines form a nice couplet:

> Line 1: "In the limitless sea of life, sojourn we must.
> 人海茫茫寄此身
> Line 2: In this universe, we're but a speck of dust."
> 大千世界一微尘

The "limitless sea of life" (人海茫茫) in Line 1 parallels Line 2's "this universe" (大千世界). The enormity of both the "limitless sea" and this "universe" is contrasted with us who are but a "speck of dust" (一微尘).

Lines 3 and 4 then remind Jing Bin that life is as brief and transient as a dream and we should not take too much to heart all that have passed. The transient nature of life is expressed by the Chinese phrase 浮生 which literally means "floating life" or existence. The expression captures in just two words the whole philosophy of the vanity and uncertainty of life and human existence.

In Lines 5 and 6, while she is staring at her own face in the snapshot she reminds herself she is still the same Jing Bin who has always been. She should not let the present sorrowful events pile cumulatively onto those in the past (新愁旧恨). She should wipe these out without a trace. Line 5 uses the metaphor "Autumn streams and mountains in Spring" (秋水春山) to describe the beautiful face of a lady. The expressions are "eyes are like Autumn stream" (眼如秋水) and "eyebrows like mountains in Spring" (眉如春山).

The climax of the poem is in the last two lines:

Line 7: "We gaze at each other, but who is whom really?   相看不厌知谁所
Line 8: For the one reflected within, I feel great empathy." 顾影还怜镜里人

Jing Bin gazes intently at her own photo wondering surrealistically who is really whom. Is she the real Jing Bin looking into the image of herself in the photo or is the person in the photo the real Jing Bin looking at her image? It is like Zhuangzi's question about who is really Zhuangzi (庄子), he or the butterfly in his dream. The last line says that irrespective of who is whom, the two must share a strong empathy between them. The "real" and the "surreal" could after all, be one and the same in life. Line 3 of the poem puts it succinctly: "Our life has always been transient as a dream 浮生自古原如梦".

Chapter 38

题静滨女士玉照

山下蘼芜任去留，
北堂萱草可忘忧。
芳颜如玉心非石，
4 笑口常开泪不流。
无限云烟凭过眼，
许多恩怨溯从头。
情怀万种都抛却，
8 毕竟君家有莫愁。

Colophon for the Portrait of Ms Jing Bin

Let go the past of an unhappy marriage.
Go home to mother who'll give you solace.
Lustrous as jade, but your heart's not a pebble;
4 A brave smile put on and tears do not flow.
Adversities come, like clouds and smoke they'll go.
The kindness and grievances you can recall;
Myriad memories, emotions, discard them all,
8 For within yourself, there's a Lady Mo-chou.

Paraphrase

L1: Let go of the past, let go the reminder of the unhappy marriage.
L2: Go home to mother from whom you will receive solace, like the herb *xuan-chao*, that will enable you to forget your worries.
L3: You are lustrous as jade outside, but your heart is not like a pebble to be kicked around by fate.
L4: We know you often put on a brave smile and manage to hold back your tears.
L5: Adversity, just as it comes, will eventually vanish in a puff of smoke or go by like the passing cloud.
L6: As you recall from the very beginning, the many acts of kindness enjoyed and grievances endured,

L7: You can throw out these myriad memories and emotions of the past;
L8: For you still have within yourself the goodness of your own heart and the compassion for others, just like the legendary Lady Mo-chou.

Background

Summary

The poem in this Chapter was composed probably not long after the poem in Chapter 37. At the request of Jing Bin, both poems were written and dated "New Year Day, 1958" (一九五八年元旦). Like the poem in Chapter 37, it was meant to be inscribed on a photo of Jing Bin. Unlike that poem, this was written as a message from our mother to Jing Bin to console her.

The Background in Chapter 37 has traced how Jing Bin who came to know our family in early 1949, became an instructor in Mother's tailoring school and then left to start her own school in Kuala Lumpur. There she met someone, eventually returned to live in Ipoh, got married and had children.

Her marriage began to go wrong. As the state of her marriage worsened, she came to see Mother often and this poem was composed by Father as a message of consolation. The poem was written as a message from Mother to Jing Bin.

Jing Bin's Second Marriage

Jing Bin went to Kuala Lumpur in October 1949 to start her own tailoring school at No. 40 Kampong Attap. She took her good friend, Ms Jiang Bao Qin, along as a partner in the business. Miss Jiang was also a graduate and later an instructor from Mother's tailoring school in Ipoh.

It is not clear how long Jing Bin had the tailoring school in Kuala Lumpur. But it was during this period, some years into her widowhood, that someone came into her life again. Her suitor used to visit Kuala Lumpur regularly to see her. She was, after all, an attractive lady. The period of courtship was perhaps the happiest days in Jing Bin's life for a long time. She had her own tailoring school and was in love again. Everyone called him "Lao Chen" 老陈 (an informal address for someone with the surname Chen). Everyone liked Lao Chen.

Jing Bin then came into some money and bought a house in Jalan Yang Kalsom in Ipoh. In any case, she returned from Kuala Lumpur to live in her house in Ipoh. She and Lao Chen got married and lived happily for a while.

Poor Jing Bin's marital bliss was not to last. A few years into the marriage, their relationship began to break down. Jing Bin would come to Mother and Father to cry out her sorrows. Everyone around her would say, "How could this ever happen to Lao Chen? He is such a nice person!" The process of divorce became acrimonious at times. The children they had together were not enough to save the marriage. They finally parted company for better or for worse.

The poem in this Chapter was written for Jing Bin during the dark days of her impending divorce from Lao Chen, the second tragedy in the life of this intelligent young lady. She was only about 37 at that time.

Jing Bin had always been public-spirited from a young age. She had at various times worked with The Salvation Army orphanage and sewed for a girls' home. She was fond of children and helped to care for some of the orphans. These were children whose parents had been the unfortunate victims in a "war" waged by the British colonial government in Malaya against the communist guerrillas during the period 1948–1960 known as the "Emergency".

Jing Bin was also a very filial daughter. Her mother lived with her until she died at a ripe old age.

Appreciation

A sad poem but with words of consolation and encouragement for Jing Bin, who at 37 has undergone so much personal suffering. Jing Bin was a young and intelligent lady who was fond of Qing Shan's works. This is the second of two poems written for her. The poem's first two lines use two allusions which would be known to someone like Jing Bin.

Widowed in her twenties, Jing Bin, now 37 (in 1958), has remarried but her marriage is in trouble. Divorce is inevitable. Line 1 goes straight to the core of the poem with the words, "Let go the past of an unhappy marriage 山下蘼芜任去留". The literal meaning in English would be "At the foot of the hill, let the *mí wú* 蘼芜 remain there". The term *mí wú* is the name of a herb and is used here as a metaphor for an "abandoned wife". The allusion comes from an old ballad "上山采蘼芜" compiled during the Chen 陈 dynasty (557–589) of the North-South epoch 南北朝. It tells of a wife who was "divorced" by the husband. The woman went up the hills one day to gather *mi wu*. As she was coming down, she met her former husband who was on his way up. She sat by his side and thoughtfully asked how was his "new" wife. The ballad is in the form of a dialogue of question and answer. The husband said that although the "new" wife was just as pretty but she was a far cry from the "old" wife in weaving skills. Any one reading this ballad will empathise with the abandoned wife. In ancient times, a wife was sometimes "divorced" not on the initiative of the husband. Her mother-in-law could take the initiative by giving the poor wife a written notification, sending her back to her own mother. Hence, Qing Shan's use of the expression *mi wu* evokes a measure of sympathy in us for poor Jing Bin.

In Line 2, "Go home to mother who'll give you solace 北堂萱草可忘忧". The literal translation is "In the Northern Hall (北堂), *xuān cǎo* (萱草) will enable you to forget your sorrow (可忘忧)". "Northern Hall" means "mother" and *xuan cao* is a herb that will make one forget one's sorrow. In ancient times,

Qing Shan's poem, inscribed below the photo of Lu Jing Bin 卢静滨, is written as a message of consolation from Qing Shan's wife, Yi Song. Jing Bing was a graduate of Yi Song's tailoring school in Ipoh. "*Myriad memories, emotions, discard them all*".

The statue of the legendary Lady Mo-chou 莫愁 who supposedly lived in the fifth or sixth century. Widowed at an early age she devoted her life to charitable works. A statue of her stands at Mo-chou Lake near Nanjing. Qing Shan's consoling line in the poem for Jing Bin: "*For within yourself, there's a Lady Mo-chou*".

38 Colophon for the Portrait of Ms Jing Bin

a rich household traditionally had the women's quarters located in the north side of the residential complex. "Northern Hall" later became a metaphor for "mother". *Xuan cao* is a herb known as "tawny daylily" which, it is said, will enable those who consume it to forget their sorrows. In this line, Qing Shan advises Jing Bin to go home to her own mother who will give her comfort and help her forget her sorrows. Jing Bin is known to be very close to her own mother who lived with her until she died at a ripe old age.

Lines 3 and 4 describe Jing Bin as an attractive girl who is outwardly "lustrous as jade" (芳颜如玉), but her heart is not a pebble (心非石) to be kicked around cruelly by fate or men. She is capable of feeling all the pain and sorrow like anyone else. Despite these sufferings, Line 5 says she still has to put on a brave smile (笑口常开) and hold back her tears so that none will flow (泪不流). With these two lines, we too feel the poignancy of her suffering; for there is no greater pain than pain that has to be borne with a smile.

Although she is only 37, so much adversities have come into her life; but they will also pass away, like clouds and smoke. The many memories and emotions that repose in her, she should now discard them all (Lines 5–7).

In the last line of the poem, Qing Shan gives the reason why she should put her past behind her. She has in her own home, or more accurately within herself a "Lady Mo-chou". This is both an allusion and a "pun". First, the allusion. There are many folklores about Mo-chou 莫愁. One tells of a beautiful and intelligent girl by that name. She lived during the North-South epoch (420–589). Her father died unexpectedly and the poor girl had no money even for his burial. But young Mo-chou chose to sell herself to raise the money needed to bury her father. A wealthy man from Jinling (the ancient name of present-day Nanjing) bought her to marry his son. But soon after the marriage, Mo-chou's husband was conscripted into the army and was killed in battle. Mo-chou, anguished by the deaths of the two men in her life, chose to devote herself to a life of welfare work to help others. Mo-chou was beloved by the people and after her death, they named a lake after her, Mo-chou Lake 莫愁湖. The lake is located near Nanjing and is on the tourist map today. Jing Bin has worked as a volunteer with The Salvation Army orphanage in Ipoh and Qing Shan compares her with Mo-chou. With this comparison, he is telling her that despite all her personal tragedies, there remains a higher purpose in her life, and in her devotion and compassion for others, as personified by the legendary Lady Mo-chou. Coincidentally (perhaps), Jing Bin's surname of Lu 卢 happens to be the family name of Lady Mo-chou. Finally, Qing Shan employs a pun effectively to convey a piece of sound advice to Jing Bin. The name 莫愁 *mo-chou* is deliberately chosen as the last two words of the poem to signify his parting message to Jing Bin. The two words 莫愁 *mo-chou* means "don't grieve"!

Chapter 39

题 张 纫 诗 女 士 牡 丹 诗 画 册 后
<small>tí zhāng rèn shī nǚ shì mǔ dān shī huà cè hòu</small>

南荒几见牡丹开，
<small>nán huāng jǐ jiàn mǔ dān kāi</small>

一捻脂痕纸上猜。
<small>yī niǎn zhī hén zhǐ shàng cāi</small>

国色岂真尘世有？
<small>guó sè qǐ zhēn chén shì yǒu</small>

4　天香疑透鬓云来！
<small>tiān xiāng yí tòu bìn yún lái</small>

高人笔下无凡卉，
<small>gāo rén bǐ xià wú fán huì</small>

大匠门前愧弃材。
<small>dà jiàng mén qián kuì qì cái</small>

惆怅胡姬太消瘦，
<small>chóu chàng hú jī tài xiāo shòu</small>

8　攀缘无计傍楼台。
<small>pān yuán wú jì bàng lóu tái</small>

Poem as Epilogue for Ms Zhang Ren Shi's Peony Album

A peony in the desolate South we've seldom seen.
A twist of red on paper we guess is how to begin.
Could such an alluring beauty on earth really exist?
4   Its fragrance subtly pervading a lady's hair.
This is no ordinary flower created by the expert's art.
Embarrassed am I with the poetry composed on my part.
Alas, our own orchid looks much too frail and slight;
8   Undeserving to escort the peony, to share the limelight.

Paraphrase

L1: In this desolate place in the south (Nanyang), how often do we see peonies bloom.
L2: A twist of red on paper would still have us guessing whether it is a peony.
L3: How could such an alluring flower, as beautiful as the peony, really exist in this world?
L4: Its perfume that fills the air seems to have come from the fragrance of a lady's coiffure.
L5: Indeed, it's only the brush of an expert that can create a flower of such exceptional beauty.
L6: Before such an expert I am embarrassed by my deficient skill.

L7: Regrettably, our local orchids look rather frail and twig-like (by comparison with the peony).
L8: Failing to measure up, our orchid cannot share the same limelight accorded (to the peony).

Background

This poem was composed probably in 1959 when Zhang Ren Shi, then in her forties came to Malaya from Hong Kong to exhibit her calligraphy and paintings. She was essentially a poet and calligrapher and may have taken up painting later in her life. In a place like Ipoh among the Chinese businessmen, there was more likely to be an interest in paintings than calligraphy, and even much less interest in poetry. According to Madam Peng Shi Lin, former Principal of Perak Girls' Middle School in Ipoh, the paintings Ren Shi brought along for the exhibition were exclusively of peonies. Everything turned out well for her in the end.

While in Ipoh, she painted a work of peonies with a colophon in her own calligraphy for Perak Cave. This painting is dated Spring of 1959 己亥之春.

Zhang Ren Shi (1911–1972) was a native of Guangdong. She was first married at the age of 28 into the Tang 唐 family of Zhong Shan 中山. After her divorce, she moved to Hong Kong and devoted herself to the arts. She travelled throughout Nanyang to exhibit her works.

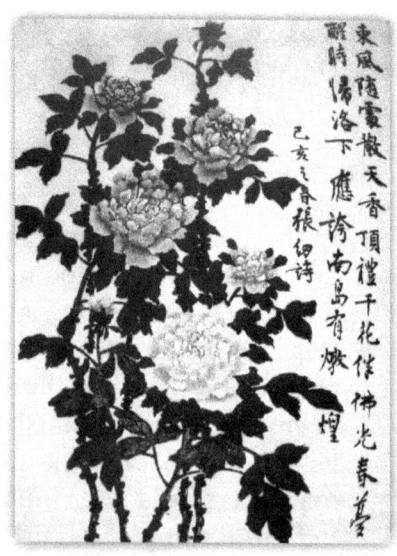

Zhang Ren Shi's painting of peony on the wall of Perak Cave in Ipoh. The colophon is dated Spring of 1959.

She appeared to have lived in Hong Kong in the 1960s. Her name was often referred to by a writer Dong Qiao (董桥, born 1962, original name *Dǒng Cún Jué* 董存爵). As a young man in Hong Kong in the 1960s, he was tutored by Zhang Ren Shi in classical poetry. In an article dated 29 March 2007, he wrote fondly of her:

> "Ms Zhang was my father's friend, a talented lady from Guangdong. Her poetry, calligraphy and painting were especially good. She passed away in the 1970s. When I first came to Hong Kong and did not know anyone, it was she, as an elder, who looked after me. When I had problems with my studies, I would go to consult her; if I did not work hard, she would reprimand me. Her study at home was named 'Yi Studio' 宜楼 as her original name was Zhang Yi 张宜."

She eventually met a man who shared her interest in poetry. He is the founder of the Vietnam Shou Xing Milk Company, Mr Cai Nian Yin (越南寿星公炼奶厂创办人蔡念因). After their marriage, they travelled to America, Japan, Taiwan before returning to settle down in Hong Kong. Ren Shi passed away in 1972 and her husband, Nian Yin, built a pavilion in Hong Kong to commemorate her, with the name "Yi Pavilion" 宜亭, after her original name.

Appreciation

The exhibition of the calligraphy and paintings of Zhang Ren Shi was held in Ipoh in 1959, soon after a similar exhibition in Singapore. A catalogue of the exhibition was published and Qing Shan and his brother-in-law, Guang Guo, were asked to include a poem at the back of the catalogue. The poems of Qing Shan and Guang Guo were published in the local paper *Jianguo Ribao* (建国日报), together with a poem of Bai Cheng Gen. Cheng Gen's poem was composed in the same rhyming scheme in response to Zhang Ren Shi's own poem.

This poem is what might be called a "courtesy" poem 应酬诗, i.e., one composed on request. Courtesy poems often do not have a ring of sincerity and consist of hackneyed expressions. It would appear that a good poet is capable of writing a good "courtesy" poem. There is another reason. Zhang Ren Shi is first and foremost a poet! The hallmark of this poem is the clever use of allusions and imagery.

Line 1 paints Nanyang as "desolate (region in the) South" 南荒 where the people have seldom seen the exotic peony bloom, a flower beloved by emperors. Line 2 follows up with a scene of the artist executing the first brush stroke as she begins to demonstrate her painting at the exhibition. She starts off with "A twist of red on paper", and the onlookers that gather round to watch, surmise that it must be a peony! 一捻脂痕纸上猜.

The Chinese expression for "a twist of red" is *yì niǎn zhī* 一捻脂 (脂 or 红 red). The allusion is a romantic story of the Tang Emperor Xuan Zong 玄宗 and Yang Gui Fei 杨贵妃. While Xuan Zhong and Gui Fei were enjoying the peonies in the royal garden one year, Gui Fei suggested she etched a mark on the petals on one of the blooms with her fingernail. Every year thereafter, the petals of the peony bloom would bear the mark of her fingernail. This species of peony became known as *"yáng fēi yì niǎn hóng"* 杨妃一捻红 (Royal Concubine Yang's twist of red).

The peony is also known as 国色 or "the country's true beauty". Qing Shan uses the term in Line 3: 国色岂真尘世有 "Could such an alluring beauty (国色) on earth really exist?" Liu Yu Xi 刘禹锡 of Tang dynasty once wrote:

> Only the peony is the country's true beauty;
> 唯有牡丹真国色
> It shakes up the capital in season of bloom.
> 花开时节动京城

Line 4 is equally romantic and carries the praise a step further. The description of the scent of the peony bloom as "celestial fragrance" 天香, comes from another Tang poem:

Its beauty during the day is sweet as wine;
国色朝酣酒
Its fragrance at night soaks the dress of thine.
天香夜染衣

The peony is therefore also called "celestial fragrance" 天香, which is another metaphor for a beautiful lady. Note that Qing Shan begins his Line 3 with 国色 (beauty) and Line 4 with 天香 (fragrance). These are precisely the same words and order used in the two lines of the foregoing Tang poem. Qing Shan's "celestial fragrance" does not soak the dress; instead it "subtly pervades through a lady's hair".

Line 5 praises Ren Shi for her talent as an artist while in Line 6, Qing Shan deprecates his own art (in poetry) as worthless. Line 7 is interesting in that he takes it upon himself to deprecate the local orchid as "too frail and slight" in comparison with Ren Shi's beautiful peony. The ultimate in humility is in Line 8 which says of the orchid as "Undeserving to escort the peony to share the limelight (on stage)".

One could not put it any better than Prof Chan Chiu Ming whose closing remarks in his critique of this poem sums it all up:

"It is so vivid that it's like a poem about 'real' peonies (rather than an exhibition catalogue of peony paintings). It uses flowers to portray the lady and the lady to portray flowers with such remarkable realism that its fragrance soaks through the paper."

Chapter 40

郑珠为刻印
zhèng zhū wéi kè yìn

镌名反体恰相宜，
juān míng fǎn tǐ qià xiāng yí

返老还童亦似之。
fǎn lǎo huán tóng yì sì zhī

七十高龄成十七，
qī shí gāo líng chéng shí qī

年光真有倒流时。
nián guāng zhēn yǒu dào liú shí

For Zheng Zhu — A Seal Engraved

A name and its seal are mirror-like the same,
Just like Old Age and Childhood, you know.
Seventy could indeed be Seventeen again,
4   Even Time could truly reverse its flow.

Paraphrase

L1: A man's name and his seal are mirror-image of each other.
L2: It is just like life; when in Old Age, a man sometimes forgets his age and thinks that he is still the young person he once was and behaves accordingly.
L3: Hence, a man of seventy could easily be "rejuvenated" into a lad of seventeen.
L4: The passage of Time could in a sense reverse its flow.

Background

Summary

This poem was written in 1959 when Father's old friend and Hinghwa (*xīng huà* 兴化) compatriot Zheng Zhu was 70. He was a long-time family friend as he had no family of his own.

Zheng Zhu was about five years older than Father, and the two of them were quite unlike. Zheng Zhu was just about able to read, but we are certain that he would just have been able to understand this poem which is short and simple. The carving of a personal seal for Zheng Zhu would have undoubtedly been arranged by Father. We remember Zheng Zhu well. As children, we all called him Zhū Bo (Uncle Zhu 珠伯).

We remember Zheng Zhu at 70 as a grumpy old man with a somewhat gruff voice. He was hunched over—even when he was much younger, we were told—but was otherwise still able to walk with sprightly steps. Old Zheng Zhu was a bachelor all his life and lived his life fully. His name had become a figure of speech in our family. Our mother would often teach the children the correct posture to stand or sit up straight, administering the warning at the same time, "Or else you will grow up a hunchback like Zhū Bo". Anyone who was well past the threshold of marriageable age and was still not married was referred to in the family as having become a "Zhū Bo". The name "Zhū Bo" was thus used as a figure of speech in the family for a "confirmed bachelor".

Image of Zheng Zhu's seal presented by Qing Shan to him. *"A name and its seal are mirror-like the same, Just like Old Age and Childhood, you know."*

We could imagine Zheng Zhu reading or having the poem explained to him and feeling rather proud of the vindication of his bachelorhood. Despite his age, he had all the vigour of a lad of seventeen. He was never shy to boast of the sexual exploits of his youth.

We are not certain when he first came from China to Malaya. But he had been a family friend in Kampar, Perak well before the

Zheng Zhu 郑珠, a bachelor even at the age of seventy, was an old friend of Qing Shan. *"Seventy could indeed be Seventeen again, Even Time could truly reverse its flow."*

Second World War. We remember him being with our family as we hurriedly left Kampar to take refuge in the rubber plantations in the Langkap area just steps ahead of the advancing Japanese army. Zheng Zhu had no family of his own and he just attached himself to us.

Our family, with Zheng Zhu tagging along, finally settled down in Ipoh when the Japanese had pacified Malaya. Zheng Zhu was given employment by some Hinghwa compatriots who had a successful motor spare parts shop in Ipoh. It was quite a convenient arrangement for Zheng Zhu and his employers. He slept in the shop premises at night and his job was that of the night watchman! Our family continued to maintain social contact with him.

Zheng Zhu Takes a Wife

Some time in Zheng Zhu's life, he decided to take a "wife". He met a lady who was younger than him, i.e., aged 67. We remember her as a small-built lady wearing the traditional Chinese "sam-fu" of silky black trousers and a floral blouse with a dark blue background. She agreed to live with him. Poor Zheng Zhu did not have a place for his matrimonial home. The Hokkien Association was kind enough to offer him the caretaker's quarters rent free and Father helped him to spruce up the place and decorate it as a "bridal chamber". When it was ready, the "young" lady was taken to her new matrimonial home. To her dismay, it turned out to be the caretaker's quarters located in the Association's Hokkien cemetery. She baulked at such a prospect and Zheng Zhu's bachelorhood thus remained intact.

Zheng Zhu Takes a Daughter

At some point in life, even old confirmed bachelors began to see the need for some "real" family ties. Zheng Zhu came to know a family with a teenage daughter, called Huang Gui Fang

黄桂芳 (or Ah Fang for short). At that time (1957), Ah Fang was helping her mother at her drinks and fruit stall parked in front of Perak Motors in Belfield Street in Ipoh where Zhu Bo worked as the night watchman. Zhu Bo often patronized the stall. Having known them for a considerable time, Zhu Bo developed a close rapport with mother and daughter. On account of this, Ah Fang's mother agreed to the "adoption" and Zhu Bo was formally accepted as Ah Fang's adoptive father (谊父). To "formalize" the occasion, a vegetarian lunch was held at the Sam Poh Tong (Ipoh Caves temple). Zhu Bo purchased a gold chain and pendant as presents for his adoptive daughter as token of the adoption. Later, he also bought her a bicycle and a sewing machine, with the hope that Ah Fang will take up sewing.

The "adoption" lunch given by Zhu Bo was held at Sam Poh Tong 三宝洞 (Ipoh Cave Temple) in January 1957. (Left to right) Ah Fong, her mother, Zhu Bo, Qing Shan, Yi Song, Peter.

Zhu Bo died when Ah Fang was 19 or 20. While Zhu Bo was still living, Ah Fang often visited him. When Zhu Bo died in 1970 or 1971 in his mid-seventies, all the funeral arrangements were made by the administration clerk in Perak Motors. Ah Fang did not even know about his death. It was seven days after that the clerk informed Ah Fang who then went to Zhu Bo's grave to make sacrificial offerings and prayers to her adoptive father.

Zhu Bo, the long-time bachelor finally had at least a "daughter" to pay respects to him.

Appreciation

This is a short and mischievous poem of only four lines about Qing Shan's old friend Zheng Zhu. From the title of poem, the occasion must have been when Qing Shan presented Zheng Zhu with a seal. The poem cleverly uses the analogy of a seal being a mirror image of the name it represents. As we grow older, we sometimes forget that we are no longer the young person we once were. Some go much further than that. Old Zheng Zhu used to live up to this fancy by regaling others with stories of the sexual exploits of his bygone years and his final attempt to get married. This poem is remarkably simple in its use of analogy and everyday language with none of the usual allusions from classical literature. It is obviously intended to be read and understood by Zheng Zhu.

Line 3 is a rather simple but skilful play on words. In English, the line "Seventy could indeed be Seventeen" sounds clever enough, but in Chinese it is even better. In Chinese, the figure seventy (70) is written in figures as 七十 *qī shí* "Seven Ten" and seventeen (17) is written as 十七 *shí qī* "Ten Seven". It is perfectly logical for the written expression of figures in the decimal system. When the two digits "Seven Ten" for 70 are reversed, they become "Ten Seven" meaning 17. The poem closes with Line 4 which makes the remarkable observation that "Even Time could truly reverse its flow"!

Chapter 41

chóu yuǎn táng chái hè jiàn zèng
酬远堂侪鹤见赠

niàn zǎi lí qún gǎn suǒ jū
廿载离群感索居，

gù rén jiàn jué bìn máo shū
故人渐觉鬓毛疏。

duō shí bù zuò huán xiāng mèng
多时不作还乡梦，

gé suì fāng chéng bào yǒu shū
4 隔岁方成报友书。

shuò guǒ jǐn cún zhī yǒu jǐ
硕果仅存知有几？

bǎi huā qí fàng fù hé rú
百花齐放复何如？

jù qín wú bǔ měi xīn zhuō
剧秦无补美新拙，

zhī hé líng yún fù zǐ xū
8 只合凌云赋子虚。

To My Compatriot Yuan Tang

    Left my friends to sojourn alone for twenty years past.
    Fewer are my old friends now and my hair's gone sparse.
    To return home is a dream I've long ceased to pursue.
4   A whole year passed, then came this letter from you.
    How many of our gallant friends survived the doom?
    What follows after the "Hundred Flowers Bloom"?
    It's futile to revile the Qin and foolish to praise the Xin;
8   Safer to write fairy tales and fanciful stories about nothing.

Paraphrase

L1: Twenty long years have I left you friends to sojourn abroad alone.
L2: My old friends are getting fewer, just as my hair is getting more sparse.
L3: For a long time now, I have not dreamed of returning home.
L4: It's only after a whole year that I now receive your letter.
L5: I wonder how many of our gallant friends have survived.
L6: Back home, after the "Hundred Flowers" policy, I wonder what will follow next.
L7: It is futile to criticize Qin (the old regime), just as it is foolish to praise Xin (the new regime),

L8: All one can (safely) write about are fairy tales and fanciful things about nothing.

Background

Summary

The poem was written probably not long before August 1959 (see note below on "Dating of this poem"). The poem is a reply to an invitation by Father's childhood friend Lin Yuan Tang 林远堂 who wrote him a poem (now lost) inviting him to return to China for a visit.

Yuan Tang recorded this in his autobiography published in 1974 some 15 years later:

> "After the Liberation [1949], I often thought of elder brother Qing Shan as he had left home [China] for so long. I once composed a poem for him as an invitation, hoping that he would return for a visit. I recall [two] lines of the poem:
>
>> *'In some far corner of the earth, if you should think of your younger brother,*
>> *Across the oceans, how could it be possible that you do not miss elder sister?'*
>
> I am a year younger than him and at that time, he had a sister living in China."
> (解放后，予思晴山兄出门日久，尝以诗代柬，盼他回国观光，记有句云：'天涯倘亦怜予季，海外能无念女嫛？'以予少他一岁，而其姊时在国内也。)

Father's reply in this poem is one of two extant poems that were written for Yuan Tang. The other is the poem in Chapter 31, "酬远堂羊毛婚纪念照题诗". Yuan Tang was born in 1895; hence a year younger than Father. They were childhood friends and grew up together. In Yuan Tang's autobiography written in 1974, he recounted a number of anecdotes about the years when he and Father were growing up together in Putian 莆田. A short episode is described here about the "word games" they played together as teenagers (see Background to poem in Chapter 31 for more about their friendship).

As teenagers, the two bought their first *qin* 琴 (stringed musical instrument) at the same time and visited each other's house to make music. Yuan Tang, Father and one other friend Pin Tuo 频陀 formed a poetry club and often got together to play and compete in word games with poems and couplets. A crowd would gather around them to watch and break into applause from time to time. In his autobiography, Yuan Tang recalled nostalgically the happy memories of their verbal games and lamented that all these came to an end when they finally had to part and each went his own way to work or for further studies.

Father and Yuan Tang kept in touch through correspondence throughout the years of separation. Even after Father died in 1960, Yuan Tang continued to write to Mother and our family until Yuan Tang himself passed away in 1975.

Dating of this Poem

The poem alludes to Mao Zedong's "Hundred Flowers Bloom" campaign which first surfaced in April 1956 with the slogan: "Let a hundred flowers bloom, let a hundred schools contend" (百花齐放，百家争鸣). It was dubbed the "Double Hundred Movement" (双百方针). The objective of the campaign was to encourage a liberal development of the different forms of arts to coexist. It was envisaged that debate and research in fine arts and literature would lead to steps for their healthy development. The fine arts and literary community and those without political affiliations were all jubilant. They thought of it as the first sign of Democracy and began to air their criticism. An overwhelming part of the criticism was directed at the

Communist Party. In mid-May 1957, Mao looked upon these critics as enemies. From mid to end-1957, it is estimated that as many as 550,000 people were labelled as "rightists" and persecuted. Line 4 of the poem: "**A whole year passed, then came this letter from you**" (隔岁方成报友书) refers to a letter sent by Qing Shan's friend, Yuan Tang, that was received only a year later. Yuan Tang's letter could have been written between mid-1957 and early 1958. As Yuan Tang's letter was received a year after, this poem as a reply could have been composed between mid-1958 and early 1959.

However, the poem appeared in the Ipoh newspaper *Jianguo Ribao* (建国日报) together with a poem about a dinner which was held on 19 August 1959, which gives another clue to the date of the poem.

The last time these two good friends saw each other was during the period 1932–1933. Line 1's "Left my friends to sojourn alone for twenty years past" (廿载离群感索居) is therefore only an approximation.

Gujiao Lou 古谯楼 — originally built during the Song dynasty (AD 983) — the iconic city gate of Putian, Qing Shan's native home. His old friend, Yuan Tang 远堂, had in 1957/58 written to him, inviting him to return to Putian for a visit.

Qing Shan's elder sister, Lai Xi 来喜, in Putian. Yuan Tang's "invitation" to Qing Shan in 1957/58 to visit Putian reminded Qing Shan that he still had a sister at home. "Across the oceans, how could it be possible that you do not miss elder sister?"

Appreciation

The poem written probably not long before August 1959 is a response to Qing Shan's childhood friend, Yuan Tang, who had sent him a poem inviting him to return to China. Yuan Tang's poem (now lost) had been sent earlier but Qing Shan only received it a year later.

The disastrous debacle of the "Hundred Flowers" campaign and the subsequent persecution of "rightists" in the second half of 1957 are still fresh in Qing Shan's mind.

The first two lines recount how long he had left China and his friends there to sojourn overseas. He recognizes that the friends left behind are getting fewer in number, just as his hair too is getting sparser. Age has caught up with them all. In Line 3, he confesses he has for some time already given up any dream of ever returning home.

In Line 4, he refers to Yuan Tang's invitation that he has just received—a year late! Qing Shan would have known all about the "Hundred Flowers" campaign. The anti-rightists campaign ended up with thousands of people sacked from their jobs, demoted, sent to re-education labour camps, incarcerated and even killed. This is followed by Mao's disastrous "Great Leap Forward", another campaign for backyard industrialization of China. After receiving Yuan Tang's "invitation" to return, Qing

Shan is concerned about the fate of his friends as he asks in Line 5: "How many of our gallant friends survived the doom?" (硕果仅存知有几?)

In Line 6, Qing Shan makes a direct reference to the "Hundred Flowers" campaign, "What follows after the 'Hundred Flowers Bloom'?" (百花齐放复何如?) He knows the predicament of his childhood friend, Yuan Tang, and all those like him. Qing Shan's empathy with their plight is captured in the last two lines of the poem:

> Line 7: "It's futile to revile the Qin and foolish to praise the Xin;　剧秦无补美新拙
> Line 8: Safer to write fairy tales and about fanciful stories about nothing."　只合凌云赋子虚

In Line 7, "Qin" refers to Qin dynasty (秦) and "Xin" (新) refers to the brief interregnum rule of Wang Mang 王莽 during the long period of the Han dynasty that followed Qin. When Wang Mang 王莽 (a commoner who usurped the Han throne) became Emperor during his interregnum rule, he styled his reign as the Xin (新) dynasty. Yang Xiong 杨雄 (53BC–AD18) wrote a composition "Revile the Qin and Praise the Xin" (剧秦美新) praising Wang Mang's new regime. Some called Yang's composition an act of self-preservation (避祸之作).

Line 8 urges Yuan Tang that if he must write, he should steer clear of politics and write fairy tales and fanciful stories about nothing. The literal meaning of Line 8 is: "You should only write a combination of *líng yún* 凌云 and *zi xū* 子虚. Both are allusions to two compositions by the Han 汉 dynasty writer Sima Xiangru 司马相如. The expression *líng yún* 凌云 literally means "soar into the clouds". Han Wu Emperor of Han dynasty loved the supernatural. It is said that after reading Sima Xiangru's composition "Da Ren Fu" (大人赋) about celestial beings, he was so taken by it that he remarked that reading it "gives the feeling of wanting to soar into the clouds" (缥缥有凌云之志). The expression "soaring into the clouds" (*líng yún*

凌云) thus became a metaphor for "fairy tales" or something far removed from reality. The expression *zi xū* 子虚 used by Qing Shan literally means "Mr Empty". It is from a poem also by Sima Xiangru. The poem narrates a discussion between two gentlemen, a Mr "Empty" ("Zi Xū" 子虚) from the state of Chu 楚 and a Mr "Non-existent" ("Wū Yǒu" 乌有) from the state of Qi 齐. Each was boasting to the other about the achievement of their king during the royal hunt. The language of the poem is beautifully written but the subject serves no purpose and is of no consequence. The expression *zi xū* 子虚 later became a metaphor for "fanciful tales about nothing".

Chapter 42

奉和白成根先生六十感怀二首

其一

大智应当享大年,
不须问舍不求田。
养生只觉心情泰,
到老从无世虑牵。
伉俪情同琴瑟友,
读书孕得子孙贤,
炎方四月如长夏,
一室春风别有天。

To Mr Bai Cheng Gen on His 60th Birthday
Two Verses in Response

Verse 1

    Bountiful wisdom, bountiful years are two of a kind.
    You need no petty land deals to weigh down your mind.
    You care for your health and hence you're happy,
4   Living to a ripe old age, with never a cause for worry.
    A loving couple with mutual respect like two good friends,
    Your profound learning nurtures good and upright children.
    The four seasons in Nanyang are like one long Summer;
8   Your household is suffused with the joy of a spring breeze.

Verse 2

    Staff in hand, your sojourn here, continue to freely roam.
    In Nanyang we've never known the sadness of Autumn.
    In the homeland, a turning point in battle we don't yet see.
4   Why not swap the homeland for your new home overseas?
    The "New Elite" who rule are mostly a murderous mob.
    The once-Noble are driven to penury, an unfortunate lot.
    Fortunate are we who remain in this our Utopia,
8   Able to enjoy a carefree life of peace in Shangri-la.

其二

策杖他乡任畅游,

南天草木不知秋。

中原久未闻三户,

海外何妨更九州。

新贵尽多屠狗辈,

故家时见卖瓜侯,

卜居幸在桃源里,

尚有桃林可放牛。

Paraphrase

Verse 1

L1: A person blessed with bountiful wisdom should equally enjoy bountiful years (longevity).
L2: There's no need for such a person to preoccupy himself with real estate deals (a metaphor for indulging in petty personal gain instead of possessing a wider vista on significant issues).
L3: He who takes care of his health well will have peace of mind.
L4: Living to a ripe old age, he will not be burdened by worries.
L5: Husband and wife are loving and like two good friends.
L6: You love reading and your learning will cultivate children and grandchildren of good character and achievement.
L7: In Nanyang, all four seasons are like one long Summer,
L8: Your entire household is filled with familial joy, like a gust of the soothing wind of Spring breezing through.

Verse 2

L1: With staff in hand, continue your sojourn here, free to roam about.
L2: In the Southern Land (Nanyang), we never know the misery of Autumn.
L3: In the Central Plain (mainland China), we've yet to see a turning point in the battle (counterattack).
L4: Why not swap the homeland for [your new home] overseas?
L5: The "New Elite" who rule are mostly a murderous mob;
L6: At home, the one-time Noble are driven to penury.
L7: Fortunate are we who remain in this our Utopia,
L8: Able to enjoy a carefree life of peace in Shangri-la.

Background

Bai Cheng Gen (白成根 Peh Seng Koon) was born in 1900 and about six years younger than Father. This poem was written in the Summer of 1959 in celebration of his 60th birthday (by the Chinese method of reckoning age). He came from Anxi 安溪, Fujian as a young man. After working for Tan Kah Kee 陈嘉庚 in Singapore, and various parts of Malaya, he finally settled down in Ipoh and opened his own business in 1934. From there on, he prospered as a rubber merchant and rubber estate owner.

Mr Bai became the President of the Perak Hokkien Association immediately after the Second World War and Qing Shan was employed by the Association as its paid Secretary in October 1945 until his death in 1960. Mr Bai was also a man of some learning and loved and enjoyed writing classical poems. Though he was Father's "boss", the two became very good friends sharing a common love for poetry. Mr Bai frequently consulted Father on the poems he wrote. Their close relationship can be seen in the 72-line poem in Chapter 42, written on the same occasion when Father presented him with a set of books, *Complete Works of Lu You*, as a 60th birthday present. Lu You was Mr Bai's favourite poet.

Appreciation

This poem of two verses and sixteen lines is rich in allusions, as it would be for someone like Bai Cheng Gen who is a keen poet himself. As the title suggests, Qing Shan's poem is, in fact, "in response" to a poem Cheng Gen had sent out inviting his friends to write.

Verse 1

The first verse expresses the usual nice things about a person who has attained this age and achieved success in life. He should rightly sit back and enjoy the rewards of family life, peace of mind, free from worldly worries. As he has attained the age of sixty, he can be said to have enjoyed "bountiful years" which would have accumulated for him "bountiful wisdom". This alludes to a quote from Zhuangzi's Chapter 1, "Wandering in Absolute Freedom" (庄子·逍遥游). Zhuangzi 庄子 said, "Little learning does not measure up to great learning; a short life does not measure up to a long life." (小知不及大知，小年不及大年). Zhuangzi explained that the fungi that sprout in the morning and die before evening do not know the alternation of night and day; cicadas do not know the alternation of spring and autumn (as they do not live beyond autumn). Qing Shan has reasoned from here that Cheng Gen's bountiful wisdom or knowledge comes from his bountiful years of sixty!

Line 2 of Verse 1 contains an enigmatic reference to "petty land deals". The actual Chinese text 问舍求田 literally means "asking about houses and seeking land to buy". This strange phrase is a metaphor meaning "to be preoccupied with activities which materially profit oneself instead of bigger ambitions like caring about national issues". The allusion is from a story in *Annals of The Three Kingdom* (《三国志》·魏志·陈登传) about Liu Bei 刘备, the king of the state of Shu 蜀. While he was in Jingzhou 荆州, he spent all his time inquiring about real estate prices with a view of making some money from land deals for himself. He did this instead of devoting his energy to solving the political turmoil that had dismembered the country into three states. Liu Bei was severely rebuked by someone by the name of Chen Deng 陈登 for "asking about houses and seeking land to buy". Line 2 says that Mr Bai is not one who does that. In fact, Mr Bai is a "Justice of Peace" and a community leader.

Verse 2

Line 1 of Verse 2 provides the springboard to its theme. It says, "Staff in hand, your sojourn here, continue to freely roam 策

杖他乡任畅游". (In ancient times, a staff was used by all travellers, not just the old or infirm.) The theme of Verse 2 alludes to the then terrible political condition in mainland China, the homeland he had left behind. It is a scathing commentary on the turbulent political conditions throughout the 1950s under the Communists who came into power in 1949. It was a time of destruction of the landlord class, persecution of the intelligentsia whose ideology was not deemed politically correct and the elimination of potential threats to the new leadership, including the former comrades-in-arm who had brought the Communists to power.

Line 3 says there is no sign of any likely change of regime in China: "In the homeland, a turning point in battle we don't yet see 中原久未闻三户". The name San Hu 三户 is used in the Chinese text as a metaphor for "turning point" or a "decisive battle". It is the name of a ford called San Hu Ford 三户津 where Xiangyu 项羽 accepted the surrender of the Qin 秦 general, leading eventually to the demise of the Qin dynasty. This allusion is also from *shiji* 史记 "The Historian's Record".

Line 4 encourages Mr Bai to give up any idea of returning to China. It reasons: "Why not swap the homeland for your new home overseas 海外何妨更九州". (The term *jiu zhou* 九州 means China. Ancient China was divided into nine administrative units.) We have not seen Mr Bai's original poem to which this poem is a response. We can surmise, however, that Mr Bai's theme would have been typically about the nostalgia for the homeland, as we can see from Qing Shan's "reply". Lines 5 and 6 paint even a darker picture to convince him why he should not return:

Line 5: "The 'New Elite' who rule are mostly a murderous mob. 新贵尽多屠狗辈
Line 6: The once-Noble are driven to penury, an unfortunate lot." 故家时见卖瓜侯

Line 6's reference to "the once-Noble" is expressed in the original Chinese text as "the melon seller nobleman" 卖瓜侯. Under the new regime in China, the fate and fortune of people are uncertain. Even those who used to have wealth or held respected positions in society are now driven to poverty. The allusion comes from the story of a nobleman Zhao Ping 召平 who had fought to topple the Qin 秦 dynasty, thus bringing about the Han 汉 dynasty. To avert the risk of being seen as a threat to the new Han Emperor, he refused the invitation to assume office and chose to retire as a commoner to cultivate melons for sale at a patch east of the capital, Chang'an 长安.

The poem closes with Lines 7 and 8 to express their common "fortune" in being able to stay overseas in a country which, by comparison, is like Shangri-la. The Chinese personification of such a place is Taohua Yuan 桃花源 or "Peach Blossom Spring". In the parable written by Tao Yuanming 陶渊明, it is a place of peace and tranquility where people live comfortably and happily. The ancestors of the residents in Taohua Yuan were supposedly refugees from the cruel and tyrannical rule of Qin Shi Huang 秦始皇.

Line 7: "Fortunate are we who remain in this our Utopia,　　卜居幸在桃源里
Line 8: Able to enjoy a carefree life of peace in Shangri-la."　　尚有桃林可放牛

Chapter 43

既和白成根先生六十感怀
二首复奉放翁全集为寿赋
卅六韵纪之

平生寡交游，
喜与古人友。
每读古人书，
4 古人在左右。
掩卷太息间，
忽惊古人走。
来去何匆匆，
8 我生幸独后。

To Mr Bai Cheng Gen, Presentation of the Complete Works of Lu You as a Birthday Gift

A 36-Rhyme Poem on the Occasions of My Completion of Two Verses to the Rhyme of Mr Bai Cheng Geng's Two Poems on His Sentiments at His 60th Birthday and My Presentation of the Complete Works of Lu You as a Birthday Gift

    All my life, I have but few friends,
    But I love to befriend the ancients.
    Whenever I read what they write,
4 I feel they're on my left and right.
    I close their works and gasp in praise;
    Suddenly I became aware they have left.
    How suddenly they come and leave!
8 I'm glad it's after them that I live.
    The ancients are from us long gone,
    Easily since a thousand years long.
    The writings that we read today,
12 Could they too have read them all?
    To have read a thousand years' writings
    Is like having lived a thousand years.
    This is what I have always said,
16 Many who hear this with me disagreed.

古人距今人，
动辄千年久。
今人所读书，
12 古人尽见否？
多读千年书，
不啻千年寿。
宿昔为此言，
16 闻者多病诟。
方讶嗜好殊，
居然亦有偶。
君身处五都，
20 心不忘二酉。
于诗喜放翁，
琅琅常开口。

断笺与残篇，
24 爱之不释手。
偶而有所作，
亦类剑南叟。
不以藻绘工，
28 弥觉性情厚。
今年甲子周，
感怀见二首。
巴人和阳春，
32 君既不嫌丑。
愿借放翁杯，
更进南山酒。
君但饮其醇，
36 糟粕且莫取。

Why is my interest and the others' so unlike,
　　　Yet here is someone who shares what I like.
　　　Though you live at a most prosperous place,
20　You still have the ancients' writing at heart.
　　　Your favourite poetry is the works of Lu You
　　　His poems trip melodiously from your mouth.
　　　Even the odd and incomplete poems left by him,
24　You find hard to resist and often quote.
　　　When you occasionally write a poem,
　　　The style is like Lu You's works,
　　　They're free of decorations and florid language.
28　Readers feel the sincere emotions all the more.
　　　This year's a full cycle of your Sixtieth Birthday.
　　　I've read your two poems written for the occasion.
　　　My response is but crude lyrics to your elegant tune.
32　As you mind not my crude composition,
　　　I shall be bold enough to borrow Lu You's cup
　　　To wish you Longevity with Nan Shan wine.
　　　Carefully savour the fragrance of the keg,
36　Be careful to avoid taking in the dreg.
　　　Lu You was inspired by Du Fu,
　　　He offered sacrifice at his Cottage.
　　　Lu You's style is from Jiang Xi School;
40　His works bear no trace of its founder.
　　　I conclude that those who are good at learning,
　　　Learn the principles, but discard the rigid rules.
　　　Once the fish is caught, forget the fish-trap.
44　Why treasure still the bamboo basket?
　　　If you follow the style of Lu You,
　　　You will come up with laudable works.
　　　He who enters the innermost of any field of study
48　Will open up the doors and windows to other ideas.
　　　To receive ideas and generate new ones is important;
　　　Guard against falling mechanically into a pattern.
　　　Learning from Lu You in this way,
52　Lu You's works will be immortalized.

放翁学少陵，
草堂供刍狗。
宗派出江西，
40 下笔无黄九。
乃知善学人，
师法不墨守。
得鱼而忘筌，
44 谁复珍竹笱？
君若学放翁，
行当翘一拇。
有如入堂奥，
48 便自开户牖。
能入贵能出，
慎防落窠臼。

如此学放翁，
52 放翁斯不朽。
南渡百余年，
神州蒙尘垢。
哀时诗中客，
56 放翁独耆耇。
虽越杖朝论，
诗胆犹如斗。
素愿有未伸，
60 时作狮子吼。
君健与翁同，
师承征所受。
养生传秘方，
64 得毋发其蔀？

The Song Dynasty was forced to the South,
While China was plundered in the turmoil.
Among the poets who cried out for the country,
56 Lu You was the oldest.
Though he was already more than eighty years old
His poetry expressed his sentiments bold.
His lifelong ambitions unrealized,
60 His cry was nevertheless a Lion's Roar.
Like Lu You, still healthy you are.
Something from your teacher you've inherited,
A recipe on how to live, a secret formula;
64 I wonder whether you can enlighten me.
As for me, I'm accomplished in nothing.
I often fail even in the everyday things I do.
In my handwriting, I am not as good as a scribe,
68 To plough the land, I'm not worth a farmer's wife.
Compared to everyone, I'm nowhere near,
I only console myself that I'm more senior.
But we do have poetry as our literary bond,
72 A relationship that'll remain forever strong.

Paraphrase

L1: All my life, I have but few friends,
L2: But I love to befriend the ancients.
L3: Whenever I read the writings of the ancients,
L4: I feel as though they are by my side.
L5: Often, when I finish reading their scrolls and am still marvelling at their works,
L6: I would suddenly become aware that the ancients have long departed.
L7: How suddenly they come and depart!
L8: Yet I am fortunate enough to live after them.
L9: The ancients are far separated from us,
L10: Easily by a time span of thousand years long.

<pre>
       jiàn zǐ   bǎi wú chéng   shì shì bù   rú   rén
        贱   子   百   无   成，   事   事   不   如   人，
       jū   héng duō zǔ   niǔ   mǎ   chǐ tú   zì   fù
        居   恒   多   诅   忸。   马   齿   徒   自   负。
       dāo bǐ   shū xiǎo lì   wéi zī   wén zì   yuán
        刀   笔   输   小   吏，   惟   兹   文   字   缘，
       chú lí   shū jiàn fù   yǔ   jūn cháng gòng yòu
    68 锄   犁   输   健   妇。   72 与   君   长   共   囿。
</pre>

Bai Cheng Gen 白成根 (also known as Peh Seng Koon) and his wife on his sixtieth birthday (1959). "A loving couple with mutual respect like two good friends, Your profound learning nurtures good and upright children."

L11: The writings that we read today,
L12: I wonder if they too have read them all.
L13: If we can read a thousand years' writings,
L14: We can consider ourselves to have lived a thousand years.
L15: This is what I have always said.
L16: Many who hear this have a serious problem with it.
L17: I have been puzzled by the fact that my interest can be so different from that of others,
L18: And am surprised to find that here is someone who shares what I like.
L19: Even though you live at a most prosperous place (*wu du* 五都),
L20: You still have the ancients' writing at heart.
L21: In poetry, your favourite is the works of Lu You.
L22: His poems often trip melodiously out of your mouth
L23: Even the odd quotes and incomplete poems by him,
L24: You find it hard to put them down.
L25: When you occasionally write a poem,
L26: The style is like Lu You's works.
L27: They place no importance on beautiful style and florid language.
L28: Readers can thus feel the sincere and deep emotions all the more.
L29: This is your Sixtieth Birthday.
L30: I have read your two poems for the occasion that express your sentiments.
L31: I have written two humble compositions in response to your elegant poems.
L32: Since you do not mind my coarse compositions,
L33: I will borrow Lu You's cup to respectfully toast you
L34: And to wish you longevity like Nan Shan.
L35: I hope you can savour its fragrance
L36: And overlook the coarseness of my compositions.
L37: Lu You was inspired by Du Fu,
L38: And had offered his sacrifice at Du Fu's Thatched Hut.

L39: Though Lu You's style originates from the Jiang Xi School of Poetry,
L40: His works do not bear any trace of the works of Huang Tingjian, founder of the school.
L41: So I conclude that those who are good at learning,
L42: Will learn the principles, but are not bound by rigid rules.
L43: He who has caught the fish, will no [longer] hold on to the fishing basket [and be encumbered by it];
L44: And he will no longer treasure the bamboo device.
L45: If you wish to follow the style of Lu You,
L46: I believe you will come up with laudable works.
L47: It's like someone who has gone sufficiently into great depth (in the study of poetry),
L48: Will know how to open up to other ideas (*hu you* 户牖 meaning "doors and windows").
L49: The most important is to be able to receive ideas to generate new ones.
L50: Guard against falling mechanically into a set pattern.
L51: Learning from Lu You in this way,
L52: Will help immortalize Lu You's works.
L53: The Song Dynasty had been forced to cross the River to settle in the South,
L54: While China was plundered in the turmoil.
L55: Among the poets who lamented at that time,
L56: Lu You was the oldest.
L57: Though he was already more than eighty years old (zhang chao 杖朝)
L58: He was bold when it comes to expressing his sentiments in poetry.
L59: His lifelong ambitions unrealized,
L60: His cry was like a Lion's Roar.
L61: You are still healthy, like Lu You was.
L62: Your teacher must have passed down some invaluable teachings,
L63: Such as a secret formula for maintaining a long life.
L64: I wonder whether you can enlighten me.

L65: As for me, I'm accomplished in nothing.
L66: I often fail even in the everyday things I do.
L67: When it comes to handwriting, I am not as good as a scribe,
L68: To plough the land, I'm not worthy even of a farmer's wife.
L69: I just can't compare with anyone in anything.
L70: I can only console myself that I am senior in age,
L71: And I do have a love for poetry and share a common bond with you,
L72: To recite verses together with you for all time.

Background

This is the second of two poems composed in 1959 for the 60th birthday of Bai Cheng Gen (白成根 Peh Seng Koon). The first poem is in Chapter 42. Bai Cheng Gen was born in 1900 and about six years younger than Father. He and Father were good poetry friends and enjoyed a very close and special relationship with each other. This can be seen from the two poems Father wrote for him.

Bai Cheng Gen was a successful businessman and at the same time a poet. In the first poem (Chapter 42), Father attributed Cheng Gen's longevity to his "bountiful wisdom" and his civic spirit instead of being just narrowly interested in working for private gain. Father went on to suggest that he should stay on happily in Nanyang instead of returning to the political turmoil in mainland China of the 1950s and 1960s. Such sentiments show the rapport they enjoy with each other.

After the first poem, Father then bought him the gift of a set of books, *The Complete Works of Lu You*, a favourite poet of Cheng Gen. This was a set of books that Father would probably have liked to keep for himself. This poem is composed as a very special 60th birthday gift. Parts of the poem even reads like a lesson on the background and style of the Southern

Song 南宋 poet Lu You 陆游 (1125–1210). More importantly, it has encouraging words on Cheng Gen's own compositions and a lesson on how to learn from the masters of poetry. The poem demonstrates even more convincingly how close their relationship was.

For further details of Bai Cheng Gen's personal background, please see the Background section of Chapter 42.

Appreciation

This rather lengthy poem of 72 lines can be broadly divided into five sections comprising:

> Section 1: Qing Shan's love of the classics
> Section 2: Bai Cheng Gen's favourite poet, Lu You
> Section 3: Apply, and not Imitate
> Section 4: Recipe for longevity
> Section 5: The literary bond between them

Section 1 (Lines 1–18) describes how close Qing Shan feels to these ancient writers who had lived such a long time ago. It is a very personal and real experience for him. The writers, of course, would not have even known of his existence and yet, as he reads their works, he feels their presence beside him (Lines 3–4):

> Line 3: "Whenever I read what they write, 每读古人书
> Line 4: I feel they're on my left and right." 古人在左右

Moreover, when he has finished reading and closes the book to gasp and marvel at their work, he feels as though they have completed their watch over him and are suddenly gone. This must be a surreal feeling. Qing Shan muses, wondering whether the ancients themselves have read all the classics that are available to us today. In a similar way, as we read Qing Shan's works today, we too have a surrealistic sense of his presence. The Chinese have a very apt expression to describe just such a feeling, "Reading his works is like meeting the man" (读其文如看其人).

So much does Qing Shan love the classics that he equates the reading of a thousand years' writings with having lived a thousand years. He is fully aware that many will disagree with him, but takes consolation in finding someone like Bai Cheng Gen who shares and understands his love of reading: "Yet here is someone who shares what I like" (Line 18).

Section 2 (Lines 19–36) praises Bai Cheng Gen for his great love for the classics and the writing and enjoyment of poetry. This is despite his living in a busy prosperous environment of a city, in the business world, filled with distractions. It is unlike the conducive environment of a learned recluse who lives in seclusion in the wilderness. Cheng Gen loves the poetry and style of Lu You. So familiar is he with Lu You's poems that "His poems trip melodiously from your mouth" (Line 22). Cheng Gen has written two verses for his own 60th birthday. Like a good teacher, Qing Shan offers encouraging words, describing Cheng Gen's compositions as "free of decorations and florid language" that help the "Readers feel the sincere emotions all the more" (Lines 27–28). On the other hand, Qing Shan declares this poem, his own composition, is "crude lyrics" responding to Cheng Gen's "elegant tune" (Line 31). Invoking the name of Lu You, Qing Shan then toasts to Cheng Gen's longevity and with "Nan Shan" wine. There is actually no such thing as "Nan Shan" wine. It merely means birthday wine. The term "Nan Shan" is borrowed from the popular birthday greeting "Shou Bi Nan Shan" (寿比南山), meaning "May your longevity be the length of Nan Shan", which is a long chain of mountain range in China. Having invited Cheng Gen to drink this "Nan Shan" wine (Lines 33–34), Qing Shan advises him to:

Line 35: "Carefully savour the fragrance of the keg,
 君但饮其醇

Line 36: Be careful to avoid taking in the dreg."
　　糟粕且莫取

Qing Shan continues with his line of humility by describing his own composition as being coarse as the dreg of a wine keg. The ground is laid here for Qing Shan's next piece of advice in Section 3 hinting to Cheng Gen not to imitate everything of others.

Section 3 (Lines 37–52) gives the advice that one should "apply and not imitate". Qing Shan uses Lu You as an illustration, Lu You's style in poetry is from the Jiang Xi School (江西诗派), a literary style popular during the Northern Song dynasty. Yet Lu You's works bear no trace of the works of its founder, Huang Jiu (黄九), also known as Huang Ting Jian 黄庭坚 (Lines 39–40). Qing Shan uses this to make the point that to follow a certain style does not mean to imitate. He comes to the conclusion (in Lines 41–44):

Line 41: "I conclude that those who are good at learning,
　　　　乃知善学人，
Line 42: Learn the principles, but discard the rigid rules.
　　　　师法不墨守。
Line 43: Once the fish is caught, forget the fish-trap.
　　　　得鱼而忘筌，
Line 44: Why treasure still the bamboo basket?"
　　　　谁复珍竹笱？

This whole lesson is from Zhuangzi who said: *"The purpose of a fish-trap is to catch fish, but when we have caught the fish, we can forget about the fish-trap… Language is used to express thoughts, but when we have expressed the thought, we can often forget about the words…"* ……筌者所以在鱼，得鱼而忘筌……言者所以在意，得意而忘言。(Zhuangzi, Chapter 26, External Things 《庄子·杂篇·外物第二十六》)

Zhuangzi is saying that words are a means to an end, viz., to convey thoughts. Hence, it is the thought or our feelings and not the words that deserve the focus of our attention. When applying this principle to composition in poetry, the clue can be found in Lu You's self-styled sobriquet Fang Weng 放翁 ("The Old Man who does not stand on ceremonies"). In the composition of poetry, Qing Shan's advice to Cheng Geng is to "follow the style of Lu You" 如此学放翁 (Line 51) and "guard against falling mechanically into a pattern" *shen fang luo ke jiu* 慎防落窠臼 (Line 50). In other words, "substance" or in the case of poetry, heart-felt feelings are more important than "form", i.e., any rigid rules of poetry.

The theme of Section 4 (Lines 53–64) is about the recipe for longevity. It touches on a period of foreign invasion of China during the second half of the Song dynasty (known as Southern Song). Lu You was among the poets who cried out for the country. He was already 80 at that time, yet his laments and cries were like a "Lion's Roar". Cheng Gen has now reached 60 and is compared to a disciple of Lu You. Qing Shan uses this opportunity to say that he must have inherited from his master, Lu You, some secret recipe for longevity and teasingly asked if he might share the recipe with him. Although Qing Shan was six years older than Cheng Gen, perhaps he would really have liked to live till 80, as Lu You did.

Section 5 (Lines 65–72) is an expression of the literary bond between Qing Shan and Cheng Gen. It begins with the usual self-deprecation. Qing Shan, a poor scholar-teacher, is in some respects not comparable with Cheng Gen the successful businessman. Qing Shan's only claim to superiority is his seniority in age. Putting all those differences aside, the poem concludes with the one important common bond between them (Lines 71–72):

Line 71: "But we do have poetry as our literary bond,
惟兹文字缘
Line 72: A relationship that'll remain forever strong."
与君长共囿

Chapter 44

呈王世昭教授三绝并序

往日读王世昭教授所著《屈原创作集》,恨不识其人,今春教授偕寄女许涵清女士南来作书画展,得见之于霹雳女中,承出示囊中古砚,云系阿房故物,许女士尤擅丹青,故并及之。

其一

书有右军诗右丞,

独承衣钵薄簪缨。

天公更欲全三绝,

故遣飞琼下太清。

Presenting Three Verses to Professor Wang Shi Zhao

I have in the past read Professor Wang Shi Zhao's dissertation "Qu Yuan". It has been my great regret that I had not been able to meet him. This Spring, Prof Wang brought his adoptive daughter, Ms Xu Han Qing, to Nanyang for a series of calligraphy and art exhibitions. I had the privilege to meet him at the Perak Girls' Middle School, where he brought out from his case an ancient inkstone said to be a relic from Epang Palace. Ms Xu is accomplished in painting, hence, this poem is also presented to her.

Verse 1

In poetry, a Wang Wei; in calligraphy, a Wang Xi Zhi.
You alone have their legacy and care not for official post.
Heaven decrees your family shall the Three Arts host
And sends the fairy Feiqiong to earth from above.

Verse 2

You've found your own Taoyuan here to remain.
After Lu Lian, who else but you can his place lay claim.
No relic has survived from Epang Palace of Qin
But for the inkstone that has followed you since.

其二

寻得桃源寄此身，
鲁连之后复何人？
阿房宫已无长物，
一瓦随君亦避秦。

其三

目光如炬笔如椽，
好为离骚作郑笺，
莫道鸡林无善贾，
天南争望米家船。

Verse 3

Farsighted your vision, mighty your pen.
To annotate Li Sao, you're a perfect choice.
Your works are enjoyed even in a faraway land
Clamouring to see your work are they in Nanyang.

Paraphrase

Verse 1

L1: In your calligraphy, we have Wang Xi Zhi; in your poetry, we have Wang Wei.
L2: You alone have inherited the true legacy of the masters of these arts, not caring for the official posts.
L3: It is as though Heaven has ordained the preservation of the three arts in your family
L4: And has dispatched the fairy Feiqiong to earth from the celestial home of the gods.

Verse 2

L1: You have found your own Taoyuan (Shangri-la), shelter from tyrannical rule and decided to remain here, your Utopia.
L2: Ever since the upright and selfless official of the State of Qi, Lu Zhong Lian, who else is one like him (but you)?
L3: No relic has survived from Epang Palace of the State of Qin
L4: Except the single piece of inkstone that has followed you in the escape from Qin (tyranny).

Verse 3

L1: Your vision is far and your pen is mighty,
L2: Which is why you are able to annotate Qu Yuan's great work "Li Sao".

L3: Fear not, even in this faraway land (in Nanyang) people know how to enjoy a good poem or painting.
L4: Are they not all clamouring to see your wonderful collection of these.

Background

This is the first of four compositions written for Wang Shi Zhao (1905–1984) during his trip to Singapore and Malaya from December 1959 to around April or May 1960. The other three "Wang Shi Zhao" compositions are two personal poems in Chapters 45 and 46 and an allegorical poem in Chapter 59. All four poems were written during the couple of months Wang Shi Zhao spent in Ipoh. He came to Singapore and Malaya to hold a series of exhibitions of his calligraphy. As calligraphy alone was unlikely to sell, he brought along his adoptive daughter, Xu Han Qing, who was a young Chinese brush painter to exhibit her works alongside.

Father addressed him as Professor Wang Shi Zhao in all the poems probably because of his high regard for him as a scholar. Prof Wang was 54 when he came to Ipoh. According to his biography in an article published in the magazine *Zhuanji Wenxue*《传记文学》 (Vol. 67, Issue No. 2), he was listed as a Presidential Advisor (to the Nationalist Government), calligrapher and poet. He was also a Guomindang (国民党) activist in his younger days pre-1949. He was the author of several books. He eventually settled in Hong Kong where he died.

One of the books he wrote was *Qu Yuan Chuang Zuo Ji*《屈原創作集》published in 1954. It is a "new" and annotated translation of Qu Yuan's famous work, "Li Sao" 离骚, into modern Chinese. This book above all appeared to be the reason for Father's great admiration for him.

For further biographical details of Wang Shi Zhao, please see the Special Section at the end of this Chapter on the "Biography of Wang Shi Zhao" and "The Qing Shan-Wang Shi Zhao Friendship".

Appreciation

As the preface to the poem explains, Qing Shan first met Prof Wang in the Spring of 1960 when he visited the school where Qing Shan was teaching. Prof Wang was accompanied by his adoptive daughter, the artist Xu Han Qing.

Three verses very appropriately deals with Prof Wang's achievement, his integrity and the calligraphy and art exhibition. Verse 1 compares his achievement in calligraphy and poetry with the great calligrapher Wang Xi Zi and the Tang poet Wang Wei. The two models are well chosen because Prof Wang shares their surname. The third of the three traditional arts, viz., painting, is implied with the mention of the fairy Feiqiong coming down to the earth. Feiqiong's surname happens to be Xu which is also the surname of Prof Wang's adoptive daughter Xu Han Qing, the accompanying artist.

Verse 2 praises him as a man of integrity and a patriot. The reference to his refuge in Taoyuan 桃源 (Shangri-la) is an allusion to the Tao Yuanming story of a place hidden from the world, where the people sought refuge from the tyrannical rule of Emperor Qin Shi Huang and lived blissfully in this Utopia. Prof Wang is also compared with Lu Zhong Lian 鲁仲连 of the Warring States era. Lu Lian (in short) had advised the state of Zhao not to bow to the Qin state which was out to conquer the other six states. This is likely to be a reference to Prof Wang's role as a Guomindang activist and his anticommunist ideology. He left mainland China for Hong Kong when the Communists defeated the Nationalists in the civil war in 1949. Prof Wang brought along with him to Malaya a family heirloom in the form of an inkstone said to be a relic from the Qin's reputed Epang Palace which was subsequently destroyed. Lines 3 to 4 of this verse make a reference to it as though he had brought it along in his escape from the state of Qin.

> Line 3: "No relic has survived from Epang Palace of Qin
> 阿房宫已无长物
> Line 4: But for the inskstone that has followed you since."
> 一瓦随君亦避秦

Verse 3 praises him for his scholarship and his work on Qu Yuan's famous work, "Li Sao". It assures him that even in the faraway land in Nanyang, there are many people who appreciate his art and they are all looking forward to seeing them. The allusions used are many, for example, the faraway land is referred to as *jī lín* 鸡林, an ancient distant kingdom. Bai Juyi's compositions were so highly prized that they could be sold to a Minister in that country. The metaphor "the poem has entered Jilin" meant that the poem's reputation has become known far and wide. In Line 4, (the literal translation) "In the south (people) clamour to look out for the Mi family's boat" 天南争望米家船 is another literary allusion. The "Mi" refers to Mi Fu 米芾, the Northern Song calligrapher. He used to sail from place to place on his official duties and brought along with him his works on the boat. The "Mi family's boat" later became a metaphor for the works of Mi Fu 米芾.

Special Section on Wang Shi Zhao

Biography of Wang Shi Zhao 王世昭 (1905–1984)

Family Background

Wang Shi Zhao was a talented Chinese classical literary scholar. He would have been better known in the Chinese literary circles and achieved much more, had he lived in a different era unlike the tumultuous years of the early 1930s and 1940s in mainland China.

As a young man and scholar who loved his country, he had a vision of saving China from corruption within the government and from foreign invasion. For that he spent most of his adulthood fighting against French colonialism, the Japanese invasion and even his own countrymen—the Communists.

Wang Shi Zhao lived a very tempestuous early life, and a good part of it was devoted to political movements, both as an active member of the Qingnian Party (青年党) and a strong sympathizer of the Guomindang (国民党). He was also a gifted Chinese classical scholar, poet, educator and a renowned calligrapher.

It is not surprising that he came from a family with scholarly backgrounds. His grandfather Wang Ren Kan (王仁堪) was a well-known *zhuang yuan* (scholar 状元), topping the Imperial Examinations in 1877 during the reign of Emperor Guangxu (光绪).

Wang Shi Zhao was born in 1905 in Fuzhou 福州, Fujian province. He started his "private-school" (*si shu* 私塾) education at the age of seven and was taught Confucianism and trained in poetry and couplets as well as calligraphy which were all part of the traditional course. This most certainly provided him with a very strong foundation in the Chinese classics.

Political Activist

In 1927, at the age of 22, Wang Shi Zhao travelled to Yunnan province (云南) to work for his cousin who was a high government official. After working there for a few years, he enrolled in Dong Lu University 东陆大学 (which was the predecessor of the famous Yunnan University 云南大学). He studied Chinese literature (which should have been easy for him, as he had already studied it in Fujian). However, the university environment provided him with a new purpose in life: to fight against the Western imperial powers' invasion of China. Shi Zhao was particularly active in the student anti-colonialism movement and contributed to many student publications.

At about the same time, the colonial power France marched troops onto a strip of land near the China-Burmese border called Jiang Xin Po (江心坡). The French were seen to have violated China's sovereignty (historically referred to as the Jiang Xin Po incident). University students all over China organized demonstrations in protest.

Dong Lu University, where Shi Zhao was a student, launched vigorous demonstrations because the event had taken place in Yunnan province. Shi Zhao who was already a political activist took on the leadership, organizing young men and women against France's invasion of China. Demonstrations took place, including an incident where he threw a homemade bomb into the compound of the French Hospital in Kunming (the capital of Yunnan) in order to harass the French. Shi Zhao's unusual leadership and organizational skills were recognized by the then new political party called Qing Nian Party 青年党 who then invited Wang Shi Zhao to join them. This young party's ideology was to reform China to become a truly democratic republic. Being a nationalistic young man and sharing this common ideology, Wang Shi Zhao joined the party without hesitation and was loyal to it throughout the rest of his life. The party later joined hands with the Guomindang 国民党 (the Nationalist Party chaired by Chiang Kai-shek) to fight against the Communists. Thus, Wang Shi Zhao took the side of the Guomindang as a staunch anti-Communist activist.

Teacher and Recruiter

After graduating from Dong Lu University in 1934, Wang Shi Zhao became a high school teacher, teaching in various places in China and overseas. His teaching career extended as far as Dutch Indonesia, French Vietnam and British Hong Kong, where he was either a Chinese teacher or a principal.

Then came the Marco Polo Bridge Incident (卢沟桥事件). The Sino-Japanese war began in 1939 and Wang Shi Zhao threw himself into military service, serving under the South-west branch of the China Nationalist Army fighting against the Japanese. While he was travelling in Southeast Asia, the war began. After hearing the news that China had declared war on Japan, he immediately went into action organizing military officer recruitment from central Thailand, Vietnam, Singapore and Malaya. He successfully recruited 142 overseas Chinese youths and subsequently led them into Guangxi province for officer training. These groups of young people later became officers in the Nationalist Chinese anti-Japanese army (中国抗日救国军), fighting bravely for their motherland.

From Activist to Refugee

In spite of all the heroic acts and personal sacrifices for the motherland during the eight years of the Sino-Japanese war, Wang Shi Zhao was not rewarded in any way. In fact, there was a downside to his personal life when the Communists took over China. As a known anti-Communist activist, Wang Shi Zhao had to escape the Communist regime. Facing various dangers, like walking through the hills and jungle on foot via the most difficult terrain, he finally reached Hong Kong. He was penniless and separated from his children and later his wife left him.

When the Communists took over China, thousands of refugees fled the country, and cramped into the small island of Hong Kong. There were no jobs, no decent places to sleep. Wang Shi Zhao managed to find a shanty hut and that became his residence for some time.

Scholar, Writer, Author

He lived on a very meagre income earned from writing from morning till night for newspaper and magazine columns. Gradually, he gained recognition for his poetry and calligraphy. In 1954, he published *Qu Yuan Chuang Zuo Ji*《屈原創作集》, a "new" and annotated translation and exposition of Qu Yuan's

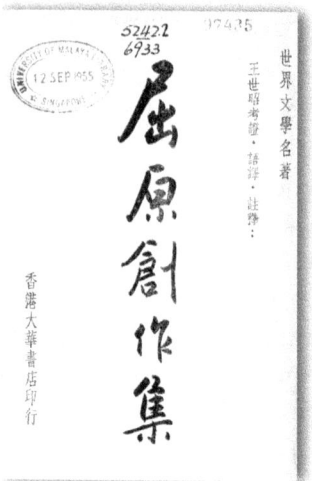

The title page of *Qu Yuan Chuang Zuo Ji* 《屈原創作集》 published in 1954, including an annotated translation of Qu Yuan's famous work "Li Sao" 离骚 into modern Chinese. Qing Shan held Wang Shi Zhao in high esteem after reading this work.

works, including "Li Sao" 离骚. (It was notably through the reading of this book that Qing Shan had such a high respect for him.) Three years later in 1957, he published *Qu Yuan Zhuan* 《屈原传》 on the life and writings of Qu Yuan.

Exhibition Tour of Southeast Asia

In the 1950s and 1960s, many artists and calligraphers in Hong Kong like Wang Shi Zhao would take every opportunity to hold exhibitions in Southeast Asia where there was a large overseas Chinese population. It was a quick and easy way for them to earn extra money. Many of them were able to sell their works and at the same time, received support from the clan associations who often helped with free accommodation and use of their premises for the exhibitions. Wang Shi Zhao was a writer, poet and calligrapher but not a painter. He came with his goddaughter, Xu Han Qing 许涵清, a talented 17-year-old Chinese brush painting artist. They held exhibitions combining his calligraphy and her paintings in 1959/1960 in Singapore, Kuala Lumpur, Ipoh, Penang, Sarawak and Kuching. The exhibitions were highly successful.

He was in his mid-fifties when he visited Ipoh in 1960. He was short and stocky but was obviously a tough and confident man. His distinctive feature was a harsh thick moustache and he even gave himself the sobriquet "Iron-moustache" (鉄鬚). His works are often signed "Iron-moustache Wang Shi Zhao" (鉄鬚王世昭).

A Lonely Conclusion

Wang Shi Zhao did not live an easy life. After escaping the Communists, he settled in Hong Kong. In the last 30 years of his life there, apart from writing for magazines and publishing books on Chinese literature, he managed to publish his travel journals on his exhibition tour of Southeast Asia, *Nan You San Ji* 《南游散记》. His personal life was not a happy one either. His children were not with him. His wife had left him. He was caught in the turmoil of the internal disharmony of his own party, the Qing Nian Party to which he was so dedicated. His only joy seems to have been the contact with his literary friends from the poetry circle like the encounter and exchange of poems with Qing Shan in Ipoh.

He died in Hong Kong 1984 at the age of 79. He passed away quietly and probably a lonely man, without his wife and children by his side.

Chen Qing Shan-Wang Shi Zhao Friendship

*"When poetry friends meet,
their only regret is not having met earlier."*
诗逢知交，相见恨晚

Wang Shi Zhao 王世昭 visited Southeast Asia and was in Singapore-Malaya from December 1959 till around April/May 1960. The purpose was to hold a series of exhibitions and sale of his calligraphy. He was in Ipoh, accompanied by his god-daughter Ms Xu Han Qing 许涵清, a Chinese painter-artist. This was when he and Qing Shan first met.

As Secretary of the Perak Hokkien Association (霹雳福建公会) in Ipoh, Qing Shan made all the arrangements for the exhibition. Since Wang Shi Zhao was a native of Fujian province, the Association gave him every moral and material support for his exhibition and sale of his works in Ipoh. Moreover, the President of the Association at that time, Bai Cheng Gen 白成根 also happened to be a poetry lover.

Both Qing Shan and Bai Cheng Gen worked diligently to introduce Wang Shi Zhao to local business leaders and to the local media, made arrangements for him to give speeches in various Ipoh schools, arranged his accommodation and even saw to it that the rental fee for the exhibition hall was waived. (The poem "Presenting Three Verses to Prof Wang Shi Zhao" 呈王世昭教授三绝并序 in this book refers to his visit to the Perak Girls' Middle School where Qing Shan was then teaching.)

Both being poets, Qing Shan and Wang seemed to have been particularly thrilled and intellectually stimulated at meeting each other. This is evident from the number of poems Qing Shan wrote for Wang Shi Zhao. Of all the poems Qing Shan wrote for friends, there were at least four written for Wang Shi Zhao. Typically, Qing Shan would write a poem for a friend to commemorate an occasion. Sometimes, he would write more than one poem for the same person but for different

Wang Shi Zhao was accompanied by his ward, Ms Xu Han Qing 许涵清, a young painter. The photo shows Ms Xu demonstrating her painting. From left (standing) are Bai Cheng Gen and Qing Shan, watching the demonstration. Mr Bai was the President of Perak Hokkien Association where Wang Shi Zhao's calligraphy and painting exhibition was held.

occasions. Wang Shi Zhao is the only person for whom Qing Shan wrote four poems in just about as many weeks when Wang was in Ipoh.

Perhaps this is not surprising as the lives of these two newfound friends were similar in many ways. Both were born into scholar families. From a young age, both were exposed to Chinese classical literature and Confucianism in family private schools (*si shu* 私塾). Both were Nationalists and strongly patriotic. Both were active in political movements against the then corrupt Chinese government. Both had devoted their lives to education and both were poets.

Ipoh, where Qing Shan had lived most of his life, was a small town. There were only a handful of people who could write Chinese classical poems and the Ipoh Chinese Poetry Society (扶风社) had only a small number of members. One could imagine how Qing Shan must have felt to be intellectually isolated in Ipoh without having someone of his calibre with whom to discuss and exchange poems. When Wang Shi Zhao came to Ipoh, Qing Shan could, at least for those few weeks, have a colleague of similar skill and interest to explore his love of poetry. Wang Shi Zhao also seemed to have recognized the quality of Qing Shan's poetry as he specifically mentioned their encounter in his book *Nan You San Ji*《南游散记》. The admiration between the two poets might be aptly described by the Chinese saying: "When poetry friends meet, their only regret is not having met earlier 诗逢知交，相见恨晚".

Qing Shan's four poems written for Wang Shi Zhao are unique and interesting, each having a specific theme. An appreciation of each of those poems is provided at the conclusion of the individual poems.

Chapter 45

诣王世昭教授旅寓问诗

诣王世昭教授旅寓问诗,并偕小女美瑜问画
於许涵清女士,诗以代贽。

学诗学画两无成,
垂老方知海有鲸,
悔把丹青供浪费,
4 枉教瓦缶作雷鸣。
问年欲唤师为妹,
序齿何妨弟赞兄,
艺苑由来无少长,
8 及门各拜一先生。

Visiting Professor Wang Shi Zhao's Lodging for Counsel on Poetry

Accompanied by my daughter Mei Yu to seek the advice of Ms Han Qing on painting, I presented this poem as a gift for our first meeting.

> Poetry or Painting we're accomplished in none.
> In old age do I realize there's an eminent one.
> Precious paints for my daughter have gone to waste.
> 4 Clay tile attempting a thunderous sound is just too base.
> My daughter by age should address her teacher "mei";
> Age alone should not bar a "di" be addressed as "xiong".
> In the realm of the Arts, age has not been the test;
> 8 We've both come, each to seek our own teacher.

Paraphrase

L1: I studied poetry and my daughter painting, but we are accomplished in neither.
L2: Only in my advanced years do I now realize the existence of persons of such eminence in the field.
L3: Regret all the painting material has been wasted on my daughter.
L4: It is pathetic for a piece of clay tile to attempt to emit a sound like thunder.

L5: Going by age, my daughter would have to address her teacher as *mei* (younger sister).

L6: The criterion of age alone should not preclude *di* (younger brother) being addressed as *xiong* (elder brother).

L7: In the realm of the Arts, age is not the criterion.

L8: Hence we, father and daughter, have come, each to seek our respective teacher.

Background

Summary

This is the second of four poems written for Wang Shi Zhao (1905-1984) during his trip to Singapore and Malaya from December 1959 to around April or May 1960. The other three "Wang Shi Zhao" compositions are two personal poems in Chapters 44, 46 and an allegorical poem in Chapter 59. All four poems were written during the couple of months Wang Shi Zhao spent in Ipoh. He came to Singapore and Malaya to hold a series of exhibitions of his calligraphy. As calligraphy alone was unlikely to sell, he brought along his adoptive daughter, Xu Han Qing, who was a young painter to exhibit her works alongside.

Professor Wang was 54 when he came. One of the books he wrote was *Qu Yuan Chuang Zuo Ji* 《屈原創作集》 published in 1954. It is a "new" and annotated translation of Qu Yuan's famous work "Li Sao" 离骚 into modern Chinese. This, above all, appeared to be the reason for Father's great admiration for him.

Father Pays his Respects

As the title suggests, Father went to visit Prof Wang and Han Qing at their lodging during their stay in Ipoh. Father had wanted to meet him personally and must have thought of the idea of asking to be accepted as his pupil as an act of humility and respect. Since there was also Prof Wang's adoptive daughter Han Qing, he could honour her by asking elder sister, Mei Yu, to be accepted as Han Qing's "pupil". Mei Yu just happened to be the member of our family who was the most artistic. This would normally be a preposterous idea since Father was that much older than Prof Wang and Father was himself a noted poet in Ipoh. It was a gesture of utmost humility and respect. Prof Wang must have been somewhat embarrassed and probably did not know how to react.

According to Prof Wang's account of the event in his own book, it was on the third day of his exhibition that Father brought his family along, including Mei Yu to "formally" meet him and Han Qing to be accepted as their "pupils". A group photo was taken of Father, Mother, first Elder Sister Mei Xuan, Elder Sister Mei Yu, Han Qing and Prof Wang. Father then inscribed this poem on the back of the photo in his own handwriting.

Following is an account of the event in Prof Wang's own words:

> " ... *I shall never forget the quality of humility in this friend. I recall that it was on the third day of the exhibition, he brought his wife Wang Yi Song, his two daughters, one was already married and the other not. He said to me, "Mr Wang, I have three requests to ask of you today: first, I have a wedding poem composed for my daughter, can you please write it in your calligraphy as an everlasting memento for her; second, you are a poet and I have already read your compositions. From your work, I can see that you are a man of integrity and principles; now that I have met you, I know you are what your reputation says. Hence I would seek you as my teacher. Please do not refuse this request. Thirdly, my daughter loves to paint, but regrets not having a good teacher. Your daughter, although still young, is already an accomplished artist. My daughter too would like to seek her as teacher. Please do not under any circumstance refuse my three requests!" With that, he brought out a "to seek a teacher" poem*

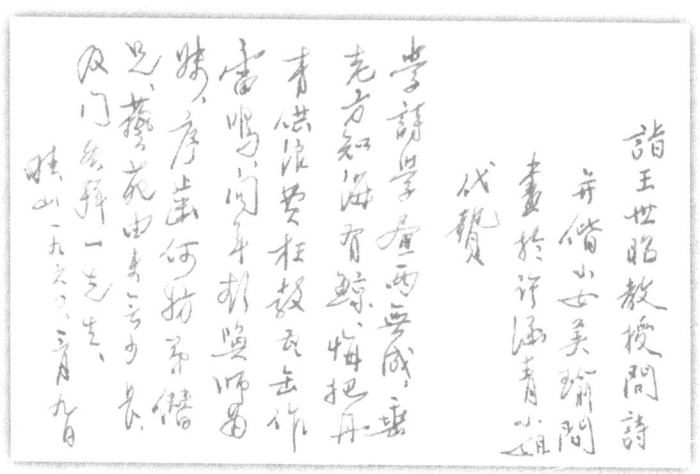

The poem inscribed by Qing Shan in his own handwriting, on the back of a photo taken at Wang Shi Zhao's exhibition, dated 9 March 1960 (see Chapter 46).

[拜师诗一首]. *The request was too great an honour for me to accept. He was an old gentleman of 63 and her daughter was already 21*. But, however strenuously I tried to decline it, he persisted. That evening, he hosted a dinner for us which I accepted as a courteous gesture to symbolize our meeting. This is a most pleasant episode in my Nanyang travels for the painting exhibition and has to be placed on record."* ["Record of Southern Travels", 《南游散记》, page 52–53]

*Note: Prof Wang inadvertently understated the ages of Qing Shan and his daughter (Mei Yu) by about three years in each case. Mei Yu had, in fact, been married two years before. Prof Wang may have been mistaken because of the request to write out the wedding poem which had been composed two years earlier in 1957. Prof Wang did, however, write out the entire poem in his own calligraphy which is still in Mei Yu's possession to this day. (Illustrated in Chapter 46)

For further biographical details of Wang Shi Zhao, please see the special section at the end of Chapter 44 on the "Biography of Wang Shi Zhao" and "Chen Qing Shan-Wang Shi Zhao Friendship".

Appreciation

Qing Shan had great respect for Prof Wang's scholarship, through reading his work on Qu Yuan and his poems. It is possible that he also had a good idea of Prof Wang's background as a Guomindang (国民党) activist in his younger days. When Prof Wang came to Ipoh for his exhibition and visited the school where Qing Shan was teaching, he met the professor for the first time and composed the poem in Chapter 44. This poem was written probably after Qing Shan first paid him a visit at his lodging and subsequently, with Qing Shan's family at the exhibition, as explained in the Background of this chapter.

The entire tone of this poem conveys a sincere respect for Prof Wang and utmost humility. This impressed Prof Wang so much that he wrote about this event in his book, *Record of Southern Travels*《南游散记》. In the first four lines, Qing Shan deprecates himself and his daughter for being accomplished in neither poetry or painting and he had to live to his age to find out there is one so eminent as Prof Wang. In Line 4, he compares himself with a clay tile pathetically attempting to emit a thunderous sound in the presence of Prof Wang.

Verse 2 of the poem is devoted to explaining the reason why, despite Qing Shan being older than Prof Wang, there is nothing wrong in calling him his "teacher". Qing Shan's reason is that in the realm of the Arts, it is not age that should be the criterion, but ability and accomplishment. The same applies to Mei Yu seeking Han Qing as her teacher. Hence, Lines 5-6 say:

Line 5: "My daughter by age should address her teacher 'mei',　　问年欲唤师为妹
Line 6: Age alone should not bar a 'di' being addressed as 'xiong'." 序齿何妨弟赞兄

(*mei* 妹: younger sister, *di* 弟: younger brother, *xiong* 兄: elder brother)

Chapter 46

送王世昭教授赴槟

其一

太空为国地为家，
大块文章尽物华。
南岭开残还北岭，
东篱秋后岂无花。

其二

巨浪排空等浊醪，
休从人海挽狂涛。
临行且尽杯中物，
纵未回天气亦豪。

For Professor Wang Shi Zhao on His Departure to Penang

Verse 1

Broad as Space your aspiration, the World is your hearth.
The beautiful blooms of your works blanket the earth.
The season ends in the south, afresh they bloom up north.
After the Autumn chrysanthemums, will no more come forth?

Verse 2

Upheavals surge like waves, as wine sloshing in a cup.
Follow not others attempting to hold the tide back.
Before you leave, let's drain the cup to bid goodbye.
Nonetheless, your heroic spirit amply fills the sky.

Paraphrase

Verse 1

- L1: Your aspiration and interest are so broad that the entire Space's your terrain, the world's your home.
- L2: The depth and beauty of your literary works blanket the entire world (i.e., are renowned).

L3: Your works having been exhibited in the south (in Ipoh), will now move to the north (in Penang).
L4: After the chrysanthemums of Autumn have bloomed, there will surely be more chrysanthemums to enjoy.

Verse 2

L1: The tumultuous events erupt once more like huge waves surging up into the sky.
L2: Do not follow the multitudes in attempting to stem back the roaring waves.
L3: Upon your departure, let me drink to you by draining this cup.
L4: Even if you're not able to save the day, your heroic bearing and spirit amply fill the sky.

Background

This is the third of four poems written for Wang Shi Zhao (1905–1984) during his trip to Singapore and Malaya from December 1959 to about April or May 1960. The draft of the poem in this Chapter, in Father's own handwriting was discovered only in 2005, among the papers of our uncle, Wang Guang Guo who had passed away in 1971.

For further biographical details of Wang Shi Zhao, please see the special section at the end of Chapter 44 which contains the "Biography of Wang Shi Zhao" and "Chen Qing Shan-Wang Shi Zhao Friendship".

After visiting Ipoh, he travelled north from Ipoh to Penang and hence, the title of this poem. Penang is known in Chinese as 檳城.

Appreciation

The third of four poems composed for Wang Shi Zhao, is a

Qing Shan's family visited Wang Shi Zhao's exhibition. From left to right: Qing Shan, his wife Yi Song 义宋, Wang Shi Zhao's ward Ms Xu Han Qing, Qing Shan's two daughters Mei Xuan 美璇 and Mei Yu 美瑜, Wang Shi Zhao. The visit was the inspiration behind Qing Shan's poem in this Chapter. So moved was Wang Shi Zhao by Qing Shan's visit that he wrote in his own book, *"I shall never forget the quality of humility in this friend..."*

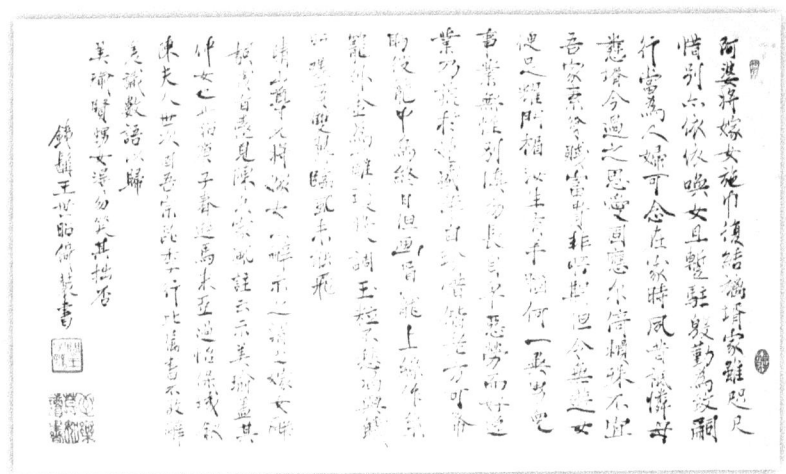

Qing Shan had, two years earlier, composed a poem, "Wedding Poem" for his daughter Mei Yu 美瑜. Qing Shan presented a copy of the poem to Wang Shi Zhao and as a further sign of respect, requested him to write it in his calligraphy for Mei Yu as a treasured memento.

farewell message to Prof Wang as he leaves Ipoh to head north to Penang in March or April 1960, on the completion of a successful exhibition of his calligraphy and the paintings of his adoptive daughter.

Verse 1 Lines 1–2 praise Wang Shi Zhao's broad and lofty aspirations for China and his rich and beautiful literary writings. Line 3: "The season ends in the south, afresh they bloom up north" refers to Wang's exhibition having been completed in Ipoh which is south of Penang where it will be reopened. It is in Line 4 that Qing Shan shows his skill in the use of allusions. The literal translation of Line 4 is: "The Autumnal chrysanthemums in the eastern hedge (东篱秋), after they have bloomed (后), is there no more flowers (岂无花) to enjoy?"

This is a reference to the Jin dynasty poet Tao Yuanming who loved to enjoy and pluck his chrysanthemums growing at the eastern hedge of his garden, as he admired the view of the southern hills. The original quote that inspires Line 4 is from Tao Yuanming's poem "Drinking Wine", Verse 5 《饮酒》(其五). The lines read:

"Plucking chrysanthemums at my eastern hedge,
采菊东篱下
I gaze leisurely at the southern hills beyond."
悠然见南山

If Wang Shi Zhao is positioned in Penang and he looks south, that will be where Ipoh is, located in a valley surrounded by hills. Qing Shan's Verse 1 Line 4 seems to ask will there be no more chrysanthemums after their autumn bloom? Chrysanthemum flowers are made into wine after their autumn blooms. The implicit answer to this rhetorical question is yes, there will be. It is an invitation to Wang Shi Zhao to come south, meet and to drink together again.

Verse 2 is a lot more philosophical. The political upheavals in China of the late 1950s (collectivisation and the "Hundred Flowers" campaign) in China are still fresh in Qing Shan's mind. Wang Shi Zhao had, as a young man, been a Guomindang political activist imbued with high ideals and aspirations in the fight against the invasion of China by foreign colonial powers and internally against the Communists. With the Communist victory in China in 1949, he was reduced to the status of a refugee in Hong Kong eking out a living as a writer and later calligrapher. This poem, written about March 1960, is composed very late in Qing Shan's own life; Qing Shan died in June the same year.

Verse 2 Line 1 describes the political upheavals that surge high into the sky like tidal waves. The second part of this line suggests that these should no longer be Prof Wang's whole purpose in life; he should just look upon these upheavals as no more than wine being sloshed about in the cup as it is being poured. Line 2's "Follow not others attempting to hold the tide back." makes this clearer as it advises him not to continue to fight a battle that can no longer be won. Instead, Line 3 invites him to "drain the cup to bid goodbye". Line 4 finally assures Wang Shi Zhao that although he has failed to achieve his aspiration to bring about a better China, his heroic spirit has already more than abundantly manifested itself: "Nonetheless, your heroic spirit amply fills the sky."

贺梁森元先生与彭士麟校长锡婚纪念

其一

十年人海几沧桑，
花样新翻时世妆，
襟袖依然旧刀尺，
开箱笑检嫁衣裳。

其二

奏记粧台第一枝，
十年窗下画双眉，
风流应笑前人拙，
只解挥毫写五噫。

In Celebration of the "Tin Wedding Anniversary" of Mr Liang and Madam Peng

Verse 1

How the world has changed in just a decade;
Many strange fashions have since appeared.
Yet your taste in clothes remains constant;
You're pleased to find that old wedding dress.

Verse 2

Recalling Zhang's impeachment for loving his wife,
Yet Mr Liang has loved his wife these ten years.
He views Zhang Chang's accusers with disdain.
They had nothing better to do than complain.

Verse 3

The mutual love you planted is thriving brilliant.
Madam Peng is a lady Zhong Ji with multi talents.
You've nurtured the tree of love in these ten years.
She can yet find time to educate others in her career.

其三

连理欣欣手自栽,

仲姬多艺更多才,

十年树木辛勤外,

余事中庭学植槐。

其四

不羡鸳鸯不羡仙,

齐眉争说孟光贤,

家珍此日从头数,

一案相承又十年。

Verse 4

Envy not the Mandarin Ducks nor the Angels above.
Praise you the virtue of mutual respect and love.
Today marks the beginning of your family treasure;
Let the Vow of Love be renewed for another ten years.

Paraphrase

Verse 1

L1: So much has happened and changed in just ten years,
L2: So many new and fancy things have appeared with the times.
L3: But your taste in clothes and fashion remains unchanged.
L4: Opening the old trunk, you're delighted at the sight of the wedding dress.

Verse 2

L1: One is reminded of the story of the impeachment petition against Zhang Chang for helping his wife with her daily make-up.
L2: Yet Mr Liang is determined to emulate Zhang and has never stopped loving and caring for his wife during the last ten years.
L3: Mr Liang is modern-minded and liberal; he will surely scoff at the stuffy people of that bygone generation,
L4: Who had nothing better to do than to use their pens to write petitions for such complaints.

Verse 3

L1: The love between the two of you, planted and nurtured by your own hands, is thriving
L2: You are like the lady Zhong Ji of ancient times who had many talents.

L3: You've diligently nurtured the tree of mutual love in these ten years
L4: And still find time to devote your talent to educating others.

Verse 4

L1: Do not envy the conjugal love of the mandarin ducks or the bliss of the immortals.
L2: Everyone praises the love and respect of the lady Meng Guang for her husband.
L3: These qualities are indeed the starting point of what the family should treasure;
L4: Let the vow be renewed for yet another ten years.

Background

Summary

Peng Shi Lin was the Principal of Perak Middle Girls' School in Ipoh where Father taught Chinese literature to the Junior, Senior Middle and Senior Normal classes in 1957–1960. Peng (a native of Hunan) was married to a Hakka tin miner in Ipoh called Liang Sen Yuan 梁森元 who was prominent in the Ipoh Hakka community which supported the school.

Peng held Father in high esteem and was herself a poet and calligrapher. This poem of four verses was written in March 1960 for her and her husband to celebrate their 10th wedding anniversary. Soon after, Qing Shan heard that the couple were about to travel to Hong Kong, Taiwan and Japan on their "second honeymoon". He then wrote another poem of six verses (in Chapter 48), thus making it a "Perfect Ten".

Appreciation

This is a poem of four verses to celebrate the couple's 10th

Madam Peng Shi Lin 彭士驎 (photo taken in 1951), i.e., Mrs Liang Sen Yuan 梁森元, Principal of Perak Girls' Middle School in Ipoh. Qing Shan taught in the school from January 1957 and stood in for Madam Peng's classes during her overseas vacation with her husband in April/May 1960.

wedding anniversary which is also known as "tin anniversary". As a start, Qing Shan has cleverly included the reference of "ten years" (十年) in each of the four verses. The allusions he uses all have some connection with marriage or the relationship between husband and wife. The central character in the main allusion that symbolizes mutual love and respect between husband and wife (举案齐眉) is a historic figure by the name of Liang Hong 梁鸿. It is no coincidence that Madam Peng's husband, Liang Sen Yuan, and the historic figure have the same surname! The poem is written for someone like Madam Peng who, as a poet herself, would have enjoyed all the metaphors and allusions used. The reference to Madam Peng's taste for the more classic fashion shows her as one who conducts herself with decorum. The reference to Mr Liang's disdain for the sanctimonious detractors of Zhang Chang 张敞 is a very apt reflection of Mr Liang's easy manner and liberal character. The poem therefore shows Qing Shan's personal knowledge of the couple and their mutual friendship.

The metaphors used are taken from the classics and some can be understood even without knowing the allusion or its source. But knowing the story behind the metaphor enhances the enjoyment. The poem has been well organized. Each verse draws allusions from one particular story. Verse 1 draws mainly from a Tang poem titled "A Poor Girl" (贫女). Verse 2 draws from the story of Zhang Chang (张敞传). Verse 3 draws from an assortment of sources and Verse 4 draws from the story of Liang Hong (梁鸿传).

Verse 1:

The allusions in Verse 1 are drawn mainly from a Tang poem titled "A Poor Girl" (贫女).

It is a poem written as the lament of a poor girl. She was a seamstress and remained unmarried. She was virtuous and talented, but plainly dressed and poor. She was obviously not dressed or made up in the latest, albeit "strange" fashion of the day. The sad part of the story is whilst she sewed wedding dresses for a living, she watched her clients with envy and self-regret. The four relevant lines from "A Poor Girl" poem are:

First quote:	谁爱风流高格调	Who would want a girl who's virtuous (but plain)?
Second quote:	共怜时世俭梳妆	All would love her dressed in some fashion strange.
Third quote:	苦恨年年压金线	Painfully I save my money year after year;
Fourth quote:	为他人作嫁衣裳	While I sew for others their wedding gear.

Qing Shan's Line 2: "Many strange fashions have since appeared 花样新翻时世妆" is adapted from the second quote from "A Poor Girl" poem. Qing Shan immediately praises Madam Peng in Line 3: "Your taste in clothes remains (just as) constant 襟袖依然旧刀尺". Qing Shan's Line 4 uses the same phrase "wedding gear (dress)" (嫁衣裳) as in the fourth quote. With this line, he describes how pleased Madam Peng is to see her old wedding dress in the trousseau trunk. This implies she values the quality of "virtue" in a girl (高格调) instead of the prevailing regard then for one who merely dresses in some latest but strange fashion (时世俭梳妆).

Verse 2

The allusions are drawn mainly from the story of Zhang Chang (张敞传). This story is told in the Appreciation of the poem in Chapter 24.

Qing Shan's Line 1 recalls the episode of how Zhang Chang's detractors submitted an impeachment petition (奏记) against him for helping his wife in her daily make-up (粧台). Having set the scene, Line 2 praises Mr Liang for helping his wife Madam Peng to do just that, viz., draw her pair of eyebrows (画双眉) in the ten years of their marriage. Line 3 describes Mr Liang's disdain for Zhang's detractors. Mr Liang, modern-minded and liberal (风流), will surely scoff at (应笑) the stuffy people of the past (前人挫). Line 4 says that such people had nothing better to do than writing petitions with such outmoded ideas as a "Song of Five Sighs" (五噫歌). The story behind this "song" is explained in the story of Liang Hong under the following Verse 4.

Verse 3

The main theme of this verse is to praise Madam Peng for having planted "the tree of mutual love" (连理) and compares her with a lady called Zhong Ji 仲姬 (1262–1319) who lived during the Yuan dynasty. She was truly multi-talented—a calligrapher, painter and poet. Note the use in Line 3 of the expression "ten years" that has been inserted in every verse to remind us of the occasion of the poem.

Line 3 says "You've nurtured the tree of love in these ten years (with exceptional diligence) 十年树人辛勤外". The tree-planting expression comes from the proverb, "Ten years to plant a tree, a Hundred years to 'plant' a man". This is a commonly-used proverb to express the length of time it takes to educate a man and bring him to his full potential. In Qing Shan's line, it is to be taken to mean Madam Peng has nurtured the tree of love for ten years (of their marriage). Line

4 makes full use of the proverb with the reference to Madam Peng being an educationist. In addition to devoting herself to her husband, "She can yet find time to educate others in her career 余事中庭学植槐".

Verse 4

The allusions are drawn mainly from the story of Liang Hong (梁鸿传). Liang Hong of Han dynasty was a clever and upright man. Many families wanted to betroth their daughters to him but he always refused. There was a girl of the Meng 孟 family in his own prefecture who was already 30 years old. She was unattractive, but strong and hardworking and she was determined to marry Liang Hong because he was an upright man. Liang Hong decided to marry her and gave her the name 孟光. The most important and relevant part of this story is that they were loving and courteous to each other all their life.

Their mutual courtesy is legendary and immortalized in the expression, "Raise the platter to eyebrow level" (*jǔ àn qí méi* 举案齐眉). It is an act of utmost respect and courtesy normally practised by a host facing his guest at a meal. It describes the act of raising the cup or platter of food with both hands and holding it up eyebrow level facing each other. The guest will reciprocate likewise. Although they were extremely poor, Liang Hong's wife Meng Guang would serve food to him, as if he was her master or an honoured guest. She would "raise the platter to brow level". This gives rise to another expression *xiāng jìng rú bīn* 相敬如宾 which means "treat each with the same courtesy as you would accord a guest", describing the mutual courtesy husband and wife accord each other.

There is yet another story about Liang Hong and his "Song of Five Sighs" (五噫歌). When he was in the old imperial capital Luoyang, he ascended a hill outside which overlooked the capital. The spectacle in front of him consists of the grand and opulent palaces of royalty and the wealthy. This was in contrast with the poverty and hard life of the general population around. He composed a poem lamenting the hardship of the people. Each line ended with a "sigh" 噫! It became known as the "Song of Five Sighs" (五噫歌). When Liang Hong heard that the emperor got to know about his composition, he was very uneasy and left the area immediately. Hence, "to compose a Song of Five Sighs" has become a metaphor for a farewell poem or a poem people regard as "outmoded or inappropriate for the times". The allusion is used in Line 4 of Verse 2.

Verse 4 is flexible enough to be interpreted as referring to Mr Liang or the couple. Line 4 is perhaps the most attractive verse with general application. In fact, Peter selected this verse with only very minor adaptation to be read at the wedding of one of his sons.

Line 1 is superbly delightful: "Envy not the Mandarin Ducks nor the Angels above 不羨鴛鴦不羨仙". The line in its original form is: "Rather be Mandarin Ducks than to envy the Angels 願作鴛鴦不羨仙". Its origin is in an early Tang poem by *lú zhào lín* 卢照邻 (635 (?)–689 (?)). Qing Shan, in his usual way, gives a new twist to its meaning. In his line, he says that the conjugal love between Mr Liang and Madam Peng surpasses the happiness of both Mandarin Ducks and Angels. He tells the couple, "You need envy neither!"

Line 2 uses the expressions "level of eyebrow 齐眉" and "Meng Guang 孟光" to denote the virtue of mutual respect and love. Line 3 sees this virtue as a family treasure to be cherished and perhaps handed down as an example to children. Line 4 uses "the mutual raising of the platter 一案相承" to symbolize the renewing of the vow for another ten years.

再贺森元先生与士麟校长锡婚之庆

森元先生与士麟校长锡婚之庆,既作"十年"四首贺之,倾闻其将赴香港、台湾、日本度蜜月,复赓六章,以全十美,且壮其行。

其一

日暖风和小洞天,

香江曾记昔游仙,

多应蜜月犹嫌短,

欲补辞书铸蜜年。

Another Six Verses to Wish Mr Liang and Madam Peng Bon Voyage

On the celebration of the "Tin" Wedding Anniversary of Mr Liang Sen Yuan and Principal Shi Lin, I had composed a four-verse poem to congratulate them on their ten years together. I now hear that they are going to Hong Kong, Taiwan and Japan for their "second honeymoon", I add another six complementary verses to make a "Perfect Ten" to wish them *Bon Voyage*.

Verse 1

Japan and Taiwan, endowed with scenery sublime,
Hong Kong was where you once roamed in bliss divine.
Your past honeymoon perhaps ended too soon.
A few more verses to add up to a year of honeymoon.

Verse 2

You'll soon replay the "Three Musketeers" of Tang;
In the Southeast Sea lies the island of Taiwan.
I imagine that's the place where Yi-mei will land;
Welcoming her there, San-lang will be on hand.

其二

新写风尘三侠图,
东南海外访扶余,
悬知一妹停骖处,
定见三郎候鹿车。

其三

过江名士尽风流,
台北台南好唱酬,
十样蛮笺胜珠玉,
诗囊满载盼归舟。

其四

草长江南莺乱飞,
故园桃李正芳菲,

Verse 3

Many literary stalwarts there have crossed the river.
Taipei or Tainan, you will find them a worthy equal.
Their literary works are precious as pearl and jade.
Hope to see their poems in your homecoming boat all laid.

Verse 4

At home, the grass grows and orioles fly without a care.
The peach and plum, their fragrance begins to fill the air.
In Japan, be not bewitched by the cherry bloom,
To forsake and not return to the Spring at home.

Verse 5

Back home, I too have my old wife, a loving lady.
For thirty years she has toiled hard for the family.
Repeatedly I've failed to deliver her that trip abroad.
With helpless sighs I gazed at the misty ocean broad.

Verse 6

I thank my friends for their praise of my composition;
My "Wedding Counsel" poem enjoys now a reputation.
While my vision is still not blurred and my pen still firm
I shall re-grind the old inkstone and write a new poem.

Paraphrase

Verse 1

L1: Japan (日) and Taiwan (小洞天) are indeed beautiful as the abode of the celestial beings; the days are warm (日暖) and the breeze soothing (風和).

东游恐被樱花误，

忍负春风缓缓归。

其五

亦有齐眉老孟光，

卅年苦作嫁衣裳，

负伊多少湖山约，

万顷烟波只望洋。

其六

曾临玉版感新知，

藻镜青垂嫁女辞，

眼未全花笔犹健，

重磨旧墨写新诗。

[Japan is ri ben 日本; the expression used is ri nuan 日暖 meaning warm and is a pun on ri ben. Taiwan is an island; according to Daoism, there are 36 beautiful places which are the home of the gods, including three islands. By analogy, Taiwan, being an island, is implied here to be one of these.]

L2: It was in Hong Kong, I recall, the two of you once roamed carefree like a pair of celestial beings.
[Hong Kong or xiang gang 香港, meaning fragrant harbour, is changed to xiang jiang 香江 meaning fragrant river; the word "river" is more in line with natural scenery.]

L3: Your re-visit is perhaps due to the "honeymoon" being much too brief.

L4: That being so, I wish to compose additional verses to make it up to a year of "honeymoons".

Verse 2

L1: You will soon re-enact the Tang story of the camaraderie of the "Three Musketeers".

L2: In your forthcoming trip, you will be visiting the Kingdom of Fuyu (implicitly Taiwan) [In the story about "The Itinerant Three Musketeers", the hero "Curly-Beard" was rewarded by the Emperor with the Kingdom of Fuyu situated in the southeast of China. By analogy, this refers to Taiwan, as the island is southeast of mainland China].

L3: I envisage where "Yi-mei" the sister (among the Three Musketeers) disembarks,

L4: There will be "San-lang" (the "Curly Beard" hero among the Three Musketeers) there to welcome you husband and wife.

Verse 3

L1: Like the Eastern Jin adventurous (过江) hero "Curly Beard", there are many such persons in Taiwan too.

L2: Whether in Taipei or Tainan, you'll find many who could spar with you in the composition and recitation of poetry.

L3: Their rich and exciting compositions are precious as any pearl or jade.
L4: I hope that you will return, laden with hoards of compositions and poems.

Verse 4

L1: It's beautiful too back home in the south, the grass grows green and the orioles fly hither thither.
L2: In the garden back home (the school), the peach and plum (the students) have begun to fill the air with their fragrance (eagerly awaiting to be taught and taken care of).
L3: In touring Japan, you could perchance inadvertently become mesmerized by the cherry blossoms,
L4: And thus forsake the gentle Spring back home, reluctant even to return!

Verse 5

L1: At home, I too have an old wife respectful and virtuous as Meng Guang.
L2: For thirty long years she has toiled for others, like the legendary poor girl of the poem who sewed for others their wedding gowns.
L3: How many times have I failed to live up to my promise of a vacation abroad with her.
L4: I keep looking across the vast ocean and watch with helpless sighs.

Verse 6

L1: I composed a poem to thank my (old and new) friends for their praise of my composition.
L2: Their praise of my "Wedding Counsel" poem has greatly enhanced its reputation.

L3: While my vision is still good and my hand firm enough to hold the pen,
L4: I shall re-grind the old inkstone and compose more new poems.

Background

Summary

This poem is a sequel to the poem in Chapter 47 which was first composed for Madam Peng and her husband to celebrate their 10th wedding anniversary in 1960. Soon after, Father heard that the couple were about to travel to Hong Kong, Taiwan and Japan on their "second honeymoon". He wrote this six-verse poem in order to make it a "perfect ten" for the couple.

About three months after the composition of this poem, Father was admitted into hospital in late May 1960. He died about a week later on 6 June. Some say that it was overwork during the period while Principal Peng was away and he had to stand in for her literature classes. In her article published in May 2002 in *Nanyang Siang Pau* 南洋商报, she expressed a profound sense of regret over this.

Madam Peng Shi Lin

Madam Peng (1923–2004) was born in Changsha (长沙), Hunan (湖南). Her father was a merchant and it was quite remarkable that he could bring up a daughter so steeped in Chinese literature during the period of turmoil in China of the 1920s and 1930s.

Madam Peng read Chinese Literature in Guangzhou Cultural University (广州文化大学) and met Liang Sen Yuan (梁森元) who was then studying Foreign Relations (外交系). Mr Liang was the son of a tin mining family of Hakka (客家) origin in Ipoh (怡保). After graduation, they did not contact each other. Later, Madam Peng and her sister left China to enter Hong Kong. On account of the turbulent times, the two girls brought along some gold bars for their living expenses. They were closely questioned and detained by the Hong Kong Customs. They were on suspicion of being smugglers. As neither were fluent in Cantonese, no amount of explanation could convince the Customs otherwise. Fortunately, they were able to contact Sen Yuan who came to their rescue. On his personal surety, the two girls were allowed in with no further problem. Their friendship developed from there and they were married in 1950. Madam Peng and Mr Liang Sen Yuan were happily married for 54 years and they brought up four sons and a girl.

Not long after her arrival in Ipoh, Madam Peng started her teaching career in the Perak Girls' Middle School which was sponsored by the Hakka community in Ipoh. Three years later in 1954, the then 31-year-old Madam Peng was appointed Principal of the school. She was the very model of a school principal and perhaps also a role model for women. She kept her hair short, never painted her nails and the slits of her "cheongsam" (旗袍) were of proper length. She held the position of Principal until her retirement in October 1978.

After her retirement, she was active in the local literary circle and was the President of the Ipoh Fufeng Poetry Society (怡保扶风诗社), among other activities. She devoted her time to reading, painting, calligraphy and writing. She published a series of handy-sized books "Emerald Garden" (翠园), named after her residence in Ipoh. They consist of short articles, essays and anecdotes of her life experiences and views. She wanted to encourage young students to read more and was thoughtful enough to ensure that the books would fit easily into their school satchels or pockets. She and her husband lived in a beautiful house near the golf course in Ipoh and hence the name Ju Cui Yuan (掬翠园) meaning "Emerald Garden in the Palm of Hand". She loved the "hill city" of Ipoh and she once explained, rather poetically, her feelings about her "new" hometown Ipoh: "The emerald green of the hill city can be held in the palm of your hand" (山城翠绿可掬于掌中).

She passed away in 2004 at the age of 81, survived by her husband Sen Yuan and children.

Father and Peng Shi Lin

Father was only too glad to have found in Madam Peng another person with a genuine love for poetry. The other notable person was Mr Bai Cheng Gen 白成根, then President of the Perak Hokkien Association (reference poems in Chapters 42 and 43 written for his 60th birthday).

Not long before the publication of our book, *Lychee Fragrance*《荔子情》in 2002, Madam Peng wrote in an article some details about this poem, composed by Father for her 10th wedding anniversary and her vacation on her second "honeymoon". Her article was published in the *Nanyang Siang Pau* 南洋商报 in May 2002.

Madam Peng Shi Lin and her husband, Mr Liang Sen Yuan 梁森元, on their overseas vacation to celebrate their 10th wedding anniversary in April/May 1960. Qing Shan was hospitalized in late May and passed away in early June 1960.

Following are excerpts from the 2002 article by Madam Peng containing several insights:

- *Father was Engaged to Teach*

    "I sometimes sit by myself in the study and think of events concerning people who have passed on. These events are hazy in my mind as though they have come and then gone in the wink of an eye. There are, however, a handful of teachers who stand out shining like stars in the 'night sky' of my mind. Mr Chen Qing Shan is one of these persons."

"When I became Principal of Perak Girls' Middle School, the Senior Middle classes had ceased for some time, leaving only the Junior Middle. Senior Middle classes could only resume with the completion of the new school premises in 1957. In preparation for this, I had to find good teachers for the new classes. I began to look all over Malaya for them. One day, I went to the Perak Hokkien Association for a chat because the Ipoh Fufeng Poetry Society is located there, as a few 'friends of the school' who loved to compose poems often meet there. On reflection now, I should call them 'scholar-merchants' (儒商). I raised the subject of the resumption of Senior Middle classes at the school and said I was short of a good Chinese literature teacher. They all strenuously recommended Chen Qing Shan: he had an in-depth knowledge of the Chinese language, was good in poetry and prose, and was a person of high principles. I was in such dire need of a good teacher that I immediately took up their recommendation to look for Mr Chen."

"Mr Chen is from Putian, Fujian. His wife Wang Yi Song has established a well-known tailoring school for girls in Ipoh's Leong Sin Nam Street. I went to the tailoring school to meet Mr Chen. Mrs Chen came out to meet me and directed me to a small room to see Mr Chen."

"Mr Chen was a lean but kindly old man; he spoke gently but with a pair of bright and shining eyes and a serious look. I explained to him my purpose for the visit. After listening to me, he very humbly said, 'My learning is inadequate and may not be able to measure up to the position.' I replied, 'Mr Bai Cheng Gen, President of Perak Hokkien Association has strongly recommended you. I am sure he is right. I have long known your wide and profound learning, especially from the poems published in the papers.' Only then did Mr Chen agreed to consider the proposition."

- *Madam Peng's Second Honeymoon*

   "Time passed by very quickly. In a flash, by 1960, I had already completed ten years in the school. In that year, my husband and I planned to visit Hong Kong, Taiwan and Japan. I discussed with Mr Chen whether he could stand in for me in my Senior Middle Three Chinese Literature class. Mr Chen agreed without any hesitation. At that time, he himself had two classes of Junior Middle Three and one class of Senior Middle One Chinese Literature classes. I was worried that he might be overstrained by the load but he said it was not a problem. Moreover, I asked him not to mark the students' essays as they could wait for my return. Before I went on the trip, Mr Chen was quite exuberant and even wrote a seven-word six-verse poem to wish me Bon Voyage."

Madam Peng, in her 2002 article, quoted Verses 5 and 6 of this poem in entirety. Verse 5 is especially poignant. Father was happy to see the young couple, Madam Peng and her husband, go on their second honeymoon for their 10th wedding anniversary. He regretted his own inability to take his old wife of 30 years on that long promised trip abroad. *Nanyang Siang Pau* used Line 3 of Verse 5 as headline caption for the article, probably because of its poignant quality. Lines 3 and 4 of Verse 5 are quoted together for completeness sake:

   Line 3: "Repeatedly I've failed to deliver her that trip abroad.   负伊多少湖山约
   Line 4: With helpless sighs I gaze at the misty ocean broad."   万倾烟波只望洋

- *Madam Peng's Regret*

   "In the four weeks my husband and I were touring Hong Kong, Taiwan and Japan, we were extremely happy. We started off in April and returned in May. When we got back, I was shocked to

Madam Peng Shi Lin and her husband Mr Liang Sen Yuan in year 2003. Madam Peng passed away in July 2004.

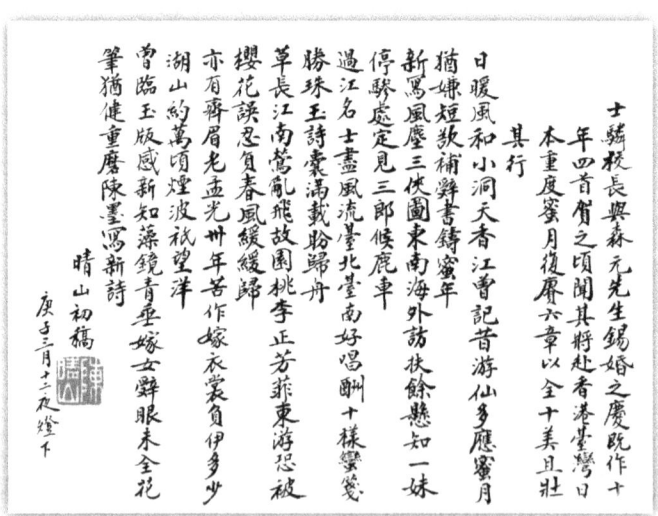

The poem written out personally by Qing Shan for Madam Peng Shi Lin. It is dated "Night of the 12th day, 3rd month, Geng-zi year [1960]" (庚子三月十二日夜灯下).

hear that Mr Chen had become ill. I went to the tailoring school at Leong Sing Nam Street to see him. He was even thinner and coughed incessantly. In June, he succumbed to liver ailment and passed away. I was full of regret. I should never have gone on that vacation, especially I should not have asked him to take my classes for me. This must have overstrained him. My tears that moment flowed in torrents."

Appreciation

This poem is like a story with a happy beginning but a very sad ending. This is how it will read for someone who has a first-hand knowledge or experience of the circumstances of its writing. This poem and the one in Chapter 47, were written to celebrate Madam Peng's 10th wedding anniversary and to send her off on her second honeymoon vacation overseas.

Verse 1 describes the beautiful scenery in the three countries that awaits the relatively young couple (then in their thirties) on their second honeymoon. The verse contains some clever puns with the names of the three countries Japan, Taiwan and Hong Kong as explained in the Paraphrase. It teases Madam Peng playfully that perhaps their first honeymoon was not long enough and these additional verses would help to extend their "honeymoon" (蜜月) into a "honey-year" (蜜年).

Verse 2 continues in this playful vein. Madam Peng and her husband are planning to visit Taiwan where they would meet Yi Jun Zuo 易君左, a poet, calligrapher and painter who visited Ipoh in August 1959 (Chapter 57). Both he and Madam Peng have met each other then. Both originated in Hunan Province and hence share a degree of kinship with each other (Madam Peng and Jun Zuo would later become "sworn" brother and sister). Verse 2 describes Madam Peng, her husband and Yi Jun Zuo as the "Three Musketeers". This is a reference to a fictional late Tang story popularly called "The Itinerant Three Musketeers" (风尘三侠). The story is from the *Biography of the Itinerant*

Curly-Beard《虬髯客傳》. The story features its three central characters, Li Jing (李靖) and his purported wife Hongfu (紅拂), and an ambitious itinerant known only as "The Itinerant Curly-Beard" who taught Li Jing military strategies. In the story, the wife Hongfu was known as "Yi Mei" ("sister", 一妹) and the Itinerant Curly-Beard was known "San-lang" ("brother", 三郎). The fictional Li Jing's name is borrowed from a historical early Tang general by that name.

Verse 3 writes about the many literary stalwarts that have "crossed the river" and are now in Taiwan. Madam Peng's sworn brother, Yi Jun Zuo, would be one of them! This refers to the many notables who have left or escaped from mainland China after its fall to the Communists. The Verse shows Qing Shan's respect for the literary stalwarts who now live in Taiwan when he expresses the hope that Madam Peng would return with a boatload of good compositions.

Verse 4 begins to turn to a more serious tone as Madam Peng is reminded of the equally beautiful environment back home in Malaya, a scene of eternal Spring and Summer where the grass is always green and the birds freely fly. Line 2 reminds her that "The peach and plum, their fragrance begins to fill the air". This is an oblique reminder that her students await her return so that they can be cared for. The verses closes with the reminder to return home.

Verse 5 is perhaps the most poignant of the whole poem. Qing Shan is happy that Madam Peng takes a good vacation by travelling abroad. He even goes out of his way to take on additional load of work to make it possible for her to travel for a whole month during school term. While he is happy to do that, he inevitably compares the position of himself and his wife with that of Madam Peng and her husband. He is reminded of his own wife; they have been together not ten but thirty years. In all these thirty years, he and his wife have had to toil with hardly any vacation. He has promised her that one day, he would take her on a vacation abroad, but for reason of both time and money he has repeatedly failed to deliver on that promise.

Verse 6 brings him back to the joy he knows or can easily afford, viz., his poetry. He appreciates the positive comments from his friends for his latest composition, a "Wedding Counsel" poem (in Chapter 11, "嫁女词示美瑜"). He sees their endorsement of his poem as an enhancement of its value. The poem closes in a subdued but resolute two lines. He will continue to write so long as he can see and hold his pen and grind his inkstone!

> Line 3: "While my vision is still not blurred and my pen still firm　　眼未全花笔犹健
> Line 4: I shall re-grind the old inkstone and write a new poem."　　重磨旧墨写新诗

It is a tragic irony that Qing Shan passed away barely three months after the writing of this poem.

Chapter 49

呈贺洪禄宽先生七秩双寿
_{chéng hè hóng lù kuān xiān shēng qī zhì shuāng shòu}

其一

画堂春暖烛双辉，
并坐齐看舞彩衣。
老尚多情征上寿，
4 心从所欲自忘机。
风流名士饶佳话，
矍铄如君信古稀，
杖国杖乡何足数，
8 清晨入市步如飞。

Presented to Mr Hong Lu Kuan for His 70th Birthday, a Double Celebration with His Wife

Verse 1

    A pair of candles in the reception hall are shining.
    The birthday couple watches the children preparing.
    Abiding love through old age is a sign of longevity;
4   Without a care, you do what you please at seventy.
    With no interest in petty gossip in town all around,
    It's rare indeed to be seventy, all healthy and sound.
    Sixty or seventy, the gap is not worth recounting;
8   You whiz to town with flying steps early morning.

Verse 2

    The exuberant spirit of your youth you retain,
    To change the world, revive the nation, your aim.
    Sheathe your sword now and enjoy your life;
4   Right or wrong, put the question now aside.
    Your talent is a match for the Eight Dragons.
    It has no need for the patronage of anyone.
    You're both still in love in this twilight year.
8   There's Shangri-la beyond Taoyuan, that's clear.

其二

少年慷慨志犹存，
欲转乾坤唤国魂，
韬晦自甘先养寿，
是非难说暂无言。
一夔足敌八龙誉。
百里宁缘五羖尊，
日暮鹿车聊共挽，
桃源之外有桃源。

Paraphrase

Verse 1

L1: In the warmth of Spring, a pair of grand candles are shining in the family reception hall.
L2: You and your wife watch your children and grandchildren prepare for the celebration.
L3: That you are still so loving with each other in old age, is a sign foretelling Longevity.
L4: A person at seventy is entitled to do as he wishes; naturally he should not be too bothered by what others say,
L5: For example, all the petty gossip about the lifestyle of the more liberal-minded and well-known personalities around town.
L6: To be hale and hearty at seventy is rare indeed.
L7: Your wife is sixty and you seventy, but the difference is not worth recounting;
L8: Just look, you're still able to whiz your way to town in the early morning with "flying" steps.

Verse 2

L1: The exuberant spirit of your youth undoubtedly still remains.
L2: You had wanted to change the world and arouse the national spirit,
L3: But now it's time to sheathe your sword, call it a day and peaceably enjoy your life.
L4: One can't say, at least for the time being, whether this is really the right thing to do.
L5: Such literary talent you have is more than a match for any scholar worthy of the name Eight Dragons.
L6: You are talented like Boli Xi who owed his success to his talent rather than to his having been redeemed with five ram skins by an influential person.

L7: In the twilight years, you and your wife are still as loving to each other.

L8: There is truly another "Shangri-la" beyond Tao Yuanming's "Shangri-la" (Taoyuan).

Background

This poem was written in 1960 and is one of two poems written for or about Hong Lu Kuan 洪禄宽 (born 1891). The other poem is in Chapter 56 composed in 1957. The title of the poem "Double (Birthday) Celebration" (双寿) and Line 7's "Sixty or seventy ..." (杖国杖乡...) indicates precisely the occasion. It is for Lu Kuan's 70th and his wife's 60th birthdays. Lu Kuan married his wife Zheng Bi Yu (郑碧玉) after he came to Malaya. The couple first had two sons, followed by a daughter (born 1926).

He was about three years older than Father. Lu Kuang was a rubber merchant in Ipoh and a committee member of the Perak Hokkien Association of which Bai Cheng Geng 白成根 (six years junior to Father) was the President. Father was the paid Secretary of the Association, but the relationship between the three was one of genuine friendship, bonded by their common love for classical poetry. There are several poems written by Father for his two poetry friends and vice versa.

Hong Lu Kuan, one of Qing Shan's poetry friends who celebrated his seventieth and his wife's sixtieth birthday in 1960.

Like Father, Lu Kuan would have studied in a traditional private school in China and acquired the skill and love for classical poetry. As poetry friends, the three of them frequently composed poems which appeared in the local newspaper. In 1960, these three poetry friends each wrote a poem which appeared in a collection of poems titled, *Yunnan Garden Anthology of Poems*《云南园吟唱集》published by the Chinese Literary Society of Nanyang University in July 1960. (See Father's poem in Chapter 58.)

For more details of the background of Hong Lu Kuan, refer to Background in Chapter 56.

Appreciation

The occasion for the poem is a double celebration for Lu Kuan's 70th birthday and his wife's birthday. We know this from the title which includes the words "Double (Birthday) Celebration" 双寿.

Verse 1

We also know from Verse 1 Line 7 that it is the wife's 60th birthday. Her birthday need not fall on the same day for a double celebration. When one gets to that age, what is in a few months?

Given Lu Kuan's background in poetry, this poem is rich in allusions. In Verse 1 Line 4, Qing Shan starts off using a quote from Confucius who said of himself:

> "…At fifty, I knew my destiny; at sixty, I listen to what is not agreeable with me; at seventy, I do what I please but without transgressing the norm." (五十而知天命，六十而耳顺，七十而从心所欲，不逾矩).

In Line 4, Qing Shan uses the very same words: "…you do what you please…" (从心所欲)", as though this expression has become a metaphor for the age of seventy.

In Line 6, Qing Shan merely uses the "code words": "It is rare indeed to be…" (古稀 shortened from 古来稀). This will be understood by Lu Kuan to mean the age of seventy. It comes from a well-known line from Du Fu's poem:

Our drinking debts are truly everywhere;
酒债寻常行处有
Seventy in life has always been very rare.
人生七十古来稀

In recognition of the other birthday celebrant in the poem, viz., Lu Kuan's wife who is sixty the same year, Qing Shan says in Line 7, that between seventy and sixty, "the (age) gap is not worth recounting". Again, he uses a "shorthand" from the classics (*The Book of Rites* 《礼记》) to express the age of Seventy (杖国) and Sixty (杖乡). According to the customs of the Zhou dynasty which venerated the aged, "those who are Fifty may use the walking stick at home, while the Sixty in the village, the Seventy throughout the country and the Eighty (*zhang chao* 杖朝) in the Imperial Court. If the Emperor should want to consult someone who is Ninety, His Majesty has to visit the home of the person with a present of pearls." (五十杖于家, 六十杖于乡, 七十杖于国, 八十杖于朝, 九十者, 天子欲有问焉, 则就其室, 以珍从).

The last line of Verse 1 praises Lu Kuan for still being fit and healthy. It is written in a light-hearted and humorous way: "You whiz to town with flying steps early morning" (清晨入市步如飞).

Verse 2

Verse 2 praises Lu Kuan as a person of noble spirit, literary talent and commends his long and happy relationship with his wife. Even at seventy, Lu Kuan still exhibits some of the exuberant spirit of his youth, wanting to change the world. Qing Shan tells him in Line 3 to slow down, "Sheathe your sword now and (start to) enjoy your life". Line 4 poses a question for Lu Kuan to reflect whether all his efforts have achieved any good, but quickly suggests that the judgment should be deferred.

Lu Kuan's talent is compared with three sets of historical figures: Kui (夔), Ba Long (Eight Dragons 八龙) in Line 5 and

Boli Xi 百里奚 in Line 6. Kui is the name of a royal musician who was exceptionally talented in playing the *pan* 磐, a stone percussion instrument. When Emperor Shun 舜 (2255BC) wanted to send him round the country to spread the music, his court officials were worried that Kui would not be up to the task all by himself. It was suggested to the Emperor that other musicians be appointed to accompany him. The Emperor had such high regard for Kui's ability that he dismissed the suggestion with the words, "One Kui would be enough" (一夔已足). The "Eight Dragons" are the eight sons of someone by the name of Xún Shū 荀淑 (83-149). They were talented and of high moral character and became known as the "Eight Dragons". Hence, Line 5 says of Lu Kuan: "Your talent (alone is sufficient match) 一夔足 for the reputed Eight Dragons 八龙誉".

Line 6 is rendered in English as "It (your talent) has no need for the patronage of anyone". The literal meaning of this line is "Boli Xi (did not achieve success or honour) because of the five ram skins" 百里宁缘五羖尊. In other words, his success was due solely to his own talent. Boli Xi lived in the 7th century BC. He was a very able statesman politician during the Spring Autumn period. He came from a very poor family and eventually found himself a captive and slave in the state of Jin 晋, his identity unknown. When the King of Qin 秦 heard that Boli Xi was a very capable man, he wanted to redeem him from Jin for a very large ransom. He was advised by his ministers to offer only five ram skins (五羖) for Boli Xi, lest the King of Jin becomes aware of his real value. Five ram skins were about the value of a slave. The ruse worked and Boli Xi was ransomed; he became a very successful and renowned Minister in the state of Qin.

The concluding two lines praise Lu Kuan and his wife for being so loving to each other even in their twilight years. Their bliss is compared with another "Shangri-la" that exists beyond Taoyuan, the "Utopia" of Tao Yuanming's story, "Peach Blossom Spring". (Refer to Appreciation in Chapter 42.)

Section 4
Reflections
感興述懷

A diversity of subjects: grief from the loss of a loved one, his philosophy of life, the political changes of the time. The final prose composition shows his irrepressible joy in Poetry.

Chapter 50

纪陈韵珊女士事

女士福州台城人，兄某久客槟城，悯嫂独居，南渡寻兄，将与偕返，归装待发，忽遘疾不起，临终遗嘱以所著诗殉葬。

朝见台江水，

暮见台江水，

阿嫂望夫泪阑干，

4　阿兄浪迹千万里。

小姑无郎惯独处，

此时亦识别离苦。

The Fair Maiden Chen Yun Shan of Taichen

The maiden was a native of Taichen of Fuzhou county. Her elder brother had sojourned in Penang for a long time, leaving his poor wife back home all by herself. Out of compassion for her sister-in-law, Yun Shan came to Nanyang to look for him, intending to return home with him. She and her brother were all packed and ready to leave when she was struck down by an illness and died. At the point of her death, she made a last request for her poems to be interred with her.

    Gazing at the waters of Taijiang at morn;
    Till dusk she gazed at Taijiang forlorn.
    Her sister yearns for her man, eyes in tears;
4   Her brother has gone afar for many years.
    She's used to living alone without a man;
    She knows truly now separation's pain,
    She's willing to fly across as the messenger of love.
8   Over to Penang, borne by the wind she'll soar above.
    Never has she ventured beyond her native home,
    What's more, in this humid Southern clime to roam.
    She'll perish in this wilderness seeking her brother.
12   But die she dare not, till he's found by her.
    A flush of joy when the two siblings meet!
    Sadness sets in, even before their joy recede.
    Can't bear thinking of the grief on the bank of Tai River,

愿为青鸟使遥天，
8 乘风飞到槟城屿。
生小不曾出乡里，
况入蛮烟瘴雨里？
分当朝夕委沟渠，
12 寻兄未遇不敢死。
骨肉相见展欢颜，
欢颜未敛复辛酸。
不堪遥忆台江畔，
16 红袖楼头人倚栏。
阿兄岂真忘情者，
感此亦自泪双下。
明日之日黄道辰，
20 相约买舟归去也。

16 Leaning forlornly on the balustrade, her grieving sister.
    Is her brother really a fickle man without a heart?
    At this painful thought, he too his tears impart.
    For the return is chosen a propitious day.
20 The steamer tickets are bought without delay.
    They packed all night, to set off at dawn.
    For no reason, comes an unexpected turn.
    The rising moon is blotted out by clouds;
24 Flowers are snapped by wind ere they bloom.
    After many perils, she has arrived in this foreign land.
    Weakened, she no longer can disease withstand.
    The disease has the body insidiously gripped;
28 So sudden, beyond help the body has slipped.
    The end of her mortal life is surely nigh.
    Farewell to life, to return home on high.
    Her departing words are all clearly said:
32 In Death I leave behind nothing to regret;
    Poetry is my very special love in life,
    Private as are thoughts between man and wife.
    Don't leave behind my thoughts for all to read.
36 Let my poems be interred with me, I plead.
    The scenery of Penang is pretty without exception,
    Its breezy waters, hills and moon a picture perfection.
    For all who share the karma of conjugal love to meet.
40 In this land, the mortal remains of my bones shall keep.
    O brother mine, do not for my sake here remain,
    Lest my death in a foreign land be all in vain.
    'Neath a mound of yellow earth covered by verdant grass,
44 Bids you farewell with the departing wind, a lonely lass,
    Who still grieves for our loved one waiting back home.
    My beloved sister counts each day when you'll come.
    The blood in my grave, as the tears in her room, is shed,
48 We ask you dear brother, "Have you reached home yet?"

趁夜治装待晓发，
无端变故生倏忽。
月方东上云横遮，
24 花未全开风摧折。
跋艰涉险来异地，
弱质夙难禁瘴疠。
二竖潜伏膏与肓，
28 一朝猝起谁能制。
合是红尘劫已完，
遄返玉京辞人世。
临终遗语犹历历，
32 侬今一死何足惜！
平生性癖耽咏絮，
未脱镜鸾钗凤句。

Paraphrase

L1: Gazing at the waters of the river Taijiang,
L2: From morn till dusk, she gazes at the river Taijiang.
L3: Her poor sister is all tearful, yearning for her husband.
L4: Her brother has wandered off thousands of miles abroad.
L5: She is used to living by herself without a man in the house,
L6: She can now fully understand the pains of being parted from a loved one.
L7: She is willing to be the winged messenger of love
L8: To be borne by the wind and fly to the isle of Penang.
L9: She has never ventured beyond her hometown,
L10: Much less to travel so far into the humid and unhealthy tropical South,
L11: She is likely to die in the wilderness of the foreign land on her mission.
L12: But she would never dare to die until her brother is found.
L13: What joy it is when the two siblings finally meet.
L14: Even before the initial flush of joy wears off, sadness again sets in.
L15: How could she not think of the continuing grief on the bank of the far away Taijiang,
L16: Where a lady still leans on the balustrade yearning.
L17: Is her brother really such a fickle and heartless man?
L18: On this thought, he too is overcome with tears.
L19: A propitious day has been chosen to begin the journey home.
L20: Her brother and she both arrange to buy their steamer passage home together.
L21: They pack their belongings in the night, waiting for dawn to commence their voyage home.
L22: Out of the blue and for no rhyme or reason, events take a tragic turn.
L23: Like the rising moon in the east being suddenly blotted out by a dark cloud,

休教艳语留人间，
36 悉以入棺殉葬去。
槟城山水殊佳绝，
水秀风清山上月。
名胜每多儿女缘，
40 此地正堪埋吾骨。
兄毋为我复淹留，
孤负此身丧异域。
一堆黄土草青青，
44 临风犹似送君行。
伤心更有故园柳，
翠楼人在计归程。
坟中碧血闺中泪，
48 为问行人归也未？

L24: Like the flowers being snapped by a gale before they can fully bloom.
L25: She has traversed perilous distances to arrive in this foreign land.
L26: Her constitution weakened, she can no longer withstand the ravages of tropical diseases.
L27: The disease has insidiously invaded her body;
L28: She is so suddenly struck down, who can help her now?
L29: Seemingly, the end of her mortal life is near;
L30: She suddenly left this mortal domain and returned to the celestial world.
L31: At her departure, she left word what was to become of her, clearly
L32: Saying: At my death, I leave behind no regret.
L33: Poetry has been my special love all my life,
L34: My poems too reflect intimately the pains of separation between man and woman.
L35: Please do not leave behind my poems of such intimate feelings for all to read,
L36: But inter them in my grave with me.
L37: The scenery of Penang is exceptionally beautiful,
L38: With its beautiful waters, gentle breeze and the moon shining lovingly upon the hills, a picture of perfection.
L39: Such a beautiful place will surely be a fitting meeting place for all men and women predestined for each other.
L40: This too shall be where my mortal remains are interred.
L41: O brother mine, please do not for my sake linger here a moment longer,
L42: Lest my death in a foreign land shall be all in vain.
L43: Beneath this mound of earth, covered by a carpet of verdant grass, (lies your sister)
L44: Who now bids you farewell.
L45: She grieves for our loved one back home.
L46: My sister counts the days before you return.
L47: As the blood in my grave and the tears in her room are shed,

L48: We ask you the traveller, "Have you reached home yet?"

Background

Summary

There are three compositions in this book that came to us through an elderly gentleman from Muar 麻坡 (in Malaysia's Johor state 柔佛州). He chanced upon Father's name when he attended the Ipoh Fufeng Poetry Society (怡保扶风诗社) meeting in November 1991. At this meeting, copies of a collection of Father's poems, compiled by Madam Peng Shi Lin (彭士驎), were given to the participants. This gentleman later sent us through Madam Peng a photocopy of these three compositions.

The other two were (i) a preface in prose in Chapter 61 composed for Mr Huang Yun Shan's anthology of poems, and (ii) a poem in Chapter 52, "No Title" (佚题). The three compositions were almost certainly included in Mr Huang's anthology of poems which was published in 1927.

The form of this "poem" including its theme looks like what would be called a "ballad" in English. We do not know who this poor maiden, Chen Yun Shan, really was except for what was written in the prologue of the poem. She came from the township of Taicheng (Fuzhou county). If we were to hazard a guess, this ballad may have been a real life story that was news some time in the early 1920s.

However, the Chinese immigrants who came to Nanyang from southern China are a familiar story. Even today, some 80 years after the events of this poem we continue to read news of people from Fuzhou and the neighbouring counties of Fuqing and Putian working in Singapore and Malaysia.

Appreciation

The poem is a sad and tragic story of a young woman who

travels all the way from her hometown in Fuzhou 福州 in China to Penang in search of her brother. It is not so much for herself as for her brother's grieving wife who is therefore her sister-in-law. Having found her brother, she dies before they could both embark on the voyage home. She is buried in Penang and at her request, all her poems are interred with her.

The poem has the ring and feel of a ballad. It is a kind of ancient-style poem, known as *ge xing* 歌行. The brief prologue gives tantalizingly few details of who our heroine is ("a native of Taichen of Fuzhou county") but it provides a thumbnail sketch of the tragedy and what the poem is all about.

Except for the first two lines of five words each, the rest of the poem is seven words per line. Lines 1 and 2 are like a curtain-raiser: "Gazing at the waters of Taijiang at morn; Till dusk she gazed at Taijiang forlorn". The scene opens on the banks of the river Taijiang in Fuzhou where the sister-in-law (阿嫂) is gazing the whole day long for the return of her husband. We do not know how long he has gone away and why there has not been any communication home.

In the original Chinese text, the relationship between our heroine and the other two characters of this poem is briskly but precisely established by the first two words of each of Lines 3, 4 and 5:

Line 3: Her sister yearns for her man, eyes in tears;
阿嫂 (ā sǎo)　望夫泪阑干
Line 4: Her brother has gone afar for many years.
阿兄 (ā xiōng)　浪迹千万里
Line 5: She's used to living alone without a man;
小姑 (xiǎo gū)　无郎惯独处

The precision of how the family members should address one another underscores the importance of family ties in Chinese culture and society. The three terms used are from the standpoint of Yun Shan, who would address her sister-in-law as "阿嫂 (ā sǎo)" with the precise meaning of "wife of elder brother". She would address her elder brother as "阿兄 (*ā xiōng*)" or 哥哥 (*gē ge*) in modern Chinese. In the presence of her sister-in-law, our heroine Yun Shan would refer to herself as 小姑 (*xiǎo gū*) which has the literal meaning of "little aunt 小姑". But even the word "aunt 姑" here means very precisely a "paternal" aunt, i.e., the sister of one's father. The word "little 小" further qualifies it as the "younger" sister. All this may sound very complicated, but to the Chinese, the three terms 阿嫂 (*ā sǎo*), 阿兄 (*ā xiōng*), 小姑 (*xiǎo gū*), all in alignment in the three lines, are everyday terms used in the family.

Line 5, "She's used to living alone without a man" (小姑无郎惯独处), tells us that Yun Shan is unmarried. The combination of the first two and last two words of this line, "小姑……独处", literally means "*xiao gu* lives alone". It is a Chinese proverb derived from the lyric of an old song. The proverb has become a metaphor for an unmarried maiden. Qing Shan has used the proverb skilfully because it applies to the situation both metaphorically and literally.

Line 6's "She knows truly now separation's pain" describes a common human experience: that we will truly know grief only after we have experienced it first hand ourselves or been very close to it.

So moved is Yun Shan by her sister-in-law's grief and plight that she would volunteer herself as a "messenger of love" (Line 7), "borne by the wind" (Line 8) on a mercy flight to Penang. This is, of course, only a figure of speech. Transportation in the 1920s would have meant two weeks at sea in some little ship crammed with passengers. This was how our immigrant forefathers came to Nanyang from China.

All the more we admire the courage and resolve of this young lady when we realize that she has never stepped out of her hometown Taicheng (Line 9). To venture now into the humid and unhealthy tropics of the South (Line 10: 况入蛮烟瘴雨里) is at a further personal risk which, we shall learn later, costs her her life.

But she is determined to reunite her grieving sister-in-law with her brother (Line 11). Even in the overwhelming joy of two siblings meeting in a distant land (Line 13), she is overcome once more by sadness (Line 14). She cannot bear recalling the image of her grieving sister-in-law back home on the river bank (Line 15). Yun Shan pictures her sister-in-law leaning across the balustrade gazing into the waters in the distance (Line 16) longing to see her husband sail home. Perhaps only a woman can fully empathise with the grief of another woman.

The image and memory of her grieving sister-in-law is too much for her to bear and it shakes her abruptly out of the joy of finding her own brother. "Is her brother really a fickle man without a heart?" (Line 17). On that thought, his tears too begin to flow (Line 18).

A propitious day is chosen for the journey home (Line 19). Brother and sister both arrange to buy the steamer tickets for the passage home (Line 20). They make their preparations and finish their packing late into the night; all they can do now is to wait anxiously for the morning (Line 21).

However, tragedy strikes! For no rhyme or reason, events take an unexpected turn (Line 22). All have gone well so far. But now, it is as though a beautiful moon rising from behind the hills is suddenly blotted out by an ominous dark cloud (Line 23). It is as though the half-open blooms on the branches are prematurely snapped by a gale (Line 24). She has come through countless perils to reach this foreign land (Line 25); her constitution is considerably weakened and she easily falls victim to one of the many tropical diseases (Line 26). The disease has indeed invaded her body, right to the bone (Line 27). It has struck so suddenly that she is now beyond any cure (Line 28).

She realizes that she has reached the end of her mortal life (Line 29); very soon indeed, she will have to bid farewell to this world and return to another world above (Line 30). On her deathbed, she wrote her last testament, clearly making known her wishes (Line 31). She has no regrets in having to die (Line 32). As poetry has been her special love in life (Line 33), her poems contain intimate thoughts that are inevitably like those between man and wife (Line 34). Although Yun Shan is not married, we wonder if there has once been a man with whom she was romantically attached. The poems which she is so anxious that no one else should read may have been the trove of her "love poems". We would never know. We can perhaps understand why she pleads that her poems with all her private thoughts be not exposed for all to read (Line 35). She asks that the poems be interred together with her (Line 36).

Although she does not regret death, she does lament her fate in the follow Lines 37–40:

Line 37: "The scenery of Penang is pretty without exception,　　槟城山水殊佳绝
Line 38: Its breezy waters, hills and moon a picture perfection　　水山清凤山上月
Line 39: For all who share the karma of conjugal love to meet.　　名胜每多儿女缘
Line 40: In this land, the mortal remains of my bones shall keep."　　此地正堪埋吾骨

Lines 37–38 describe the beautiful scenery on the island of Penang. So beautiful that it must possess the karma of conjugal love (儿女缘) and is a fitting meeting place for all men and women who are predestined for each other. It is also Yun Shan's destiny that she should die and be interred in this beautiful island (Lines 39–40). Although she has not the chance to experience love in life, it is most fitting that she is laid to rest in a land so filled with the karma of conjugal love.

In her dying breath, she exhorts her brother to continue with his journey home without delay, and without any further consideration for her (Line 41). Even on her deathbed, she still thinks of her poor sister-in-law waiting for the return of her husband. Yun Shan's mission is to get her brother to return. If he fails to do that on account of her death, then her death and burial in a foreign land would have been all in vain (Line 42).

The next two Lines 43–44 tell him that she will bid him farewell from her grave:

> Line 43: "'Neath a mound of yellow earth covered by verdant grass, 一堆黄土草青青
> Line 44: Bids you farewell with the departing wind, a lonely lass;" 临风犹似送君行

The poem again returns to the recurring theme of the grieving sister-in-law back home counting the days of her husband's home-coming (Lines 45–46). The final two Lines 47-48, are equally touching; they are perhaps the most poignant of the entire poem.

> Line 47: "The blood in my grave, as the tears in her room, is shed, 坟中碧血闺中泪
> Line 48: We ask you dear brother, 'Have you reached home yet?'" 为问行人归也未

Yun Shan has paid for the success of her mission of love with her own life. It is a noble sacrifice on her part (Line 47). Even in death, her love and concern for both brother and sister-in-law never cease. She from her grave, and her sister-in-law at home, continue to ask her brother (*xing ren* 行人, "the traveller") whether he has reached home yet (Line 48).

Chapter 51

吴将军画像赋一首

我生不逢将军提刀杀敌时,

无由望见瑰杰岸异之英姿。

三百年后瞻遗像,是耶非耶尚怀疑。

4 而况遗像我犹未见之。

将军事业炳一代,

本来不等丹青绘。

其人其事但足传,

8 尚论何妨凭我辈?

Portrait of General Wu

("Portrait of General Wu" was composed in the Spring of 1924 at the home of Mr Wu Xing Fu. General Wu Ying—a native of the coastal Putian—was the Provincial Commander-in-Chief during the Qing dynasty.)

    Born in an untimely era, not when the General was killing his enemies,
    Never could I have witnessed his marvellous and heroic bearing.
    Three hundred years on, we view his portrait and question whether it is his likeness.
4   Besides, I have never before seen his portrait.
    The general's achievements are well acclaimed;
    Indeed he depends not on a portrait framed.
    The man, his deeds are there to spread his fame.
8   There's no harm for us to examine his role again.
    However, in this boundless sea of humanity,
    Soulless nondescripts are indeed many;
    We meet them with no exception daily.
12   If not him, whom should we rate as worthy?
    The general can battle enemies of ten thousand
    But he lived in an era that is untimely.
    Still a fledgling, not ready for great deeds yet,
16   A drastic change in Jia-shen year he met.

不然茫茫人海里，

走肉行尸知凡几？

朝朝觌面亦寻常，

12 有谁值得留笔底？

将军之力敌万人，

将军之生何不辰！

毛羽未遂高飞愿，

16 一朝国变逢甲申。

朱明运绝山河改，

汉族衣冠留左海。

郑家父子效孤忠，

20 其志可嘉势则殆。

The Ming faced many defeats and most land was lost.
The Hans retreated to Fuzhou; t'was their final cost.
Zheng and son, loyal to the Ming they remain.
20 Valiant their spirit, but hopeless t'was plain.
A retreat (to Taiwan) would be all in vain,
General Wu's talent had nothing to gain.
No way to salvage the chessboard, a lost game;
24 Surrender he must, a break would come again.
Great talent and ambition he had from young.
Great pity it'd be, to bury them unsung.
Eager for instant result from his every deed,
28 Han talent given to Manchu use is sad indeed.
General Wu in just one battle took Xiamen,
Followed by victories in Penghu and Taiwan.
Alas, the General's achievements seemed magnificent!
32 But was this truly his righteous ambition?

Paraphrase

L1: I did not live in the period when General Wu was going about putting the enemies to his sword.
L2: I have never had the opportunity to witness his marvellous and exceptional stature nor his heroic bearing.
L3: Now three hundred years later his portrait is being reviewed (with his role in history).
L4: Moreover I have never before seen his portrait.
L5: The general's brilliant military achievements were already renowned throughout his time
L6: To begin with, his fame does not depend on a portrait.
L7: The man and his achievements are sufficient to spread his fame.
L8: But there's no harm in our examining his role once again
L9: We do not know in this vast sea of humanity
L10: How many soulless, colourless nondescripts are there.
L11: We meet them every day

杖藜皂帽恐徒然，

英雄用武非所在。

一局残棋不可收，

降志辱身原有待。

将军年少负奇才，

不甘长弃没尘埃。

功名事业急自见，

楚材晋用良可哀。

将军一战平全厦，

将军再战下澎台。

呜呼！将军之功诚伟矣！

是岂将军之志哉！

L12: (If we do not write about General Wu) Whom should we write about that is worthy?
L13: The general has the strength and courage to stand up to ten thousand enemies,
L14: But he lived in an inopportune time.
L15: At a time when he was still a fledgling, not capable yet of great deeds,
L16: The country met tragically with a dynastic change in the year of Jia-shen three hundred years ago,
L17: (Zhu Yuanzhang's) Ming dynasty met a fateful end and the entire land was lost.
L18: The Han loyal followers of the Ming emperor retreated to their last stand in Zuohai (city of Fuzhou)
L19: Only Admiral Zheng Chenggong and his son remained loyal to the Ming.
L20: Admirable though their valiant spirit, the situation was already lost,
L21: Retreating (to Taiwan) would all be in vain.
L22: General Wu (by following suit to retreat and stay put in Taiwan) would find no opportunity to exploit his talent.
L23: There was no way to salvage a lost game on the chessboard.
L24: He surrendered (to the Manchus) in order to await an opportunity (to rise).
L25: After all he was endowed with remarkable abilities and great ambition from young.
L26: It would be a pity if such talent lay forever buried, unseen and unused.
L27: In his eagerness to realize the potential of his own talent,
L28: It is lamentable that he allowed the talent of the state of "Chu 楚" (employed here as a metaphor meaning the Han Chinese) to be used for the cause of the state of "Jin 晋" (as a metaphor for the Manchus).(*chu cai jin yong* 楚材晋用)
L29: The arrival of General Wu into the battle brought about the pacification of the whole Xiamen region.

L30: Followed by his taking of Penghu in Taiwan (from Zheng Chenggong)
L31: Alas, is the general's success truly so noble an achievement?
L32: Are all these truly the general's intended ambition?

Background

This is an interesting poem for several reasons. It has been dated as "Spring of 1924" in the house of Wu Xing Fu 吴星夫. The subject is about General Wu Ying 吴英 (1637–1713), a Provincial Commander-in-Chief and a native of Putian in Fujian. Putian is Father's native county. The poem first appeared in (the literary publication of) Putian's "Hu She" 壶社, a poetry club.

The poem was obtained from an old gentleman, Lin Jing Xin 林井心 of Putian in 1987 who told us the following:

  i. Mr Song Hu Ming 宋湖民, an old prominent literary figure of Putian, had said of this poem, "This composition is written with the free and vigorous strokes of the pen, the last two lines are especially profound. This is indeed a masterpiece." (此作结笔力横恣，而结尤见地高超，真大家诗也。)
 ii. "Hu She" 壶社 was a poetry society in Putian during the period 1920–1940. The members were people steeped in the classics; they were over 30 and 40 years old. They were all leading scholars of the time, comprising Hanlin academics, Jinshi, Juren, Xiuchai, etc., (翰林、进士、举人、秀才) of the late Qing era, numbering about 20 to 30 people. Chen Qing Shan, about 30 years old then, was one such eminent talent among them.

Father had returned to Putian for six months in the second half of 1923 to get married. In the "Spring of 1924," he was actually in Nanyang and this article must have been mailed to

Hu She from Nanyang. It is stated in the published version of the poem: "Manuscript sent in by Chen Qing Shan" 陈晴山来稿.

What then is the reference to "the house of Wu Xing Fu"? We understand that the small group of Hu She members would gather in the house of Mr Wu Xing Fu 吴星夫 and were given a subject for composition. The subject for that occasion happened to be "General Wu" (吴将军). It is possible that Father had actually attended such a meeting in Mr Wu Xing Fu's house while he was still in Putian in the second half of 1923 and the members were given time to then submit their compositions for eventual publication in the ensuing months. By then, Father had already returned to Nanyang.

Wu Xing Fu was a Putian shipowner whose residence was often open to literary and cultural activities during the first half of the 20th century.

General Wu Ying (1637–1732) was born in the last years of the Ming dynasty. He was a capable and ambitious young general in Putian. Although the Manchus established their rule over China as the Qing dynasty in 1644, the Ming dynasty loyalists continued to resist the Manchus in the southern provinces like Fujian for another 40 years. General Wu Ying once served under the Ming loyalist Zheng Chenggong.

Appreciation

The circumstance of the composition is interesting enough. The "Portrait of General Wu" is a given subject for a poetry society meeting in Putian, very likely, in late 1923. The meeting is held in the house of Mr Wu Xing Fu (吴星夫), a Putian shipowner whose residence is often open to such literary and cultural activities. The choice of subject is perhaps not coincidental, given that Mr Wu shares the same surname as the historical figure General Wu Ying (吴英 1637–1712), a native of Putian.

We do not know what the other members of the society wrote. It is an evaluation of the role of General Wu Ying. As the historical Wu Ying is a native of Putian and for many, a local folk hero, it is possible that some poems written for this occasion would sing his praises. The treatment given to the subject by Qing Shan is unusual.

The poem is in a form known as *ge xing* 歌行, a structure of 32 lines; the first 16 lines with a "rhyme" in every fourth line; the second 16 lines with a "rhyme" in every eighth line. For those interested in a detailed description of the structure, please refer to the Appreciation (赏析) section of the poem in the Chinese edition of this book.

The poem can be divided into three sections. The first section (Lines 1–12) explains the purpose of the poem, viz., to examine the role of General Wu while reflecting before the portrait of this local hero. Qing Shan begins with a masterly first line. It declares that he was "Born in an untimely era, not when the General was killing his enemies." Qing Shan is apparently referring to himself, but he is really pointing to General Wu being born in an untimely era. We will see the reason as the story unfolds in the poem. Besides, we are looking at his portrait 300 years later and we do not even know for sure whether this is a true likeness of him. This is another line with a hidden meaning: is what we see really what it is, so asks Qing Shan in this first section.

The second section (Lines 13–24) explains why General Wu, a Ming general surrenders to the invading Manchus. General Wu is a subordinate of Zheng Chenggong, the loyal Ming general. Zheng and his son are holding out and protecting what is left of the royal household of Ming. General Wu is still young, a "fledgling, not ready for great deeds yet" (Line 15: 毛羽未遂高飞愿). Unfortunately, this tragic change has overtaken the whole country and the Ming loyalists are driven south to Fuzhou. Zheng retook Taiwan from the Dutch intending to continue waging war against the Manchus from there. The young General Wu's remarkable ability and great potential might never have been realized if he had retreated with Zheng to Taiwan

The residence of Wu Xing Fu (吳星夫) in Putian, a wealthy commercial shipping fleet owner. His residence was often open to literary and cultural activities throughout the first half of the 20th century. (This photo was taken in 2002.) "Portrait of General Wu" was the subject chosen for a poem at a meeting held here by the local poetry society "Hu She" (壺社) in the Spring of 1924.

The facsimile of the page in which the poem "Portrait of General Wu" first appeared in the literary publication of Putian's poetry club "Hu She" 壺社. As in old classical writings, it has no punctuation. The punctuation marks that are visible were inserted by hand for us by an old Putian poet Lin Jing Xin 林井心 in 1987 when he gave the poem to us.

and died there defending a losing side. If not for the Manchu invasion, General Wu could have developed into a great Ming general. Hence, General Wu is said to have "lived in an era that is untimely" (Line 14: 将军之生何不辰). This is the real message when Qing Shan says of himself at the beginning of the poem that he was "born in an untimely era, (and) not (at a time) when the General killing was his enemies" on behalf of the Manchu invaders (Line 1: 我生不逢将军提刀杀敌时).

In Line 21, Qing Shan demonstrates a masterly use of allusions to describe "A retreat (to Taiwan) would be all in vain" (杖藜皂帽恐徒然). It would be "in vain" at least for General Wu! In this line, Qing Shan shows his skillful use of the allusion to describe "retreat". The first four words 杖藜 (holding a walking staff) and 皂帽 (wearing a common black cap) are originally used in a positive sense to describe the wise and principled men who escape the turmoil and an oppressive regime by retreating into the wild to live as recluse. It is used here with a touch of sarcasm to suggest that a retreat to Taiwan would certainly not have served the ambition of the young General Wu.

Line 24 lays bare the truth about General Wu: "Surrender he must, a break would come again" (降志辱身原有待). The expression used in Line 24 "*jiang zhi ru shen* 降志辱身", in place of the simple word "surrender" is particularly damning. It literally means "to compromise your righteous aspiration and disgrace yourself". It is taken from Confucius who was praising some exemplary figures in history who "did not compromise [their] righteous aspirations and did not humiliate [themselves]" (不降其志，不辱其身). Qing Shan has turned it around as an implied rebuke of General Wu.

The third section (Lines 25-32) is openly critical of General Wu Ying for surrendering to the Manchus and retaking Taiwan from Zheng Chenggong.

Line 25: "Great talent and ambition he had from young.
　　　　　将军年少负奇才
Line 26: Great pity it'd be, to bury them unsung.
　　　　　不甘长弃没尘埃
Line 27: Eager for instant result from his every deed,
　　　　　功名事业急自见
Line 28: Han talent given to Manchu use is sad indeed."
　　　　　楚材晋用良可哀

What subtleties in the earlier lines are now cast aside. General Wu is now pictured as a talented but ambitious young man. His opportunity for greatness is to defect to the Manchus, lest all his talent and potential remained buried unsung (没尘埃). How lamentable it is that by switching sides, as a Han Chinese, his talent is given over to the foreign Manchu invaders!

The last two lines sums up the poem brilliantly:

Line 31: "Alas, the General's achievements seemed
　　　　　magnificent!
　　　　　呜呼！将军之功诚伟矣！
Line 32: But was this truly his righteous ambition?"
　　　　　是岂将军之志哉！

If only he had been born in a more opportune time in history!

Chapter 52

佚题

我生良不辰，
数奇遘阳九。
顾此七尺躯，
4 不能庇一妇。
秦嘉浪迹频，
黔娄落拓久。
万里累相随，
8 弱质劳奔走。

"No Title"

      Oh! Unlucky must have been the day I was born.
      My turn of fortune has gone so badly wrong.
      Look at me, a seven-foot man standing tall
4   Yet unable to protect his wife at all.
      Like Qin Jia, I have to wander far and about,
      Like Qian Lou, I am always down and out.
      She came with me this far; I've burdened her.
8   Frail in health, yet hardship she has to endure.
      Before the journey's end, untimely she left me.
      Weak though she was, could I from blame be free?
      Oh, how shall we ever fathom our ultimate fate?
12 My inner conscience tells me my blame is great.
      When I reflect on the land we have at home;
      We have enough to live on and to farm our own.
      I regret not heeding the words she conveys,
16 To stay home and live out together our days,
      Like Lao Lai, to enjoy our lives together alone.
      Who can say into old age we wouldn't have grown.
      The grief for my wife will never be wiped clean.
20 Sharing my grief, my old friends have been.
      I thank the sincere solace from my old friends;
      So earnestly expressed are all their concerns.
      Their advice to care for my health I value and follow;
24 Good advice like good medicine is bitter to swallow.

中道忽弃捐，

藐躬岂无负？

天命不可知，

12 寸心良自咎。

念此旧田园，

种桑亦数亩。

悔不听妇言，

16 故山长相守。

偕隐学老莱，

安知不白首？

悲怀不能忘，

20 殷忧贻我友。

感子故意长，

惠我抑何厚。

珍重金石言，

24 良药宁苦口。

春蚕未尽丝，

作茧自纷纠。

再拜读君诗，

28 有如醒宿酒。

达人贵知命，

眼泪非所有。

况因见女流，

32 对镜滋可丑。

Like the silkworm I continue to spew my grief,
Entwining myself to end up a life too brief.
I've read your consoling poem over and over;
28   It's like waking from a stupor the morning after.
The enlightened would accept the inevitability of Fate.
It serves no purpose to continue with tears to shed.
Much less for the sake of a woman, it might be said.
32   The mirror shows how bad my face the crying has made.
Pre-Creation, in the beginning of time before Chaos,
Till the world is consumed by fire, reduced to ashes.
In our whole universe and its boundlessness
36   Our very existence is one of randomness.
A lifetime is but a 36,000 days' time span,
Like flipping our palm as quick as we can.
We're co-sojourners in this world on life's journey.
40   It's part of life, whether untimely death or longevity.
The death of one's wife is sad, but Zhuangzi is singing:
Of the philosophy of life, he shows a deep understanding.
I alone am too dumb to follow Zhuangzi's reasoning.
44   Do you think I'm not ashamed of my shortcoming?
The encouraging words my good friends impart
Will always be engraved indelibly in my heart.

Paraphrase

L1: Oh, I must have been born on a most inauspicious day
L2: And encountered the worst of fortune there is.
L3: Just look at me, a person standing tall at seven feet
L4: Who can't even protect his own wife.
L5: Like Qin Jia, I often have wandered far.
L6: Like Qian Lou, I'm poor and always down and out.
L7: How I have burdened her to come with me this great distance.
L8: Already frail in health, she endured the hardship to come along.

上溯混沌前，
下穷劫灰后，
茫茫宇宙间，
36 吾生也特偶。
三万六千日，
有如一反手。
同宿逆旅中，
40 彭殇孰为寿？

是以鼓盆歌，
达观有庄叟。
而我独墩墩，
44 亦复自惭否？
我友镂良箴，
永以铭座右。

L9: But her poor life ended before the journey's end,
L10: Feeble though she is. How could I be free from blame?
L11: Oh Heaven, we shall never fathom our ultimate fate.
L12: My very conscience tells me I'm entirely to blame,
L13: (Especially) When I think of the land we have at home
L14: Which we can at least farm to support our livelihood.
L15: I regret not listening to her words
L16: To remain in our native home to live out our days together,
L17: To taste the familial joy like the proverbial Lao Lai.
L18: [If only I had heeded her], who can say that we could not have grown old together.
L19: The grief in me [for my wife] can never be wiped out.
L20: My old friends too share this grief with me.
L21: I appreciate the consolation of old friends sincerely expressed.
L22: Their kind concern for me is so sincere;
L23: Their advice for me to take care of my own health I greatly treasure.
L24: Good advice like good medicine is often bitter to take.
L25: I continue to spew out my grief like the silkworm which has not exhausted spitting out its silken thread.
L26: Still spinning its silken thread (around itself) into a cocoon at the risk of binding itself in pain and disaster.
L27: I read and re-read your poem.
L28: It becomes clear as awakening from a drunken stupor the morning after.
L29: An enlightened person would accept the inevitability of Fate (and move on from there).
L30: It serves no purpose to continue shedding tears,
L31: Much less it might be said, to shed tears for a woman.
L32: Looking at myself in the mirror, the crying has made my appearance look terrible.
L33: When we trace back from the Chaos in the beginning of time before Creation
L34: To the final Doomsday, when the world is consumed by fire and reduced to ashes,

L35: In the boundlessness of the universe
L36: Our existence is but by random chance
L37: A lifetime covers only a span of 36,000 days.
L38: It's like a quick flip of the palm.
L39: We're all co-sojourners travelling hurriedly in this world.
L40: Longevity (彭) or an untimely death (殇) are all part (孰为) of Life (寿)
L41: The tragic death of one's wife is truly mournful, but Zhuangzi is happily tapping on the plate singing.
L42: That Zhuangzi is so philosophical about Life shows his deep understanding of Life.
L43: I'm the only one who's too dumb (to follow that philosophy).
L44: Do you not think I'm ashamed of my shortcoming?
L45: The words of encouragement from my good friends
L46: Will always be engraved indelibly in my heart.

Background

Summary

Father first came to Nanyang in 1917. He returned to China in mid-1923 to get married to Wu Niao Mei 吴裊妹 and returned with his wife to Nanyang (Kampar) at the end of the same year. He was away for a total of six months. Not long after his return, his wife died in childbirth together with the child probably in the second half of 1924. Both mother and child were buried in Kampar, Malaya.

This composition is the earliest poem we have of Father's poetry. Written almost certainly in 1924, the poem was composed while Father was mourning the death of his first wife and in response to the poems and messages of consolation from his friends. It came to us from the same source as that of the Preface in Chapter 61, "Preface for Mr Huang Yun Shan's 'Tian

Nan Yin Cao'" (天南吟草) and another poem in Chapter 50, "The Fair Maiden Chen Yun Shan of Taichen" (纪陈韵珊女士事).

These three compositions came to us through an elderly gentleman from Muar 麻坡 (in Malaysia's Johor state 柔佛州). He chanced upon Father's name when he attended the Ipoh Fufeng Poetry Society (怡保扶风诗社) meeting in November 1991. At this meeting, copies of a collection of Father's poems, compiled by Madam Peng Shi Lin (彭士驎), were given to the participants. This gentleman later sent us, through Madam Peng, a photocopy of these three compositions.

Title of the Poem

The three compositions were given to us as photocopies of pages from a book. Like the early form of classical Chinese compositions, these did not use punctuation marks. This particular poem had the heading: "The original poem sent to me by Qing Shan" (晴山见酬原作). The poem is from a page in Mr Huang Yun Shan's book of poems 'Tian Nan Yin Cao' (天南吟草)." In the Preface in Chapter 61, Qing Shan described his close rapport with Mr Huang who most probably wrote him a poem in 1924 to comfort him. The poem was likely to have been composed and sent as a response to Mr Huang's poem of consolation and was then included in Mr Huang's book which was published in 1927.

A very early photo of Qing Shan (晴山) in the 1920s.

Father's First Wife

Unfortunately, we know little about Father's first wife Wu Niao Mei 吴裊妹. She appeared to have two brothers who were in Ipoh. We recall now that when we were very young, there were two brothers whom we were taught to address as "uncle" 阿舅 in our Hinghwa (兴化, 莆田) dialect, which is the same as jiu jiu 舅舅 in Mandarin. In either form, it denotes a genuine relationship. The two brothers returned to China after the Japanese Occupation ended.

We also recall in the early 1950s we once went with Father to a cemetery just outside the township of Kampar. We did not know it then, but it was to visit the grave of his first wife and to repaint the engraved wording on her gravestone. We were very young and did not quite know what it was all about. We went in a hired taxi. When we reached the foot of the hill where the cemetery was located, Father took Michael up the hill. He had a small tin of red paint and a writing brush pen with him. Peter, who was three years older, stayed behind in the car with Mother to wait. This is how Michael remembers the event today, even after nearly 60 years!

In Michael's own words: *"Father took me with him to walk up the hill along a little dirt path. It must have been quite some time since his last visit, because he made a few wrong turns. Father was in his usual attire, wearing a white cotton jacket but without a tie. It was early afternoon and a hot day. As we trudged our way up the hill, he reached into his pocket frequently for his handkerchief to wipe the sweat off his forehead. It was about mid-hill, off the main walk path that he finally found the tomb. Strangely enough, I still have a vivid image of the tomb clearly in my mind. It was made from a grey-coloured stone (probably unpolished granite), the type commonly used for "milestones" along major roads in Malaysia before the highways were built. The tomb (坟墓) was typically Chinese-style, a dome-shaped mound. It was of a modest size, about 18 inches wide and 26 to 30 inches high. Father then dipped the brush pen into a small tin of red paint, and refreshed the engraved wording. I must have been in my third grade in school and recognized a few words on the tombstone as 'Loving Wife ____, Mother and child herein interred' (爱妻____ 母子合葬). Father's name Chen Qing Shan (陈晴山) was also on the tombstone, all wordings* engraved vertically. When Father and I returned to the taxi at the foot of the hill, Peter and Mother were both waiting there. I recall seeing Mother very quiet."

Appreciation

This is a very early poem of 46 lines, composed when Qing Shan was mourning the death of his first wife. He had been married only about a year when she died (in 1924) in childbirth. It is full of sorrow and remorse as he tearfully admonishes himself for not having heeded his wife's plea to stay back in China.

The poem may be divided into three sections, with the first comprising Lines 1–20. He first blames himself for having been born on an unlucky day and feels guilt in his inability to "protect" his wife. "Look at me, a seven-foot man standing tall, Yet unable to protect his wife at all" (顾此七尺躯，不能庇一妇). He regrets his unfortunate circumstance, having to leave home (away from China) to earn a living, comparing himself with Qin Jia 秦嘉. The poet Qin Jia lived during the Han dynasty; he died a long way from home while serving in an official position. Qing Shan also laments that he is a poor man, and compares himself with Qian Lou 黔娄, a philosopher of the Warring States period; Qian Lou's poverty was legendary as he declined all official posts and chose to remain poor (but free from obligations).

The most poignant lines of this poem are perhaps in Lines 11–16.

> Line 11: "Oh, how shall we ever fathom our ultimate fate. 天命不可知
> Line 12: My inner conscience tells me my blame is great. 寸心良自咎
> Line 13: When I reflect on the land we have at home; 念此旧田园

Line 14: We have enough to live on and to farm our own.
   种桑亦数亩
Line 15: I regret not heeding the words she conveys,
   悔不听妇言
Line 16: To stay home and live out together our days,"
   故山长相守

Qing Shan's father was a scholar. Although he was not rich, he at least had a small acreage of land rented out for others to farm. The reference to "the land we have at home" is more than a figure of speech. It is probably not enough to support the family and Qing Shan is compelled to return to Nanyang, despite the plea of his wife to stay. If only he had listened to her, they might have been able to live out their old age together!

The second section runs from Lines 21–28. The lines herein convey his gratitude towards his friends for consoling him and advising him to look after his own health. However good the advice is, like good medicine, it is not always easy to take. In Lines 25-26, Qing Shan uses the analogy of a silkworm relentlessly spewing out its thread, except that his thread is his grief. The silkworm will not stop until its thread is exhausted. This is inspired by the Tang poem of Li Shangyin (李商隐) whose line reads: "The Silkworm's thread exhausts only on death's relief" (春蚕到死丝方尽). Qing Shan extends the analogy by describing how his inexorable grief may end up harming himself.

Line 25: "Like the silkworm I continue to spew my grief,
   春蚕未尽丝
Line 26: Entwining myself to end up a life too brief."
   作茧自纷纠

The silkworm spins its thread round itself to entwine itself into a cocoon. We see in this line how Qing Shan, even in this very early poem, has begun using his technique of extending or turning an allusion into a fresh new expression.

The third section runs from Line 29 to the end of the poem. It portrays a contradiction of feelings in Qing Shan. On the one hand, he tries to rationalize that an "enlightened or truly wise person" (*da ren* 达人) will know the true nature of Life and the inevitability of Fate (Line 29). Besides, it serves no purpose to cry, much less to cry over a woman (Lines 30–31)! In the next few lines, Qing Shan tries to "downplay" the significance of Death by pointing out in Line 36 that our very existence is a random chance (吾生也特偶). After all, our human life is but a duration of 36,000 days long (100 years), which passes as quickly as the flip of our palm. Finally, he pulls out the ultimate card in the argument by quoting Zhuangzi who even sings and taps on the plate to beat time while "mourning" the death of his wife (Line 41: *shi yi gu pen ge* 是以鼓盆歌). This is because Zhuangzi, being an enlightened person knows all that.

Death is part of a never-ending cycle of change, like the changing of the seasons, the alternating changes between night and day. There is nothing to be happy about Life and nothing to be sad about Death.

After all those brilliant arguments, Qing Shan still comes back to the reality — he still grieves for his wife. It must be because he is too dumb to understand the profound philosophy of Zhuangzi (Line 43: *er wo du dun dun* 而我独墩墩)!

Chapter 53

咏李香兰

多时不听卖糖歌,
铁锁琅珰响佩珂。
几许时人齐下泪,
伤心非独一星娥。

A Song to Li Xiang Lan

No more the "Candy Song" you once sang.
Iron padlocks against the jade pendant clang.
Many are those who with their tears do part.
You're not alone with a grieving heart.

Paraphrase

L1: It's a long time since we've heard you sing the "Candy Song".
L2: What we hear now is the clanging of iron padlocks against the jade pendant.
L3: There are many out there who are saddened to the point of tears for you.
L4: And you, the beautiful star of heaven is not the only grieving one.

Background

Li Xiang Lan was a popular actress and singer in China and among the Chinese population throughout Southeast Asia countries like Singapore and Malaya before the Second World War. A song made famous by her in one of her films was called "The Candy Song" 卖糖歌 and it became her signature tune. The film *Wàn Shì Liú Fāng* 《万世流芳》 was about the anti-opium campaign waged in 1839 by Lín Zé Xú 林则徐 in Guangdong. In the film, Li Xiang Lan played the role of a candy-selling girl spreading the message against the evils of opium smoking.

She was born in 1920 in Manchuria where her father was an employee of the Japanese-run railway. She was beautiful, had a good operatic voice and was fluent in Japanese and Chinese. The Japanese used her during the war years as a symbol of Chinese-Japanese friendship. Shortly after the end of the Second World War, she was arrested by the Chinese government on charges of collaboration with the Japanese. The treason charges were dropped when it emerged that Li Xiang Lan was actually not Chinese at all. She was in fact Japanese, even though she was born and raised in northern China. She was eventually deported and lives today in the United States.

Her arrest and trial for treason would have taken place between September 1945 (Japanese surrender) and the dropping of the charges against her in February 1946. The poem is likely to have been composed shortly after news of her arrest perhaps in late 1945 or even early 1946. The date of composition is likely to be well before the end of the trial in February 1946 when it was revealed that she was not Chinese after all.

Li Xiang Lan was immensely popular in Singapore and Malaya and had a great number of fans. By his own word, Father was a movie fan (refer to the paraphrase of poem in Chapter 15), but the poem must also have been a reflection of the public reaction to the news of her arrest and trial at that time.

Appreciation

In four brief lines, this poem expresses a great deal of emotion over the "fallen star" of the beautiful and popular Li Xiang Lan. It is like a poem with one message written in normal ink and a different message hiding underneath in invisible ink.

The popular reaction to her arrest could also be a mixed bag of emotions. "No more the 'Candy Song' you once sang 多时不听卖糖歌". Line 1 is not as clear-cut as it looks. Is it an expression of sadness and regret that "no longer do we hear you sing the Candy Song"? Or is it a rebuke which says "no longer do we <u>want to</u> hear you sing the Candy Song"? Their beloved Li Xiang Lan is being tried for treason against China!

In Line 2, we can almost "hear" the sound of her incarceration: "Iron padlocks against the jade pendant clang 铁锁琅珰响佩珂. The Chinese expression *láng dāng* 琅珰 used in the line has two meanings. It is an onomatopoeia (word or phrase that suggests the sound described) and also means "prisoner's chain". The use of the expression "jade pendant 佩珂" defines her beauty and femininity.

Line 3 apparently describes the tears shed for the popular Li Xiang Lan at her arrest. Qing Shan could also be subtly pointing out to the suffering of the Chinese people in China and Southeast Asia at the hands of the Japanese.

Line 4 continues with the dual message: "You're not alone with a grieving heart 伤心非独一星娥". The visible message is "you do not grieve alone, because your thousands of fans grieve with you". The "invisible" message is "you do not grieve alone. Thousands of Chinese also grieve because of their suffering as a result of your betrayal."

This is quite a remarkable poem with two parallel messages, a hallmark of Qing Shan's poems.

Chapter 54

题劫灰集后寄酬西浪

三年八月叹沦胥，
坑外同为漏网鱼。
顾我已无长物在，
4 多君犹有劫灰余。
风云色霁回天后，
金石声闻掷地初。
腹内诗书烧不尽，
8 祖龙毕竟霸才疏。

卅六年一月年三日

Postscript for Jiehui Anthology of Poems Sent to Xi Lang

Oh, cruelly occupied we've been for three years eight months.
Out of the pit of hell, through the dragnet we've come.
I have not a shred on hand that's worth anything;
4   Despite the turmoil, you have salvaged your writing.
War has ended, the haze dispersed, fair sky is seen.
Your writing's like the first note, a sound so pristine.
No fire can ever destroy within us, our poetry.
8   Emperor Qin can't match us even with his tyranny.

Paraphrase

L1: Alas, how we have endured the three years and eight months of death and destruction
L2: Out of the pit of hell, we are all lucky enough to have slipped through the dragnet of death.
L3: I have not a shred of anything left on hand.
L4: We are fortunate that your writings have managed to survive.
L5: The war has ended, the haze dispersed, the fair sky can be seen once again.
L6: It's like hearing the first note struck of the musical stone chime.

L7: The poetry within us is ultimately indestructible even by fire.
L8: Even the tyranny of Emperor Qin is no match to our poetry.

Background

This poem came to us rather fortuitously one day in 2005. Our cousin sister Wang Xia Xian 王霞仙 had put aside some old documents and books which she thought might be of interest to us. Among the papers were some handwritten drafts of Father's poems and a copy of Xi Lang's *Jiehui Anthology of Poems*. The date of publication is uncertain, but the last epilogue written is dated 30 May 1946 and the book was printed in Hong Kong.

Li Xi Lang (died 1972) was a well-known Malayan-Singapore Chinese literary writer in the 1920s, renowned for his classical poems for which he earned the name "Poet of the South" (南国诗人). He appears to have lived in Singapore.

There were two copies of this book among the material handed over to us. One was personally inscribed with a seal by Xi Lang for Father. The other was similarly inscribed for our fourth uncle Guang Guo 光国 (Xia Xian's father). This poem was personally inscribed by Father on the last page of Guang Guo's copy of Xi Lang's anthology; the inscription even bears Father's seal. It is reasonable to assume that a copy of the poem was sent to Xi Lang.

Appreciation

At the end of the Japanese Occupation in August 1945, a flurry of publications of poems began to appear as the dust is blown off writings that had been secretly composed and kept during the three years eight months of the occupation. Xi Lang's collection of poems by himself and some from his friends is just one of several that appear.

Most of the poems in the anthology describe the writers' tribulations during the dark years of the Occupation or like Qing Shan's poem, expresses great relief at the end of the ordeal. The "signature" of this genre of poems is the expression "three years eight months", as though everyone had been counting the entire ordeal by the day. This poem's opening line is no exception; "Oh, cruelly occupied we've been for three years eight months". Many innocent people were killed during the Occupation.

Line 2 uses two picturesque metaphors to describe the survivors' relief and experience: "Out of the pit of hell, through the dragnet we've come." The "pit" is both a current and historical allusion. In the early days of the Occupation, untold atrocities were committed by the Japanese. Purges of the Chinese were conducted; the victims were rounded up, massacred and buried in "pits" of mass graves. The historical allusion refers to Emperor Qin's reputed burial of the scholars alive. The use of the metaphor of having slipped (come) through the dragnet is very appropriate. The Japanese conducted mass "screening" exercises known as "sook ching" (*su qing* 肅清) to identify and eradicate anti-Japanese elements. The population

The memorial plaque commemorating the sacrifice of the anti-Japanese fighters during the Occupation from 1942 to 1945. The memorial is still tended till today 70 years later, at the village of Langkap in Malaysia. "*Oh, cruelly occupied we've been for three years eight months. Out of the pit of hell, through the dragnet we've come.*"

was assembled in a large holding area and each person was made to file pass a hooded informant. His word can mean life or death. Those who managed to come through, were like fish that have slipped through the net. Anyone who has lived through those terrible times will instantly know what the line means. In those two lines, Qing Shan has managed to paint the experience of three years eight months of hell.

In Lines 3-4, Qing Shan describes how he had survived, with nothing but his life. He contrasts this with Xi Lang who had survived with his precious collection of poems. With his writings intact, their publication would sound like the first note of the stone chime, clear and pristine, reverberating through a clear and beautiful sky (Lines 5-6).

In a final shout of defiance, Lines 7–8 declare that the poetry that is in us can never be completely destroyed by fire—another reference to Emperor Qin who stands accused by history of a double crime: "burn the books and bury the scholars" (焚书坑儒). The poem ends with the line "Emperor Qin can't match us even with his tyranny" as though thumbing his nose at the defeated and departing Japanese.

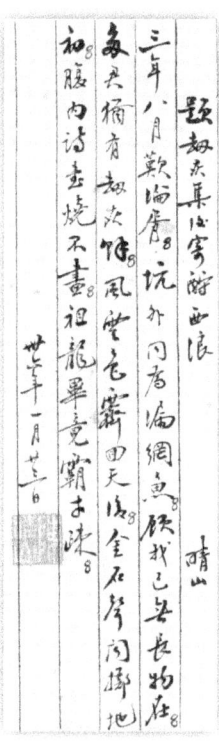

← The poem inscribed personally by Qing Shan on the last page of the copy of Xi Lang's anthology of poems that had been given by Xi Lang to our fourth uncle Wang Guang Guo. The poem is dated 23 November, 36th Year of the Chinese Republic (1947).

The book cover of Xi Lang's book *Jiehui Anthology of Poems*.

Chapter 55

gǎn huái
感怀

tiān yá hé chù nài sī liàng
天 涯 何 处 耐 思 量？

shí dé wēn róu biàn shì xiāng
识 得 温 柔 便 是 乡。

yuè rèn xīng suí guāng bù jiǎn
月 任 星 随 光 不 减，

huā suī zǐ jié yè yóu xiāng
4 花 虽 子 结 叶 犹 香。

piān zhōu wèi xǔ wǔ hú gòng
扁 舟 未 许 五 湖 共，

dòu mǐ rěn lìng sān jìng huāng
斗 米 忍 令 三 径 荒？

hé jìng fēi yīn méi yǔ hè
和 靖 非 因 梅 与 鹤，

gū shān qǐ biàn zú cháng yáng
8 孤 山 岂 便 足 徜 徉？

Reflections

In a distant land, where do we long to be?
Home is love and warmth, wherever it is.
With the stars about, the moon is not less brilliant.
4   The flowers bear fruits, the leaves are still fragrant.
My little boat can't leisurely drift the five lakes.
To make a living, my own garden's overgrown.
He Jing would be no recluse, but for his plum and crane.
8   The recluse couldn't be kept there by Gu Shan alone.

Paraphrase

L1: When in the far corners of the earth, what is the place we most long to be in?
L2: Home is wherever we find love and warmth.
L3: Although surrounded by numerous twinkling stars, the moon is not any less bright.
L4: Although the flowers have turned into fruits, the leaves still retain their fragrance.
L5: My circumstance doesn't allow me to drift leisurely over the five lakes living as a recluse.
L6: For the sake of making a living, can I bear to leave home and leave my own garden uncared for (as *Tao Yuanming* once did)?

L7: *He Jing* would not have been able to roam and lead the life of a recluse in the wilderness, had it not been for the plum and crane as his companions (which are like "wife" and "children" to him),

L8: However nice Gu Shan (a place in Hanzhou) may be, it alone would never have been good enough a reason for *He Jing* to live there by himself as a recluse.

Background

Father first came to Malaya in 1917. He returned to China in 1923 to get married and again in early 1930s (with the family). The second stay was only for two to three years as he had to flee China to avoid arrest by the Putian Governor for what he wrote. Then came the Second World War and Malaya/Singapore were occupied from 1942 to 1945, during which time there was no postal communication between Malaya and China. It was only when the war ended in August 1945 that he learned his father had died in China in 1940.

When World War II ended, the civil war in China between the Communists and the Nationalists (Guomindang 国民党) intensified, and in 1949 the Communists took total control of the entire country. It is likely that by 1949 it became clear to Father that he was unlikely ever to return to his native Putian in China, although nostalgia for the "old country" still persisted. Nanyang would finally be his new home. This poem is likely to have been composed in 1950 about the time he and Mother were applying for citizenship of the Federation of Malaya (established in 1948).

Appreciation

Lines 1 and 2 are perhaps the two most beautiful lines of the poem. Line 1 is a common sentiment expressed by the Chinese, who like Qing Shan, left home in China a hundred years ago to work or seek their fortune. All had the intention of returning to their "native land" one day, but most never made it.

In the first one, two or even three decades overseas, they longed for their homeland. For Qing Shan, the end of the civil war in China and the beginning of Communist rule in the mainland in 1949 marked the turning point.

Line 1: "In a distant land, where do we long to be?
天涯何处耐思量
Line 2: Home is love and warmth, wherever it is."
识得温柔便是乡

The question posed by Line 1 is not directly answered. The implicit answer is "Home" is where we long to be! Line 2 then defines what really is "Home". It is not the place where you are born or come from originally. "Home" is "everywhere" and "wherever" you find love and warmth with your wife and children and with your friends.

TO WHOM IT MAY CONCERN

Bearer Mr. Chen Thing San of No.9, Leong Sin Nam Street, Ipoh, is personally known to me.

He has been a Resident in the Federation for a period of not less than 20 years.

Dated at Ipoh this 30th day of October 1950.

Peh Seng Koon

Qing Shan's application for Malayan citizenship in 1950 required the minimum of a 20-year residence in the country. This is the certificate to that effect, signed by the community leader Mr Bai Cheng Gen (also known as Peh Seng Koon), one of his poetry friends and "boss".

55 Reflections

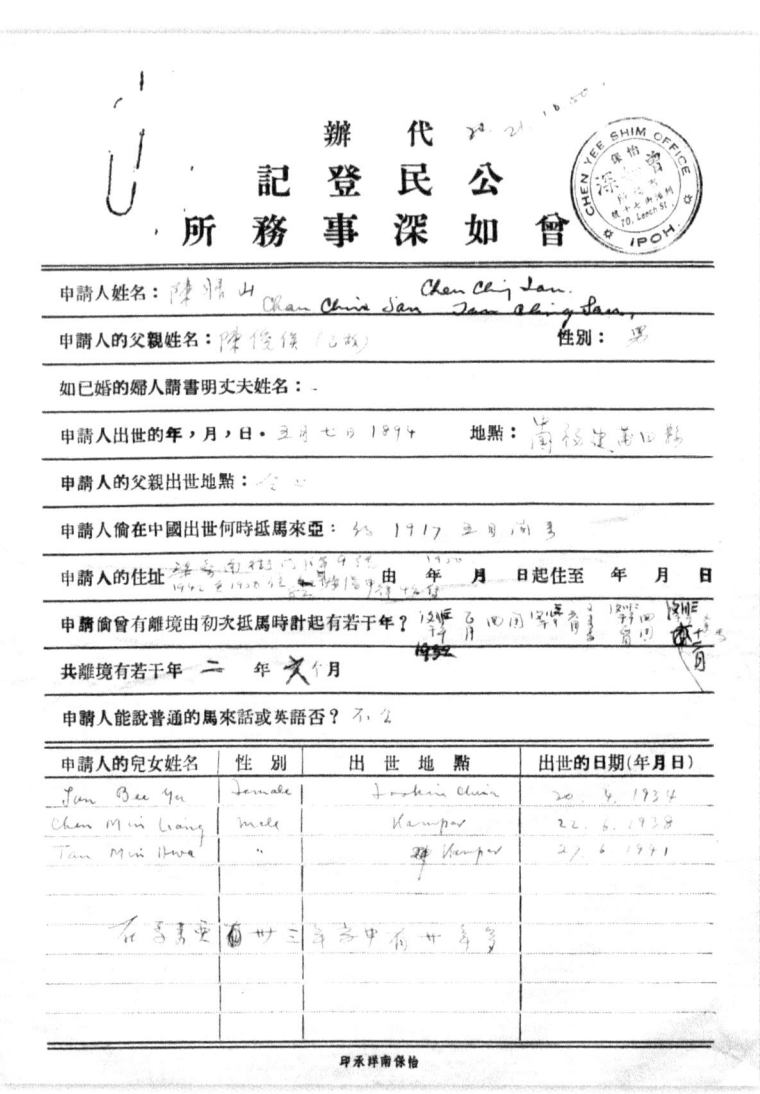

Qing Shan's application for Malayan Citizenship. This was a turning point for him.
"In a distant land, where do we long to be? Home is love and warmth, wherever it is."

In Lines 3 and 4, Qing Shan uses the metaphor "moon" and the "stars" that accompany it to represent his wife and himself. His wife is not any less "brilliant" (beautiful) after marrying him. This analogy is taken further in the next line. "The flowers bear fruits, (yet) the leaves are still fragrant". It says that even after bearing children, his wife is just as alluring to him. Qing Shan's home is wherever his family is, for they give him love and warmth.

Lines 5 and 6 explain his own circumstance that has prevented him to freely do what he wants. It is to leisurely drift from place to place, like the learned men who chose to live in seclusion, free from all worldly affairs. Even Tao Yuanming, at one time, had to forsake this carefree life in order to earn a living. For the sake of "five bushels of rice" (五斗米), he had to bear the thought of leaving his garden at home unattended and overgrown with weed (忍令三径荒). Tao Yuanming eventually thumbed his nose at all this and returned to his own family to enjoy the chrysanthemums and tend to his garden. There is a hint of regret in Qing Shan who wishes he had the same courage and resolve to be able to do that.

The last two Lines 7 and 8 use the allusion of Lin He Jing 林和靖 (of Song dynasty) who refused to serve as an official in the corrupt and tyrannical political environment of his time. He chose instead to live in seclusion in Gu Shan 孤山 in Hangzhou's West Lake for 40 years. He had only his plum trees and the cranes (梅鹤) for his companions. They are like his wife and children to him. Line 8 further explains that however attractive Gu Shan might be, it is the plum trees and the cranes, He Jing's "wife" and "children" that kept him there for 40 years.

Chapter 56

过禄宽新居
guò lù kuān xīn jū

吾闻天地之大无不容，
世或处之若樊笼。
又闻壶公昔向壶中宿，
4 壶中日月天地之大乐融融。
可知境由心造耳，
身寄一壶心千里。
不然虽有广厦千万间，
8 欲求容膝之安亦难矣！

On Passing by Lu Kuan's New House

    The world is so large it can hold everything;
    Yet people feel restricted as though caged in.
    The Old Man of the Bottle returns to his bottle nightly.
4   In the magic world of mansions he lives blissfully.
    How large or small a place, is made up in our mind.
    Even confined in a bottle, we can be open-minded and kind.
    The narrow-minded have many mansions yet feel confined.
8   They have problem living in a small place with ease of mind.
    We are not all like Wu Ba, the legendary giant
    Whose girth is ten hand spans; a large drum serves for his pillow.
    Even if a man's height is a huge seven feet,
12 A simple structure will meet his need.
    What need for large mansions that reach to the sky?
    Price of land shoots up as people clamour to buy.
    With no more room on earth, we'll soon call on Heaven
16 To let us buy a hill on the moon even.
    The owner of this idyllic house leads a contented life,
    Tending his little cottage, happy with family and wife.
    He has left land for others on which to build.
20 To have anyone without shelter is not his will.
    His house is tiny as a snail shell, says he humbly.
    More than the magic world of the Bottle, happy is he.

世人岂皆毋霸巨,
腰可十围头枕鼓?
纵令昂藏七尺躯,
12 一椽已足蔽风雨。
胡为甲第起连云,
求田问舍尚纷纷?
地已无皮天可上,
16 买山更向月球奔。
桃源主人能知足,
挈妇抱孙营小筑。
留将余地与他人,
20 但愿道旁无露宿。

The loving couple tend their flowers and trees;
24　They even have space in front for a small carriage.
　　　Sir, do you not see how desolate the once famous gardens are these days?
　　　Abandoned, dusty and overgrown with weeds, they've seen better days.
　　　But in Sichuan today, there still stands Ziyun Pavilion.
28　Ziyun's name and fame have a thousand years endured.

Paraphrase

L1:　The world is so large there is nothing it cannot accommodate
L2:　Yet people living in this wide spacious world still feel restricted, as though living in a bird cage.
L3:　It's said that the legendary Old Man of the Bottle returns daily into his bottle for the night.
L4:　In his bottle is a complete magical world of its own, with magnificent buildings, fine food and everyone lives blissfully.
L5:　Whether a place is large or small is the making of our own state of mind.
L6:　We may live bodily in a confined space as the legendary bottle, but our mind can still be generous and accommodating.
L7:　On the other hand, those who possess many large houses,
L8:　Will never feel at ease living in a small place.
L9:　Not everyone is as big as the legendary giant called Wu Ba Ju
L10: His girth was ten-palm spans wide and he was big enough to use a huge drum for his pillow.
L11: Assuming a man is huge seven feet tall,
L12: Even a simple structure will suffice to shelter him against the elements.
L13: Why build mansions so high that will even touch the clouds?

主人自谓为蜗庐，

乐趣却胜壶中居。

莳花种树偕妻子，

24 门前长可挽鹿车。

君不见，洛阳名园皆寂寞，

草蔓烟荒日色薄？

西蜀犹有子云亭，

28 千载之下留其名。

L14: Or allow the buying of land and house to result in great market turmoil.
L15: If there were no more room on earth for us to build, we might have to expand skywards
L16: By buying a hill or even acquiring land on the moon.
L17: Lu Kuan who lives in his own Shangri-la leads a happy contented life
L18: Enjoying the company of his wife and grandchildren (familial joy), tending his little cottage
L19: Whatever land that's not built on by him is left to others to build.
L20: He does not wish to see anyone left without shelter.
L21: The owner of this house, in self-deprecation, says it is but tiny as a snail shell.
L22: But I see that his joy surpasses that of the legendary "Old Man" living in his "Bottle".
L23: Together with his wife planting flowers and tending the trees;
L24: Always together as a loving couple, they have space even for a small carriage (car).
L25: Sir, do you not see how desolate now are all those once magnificent gardens of royalty and the rich?
L26: They are overgrown by weeds and abandoned, having seen better days.
L27: But in Sichuan, there still stands today the Ziyun Pavilion 子云亭 (dedicated to the memory of the Western Han scholar Yang Xiong 杨雄, also known as Ziyun)
L28: Ziyun's fame has endured more than a thousand years.

Background

Summary

One of Father's poetry friends, Hong Lu Kuan 洪禄宽, moved into his new house in 1957. This poem does not look like the typical poem for celebrating a new house, nor does it seem to be written in response to a request from Lu Kuan. Father might have responded to a poem by Lu Kuan himself about his new house.

Lu Kuan was a rubber merchant in Ipoh and a committee member of the Perak Hokkien Association of which another poetry friend Bai Cheng Geng 白成根, was the President. He was a man of reasonable means. Qing Shan was the paid Secretary of the Association, but the relationship between the three was one of genuine friendship, bonded by their common love for classical poetry. There are several poems written by Father for his two poetry friends and vice versa.

The house that Lu Kuan bought is located at No.1 Jalan Gopal Singh in Ipoh. According to his daughter Cui Lan 翠兰, it cost 25,000 dollars. It was part of the first residential housing estate in Ipoh built by the "Housing Trust" for sale to the public. As a businessman of some means, Lu Kuan was able to buy this bungalow with modern flush toilets and all! Our family too had wanted to book a very small single-storey house of 9,000 dollars in the same housing estate at that time. For a number of reasons, including money, we were not able to. We had to be contented with one room for the whole family, but Father was fortunate enough to be provided a room partitioned off in his large office at the Perak Hokkien Association where he worked.

One of Mother's former tailoring students Jiang Shu Hua 蒋淑华 moved into a house in the same residential estate. We recall taking our parents to visit her and passed by Lu Kuan's house in 1957 on one occasion.

Hong Lu Kuan's house is still there, now lived in by his grand-daughter and her family.

Hong Lu Kuan

He was born in Fujian around the year 1891. He was hence three years older than Father. He studied in the old-style private school in China which explains his love for poetry. It is unusual for successful businessmen to be interested in poetry. Perhaps in Lu Kuan's case, he was a person who loved poetry and who subsequently became a successful businessman and not vice versa. Among Father's "poetry friends", two other examples were Bai Cheng Gen (Chapters 42 and 43) and Bai Yang Feng (Chapter 34).

Even Lu Kuan's daughter, Cui Lan, was not aware that her father could compose poems until she was in her twenties when she saw her father's poems appearing in the local newspaper. Cui Lan recalled he used to recite the "300 Tang Poems" 唐诗三百首 in the Fujian dialect. She also remembered that her father would mention Qing Shan's name whenever there was any poetry involved or formal documents to be prepared.

Lu Kuan came from a poor family and used to sell *you tiao* 油条 by the roadside when he was young. He migrated to Malaya whereas his three other "classmates" later migrated to Singapore. He started life as a clerk in Ipoh with a cloth merchant whose shop name was Wan Shun De 万顺德. This is an indication that he was sufficiently educated.

He later joined two friends to open a drapery shop in Kuala Kangsar, but there was a fire and the entire business was lost. He returned to Ipoh to open a wholesale grocery shop in 1926/1927 called Kuan Ji 宽记 (after his own name) in Chamberlain Road. Two years later, he founded his rubber trading business in Hume Street with the name Nan Chun Zhan 南春栈.

After the Japanese Occupation, Lu Kuan did not have much money left. A great deal of money was paid to the Japanese as war compensation in the form of a poll tax imposed on the Chinese population in Malaya and Singapore.

Appreciation

The title of this poem raises an interesting question: "On Passing by Lu Kuan's New House". Since Qing Shan was a poetry friend of Lu Kuan, had he not visited Lu Kuan's house? Or had Qing Shan merely "passed by" the house as the title suggests. (It was not the custom to have "housewarming" parties in those days.) Qing Shan probably had not been to the house but had passed by it on one occasion. The poem may, at first sight, read like the detached comments of a "passerby", but more likely, it is a poem written after he read Lu Kuan's own poem about his new house. It is quite likely Lu Kuan could have said, in all humility, that his new house was "small as a snail shell 主人自谓为蜗庐" and that might have provided Qing Shan with the platform for this poem.

The poem of 28 lines can be said to comprise two sections. The first section from Line 1 to Line 16 proclaims the philosophy that our environment is what we make of it in our own mind. It criticizes those who keep wanting to acquire more property and bigger houses. Lines 7–8 criticize "The narrow-minded (who) have many mansions 广厦千万间 and (yet) feel confined". "They have problem living in a small place with ease of mind". The lines say that irrespective of the size of the house, the important thing is that we are content with what we have. This is a reflection of the common Chinese saying, "To know Contentment is constant Happiness" 知足常乐, a quote from the Chinese philosopher Lao Zi 老子.

The poem uses the amazing story of the Old Man of the Bottle 壶公 taken from the *Later Han Chronicles* 《后汉书》. A local official by the name of Fei Zhang Fang 费长房 once saw a strange-looking old man selling medicine by the roadside. He had a bottle swung round his neck. Every evening when the crowds had dispersed, he would "jump" into his bottle. Zhang Fang knew he was an extraordinary man and wanted to meet him. He brought along gifts of wine and food. The old man knew what Zhang's intention was and invited him to come again the next day to take a trip home into his bottle with him. When the two got in, it was like a magic world. It was a glorious place full of beautiful mansions and there were lots of exotic food to savour. After a sumptuous meal together, it was time for Zhang Fang to leave and the Old Man made him promise not to tell anyone about this. Contentment is all in the remarkable world of our own mind and making.

The second part from Line 17 onwards praises Lu Kuan for being a modest man, content with the house he has. He is content with the familial joy. The literal translation of Line 17 is: "to hold his wife's hand, carry the grandchildren in his arms and tend to his little cottage 挈妇抱孙营小筑". Line 19 praises Lu Kuan for not indulging in a big property, thus "He has land left for others on which to build". This is in contrast with "the narrow-minded" in Line 7 who "have many mansions 广厦千万间" and yet "feel confined". The expression "many mansions" comes from Du Fu's poem, "My thatched cottage is blown off by the autumn wind 茅屋为秋风所破歌". The Tang poet Du Fu was living as a recluse and his poem describes how the thatch of his cottage was blown off by the autumn wind and he was unable to retrieve it from the children who ran off with part of his roof! As a result, his cottage leaked everywhere in the autumn rain, making it difficult for him to sleep. In the closing lines of the poem, he lamented:

> "How could we get the many mansions that are here
> 安得广厦千万间
> To spread out and bring a poor recluse a little cheer."
> 大庇天下寒士俱欢颜

Line 20 praises Lu Kuan for not wanting to see anyone left out and without shelter. This contrasts with Line 8 which criticizes those who can never find ease living in a small place. Line 8's literal meaning is "To seek ease of mind in a small place would be difficult 欲求容膝之安亦难矣！" The metaphor used for "a small place" is 容膝 which literally means "that can accommodate knees" or simply "knee space". In other words, "just big enough to accommodate one's knees without knocking into the next person". Qing Shan's line has deliberately chosen these two identical words *róng xī* 容膝 used in Tao Yuanming's famous essay "Homeward Bound" 归去来兮辞 to complement a later allusion. The two lines from Tao Yuanming's essay are:

"Leaning on the south window, putting the world aside,
倚南窗以寄傲
In my tiny space at home, completely at ease am I."
审容膝之易安

Tao Yuanming, the pastoral poet, had just resigned from his official post after only three months. He "retired" to his own home. His two lines describe his feelings of ease and relief upon returning home. Qing Shan has chosen another Tao Yuanming allusion in Line 17 by referring to Lu Kuan as the "owner of Taoyuan 桃源" or "Peach Spring". The reference is to TaoYuanming's prose essay with the title "Peach Blossom Spring", viz., "Taohua Yuan Ji 桃花源记". It is the story of a beautiful and peaceful place hidden from the outside world. Everyone in Taoyuan lived in perfect happiness and contentment, or a "Utopia".

Line 23 describes Lu Kuan and his wife as the old and loving couple happily tending their garden. Line 24 says that the house (even though Lu Kuan claims it to be small) has sufficient space to park a small "carriage" (car). The literal meaning of Line 24: "In front of the house (门前), there is sufficient space (长可) to pull a deer carriage through (挽鹿车)". Line 24 is another example of Qing Shan's mastery in the use of allusion to imply a futher meaning. The expression "to pull a deer carriage through (挽鹿车)" is an adaptation of the proverb "together, pull a deer carriage (共挽鹿车)". It is a metaphor that praises a husband and wife couple who stay loyally together "through thick and thin", "for better or worse". The proverb comes from the Later Han Chronicles, "The Story of Bao Xuan's Wife". 《后汉书·鲍宣妻传》. Bao Xuan's wife Shao Jun 少君 was the daughter of a wealthy family. Her father was in fact Bao Xuan's teacher who admired the student Bao Xuan 鲍宣 for all his talent and qualities. Hence she was betrothed to Bao Xuan. When Bao Xuan first saw Shao Jun dressed in all her finery, he said, "I am from a poor family; we can never be a good match." Shao Jun replied, "My father admires your qualities and so do I. That is why I am betrothed to you. I shall live by your principles and do as you command." Shao Jun then discarded her fine clothes and put on a coarse tunic. This greatly pleased Bao Xuan. The couple then went to Bao Xuan's village to meet his parents. They travelled there by pulling along a "deer carriage". (It was termed a "deer carriage" probably because it was a carriage small enough to be drawn by a deer which was a smaller, more common and affordable animal than a horse).

To add further praise to Lu Kuan, Qing Shan refers indirectly to a famous essay titled "陋室铭" (Lòu Shì Míng) by the Tang poet Liú Yǔ Xī 刘禹锡 (772–842). Lines 25–26 of Qing Shan's poem point out that the once famous gardens in the ancient capital Luoyang now lie abandoned and in decay. This contrasts with the name Ziyun Pavilion 子云亭 commemorating the great Han scholar Yang Xiong 杨雄 (53BC–AD18), who was also known as Ziyun (Lines 27–28). The pavilion no longer exists today but one location in modern day Sichuan, believed to be where Yang Xiong's modest home once stood, continues to be remembered. The memory of Yang Xiong as symbolized by the name Ziyun Pavilion was singled out for mention by Liú Yǔ Xī in his essay Lòu Shì Míng. Qing Shan's poem closes with Line 28: "Ziyun's name and fame have a thousand years endured 千载之下留其名".

This essay, as with all the other allusions used in the poem would be well known to a poet like Lu Kuan. The last line from the essay of Liú Yǔ Xī, although not quoted by Qing Shan could just as well sum up his answer to Lu Kuan's humble description of the modest size of his new house:

"If a Superior Man lives in it, what's so humble about it 君子居之，何陋之有?"

Chapter 57

题易君左先生诗书画个展特刊

沁园春唱彻云天,

艺海何期有鲁连。

一帜独标征亮节。

4 四魂不绝得真传。

等身著作名山业,

满目琳琅异国缘。

为报鸡林行贾道,

8 此中只少美新篇。

Colophon for Mr Yi Jun Zuo's Calligraphy and Painting Exhibition Catalogue

    Your "Qin Yuan Chun" is sung and highly praised.
    In the Arts, a modern Lu Lian, our hopes are raised.
    Your poem's a rallying call for the noble spirit;
4   Your father's literary skills you inherit.
    You've authored many well-known works and poems.
    Fortunate are we in foreign land to enjoy these gems.
    To let you know your works are held in high esteem,
8   Not a single piece we find that fawns the new regime.

Paraphrase

L1: Your poem "Qin Yuan Chun" is highly praised and sung throughout the land.

L2: In the world of the Arts, could there be another personage like Lu Zhong Lian who refused to bow down to the ambition of Qin?

L3: Who single-handedly hoisted the banner rallying to the call to uphold the spirit of unsullied nobility .

L4: Indeed you have inherited from your father his great spirit and literary skills as exemplified in his work "Si Hun Ji", an anthology of his poems.

L5: You yourself have written a collection of well-known literary works.
L6: We who live in a different country overseas are fortunate to be able to behold these gems of calligraphy and paintings of yours.
L7: I should like to point out your works are highly esteemed in Nanyang,
L8: For the outstanding reason that there is not a single piece that fawns and flatters (the new regime).

Background

Summary

In the 1950s and 1960s, we had a number of painters and calligraphers from Hong Kong and Taiwan coming to Singapore and Malaya to hold exhibitions of their works. Many had fled mainland China on the takeover by the Communists in 1949. These are also scholars who are usually steeped in the traditions of classical literature and therefore accomplished poets. The Chinese often rolled all these three accomplishments into the expression *shi shu hua* (poetry, calligraphy and painting), as though they were inseparable. Yi Jun Zuo, for whom this poem was written, was just such a poet, calligrapher and painter who visited Malaya in the late 1950s.

The front cover of Yi Jun Zuo's (易君左) book, "Eighteen Years in the Far Corners of the Earth" 《海角天涯十八年》. Qing Shan's 1959 poem for him was highly praised in Jun Zuo's book. Qing Shan's admiration of Jun Zuo's patriotism is summed up in his lines: *"Your 'Qin Yuan Chun' is sung and highly praised. In the Arts, a modern Lu Lian, our hopes are raised."*

This poem was highly praised in Yi Jun Zuo's book (Volume 2, page 333 of his three-volume 《海角天涯十八年》 *Haijiao Tianya Shiba Nian*) published in December 1970. The poem was composed in about August 1959 during Jun Zuo's exhibition of his works in Ipoh.

Yi Jun Zuo (1898–1972) came from a well-known family background. His father had served in government appointments during the late Qing 清末 and early Mingguo 民初 periods. He had a varied career, in a publishing company, as a school teacher and an officer in the Jiangsu Education Department. He wrote extensively, including works that gained either notoriety (Yangzhou Gossips 闲话扬州) or fame, i.e., the poem to the tune of Qin Yuan Chun 沁园春. Yi Jun Zuo's poem was composed in response and as a retort to Mao Zedong's poem written to the same tune.

He left mainland China in 1949 to live in Taiwan. He died there in 1972 at the age of 73.

Mao's Poem

On 15 August 1945, the Japanese Emperor announced Japan's surrender. Mao arrived in Chongqing 重庆 on 28 August 1945 for peace talks with Chiang Kai-shek. On 6 September, Mao copied his "Snow" poem and gave it to a noted poet and scholar Liu Ya Zi 柳亚子. Liu copied Mao's poem "Qin Yuan Chun—Snow" (沁园春——雪) and wrote a response and sent both poems to *Xinhua Daily*. Liu's poem was published, but not Mao's. The public's curiosity was aroused and readers wanted to read Mao's "Snow" poem. Eventually, the supplement of *Xinmin Daily* published Mao's poem on 14 November with a piece of editorial compliments. The media saw fifty poems written in response to Mao's poem and over twenty commentaries.

It was said that Chiang Kai-shek was irritated by the publicity and praises heaped on Mao's literary work and asked his top consultant Chen Bulei 陈布雷 what he thought of Mao's poem. Chen was highly complimentary. Chiang then sent out an internal notice to scholars asking them to compose responses in the hope that more outstanding work would be composed to eclipse Mao's new-found reputation as a man of letters. According to a source, none could be found to match, with the exception of a few like the composition of Yi Jun Zuo's response. Yi responded with a poem to the same tune and a preface attacking Mao.

Yi Jun Zuo was then involved in the publicity work for the Nationalist Party (Guomindang 国民党). Mao's poem was supposedly written in 1936 during the Long March but seemed to have surfaced only in 1945. It was highly praised as "…imbued with great momentum, with a spirit that can conquer the mountains and rivers. It is a rare monumental work of art (气势磅礴、气吞山河，可称盖世之精品). In particular, in the last nine lines of his poem, Mao was seen as comparing himself with the great emperors and figures of history, each of whom was lacking in one quality or another. He is seen as implying that he, Mao alone, had the combined qualities of them all and more. This is what Mao wrote that infuriated Chiang Kai Shek who accused him of harbouring imperialist ambitions and aspiring to be emperor.

Mao's Poem that stirred up the storm. (The English version is supposedly an "official" translation with the original Chinese text as follows):

To the tune of "Qin Yuan Chun — Snow" 沁园春－雪

North country scene: 北国风光
A hundred leagues locked in ice, 千里冰封
A thousand leagues of whirling snow. 万里雪飘
Both sides of the Great Wall 望长城内外
One single white immensity. 惟余莽莽
The Yellow River's swift current 大河上下
Is stilled from end to end. 顿失滔滔

The mountains dance like silver snakes 山舞银蛇
And the highlands charge like wax-hued elephants,
　原驰蜡象
Vying with heaven in stature. 欲与天公试比高
On a fine day, the land, 须晴日
Clad in white, adorned in red, 看红装素裹
Grows more enchanting. 分外妖娆
This land so rich in beauty 江山如此多娇
Has made countless heroes bow in homage.
　引无数英雄竞折腰
But alas! Qin Shihuang and Han Wudi 惜秦皇汉武
Were lacking in literary grace, 略输文采
And Tang Taizong and Song Taizu 唐宗宋祖
Had little poetry in their souls; 稍逊风骚
And Genghis Khan, Proud Son of Heaven in his time,
　一代天骄, 成吉思汗
Knew only shooting eagles, bow outstretched.
　只识弯弓射大雕
All are past and gone! 俱往矣
For truly great men 数风流人物
Look to this age alone. 还看今朝

In a nutshell, Mao's poem describes the immense and majestic scenery of snow, rivers and mountains that confronted him during the Long March. In the second part, it enumerates the past emperors: the Qin dynasty's First Emperor, Han dynasty's Emperor Wudi, Tang dynasty's Emperor Taizong, Song dynasty's Emperor Taizu. Great as they were, they all had some shortcoming. Even Gengzhis Khan is cited—as someone who knows only how to draw a bow. It concludes by saying that even these great personages of history will need to look to this age (for someone like Mao who possesses all their qualities and more).

Appreciation

The theme of Qing Shan's poem is in praise of Yi Jun Zuo's patriotism in standing up to Mao Zedong's ambitions as expressed in his 1936 poem "Qin Yuan Chun—Snow 沁园春——雪" that surfaced in 1945. We should first examine what it is that Yi Jun Zuo wrote.

A Response to Mao's Poem

Although some ten years separated Mao's poem (1936) and Yi's poem (1945), it was only in 1945 that Mao chose to let the poem surface at the time of the peace talks at Chongqing. In this sense, it might as well have been written in 1945. Yi's poem begins with scenes filled with the destruction throughout the country wrought by the civil war and the war against the Japanese. The next part of the poem compares Mao with two notorious figures in Chinese history. One is Huang Chao 黃巢 who led a rebellion against the Tang Emperor in 875. His army, it was said, ate people as food. The other is the invincible Qin dynasty General Bai Qi 白起 (died 257 BC) who reputedly buried alive 400,000 of his enemy's troops after they surrendered. It attributes to Mao the destruction of the country through the plunging of the country into civil war. Whatever his slogans, however beguiling his pretences are, he will not escape the inevitable judgment of history (青史无私细细雕). It warns Mao not to allow a single moment of "weakness", viz., his ambition, to turn into his everlasting guilt (一念参差，千秋功罪).

Qing Shan's Poem

The first line praises Yi Jun Zuo for his 1945 poem to rebut Mao and to rebuke him for harbouring ambitions to be emperor. The second line compares Jun Zuo with the historic figure

Lu Zhong Lian (鲁仲连), a strategist of the Warring States era (战国). When the state of Qin 秦 laid siege to the capital city of Zhao 赵, Lu Zhong Lian saw through the stratagem of the King of Qin to conquer all the other states to make himself emperor of the entire land. He was determined "not to submit to the ambition of Qin to be emperor" (义不帝秦) but used his strategy to help the state of Zhao to have the siege lifted. Line 2 personifies Jun Zuo as a modern day "Lu Zhong Lian" in the literary field (艺海何期有鲁连) who by his poem has exposed the ambition of Mao to be emperor. Line 3 likens him to a standard bearer rallying to the call to uphold the spirit of unsullied nobility (一帜独标徵亮节). Line 4 explains that Jun Zuo must have inherited his literary talent from his father who authored the well-known writing *Si Hun Ji* (四魂集).

Lines 5–7 praise Jun Zuo's own numerous publications, for their fame is well-known and held in high esteem. The last line is perhaps the highest praise for Jun Zuo and the sharpest rebuke to those who support Mao. It says that in all Jun Zuo's writing, "Not a single piece we find that fawns the new regime" 此中只少美新篇! This is an allusion to the Han dynasty writer Yang Xiong 杨雄. The Qin dynasty (秦) was succeeded by the Han dynasty. When Wang Mang 王莽 (a commoner who usurped the Han throne) became Emperor during the interregnum rule, he styled his reign as the Xin (新) dynasty. Yang Xiong 杨雄 wrote a composition "Revile the Qin and Praise the Xin" (*ju qin mei xin* 剧秦美新) praising Wang Mang's new regime. It is said that Yang Xiong's composition was an act of self-preservation. This allusion is also used in the poem in Chapter 41 (Line 7).

Chapter 58

闻云南园雅集有感，寄列座诸君子

其一

月令犹存觞咏中，
扶持大雅仗诸公。
催诗岂待今宵雨？
4 修禊遥追六代风。
石焰惊天呈浩劫，
金声掷地振群聋。
祖龙休拨坑灰火，
8 吾道长城有学宫！

To the Yunnan Garden Gathering of the Literati

Feelings Upon Hearing the News of the Yunnan Garden Gathering of the Literati, Addressed to the Assembly of Scholars

Verse 1

    Our literary heritage is preserved through wine and song.
    Guardians of the Book of Poetry are you, noble Sirs!
    Why wait till the storm breaks out to chant your poem?
4   To exorcise evil, you can learn from our distant ancient past.
    A meteorite explodes across the sky; calamity has befallen us.
    Your clarion calls awake the people, muddled and benumbed.
    Emperor Qin, desist! Burn not the books, bury no more scholars.
8   The protective Great Wall of our Chinese culture, Nantah stands.

Verse 2

    The Gathering at Orchid Pavilion is a day long gone,
    By the lake, they gathered to write and sing "Yonghe Spring".
    The tradition of that bygone day will live a thousand years;
4   The Gathering today evokes many a hundred new feelings.
    The wine cups upon the winding stream are now filled with tears;

其二

雅集兰亭迹已陈,
临池犹写永和春。
当年佳话千秋在,
4 此日清游百感新。
曲水觞流惟饮泪,
茂林斧过尽为薪。
不堪重忆山阴道,
8 道上难逢薄醉人。

Once lush forests, swept by the axe, become mere wood to burn.
Painful to recall the walk to the Orchid Pavilion that happy day
8   For you will not meet one happy soul along the same old way.

Paraphrase

Verse 1

L1: The spirit of the Yueling chapter in Liji continues to be preserved in our culture of wine and poetry.
L2: We rely on you noble Sirs to preserve the purity of our Chinese heritage (*Book of Poetry*).
L3: Why do you need to wait till you confront a political upheaval (storm) before expressing your will in poetry?
L4: To exorcise evil, you can learn from our distant ancient past.
L5: A meteorite has exploded across the sky, calamity has befallen us.
L6: Your clarion calls will awaken those already muddled and benumbed.
L7: Emperor Qin, desist! Burn not the books, bury no more scholars.
L8: We have Nantah as our Great Wall to protect the great heritage of our Chinese culture.

Verse 2

L1: The Gathering at Orchid Pavilion is a day long gone,
L2: They had gathered by the lakeside to write and recite the song of "Yonghe Spring".
L3: However, the tradition of the Orchid Pavilion Gathering has lived on for a thousand years.
L4: But the Gathering today evokes in us many new and different feelings.

L5: We continue to place the wine cups in the flowing stream, but the cups are filled with bitter tears.

L6: The heritage of our lush green forests are all cut down and turned into mere firewood for burning.

L7: It is painful to recall that breezy day with people strolling happily along the path to the Orchid Pavilion.

L8: Along this same path today, it will be difficult to meet anyone who is, perhaps in a mild stupor, happy as those who had once gathered at Orchid Pavilion.

Background

Summary

The poem is clearly titled "Addressed to the Assembly of Scholars". This assembly of scholars refers to the professors and students of Chinese Language and Literature at Nantah. The poem was written for the publication, *Yunnan Garden Anthology of Poems* 《云南园吟唱集》, in connection with the University Week (大学周) which began on 30 March 1960, as part of the celebration of the first convocation of Nantah held on 2 April 1960. We met the editor Mr Huang Ying Liang (黄应良) some ten years ago. He was a final year student at Nantah in 1960 and remembered that most of the poems were received only after the convocation, which explains why the publication was ready only in July 1960, several months after the exhibition.

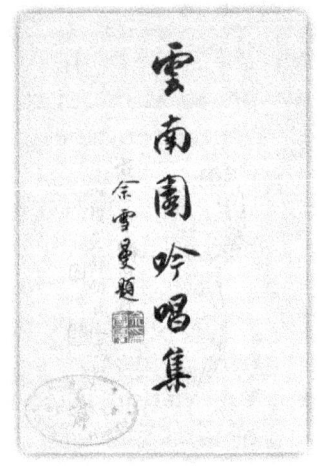

The front cover of *Yunnan Garden Anthology of Poems* 《云南园吟唱集》, a collection of Chinese classical poems published by the Chinese Literary Society of "Nantah" (Nanyang University) sometime after July 1960. Qing Shan's poem appeared on page 7 of the publication.

This is one of Father's last compositions before he died on 6 June 1960. It was not until some time after his death that the publication in which the poem appeared was printed and a copy mailed to our family. Father never saw this poem in print.

Nantah

Not long after the Communists took over mainland China in 1949, Nantah was founded to cater for the large numbers of Chinese high school students graduating each year in Malaya and Singapore who would otherwise have to go to Taiwan or Hong Kong for their tertiary education in Chinese. Nantah, thus, became an overseas centre of learning for Chinese studies and culture.

During Nantah's fund-raising campaign throughout Singapore and peninsula Malaya in the 1950s, thousands of ordinary Chinese, from the wealthy businessmen to the poor trishaw riders contributed generously. Mother's tailoring school held

The arch in the garden of the former Nanyang University. It is a replica erected in 1995. The original arch still stands in its original position nearby, now by the side of a public road.

The garden in the former Nanyang University.
"*The Gathering at Orchid Pavilion is a day long gone.
By the lake, they gathered to write and sing 'Yonghe Spring'.*"

The Library of the former Nanyang University (Nantah).
"*Emperor Qin, desist! Burn not the books, bury no more scholars.
The protective Great Wall of our Chinese culture, Nantah stands.*"

a charity sale of clothing and the proceeds were donated to Nantah's building fund. Apart from this very remote connection, Father actually had no other connection with Nantah.

Our maternal uncle Wang Guang Guo 王光国 probably knew Prof She Xue Man 佘雪曼 (1907-1993) who was then the Head of the Chinese Department in Nantah. Several prominent poets from Ipoh also contributed to the Nantah magazine. Prof She appears better known as a painter and calligrapher than as a poet.

Appreciation

In writing this poem for the Chinese scholars of Nantah for their special literary gathering, Qing Shan refers to their gathering as *xiū xì* 修禊. It was an ancient tradition in China for people to go for an outing by the water, during the third day of the third lunar calendar month, where they would enjoy themselves at a picnic, take in the orchids, and rid themselves of any bad luck. (The day of Nantah's first convocation ceremony 2 April 1960 fell on the seventh day of the third lunar calendar month.) It was at such an outing some 1,600 years ago that the famous calligrapher Wang Xi Zi (王羲之, 303-361) once gathered his literary friends at the Orchid Pavilion (Lan Ting 兰亭). By alluding to the "Orchid Pavilion Gathering of the Literati" (兰亭雅集) in Verse 1 Line 1, Qing Shan shows great respect to the scholars gathered at Nantah.

The poem reminds them not to forget the founding purpose of the university, which is the preservation of Chinese culture, "Guardians of the Book of Poetry (Chinese heritage) are you, noble Sirs!" says the poem (Verse 1 Line 2). The righteous call to the scholars to stand firm in the face of the evil forces is echoed in Verse 1 Line 8: "The protective Great Wall of our Chinese culture, Nantah stands (南大 Nanyang University)." These are powerful words of defiance.

Verse 2 Line 5 is rather interesting: "Once lush forests, swept by the axe, become mere wood to burn 茂林斧过尽为薪". On the face of it, this is another of Qing Shan's clever puns. Firstly, a person without education is transformed through learning into someone useful, as befitting the role of Nantah as a university. Secondly, Nantah stands on land that was once covered by a rubber estate which had been cleared to build the university. The late Dr Pan Shou was closely connected with the early history of Nantah. When he first read this poem about 14 years ago he exclaimed, "The line is saying much more than that! The reference is to the Da Zheng Feng (大整风) movement persecution of the literati in mainland China in the mid-1950s. This was followed by the Great Leap Forward, the collectivisation movement and the failed attempt to promote (backyard) industrial production."

The clue given by Pan Shou, brings yet another dimension to these seven words. Firstly, the rich literary heritage of China was being destroyed and would be worth no more than the paper they are printed on. Secondly, the attempt to industrialise China through the proliferation of backyard foundries to produce iron, caused forests to be cut down as fuel for the furnaces and this led to widespread deforestation.

Many of the lines in this poem then fall into place. It is now clear what the metaphor in Verse 1 Line 5 means when it says: "A meteorite explodes across the sky; calamity has befallen us 石焰惊天呈浩劫". The meteorite (石焰) that explodes over China is Mao Zedong's persecution of the literati. This line provides a clue that Qing Shan's poem is likely to be based on an allusion from a poem, "Thermal Spring Song" 温泉行 by Song dynasty 宋 poet Li Fu 李复. The last two lines of Li Fu's poem revile the Tang Emperor Ming Huang for bringing the country to a ruinous end 唐明皇误国:

The Emperor, vile and contemptuous of the gods and　　　
Heaven,　　　　　　　　祖龙心秽慢神天

His hair dripping with stinking sweat, his body covered with poison.　　毛发流腥身被毒

The surname of Mao Zedong has the literal meaning "hair" (*mao* 毛). With the allusion to Li Fu's poem, Qing Shan is making an oblique reference to Mao.

As indeed in Verse 1 Lines 7 and 8, Qing Shan makes it clear with his own words:

"Emperor Qin, desist! Burn not the books, bury no more scholars.　　祖龙休拨坑灰火
The protective Great Wall of our Chinese culture, Nan-tah stands."　　吾道长城有学宫

Qing Shan cries out in anger and anguish. He is "pointing to the mulberry to revile the locust tree" (指桑骂槐). Whilst the finger is pointed at Emperor Qin (refered to as *zu long* 祖龙), the real object of the rebuke is Mao Zedong who is ultimately responsible for the Da Zheng Feng movement against the scholars in mainland China.

Qing Shan fiercely loves Chinese literature throughout his life. He is saddened when he learns of the damage that Da Zheng Feng has done to the Chinese culture of five thousand years. The exasperation in Verse 1 Line 3 also becomes more apparent: "Why wait till the storm breaks out to chant your poem [to register your will]? 催诗岂待今宵雨?"

Qing Shan exhibits two sets of conflicting feelings: firmness and anger, softness and sadness. First, he angrily raises his thick eyebrows (横眉), pointing his finger and orders, "Emperor Qin, desist! Burn no more books; bury no more scholars. The protective Great Wall of our Chinese culture, Nantah stands." Then, lowering his head (俯首), he sadly sighs, "Painful to recall the walk to the Orchid Pavilion that happy day; For you will not meet one happy soul along the same old way."

Chapter 59

龙市——呈王世昭教授

昔楚有叶公,
平生颇好龙。
龙孙与龙子,
4 一时入彀中。
势难别优劣,
亦莫辨雌雄。
一龙自天降,
8 风举而云从。
行空若天马,
入门如长虹。

Dragon Market
— A Poem for Professor Wang Shi Zhao

In ancient Chu there was a Ye Gong.
He loved all dragons that come to him.
Dragons of every age and shape
4   Were soon in cage with no escape.
To know their quality was quite an art;
Their gender wasn't easy to tell apart.
Then came a dragon out of the blue,
8   The clouds followed as the wind blew;
Like a divine horse it came down below,
Its noble spirit trailing like a rainbow.
Ye Gong rounded them up, all he fancied,
12   Caught them in cages as they scurried.
He met a horse and dragon dealer one day.
Dragons at the price of eels, would he pay?
Tightly packed are dragon scales, the dealer said.
16   Dragon meat is not fleshy, he was afraid.
The meat is cooked in a cauldron, said Ye Gong.
With ginger and onions as spices added on!
But price and quality the two must fit;
20   Neither taste nor meat is much to eat!
The dragons flew off in shock and fright.
Not a single dragon was then in sight
But for the one proud and majestic dragon,
24   With pent-up feelings yet unspoken.

既聚于所好，
12 杂置诸樊笼。
一朝逢驵侩，
论价鳝鳅同。
鳞甲嫌太密，
16 肌肉嫌未丰。
云将调鼎鼐，
佐之以姜葱。
锱铢较轻重，
20 口腹恐不充。
群龙骇且走，
庭院为之空。
一龙独矫首，
24 若有感于衷。
获麟叹西狩，
我道宣终穷。

"The Qilin is hunted again," it seemed to say,
"The righteous path I tread is gone today!"

Paraphrase

L1: In the ancient state of Chu, there was a Ye Gong (Mr Ye);
L2: He just loved dragons.
L3: Dragons old and young were all enticed by him.
L4: In a short while, they all fell into his trap.
L5: There were so many of them that it was difficult to tell their different qualities.
L6: Equally difficult was to distinguish their genders.
L7: Quite out of the blue a dragon descended suddenly from the sky.
L8: It unleashed the wind and stirred up the clouds.
L9: It came down majestically like a celestial horse.
L10: It entered Ye Gong's house, breathing a noble spirit which trailed the length of a rainbow.
L11: Ye Gong rounded up all the dragons he fancied
L12: And put them into various cages.
L13: One day, he met a horse and dragon dealer.
L14: Ye Gong wanted the price of the delectable eels for his dragons.
L15: The dealer countered that dragon scales were too tightly packed and numerous.
L16: Moreover, dragon meat was not sufficiently fleshy.
L17: Ye Gong explained that dragon meat can be cooked in a large cauldron (*ding*) cooking pot,
L18: Richly flavoured by ginger and onion.
L19: The dealer countered that the price must be commensurate with the quality of goods.
L20: There is neither enough taste nor meat for anyone to eat.
L21: When the dragons heard the haggling that was going on, they bolted in fear and alarm.
L22: Ye Gong's yard was then empty of dragons

L23: Except for the one proud and majestic dragon that had descended from the sky.
L24: It was filled with pent-up yet unspoken emotions
L25: As though saying, "The hunt for the sacred Qilin is about to be re-enacted."
L26: "The righteous path that I have followed is about to be obliterated."

Background

This is a poem with a rather enigmatic title "Dragon Market". When we first saw a hand-copied version of this poem transcribed by someone, it had no reference to Wang Shi Zhao 王世昭. We could tell that it was an allegory but were not quite sure to whom or to what it refers. It was not until recently that we discovered Father's own handwritten draft that the full title was revealed: "Dragon Market—Presented to Prof Wang Shi Zhao". Everything then fell into place.

This is one of four poems written for Prof Wang Shi Zhao. They were all written during February to March 1960 when Wang visited Ipoh with his adoptive daughter Xu Han Qing 许涵清 and held an exhibition of his calligraphy and her painting. The other three poems are in Chapters 44, 45 and 46.

Prof Wang was known to be ideologically anti-Communist. His native home was in Fujian province and he had moved from mainland China post-1949 to live in Hong Kong. There, he published or edited a magazine called *Chun Qiu* 《春秋》 (Spring Autumn).

By virtue of Father's handwritten draft addressing the poem to Prof Wang, there is no dispute that this poem is about Wang's staunch stand against communism. There may not be full agreement on one or two details of the allegory but there is no disagreement as to who the "target" is and what event in recent Chinese history is being alluded to.

One should remember the date of this poem, viz., February to March 1960. At about the same time, Father wrote the poem in Chapter 58, "To the Yunnan Garden Gathering of the Literati" (闻云南园雅集有感，寄列座诸君子) which has a similar theme. It laments the destruction of the five thousand years of Chinese culture in mainland China which is compared with the burning of books and burying of scholars (焚书坑儒) by Qin Shi Huang 秦始皇 (259~210BC). The allegory of this poem "Dragon Market" refers pointedly to a more recent event in modern Chinese history, viz., the so-called "Hundred Flowers Campaign 百花齐放" in 1956–1957. Intellectuals were first asked to freely voice their opinions 大鸣大放. When criticisms got out of hand and went beyond what Mao regarded as healthy criticism, the aftermath was brutal. As many as half a million were identified and singled out as "rightists", persecuted, imprisoned, sent to "rehabilitation" centres and many were killed.

For further biographical details of Wang Shi Zhao, please see the special section at the end of Chapter 44 on the "Biography of Wang Shi Zhao" and "Chen Qing Shan-Wang Shi Zhao Friendship".

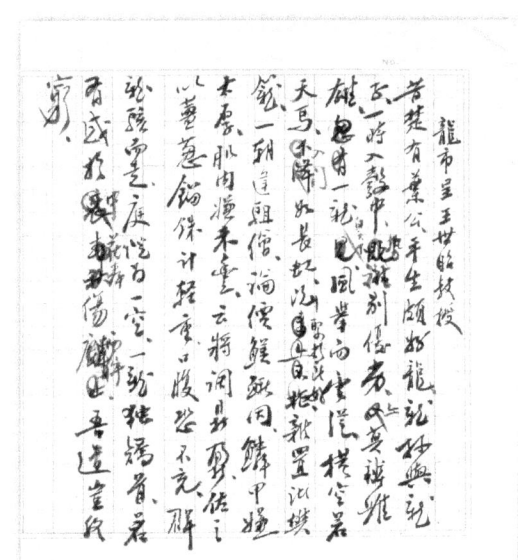

Qing Shan's handwritten draft of the poem specifically addressed to Professor Wang Shi Zhao.

Appreciation

This is an allegory and Qing Shan is a good storyteller. The story begins like an English fairy tale: "Once upon a time, in the ancient state of Chu, there was a man known as Ye Gong." It is told in a humorous way; some of the situations described are even farcical. If not for the seriousness of the real message and of the events targeted, this poem would have been merely amusing. The poem is an allegory of the ill-fated "Hundred Flowers Campaign" in China which began publicly in late 1956.

The Original Ye Gong Story

The Chinese metaphor "Ye Gong loves the dragon" 叶公好龙 is used today to describe someone who professes a great love for something only because it is desirable to be seen as such, for example, to be fashionable or to be well thought of. It is a Han dynasty story by Liu Xiang 刘向 about a historical figure Lord Lu 鲁哀公, one of the feudal lords during the Spring Autumn period (722~481BC). Lord Lu professed that he greatly welcomed able people who could help him govern. A scholar Zi Zhang 子张 heard of his reputation and went to see Lord Lu. Despite staying for seven days in the house as a guest, he never got to see Lord Lu. Disappointed, the scholar Zi Zhang finally took his leave and told the servants to pass a message to Lord Lu before he left.

Zi Zhang said, "Tell your master Lord Lu that I have heard he welcomes talent into his house. I have come a long and difficult way to see him but after seven days he has not deigned to meet me. Lord Lu's love of talent is comparable to Ye Gong's love of dragons. It is said that Ye Gong displayed his love of dragons by having images of the dragon decorate every item of his clothing, household utensils and furniture. When the "real" dragon in heaven heard about Ye Gong, it decided to visit Ye Gong's home to express its appreciation. The dragon first peered through Ye Gong's window and then parked his gigantic tail in Ye Gong's reception hall. When Ye Gong saw the real dragon, he was frightened out of his wits and ran away for his life. Ye Gong did not really love dragons; he only liked what appeared to be dragons. Similarly, I have heard your Lord values talent and I have come a long way to see him. For seven days, he has not extended the courtesy to meet me. Your Lord does not really value talent, he only loves such a reputation. I take my leave."

Qing Shan's Version

Qing Shan's story is a modified and modernized version of the original. In his story, the dragons in heaven, having heard of Ye Gong's fondness of dragons; all came down to his house. Ye Gong had the dragons all kept in a cage. In addition to these "lesser" dragons that were not in the original story, there was one majestic dragon which came in a gust of wind and rolling clouds, trailing down like a long rainbow. Ye Gong took them all in.

The next important departure and modernization of the original story is Ye Gong's haggling with a dragon dealer over the price he wanted for all the dragons. The dealer complained about the scales and meat of the dragons but Ye Gong pointed out how delicious dragon meat can be when cooked and spiced with ginger and onion. When the dragons heard this unseemly haggling going on, they all flew away except one.

This was the divine-looking majestic dragon. It alone remained holding its head high, yet feeling rather sad. It seemed to have a great deal of pent-up and unspoken emotions, as though saying, "The hunt for the sacred Qi-lin (unicorn 麒麟) is being enacted again. The righteous path that I follow will be totally destroyed today!"

"Hundred Flowers Campaign"

It is very clear that the event in the poem refers to the "Hundred

Flowers Campaign". There are at least two schools of thought regarding the original motivation of the campaign. One school believes that it was an entrapment devised by Mao Zedong to flush out the dissidents for their elimination. Probably the majority of historians believe that the campaign started off as a genuine attempt to invite criticism. It was only after it got out of hand that the crackdown and persecution began.

The Main Characters and Events of Qing Shan's Story

There is little doubt that Mao Zedong was intended to be the Ye Gong of the story. Partly persuaded by Zhou En Lai, he made it known that he wanted to hear criticism from the intellectuals, just as Ye Gong was widely known to love dragons! But when the criticisms began to go beyond the limits, he pulled back and the persecution began. It became a legitimate question for some to ask whether Mao had really wanted to hear criticisms or, as an analogy to Ye Gong, merely wanted the appearance of wanting to hear them.

In Qing Shan's version, when Ye Gong was haggling with the dealer over the price of dragon meat, "The dragons flew off in shock and fright (群龙骇且走), Not a single dragon was then in sight (庭院为之空)"; in other words Ye Gong's cages in the yard were all empty (Lines 21–22). In the "Hundred Flowers Campaign" however, the intellectuals could not flee but were imprisoned or killed. The prisons were full! An explanation is possible for this apparent "discrepancy". Qing Shan's dragons that flew away refer not to the intellectuals themselves but to their thoughts, values and criticism. With their persecution, these are no longer expressed. They are heard no more and Mao's "courtyard" (庭院) is hence "empty" (为之空).

Who or what is this single dragon that remains, proudly holding high its head? We believe it represents Prof Wang Shi Zhao as a personification of the five thousand years of Chinese culture and traditional values. Prof Wang moved from China to live in Hong Kong ahead of the Communist rule. There he published a magazine called *Chun Qiu*《春秋》(Spring and Autumn) which was pro-Guomindang and anti-Communist. It appears that the allusion in the last two lines of the poems has been carefully chosen by Qing Shan. In the "unspoken" words of this majestic dragon, it laments the imminent destruction of the traditional way and values of Chinese civilization.

> Line 25: "The Qilin is hunted again", it seemed to say.
> 获麟叹西狩
> Line 26: "The righteous path I tread is gone today!"
> 我道宣终穷

The Qilin referred to in the poem is a sacred animal. Chun Qiu is the title of the "Chronicles" of the State Lu during the "Spring and Autumn era (722~481BC). It is reputedly compiled by Confucius. When Confucius saw that a Qi-lin had been killed by Lord Lu 鲁哀公 during a hunt in the western part of Lu 西狩获麟, he lamented the sign as an ill omen for an impending calamity. It was at that point that Confucius stopped compiling the "Spring and Autumn Chronicles" and ended its last chapter. It is more than a coincidence that the magazine edited by Professor Wang in Hong Kong was also known by the name of *Chun Qiu* 春秋 (Spring and Autumn)!

More Interesting Allusions Explained

This Appreciation has so far focused on the theme of the original and Qing Shan's stories and the main characters and events. Here, we will highlight a couple more interesting and colourful expressions used by Qing Shan that might otherwise be lost in the translation.

> Within shooting range
> Line 3: Dragons of every age and shape　　龙孙与龙子
> Line 4: Were soon in cage with no escape. 一时入彀中

The literal meaning of Line 4 is "At the same time (一时) they all came within (入) the shooting range of my crossbow (彀中)." The expression "they have all come within the shooting rang of my cross bow" is attributed to Tang Taizhong 唐太宗, the second Tang emperor. As he watched the large number of successful candidates of the Imperial Examinations file past, he remarked happily, "The best talent in the land are now all within the range of my crossbow 天下英雄入吾彀中矣！". The emperor used this expression to mean the talent were all within his power to use or exploit. The expression later became a metaphor for "fallen into a trap". This is seen as a very appropriate expression by those who believe that the "Hundred Flowers Campaign" was indeed an entrapment of the dissidents among the intellectuals.

Managing the Affairs of State
Line 17: The meat is cooked in a cauldron, said Ye Gong.
　　　　云将调鼎鼐
Line 18: With ginger and onions as spices added on!
　　　　佐之以姜葱

In these two lines, Ye Gong did his sales pitch by trying to convince the dragon merchant how tasty his dragon meat can be when cooked in a cauldron, spiced with ginger and onions. The literal meaning of Line 17 is "[Ye Gong] said (云), [dragon meat] when cooked and adjusted to taste (将调) in a large cauldron (鼎鼐 $dǐng\ nài$)"….. This may just seem like an amusing or even silly story about cooking dragon meat in a large cauldron, but there is more to it.

Firstly, the expression "cooking dragon meat" comes from a line in a Tang poem by Li He "Invitation to Wine" 李贺《将进酒》. The line refers to a sumptuous dinner "prepared (cooked) with dragon and phoenix meat 烹龙炮凤 $pēng\ lóng\ páo\ fèng$". There is indeed a "literary precedence" for Qing Shan's parable of an exotic dish of dragon meat and, following from this, a flourishing market for dragon meat too.

Secondly, Qing Shan's reference to the dragon meat being cooked in a large cauldron connotes more than its literal meaning. The term used in Qing Shan's poem for a cauldron is *dǐng nài* 鼎鼐 which means a large *dǐng*. It is a vessel originally used for cooking and is usually round, standing on three legs. Much larger versions of the *dǐng* were cast in bronze in ancient China and it became a symbol of authority because important historical events and the emperor's achievements were recorded on them. Their dignified and imposing style made them a favourite in the eyes of the emperors and were regarded as an auspicious symbol.

The Shang emperor 武丁 Wǔ Dīng once asked his Prime Minister 傅说 Fù Yuè how he managed to govern the country so well. Fù Yuè explained how he managed the affairs of state by using the analogy of cooking in a large *dǐng* in which he had to constantly adjust the seasoning by tasting the food until the taste is just right (鼎鼐中调味). The analogy is used today to describe the managing of the affairs of state, especially the role of a Prime Minister. Qing Shan uses the same analogy in Line 17. He puts these very words into the mouth of Ye Gong: "The meat is cooked (adjusted to taste) in a cauldron (*dǐng*), said Ye Gong 云将调鼎鼐". Qing Shan thereby further hints at his intended identity of Ye Gong, a person of great political power and responsibility like Mao.

Professor Wang Si Zhao would have enjoyed this poem tremendously.

Chapter 60

吟榻述怀

收拾雄心隐管城，
书生纸上愧谈兵。
妇人醇酒皆吟料，
诗国何妨有信陵。

Thoughts While Chanting in Bed

Put away all ambitions, go indulge in fancy writing.
A scholar all life, who can but on paper strategise.
Fine wine and women, are subjects for poetry to sing.
In the realm of poetry, why not a Prince Xin Ling?

Paraphrase

L1: Put away all lofty aspirations and high ideals, retreat into a world of fancy writing.
L2: A scholar all life who regrettably can only discuss military strategy on paper.
L3: Fine wine and women are all subjects for poetry and songs.
L4: In the realm of poetry, there's no harm in being like Prince Xin Ling.

Background

Summary

This is a poem discovered by accident in 2005. It was written probably not long before Father died in June 1960 at the age of 66. It had been in the possession of our fourth uncle Guang Guo who died in 1971 and was among the papers he left behind, until his daughter Xia Xian gave it to us among other documents.

A scholar, teacher, writer all his life, Father was in his twenties at the time of the May Fourth Movement in the early 20th century. After he left China in 1917, he spent all his life in Malaya except for some two to three years back home in his native Putian.

Re-discovery

The poem was composed late in life, very likely not long before he passed away in June 1960 at the age of 66. Father could be reading in bed or on his day couch, while he mused and reflected on his life. The literal meaning of the title is "Narrating my thoughts while chanting poetry in bed" (吟榻述怀).

We had no idea that this poem was ever written, until February 2005, some 45 years later. Our cousin Xia Xian of Ipoh handed us several handwritten drafts of poems which she had salvaged from her father's old house at Kampong Paloh in Ipoh. Her father, our uncle Guang Guo had died in 1971, coincidentally also at the age of 66. His house at Kampong Paloh in Ipoh was about to be sold and it was fortunate for us that Xia Xian had the presence of mind to recognize the value of these old manuscripts in her father's own handwriting and a few in Father's. Uncle Guang Guo was 11 years Father's junior and in the pre- and post-Second World War years, the two had been very close "poetry friends" despite their difference in age. In matters of literature and poetry, Guang Guo looked up to Father and often consulted him. Father had, in fact, once been the young Guang Guo's tutor in the latter's native village of Jiangdou in Fuqing.

Not long after Father's death, this poem together with three others by Father were discovered by Guang Guo among Father's papers. Guang Guo must have been very excited about the discovery of the four poems, just as we are today upon their "re-discovery".

Qing Shan's younger brother-in-law, Guang Guo 光国 (1905-1971), who was 11 years younger than Qing Shan. They were nonetheless "poetry friends", although Qing Shan had been Guang Guo's tutor in China. The poem in this chapter was discovered by chance by Guang Guo from among Qing Shan's papers after his death. Upon this discovery, Guang Guo was so overcome by deep-felt sorrow that he composed a poem which is quoted in this chapter.

Ambitions Unachieved

As Father reflected on his own life, while lying in bed he probably had a certain sense of frustration. Born in 1894, he would be like others of his generation greatly fired up by the ideals following May Fourth. Like the "giants" among the literati of the time such as Lu Xun 鲁迅, Mao Dun 矛盾, Father too would have had the ambition to wield his pen to contribute to the social and political changes in his motherland of China. He wrote, but was in Malaya most of the time, except for two to three years.

In the years from 1932 to 1933, while he was the Chinese literature teacher in Li Qing High School in his native county Putian in China, he started a paper and edited two weekly papers. Father had a sharp pen and wrote biting commentaries on the corruption and unjust taxes imposed by the local Governor Li Wan Chun. Soon Father was placed under arrest but he managed to escape and went into hiding. The corrupt Governor arrested Mother instead and had her remanded in the police lockup. Elder sister Mei Yu was still being suckled and had to be taken to the lockup for breastfeeding a few times daily. The whole Putian city rose up in support of Father; widespread strikes by students and teachers were organized and Governor Li backed down and Mother was released. Father then returned secretly to Malaya, and was rejoined by Mother and the children two years later. The pen is not always mightier than the sword.

Few could make a living as a writer in those days and neither could Father. As a poor scholar, writer and teacher, he had to take on the more menial and less glamorous clerical and bookkeeping jobs in order to support the family, especially during the Japanese Occupation years of 1942–1945. With the responsibilities of the family upon his shoulders and the realities of daily living at stake, all youthful ideals and ambitions fell by the way side. They remained unachieved.

Consolation for Qing Shan

So moved was Guang Guo by this poem that after much thought, he composed a poem to express his own feelings, in consolation, and appended to it Father's poem. Guang Guo wrote thus:

> [Paraphrase of Guang Guo's poem]
>
> "I came across by chance this poem left behind by my late elder brother-in-law Qing Shan. After reading it, I was overcome by deep-felt sorrow for a long time, and so moved, I compose this poem:
>
> *'From the small bag left behind, I chanced upon a poem [by Qing Shan]. It is as though I still see him standing right in front of my eyes, with his familiar voice and countenance. It has always been that even the most resolute visionary who possesses lofty ideals finds it difficult to become a sage. Why then should a scholar be so determined to pursue such an aspiration. When our world of poetry loses such a stalwart [like Qing Shan], who*

is there left to continue with the sweet music of elegant poetry? After Tao Yuanming, there are but few who are resolute and principled enough to thumb their nose at officialdom, resign their post and return home to tend to their garden. Alas, we can today only stand sadly by the empty hedge where the chrysanthemums once bloomed, as we gaze gloomily unto the sky.'"

偶拾晴山兄遗诗一首，读后怆然久之，感而赋此：

偶从遗橐拾诗篇　　謦欬如生到眼前
狂士由来难作圣　　文人何必亦希贤
骚坛痛折中流柱　　洛社谁赓白雪弦
陶后不堪山径废　　伤心黯对菊花天.

Guang Guo's poem was meant to console Qing Shan (who had by then passed away), but in reality it was more to console himself. Qing Shan's poem must have struck a chord while Guang Guo reflected on his own life. Guang Guo had been a teacher most of his life, but during the Japanese Occupation and for several years after, he had to take on clerical and bookkeeping jobs in the local bus company owned by his Fuqing compatriots who were barely literate. He was a poet and a good calligrapher, with highly regarded accomplishments in the literary circle. However, in the "secular" world of commerce in which he had to work to support his family, he was just another employee, as Tao Yuanming was but a petty official. Guang Guo too had ambitions unachieved.

Are the Ambitions of Youth the Only Thing?

Both Qing Shan and Guang Guo, by their own estimations, had not achieved the ambitions of their youth. But they were not without their own accomplishments. Qing Shan had written prolifically in many forms ranging from essays, short stories, plays and poems in classical form. Unknown to him then, his literary works would eventually be identified in the 1970s and

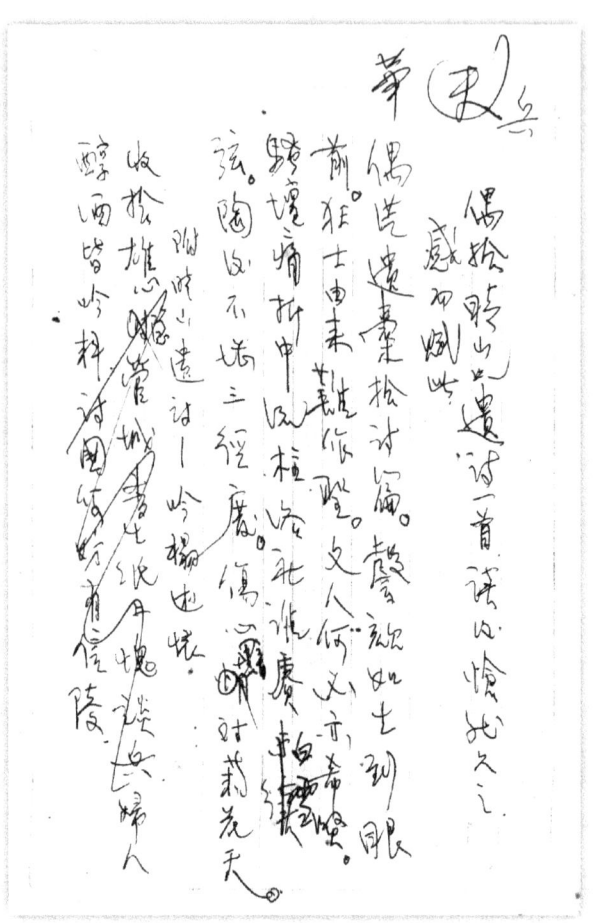

A handwritten draft by our fourth uncle Wang Guang Guo. It contains a poem written by Guang Guo, followed by the draft of the poem composed by Qing Shan. The circumstance of Guang Guo's first discovery of this poem by Qing Shan is explained in the Background of this chapter.

1980s by the Singapore literary historian Fang Xiu as pioneering works in the New Revolutionary Literature Movement of Singapore and Malaya. Two of his works are included in full in Fang Xiu's publications. Guang Guo had a collection of his poems published on the 12th Anniversary of the Malaysian

Poetry Society in 1987 and his calligraphy appears in various places in Ipoh, including the Perak Caves which is decorated with the paintings and calligraphy of well-known painters, calligraphers and scholars such as Zhang Da Qian 张大千, Yu You Ren 于右任, Hu Shi 胡适, etc. Both Qing Shan and Guang Guo returned to teaching Chinese Literature part-time in the two premier high schools in Ipoh, Perak Girls' High School and Yoke Choy High School respectively. Chinese Literature was the subject they loved. They were both loved and respected by a large number of their students. The ambitions of youth are not the only thing in life.

Appreciation

This is a very short poem of only four lines but it sums up the lifetime frustration of a scholar.

The opening line, "Put away all ambitions, go indulge in fancy writing" (收拾雄心隐管城) paints the picture of the scholar packing up and putting away all the ambitions and high ideals of his youth. Now in his sixties, his ambitions can only be described as "unachievable". He might as well withdraw into his own literary world to wield his pen writing whatever fancies him.

Line 2, "A scholar all life, who can but on paper strategise" (书生纸上愧谈兵). That is often said of a scholar and what Qing Shan thinks of himself. Here Qing Shan uses a simple and well-known expression, "discourse military stratagem on paper" (纸上谈兵). It is used to describe an armchair expert who may be good on theory but may lack practicality. Qing Shan's self-deprecatory regret for having been a scholar is also reflected in the poem in Chapter 10 in his 1947 poem, "Admonition to My Daughter Xuan" (示璇女) in which he said,

"Long have I suffered pursuing a scholar's path.
早被儒冠误到今
Good in nothing but the classics, is not enough."
百无一就但长吟

Line 3, "Fine wine and women are subjects for poetry to sing" (妇人醇酒皆吟料), uses the expression "women and fine wine" (妇人醇酒). The expression is introduced here because it is associated with a Prince Xin Ling (信陵) whose name appears in Line 4. Xin Ling was a Prince of the state of Wei (魏) and brother of its King during the Warring States period. An able military strategist and commander, he successfully defended his own and neighbouring states against the ambitious state of Qin (秦). As a result of false rumours spread by Qin that he had aspiration to be King of Wei, he lost favour with his brother and was replaced as military commander. He feigned illness and refused to attend court. Instead he decided to retreat even deeper into his own sanctuary. He lived it up in the last four years of his life by indulging in "fine wine and women" and eventually died. Even having been a successful military strategist and commander, Xin Ling was no better off than when he started. It is as though his aspirations were unachieved. Qing Shan, his own aspirations unachieved, compares himself with Xin Ling. He too decides to retreat into his own world of "fine wine and women". However, it is evident in his poetry that he has a deep love and affection for his wife and enjoys literary activities with his friends. His "fine wine and women" are the subjects and themes for his poetry. He calls it "subject material for chanting (poetry)" 吟料. This is a pun because it rhymes with 饮料 (beverage or "drinks" including wine). Both have the same pronunciation.

Line 4, "In the realm of Poetry, why not a 'Prince of Xin Ling'" (诗国何妨有信陵), is difficult to understand without first knowing who Prince Xin Ling is, as explained in the foregoing paragraph on Line 3. Qing Shan says here that in Poetry, there is no harm in emulating someone like Prince Xin Ling. When all is said and done and we decide to "call it a day", the poet too can, metaphorically speaking, indulge in "fine wine and women" in his own way by singing and chanting his poetry.

Unfortunately, by the time Qing Shan wrote these lines, there was not a great deal of time left for him to enjoy chanting his poems. But that is not an accurate picture either, because he had enjoyed and indulged in his poetry virtually all his life. An "Epilogue", written in 1957 (see Chapter 63, "My Seven Principles of Poetry"), shows very clearly how much joy he had by indulging in ripostes and verbal jousting with his poetry friends. This indeed was his "fine wine and women" which he might have enjoyed even more than Prince Xin Ling. We do not think Qing Shan had missed anything.

Chapter 61

为黄君愠山先生之《天南吟草》序

民国十三年,余重游南洋,始晤黄君愠山于怡保。时君方长培南学校,余亦任职金宝,休沐之暇,辄相过从。余与君性不相若,君善饮而余不能,君旷达而余则郁郁寡欢。所谓有口不言愁,有愁但饮酒者,愧弗如之。顾于诗,君独引为知音,有所作必见示。余不能诗,自是亦稍稍为之,邮筒相寄无虚日。每一良晤,恒促膝作长夜谈,诗以外鲜及他事。时或推敲所作,一字未

Preface for Mr Huang Yun Shan's "Tian Nan Yin Cao"

In the 13th year of the Republic (1924), when I re-visited Nanyang I first met Mr Huang Yun Shan in Ipoh. He was then the Principal of Poi Lam School (培南学校) and I was working in Kampar. When we were free during our vacation, we often met up with each other. By comparison, he and I were totally different. He drank well but I had no capacity for liquor; he was gregarious whereas I was gloomy and depressed. Gregarious though he was, he would not express his own sorrow to others, preferring to drown his sorrow in drinks. There are people who, when beset by sorrow, are still able to drink. I regret I am not one of them. In poetry, he regards me as one with whom he has the closest rapport; he would show me all his compositions. I did not know how to compose poems then, but after getting to know him I began to dabble in poetry writing. We corresponded with each other and there was never a dull day. Whenever we met we would spend the whole night in discourse, to the exclusion of any other subject but poetry. Sometimes in polishing a composition while we have yet to settle on the best word for a line, we would sit upright facing each other deep in thought. The moment the right word finally dawned on us, we would resume eye contact with each other

安,则相对兀坐;既得,复相视而笑;有所可否,皆出于诚,不面谀也。君为郑苍亭先生高足,渊源所自,非予浅学所能窥,而彼此相得有如是者,其佛家所谓缘与?

君乡人之游此地者,皆善居积,君身外独无长物。今者,治任将返,行箧中仅诗集一卷存焉。人称其廉,君亦自以为拙。"贾楚无长袖,投秦剩敝裘。"盖已自写其况矣。人之志趣不同,取舍各异。君南来于物质虽无所取,而平日登高览胜,剔怪搜奇,所谓"异域江山囊底收"者,所得已不少于人矣。

君自言曩为诗多壮语,南渡后百忧丛集,转抱悲观;以予所见,殆不若是。君为人不斤斤于得失,不戚戚于贫贱。黄金处处同,新诗几人有?斯亦可

and break into a smile at the same time. Be it criticism or praise, everything was said in all sincerity; neither of us would praise the other out of politeness, just because we were face to face. He studied under the well-known poet Mr Zheng Cang Ting (郑苍亭); hence the depth of his knowledge was not what a person like me, without much learning, could easily fathom. The fact that we should be thrown together is what Buddhism refers to as *yuan* (缘 destiny).

The compatriots from his native county in China who came to Nanyang have all amassed great wealth. Mr Huang, on the other hand, has no material possession to speak of. As he is about to return home on the completion of his assignment here, all he has in his trunk is the manuscript of an anthology of poems. People regard this as the hallmark of "Honesty", but Mr Huang himself regards this merely as the result of his being less than artful in life. He describes his own position with a quote [probably from his poem], "A schoolmaster's rod and not long sleeves have I, Thus shall I return home now, all high and dry." Everyone has his own purpose and interest in life. Although Mr Huang's sojourn in Nanyang has brought him no great material possession, he has travelled widely and seen much including numerous exotica of life here. As one might say, he has all "the rivers and mountains of these foreign lands 'in the bag'". He has thus accomplished not less than what many people have done.

He says that, in the past, his poetry was bold and full of optimism; but since coming to Nanyang, beset by worries, his compositions have become tinged with pessimism. From what I can see, this is hardly the case. In his dealing with others, Mr Huang does not quibble over each other's relative gain or loss. He never worries about being poor. The wealthy, they are the same everywhere; but how many are there who can create poetry? Mr Huang can be justly proud of himself. Why should he lament? I have compiled Mr Huang's poems into an anthology "Tian Nan Yin Cao" (天南吟草) which is about

以自豪矣!复何悲?为君辑所为诗成《天南吟草》一卷,将付剞劂,因为主序如此。

陈晴山
民国十六年六月廿八日于金宝

to be sent to the printers. Hence I have now written this as its main Preface.

Chen Qing Shan

28 June, 16th Year of the [Chinese] Republic [1927]

Kampar

Background

Summary

Written in 1927, this Preface is the earliest prose written in *wen yan* (文言 classical form) in our possession. It is dated 28 June 1927 by Father himself. It came to us through an elderly gentleman from Muar 麻坡 (in Malaysia's Johor state 柔佛州). He chanced upon Father's name when he attended the Ipoh Fufeng Poetry Society (怡保扶风诗社) meeting in November 1991. At this meeting, copies of a collection of Father's poems, compiled by Madam Peng Shi Lin (彭士驎), were given to the participants. This gentleman later sent us through Madam Peng a copy of this Preface and two other poems written by Father (see poems in Chapter 50, "The Fair Maiden Chen Yun Shan of Taichen" 纪陈韵珊女士事 and Chapter 52, "No Title" 佚题).

This Preface was written for the publication of Mr Huang Yun Shan's (黄愠山) collection of poems titled, "Tian Nan Yin Cao" (天南吟草). The two other compositions mentioned above were probably taken from "Tian Nan Yin Cao". Hence Mr Huang's collection comprised compositions by himself and those of his friends.

Father and Mr Huang had known each other since 1924. Mr Huang was leaving Malaya to return to China in 1927, after having served as the founding principal of the Poi Lam 培南 School in Ipoh.

Mr Huang Yun Shan

The Preface was written for Mr Huang Yun Shan (黄愠山), who was also known as Huang Ying (黄瑛). According to the Preface, Mr Huang was in 1924 the Principal of Poi Lam School in Ipoh. According to other sources, Poi Lam School was founded on 17 January 1925 and classes "officially" started on 7 July 1925 at 111, Belfield Street, the newly completed premises of its sponsor the Perak Hokkien Association (霹雳福建公会). This seeming "discrepancy" between 1924 and 1925 can probably be explained by the fact that the sponsor of the school, the Perak "Hokkien" association had since 1917 been maintaining a private education centre (私塾) at a shophouse at 120, 那实得 Street (the proper English name of street unavailable). Mr

Poi Lam School 培南学校 in Ipoh celebrating Children's Day in 1947. The school is sponsored by the Perak Hokkien Association and classes "officially" started at the Association's premises (111, Belfield Street) on 7 July 1925. Mr Huang Yun Shan (黄愠山) was its first principal and was one of Qing Shan's poetry friends. The Preface in this chapter was written for Mr Huang's collection of poems in 1927 shortly before Mr Huang returned to China.

This is a close-up of the preceding photo. Coincidentally, in October 1945, Qing Shan became the paid Secretary of the Perak Hokkien Association with an office located in the same premises as Poi Lam School. Mr Huang Yun Shan was Principal in 1925. The window in the photo, located at the right end of the premises was where Qing Shan had his office. The two young boys (circled in the photo) peering out of the window are Peter and Michael, then nine and six years old.

Huang was likely to have been brought out from China during this transition from an education centre to a proper school. He thus became the principal of the new school which was then named Poi Lam School. Mr Huang could have come to Ipoh in 1924 or a little earlier. According to the record of Poi Lam School, he was the school's first principal from June 1925 to December 1926. This will explain why according to Father's Preface, Mr Huang was returning to China in 1927.

Significance of the Year 1924

Father first came to Malaya in May 1917 and returned to Putian for six months from January to December 1923 to marry a Miss Wu and brought her back to Kampar. In 1924, his first wife Madam Wu died while giving birth to their first child and the baby died with her.

Father's lament over the death of his first wife is recorded in the poem Chapter 52, "No Title" (佚題). The story of how Father later came to marry our mother can be read in the Background to the poem in Chapter 12, "Three Birthday Verses for My Wife" (寿内三章).

Hence, at the age of 30, Father became a widower in 1924, the year he first met Mr Huang. Compared with Mr Huang who was a gregarious person, Father described himself as "gloomy and depressed" during this dark period of his life.

Beyond the foregoing, we do not know anything more about Mr Huang or his poetry. What Father has written already tells us a great deal about the essence of the man.

Appreciation

This is an early prose composition in *wen yan* (文言 classical form) by Qing Shan. In its original form, the composition traditionally has neither punctuation nor paragraphing. Both have been inserted for easier reading today. A misplaced comma or full stop can sometimes completely change its meaning. The punctuation and paragraphing could therefore be said to be according to our interpretation or reading of the piece.

The first section introduces Mr Huang to the reader and contrasts the character and disposition of these two poetry friends Mr Huang and Qing Shan. When they first met, the two of them could not have been more different. They were brought together by their common love of poetry. Qing Shan was then 30 years old in 1924 and it is possible that Mr Huang was older. They were obviously good friends in poetry, with sufficient mutual respect for Mr Huang to have shown Qing Shan his compositions and to have asked him to write the Preface to such an important publication as his own poems. Qing Shan says, as an expression of humility, "I did not know how to compose poems, but after knowing him (Mr Huang), I began to dabble in it."

Qing Shan was, in fact, already well-versed in the writing of poetry in his teens and twenties. This was told by his childhood friend Lin Yuan Tang 林远堂 in his autobiography. Refer to the Background to Chapter 31, "On Yuan Tang's Wool Wedding Anniversary" (酬远堂羊毛婚纪念照题诗). Moreover, by 1924 Qing Shan was already a seasoned poet as seen in his excellent poem in Chapter 51, "Portrait General Wu" (吴将军画像赋一首), which was highly praised by Mr Song Hu Ming 宋湖民, an old prominent literary figure of Putian.

The Preface continues with a scene of two poets sitting upright facing each other without a word and deep in thought while looking for the right word for a particular line in the poem. There is such a close rapport between the two of them: "The moment the right word finally dawned on us, we would resume eye contact with each other and break into a smile at the same time." There is no explanation why Mr Huang and Qing Shan should have found such compatibility in each other, except for their common love of poetry. As Qing Shan describes it in the Preface: "In poetry, he (Mr Huang) regards me as one with whom he has the closest rapport; he would show me all his compositions." It is a great joy for a writer to find someone who has such a rapport with him in his compositions. The Chinese calls such a person as his "zhi yin" (知音) or literally "one who knows the inner voice of my words".

The second section then contrasts Mr Huang, the poet, with his businessmen compatriots. By the time Mr Huang left Malaya to return to China, he had nothing of any great monetary value to show for his time in Nanyang, whereas many of his compatriots in business had amassed great wealth. All Mr Huang "has in his trunk is the manuscript of an anthology of poems." Others offered Mr Huang this consolation: "People regard this (lack of material wealth) as the hallmark of 'Honesty'". Mr Huang was realistic enough not to be taken in by these polite words and "would regard this merely as the result of his being less than artful in life." Quoting a couple of lines probably from his poem, he says:

"A schoolmaster's rod and not long sleeves have I,
贾楚无长袖
Thus shall I return home now, all high and dry."
投秦剩蔽裘

The allusions used in the two lines are interesting. The first two words of the first line "jia chu" 贾楚 can also be written as 槚楚 with the same pronunciation. It originally meant a wooden instrument for punishment; the term was later used to simply mean a schoolmaster's rod. The reference to "long sleeves" (长袖) in the same line is an allusion from Han Feizi (韩非子, died 233BC) who wrote "Long sleeves enable one to dance well; sufficiency of money enables one to succeed in trade" (长袖善舞，多钱善贾). The expression means that those who are artful and have sufficiency of capital will do well in business. As a "schoolmaster", poor Mr Huang has neither the wiles nor the capital!

The allusion in the second of Mr Huang's quote has the literal meaning, "I cast my lot with the state of Qin and return with only my ragged garments" (投秦剩敝裘). The allusion is from the story of Su Qin (苏秦 of the Warring States era) who set off for the state of Qin 秦 to persuade its King to adopt his strategy. He failed and returned home in abject poverty, having spent all his money in the venture. Mr Huang has indeed only a trunk full of the manuscript of poems to show on his return. But "wealth" is not measured only in material terms. Qing Shan then praises Mr Huang for having travelled widely while he was in Nanyang and having seen and experienced much of life there. Mr Huang has accomplished more than what many others have done.

In the third section, an observation is made of Mr Huang's poetry. Mr Huang himself thinks that his poems have become more pessimistic since coming to Nanyang because of his many worries. Qing Shan who has known Mr Huang during his entire stay in Nanyang sees him quite differently. In fact, Qing Shan praises him as a gentleman who when dealing with others, does not quibble over each other's relative gain or loss. He never worries about being poor. Qing Shan closes the Preface by asking rhetorically, "The wealthy, they are the same everywhere; but how many are there who can create poetry?" Spoken like a true poet!

Chapter 62

《海屋唱酬集》序

光汉先生既为六十自寿诗,复集朋辈和章,将付铅椠,以彰友谊,属予序之。

予曰:"诗序乎,抑寿序也?"

曰:"诗序,亦寿序也。"

"然则当求诸贤而达者,何取于予?"

曰:"何哉子所谓贤达者?大人虎变,君子豹变,先笑而后号,前倨而后恭,入主而出奴,朝秦而暮楚,此所谓贤达者欤?是固未尝一日寿也,又恶足以寿人而为吾序!"

曰:"以后种种,今日生也,庸何伤?"

Preface for Guang Han's 60th Birthday Poems

Guang Han has himself composed a birthday poem in celebration of his 60th birthday. He gathers his cohort of friends and invites them to compose a "response" to his poem which he is about to send to them as an expression of his friendship. He asks me to write a Preface.

I say to him, "Is this a Preface for the poems or for your birthday?"

He replies, "A Preface for the poems is also a Preface for my birthday."

I reply, "In that case, you should invite a prominent person to write. Why me?"

He asks, "What prominent person are you speaking of? The conduct of a prominent person is quite unpredictable; he can just as easily turn from friend to foe, like a tiger, against you. A so-called 'gentleman' camouflages his true self just as a leopard uses its spots. There are those who constantly change from one to the other; he will smile in front of you, but 'shout' at you behind your back. He is haughty if he does not think you are important, but becomes instantly reverential as soon as he finds out you are indeed somebody. He is all right with you if you agree with his point of view, but will brush you aside if you do not. He is particularly partisan and changes constantly. Is this the prominent person you speak of? They who have themselves not experienced a decent day of real

曰:"今日生矣,昨日何如?且旦日又何如也?旦之视今,犹今之视昨,则其生也亦暂耳!"

曰:"适者生存,固自寿之道也。"

曰:"诚如是,则吾与子,亦何尝弗适乎?布衣之服,陋巷之居,晚食有肉,安步有车,此吾与子之所共适也。昔吾遇子,同在丁年,今垂垂老矣。转变者鬚髮,动摇者齿牙,而皆有不变不动者在;今犹昔也,旦日可知。子其寿予,且以自寿也。"

则唯唯称谢,谨志其言而为之序:

先生福建福清籍,世居江皋乡,先外父淡如公之哲嗣也。淡如公专美术,以金石书画名家,自悔少时不能专力于学问,常以教育事业望其后。先生尤能成其志,省立第一师范学校毕业后,即随其尊人南渡,先后任波德申中华,吉隆坡尊孔、国民,怡保

living are ill-qualified to wish me longevity and to write the birthday Preface for me!"

I say, "The ancients say that whatever happened in the past is like the 'yesterday' that has passed; whatever that will happen in the future is like the today that is coming into being. It is like a new birth. Whatever others have done in the past cannot do us much harm."

He replies, "True, today is like a new birth, but what about yesterday? What about tomorrow? To look at today from tomorrow is like looking at yesterday from today, everything is in the past. In this way, our time here is but temporary."

I say, "Those who know how to adapt to the circumstances will survive. Survival of the fittest is their 'secret' of longevity."

Guang Han says, "That's very true, just take you and me — have we not also adapted to our circumstances? Our clothing is basic and we live in the humblest of places, (setting aside sufficient to ensure that) we have meat on the table every evening and we have the means of transport whenever we wish to move. This is how you and I have adapted. When we first knew each other a long time ago, we were still in our youth. We are now both getting on in years; our hair has gone grey and our teeth begin to shake, but neither of us has changed. We do not change our sentiments from day to day. We are the same today as we were yesterday. What we will be in the future is also predictable. You go ahead and write this Birthday Preface for me; it can be a birthday wish for yourself too."

(Completely agreeing with his philosophy,) I could only accede to his request. I shall remember all he has said and hence compose this Preface for him.

Guang Han is a native of the county of Fuqing (福清) in Fujian (福建) province. The family has lived there for generations. He is the son of my late father-in-law, Mr Wang Dan Ru 王淡如, a renowned engraver, calligrapher and painter. The elder Mr Wang regretted not having persisted in his studies and therefore hoped that his children would devote themselves to

育才，安顺培华，金宝培元，实兆远南华等校教职三十余年，其间长培元学校者且二十年。马来亚沦陷，率家人隐实兆远，躬耕自食。光复后，复受吉隆坡文良港中华中学聘，旋调任吉隆坡华校师资训练班讲席，兼高师班国文科教员。

姊一，适李氏，马六甲培风学校教员李凤徵女士及吉隆坡精武学校教员李占春、福建莆田东山高级职业学校教员李当春昆仲之太夫人。妹义宋，初在福清馨英女学校，助理幼稚园，归予后，复致力于妇女职业教育，现任霹雳妇女裁剪训练所所长。弟三：光坡，经商芜湖；光国，历任宋溪启明、巴生港口青年，巴力中华等校校长二十年、其夫人胡琼玉女士，今犹任教于怡保三才学校；光河，侨商怡保；皆能自立门户矣。配陈氏，有贤能，家政悉以委之，故得专心于

the field of education. Guang Han himself is a fulfillment of his father's wish. After graduating from the state-sponsored First Teachers' Training College (省立第一师范学校), he went with his father to Nanyang. He first taught at Zhonghua School 中华 at Port Dickson 波德申, followed by Zun Kong 尊孔 in Kuala Lumpur 吉隆坡, Guo Ming 国民, Yoke Choy 育才 in Ipoh 怡保, Pei Hua 培华 in Telok Anson 安顺, Pei Yuan 培元 in Kampar 金宝 and Nan Hua 南华 in Sitiawan 实兆远, etc., thus having worked over 30 years in these various schools. Within this period, he was also the Principal of Pei Yuan 培元 for 20 years. During the Japanese Occupation of Malaya, he took his family to seek refuge in Sitiawan, and there they lived off the land by planting their own food. After the liberation of Malaya, the Zhonghua High School 中华中学 in Kuala Lumpur's Setapak 文良港 recruited him to lecture in the training courses for Chinese school teachers 华校师资训练班, in addition to his position as the Chinese Literature teacher for the Senior Normal Classes 高级师范班.

He has one elder sister, married to Mr Li 李, with the following children: Madam Li Feng Zheng 李凤徵 who teaches at Pei Feng School 培风学校 in Malacca; Li Zhan Chun 李占春, a teacher at Jing Wu School 精武学校 in Kuala Lumpur; Li Dang Chun 李当春, who teaches at Dongshan Higher Vocational College 东山高级职业学校 in Putian 莆田, Fujian. Guang Han's younger sister Yi Song 义宋 was formerly a kindergarten assistant at the Xingying Girls' School 馨英女学校 in Fuqing. After her marriage to me, she devoted herself to the vocational training of women and is currently the Principal of the Perak Women's Tailoring Training Centre 霹雳妇女裁剪训练所. Guang Han has three younger brothers: Guang Po 光波 is in business in Wuhu 芜湖; Guang Guo 光国 who had taught in Qi Ming 启明 in Sungei 宋溪, Qing Nian 青年 at Port Swettenham 巴生港口, and was the Principal of Zhonghua 中华 in Parit 巴力 for 20 years and his wife Madam Wu Qun Yu 胡琼玉 who is currently still teaching at Sam Chai School 三才学校 in

职务。生男二：靖中，芙蓉启华学校教员，娶李琼贞女士，芙蓉新华学校教员；允中，吉隆坡中华学校教员。女三：梅仙，曾任江沙崇华学校教员，归杨双德，随居马六甲视学官任次；芬仙，归丹戎马林陈文槐；云仙，归新嘉坡陈庆宵；皆已儿女成行。一门内外，从事教育者凡十一人，可谓善承淡如公之遗志矣，而启之者先生也。

江皋王氏，为福清望族，其乡人侨居马来亚者尤众，皆多财善贾，以赀相尚。独先生一家，食贫力教。或怜其拙，讽使改业，谓"多金则位高，奚自苦为？"辄婉言以谢之曰："少已习此，何可改也？且吾乡人，既庶既富，亦当有以加之矣。"比闻王氏族侨，方募集巨金，谋建乡校，未始非有感于斯言也。

Ipoh 怡保; Guang He 光河, is a businessman in Ipoh. All his siblings are independent and well-established. Guang Han is married to Madam Chen 陈氏, a capable lady who takes good care of the home thus enabling him to devote himself to his work. They have two sons: Jing Zhong 靖中, a teacher at Seremban's 芙蓉 Qihua School 启华学校, married to Madam Li Qiong Zhen 李琼贞, a teacher at Xinhua School 新华学校 in Seremban; 允中 Yun Zhong, a teacher at Zhonghua School 中华学校 in Kuala Lumpur. They also have three daughters: 梅仙 Mei Xian, formerly a teacher at Chonghua School 崇华学校 at Kuala Kangsar 江沙, married to Yang Shuang De 杨双德 an Inspector of schools in Malacca; Feng Xian 芬仙, married to Mr Chen Wen Huai 陈文槐 of Tanjong Malim 丹戎马林; Yun Xian 雲仙, married to Mr Chen Qing Xiao 陈庆宵 of Singapore; all blessed with children. In his entire extended family, there are eleven altogether who are teachers. This is truly an actualisation of the wish of his father Dan Ru, with Guang Han as the trailblazer.

The Wang family of Jiangdou is a distinguished family in Fuqing county. Many from the county now live in Malaya and many among them are wealthy and successful businessmen. Mr Wang's family is an exception. They are just poor teachers. Some people sympathise with them for their stubbornness and subtly suggest that they may perhaps wish to change their occupation, saying, "It is through wealth that one attains a prominent position in life, so why do you bring this misery upon yourself?" Mr Wang would always politely thank them, saying tactfully, "This is how I have been schooled from young, there is no reason to change. Moreover, it is good that our compatriots are wealthy. Besides the pursuit of wealth, you can also make a positive contribution in other ways." We hear that the overseas community from the Wang clan donated a large sum of money to build a school in the county. There is no doubt that they had been so moved and motivated by these words of his.

先生外似平易近情，中实倔强，与余论事，常坚持成见不相下。自以为既学为人师，教育即终身事业。斯固然已，其如迂阔不合时尚何？士生于今，用非所学者亦多矣！学致其用，不厌不倦，数十年如一日者，此即所谓不变与不动者欤？

先生今年六十，而其倔强与固执犹昔，是亦多寿之征也，于其所为诗见之已。集中和者殊寡，然皆夙昔知交，由衷而发，其不知者弗与也。

先生于讲学之余，分甘之暇，时一展玩，如对故人。其或篝灯夜诵，得意忘形，呼老妻起，强之使听，口陈指画，若坐绛帷。闺房之乐，甚于画眉矣。以此优游岁月，颐养天和，百年可待也。彼身居高楼大厦，饫膏粱而裹文绣，徘徊于纸醉金迷之室，周旋于粉白黛绿之

Outwardly, Guang Han appears to be an easy-going and amiable sort of person, but inwardly, he can be stubborn. When he and I are engaged in serious discussion, he often remains steadfast in his views and refuses to budge. He has always devoted his entire learning to be a teacher; it is natural that education is his chosen vocation for life. This is quite right. How can this be regarded as being stubborn? There are many men of learning today who no longer do what they have been trained for. Guang Han puts to good use what he has learned, and persists tirelessly in it. Even a decade seems like a day to him. Is this is not the same steadfast spirit that he has spoken of earlier (that persists in our friendship)?

Guang Han is sixty this year, but his stubborn character has not changed. Obstinacy can be a clear sign of longevity. Similarly his poems too show the stubborn side of his character. Although his cohort of poet friends are not many, they are all his close friends and speak from their heart. Those who are not so intimate with him have not been invited to respond. When he is not busy with his teaching, he shares the joy of his learning with others. Whenever he opens his book, it is like meeting an old friend. When he recites his poetry or reads late into the night, he gets so carried away that he wakes up his wife and insists she listens to him. He sits there like a schoolmaster, gesticulating with his hands to make his point. Such marital bliss surpasses even the most joyous of love between husband and wife. Thus do they enjoy their years together with a harmonious relationship which they can look forward to for another hundred years. Those who live in large mansions, dine on the best and drape themselves in finery, those who love money, are intoxicated by wealth and those who womanise—how can they live to his age? Moreover, who among them would feel carefree enough to accompany him on his leisurely walk, with pen and inkstone on hand, and honoured with the opportunity to compose this Preface for

间者，孰能如其寿，又孰能从容暇豫，长陪杖履，捧笔砚，以从先生之后而序其诗其寿乎！此予之所不敢辞而亦不容辞者也。是为序。

中华民国卅九年岁在庚寅八月之望

莆阳陈晴山撰于怡保

his Poems and Birthday? This is a privilege I would not dare decline, nor would I allow myself to. Thus is my Preface.

Chen Qing Shan of Puyang, writing in Ipoh
On the 15th day of the 8th month Gengyin year,
39th Year of the Chinese Republic [1950]

Background

Summary

This is one of three compositions in the book which are not poems but prose, written in the classical style. It was composed as a Preface for an anthology of birthday poems for our eldest uncle Wang Guang Han's 60th birthday titled, "Hai Wu Chang Chou Ji" (海屋唱酬集). Unlike most poems, but usual for Prefaces, this work was dated. It was "signed" dated 15th day of the 8th month of Gengyin (庚寅) year (which corresponds to 26 September 1950).

Three Brothers-in-law

Uncle Guang Han was born in 1890 and married Chen Xiu Ying 陈秀英 in 1906. Leaving behind his wife and a six-year-old son and three-year-old daughter, he first came to Malaya with his father in 1914. He became the first principal of Zhong Hua Primary School in Port Dickson in 1914 at the age of 24.

Guang Han was also the elder brother of Mother, in other words, he and Father were brothers-in-law. Guang Han was four years older than Father and their relationship was closer than would ordinarily have been between brothers-in-law. Guang Han's role in matchmaking his younger sister Yi Song to Father has already been explained in the Background to Chapter 12. Moreover, Father at that time was a teacher in the school in Kampar throughout the period when Guang Han was its principal from 1923 to 1940. Both had received a traditional education in the classics and were fond of poetry. It is no wonder that Guang Han had asked Father to write the Preface for this important publication of his birthday poems. Guang Han's younger brother, our uncle Guang Guo too came to Malaya as a teacher and was equally fond of poetry and he was asked by Guang Han to write the Epilogue for the anthology of poems.

Prior to his arrival in Malaya, Father had also been a tutor to the young Guang Guo in their native village of Jiangdou 江兜 in Fuqing. While Guang Han and Guang Guo had a high regard for Father's literary talent, these two brothers had themselves inherited the artistic skill of their father Wang Dan Ru 王淡如 who was an accomplished painter and calligrapher. Guang Han and Guang Guo became well-known for their calligraphy in the local literary circle in Kuala Lumpur and Ipoh.

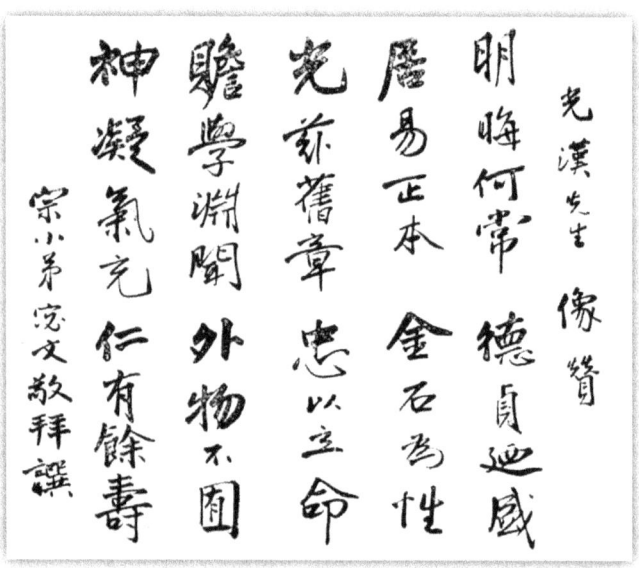

This is a poem composed by Mr Wang Fu Wen 王宓文 for Wang Guang Han 王光汉 to accompany the portrait of Guang Han in the collection of poems published in 1950 to celebrate Guang Han's 60th Birthday. Wang Fu Wen was then the Inspector of Chinese schools in the state of Perak, Malaya. Qing Shan wrote the Preface (in this Chapter) for the publication.

The portrait of Wang Guang Han, at the age of sixty, as appeared in the commemorative publication of his anthology of poems.

The extended family of Wang Guang Han. The photo was taken in December 1949 and appeared in the commemorative publication. Guang Han is seated in the centre (wearing tie) with his wife (holding a child) seated on his left.

Tenure in Pre-War Chinese Schools

The Preface singled out for mention that Guang Han was Principal of Pei Yuan School in Kampar for some 20 years. According to what was recorded in "History of Malaysian Schools founded by Hokkiens" 马来西亚福建人兴办教史料集 published in 1993, he was principal for 18 years from 1923 to 1940. This long period of tenure was most unusual in those days and the same publication pointed it out as indicative of the stability and close cooperation between the school board and the staff of Pei Yuan School.

Chinese schools in pre-Second World War Malaya were largely financed by the clan associations and "he who pays the piper calls the tune". The employment and tenure of teachers were in the hands of the school board who were usually members of the clan association board with its Chairman in the most influential position. The tenure was usually for two years and the last quarter of every year was the time for contract renewal. This was also the time of great anxiety for every teacher and his family. Would he still have a job next year? Would the family have to move again to another school in another town? By the end of 1940, Guang Han was already 50 years old and had enjoyed a good run of 18 years as Principal. His contract was not renewed. Barely a year after he left Pei Yuan as Principal, the Japanese invaded Malaya and all schools were closed.

Teacher Farmers during the Occupation

During the Japanese Occupation, he took his family to Sitiawan (about 50 kilometres from Kampar) and lived off the land like many others. By then his family had grown. Although the older children were trained as teachers, they all had to farm in order to eat.

Post War

When the Japanese Occupation ended in 1945, Guang Han moved his family to Kuala Lumpur and resumed teaching in schools and teacher training classes in and around Kuala Lumpur. His children by then were all independent. He retired from teaching and enjoyed his retirement with his wife, growing chrysanthemums, keeping a few birds and reading and writing poetry—the leisure pursuits of a scholar gentleman.

Appreciation

The Preface opens in an unusual and interesting way. After explaining very quickly what the publication is all about, it then takes the form of a brisk Socratic dialogue of question and answer between Qing Shan and Guang Han.

Since Guang Han had asked Qing Shan to write the Preface for his publication of his birthday poems, Qing Shan wanted to know, "Is this a Preface for the poems or for your birthday?" Guang Han replied swiftly, "A Preface for the poems is also a Preface for my birthday" almost saying the two are the same, why quibble over the difference. Qing Shan with no longer an "excuse" to decline the job, then went straight to the point, "In that case, you should invite a prominent person to write. Why me?"

This question appears to be planted into the dialogue to beg the denunciation of the so-called "prominent persons" of this world. *"The conduct of a prominent person is quite unpredictable; he can just as easily turn from friend to foe, like a tiger, against you. A so-called 'gentleman' camouflages his true self just as a leopard uses its spots. There are those who constantly change from one to the other; he will smile in front of you, but 'shout' at you behind your back. He is haughty if he does not think you are important, but becomes instantly reverential as soon as he finds out you are indeed somebody. He is all right with you if you agree with his point of view, but will brush you aside if you do not. He is particularly partisan and changes constantly. Is this the prominent person you speak of?"* These lessons in life come from the older Guang Han, but did he actually ever say them? Perhaps not in the same form, but they are bound to be the same sceptical views of life shared by the two brothers-in-law who must have experienced such treatment by "prominent persons" or "gentlemen" in their time.

The dialogue is written as though Guang Han is giving his younger brother-in-law a lesson on life. To Qing Shan's suggestion that those who know how to adapt to the circumstances will survive, Guang Han puts a different meaning to "adaptation" for survival. It is not about having to see which way the wind is blowing and bending our own principles accordingly or fawning upon "prominent persons". Guang Han's answer is simply to adapt our expectations to our means and putting first things first: *"…just take you and me—have we not also adapted to our circumstances? Our clothing is basic and we live in the humblest of places, (setting aside sufficient to ensure that) we have meat on the table every evening and we have the means of transport whenever we wish to move. This is how you and I have adapted."*

We see from the foregoing Background for this poem the special relationship between Guang Han and Qing Shan and this old and steadfast friendship is amplified by Guang Han: *"When we first knew each other a long time ago, we were still in our youth. We are now both getting on in years; our hair has gone grey and our teeth begin to shake, but neither of us has changed. We do not change our sentiments from day to day."*

To describe how their long friendship has remained constant throughout the years, Qing Shan uses an interesting antithesis in Guang Han's words: *"…our teeth begin to shake* (动摇者齿牙)*"* is compared with the idea that their friendship has remained steadfast: *"…but neither of us has changed* (而皆有不变不动者在)*"*.

After a long introduction, Qing Shan then begins the Preface "proper". He begins with a long paragraph detailing the background of the Wang family in Fuqing, Guang Han's education and subsequent career and that of all his children and his siblings. It is not very interesting as literature but useful for Guang Han's family as material for their family history.

The last three paragraphs of the Preface explains why Guang Han has taken on a career in education. Several of his Fuqing compatriots have become wealthy by going into business. They see Guang Han living in such simple circumstance and subtly suggest he considers doing something else that might make more money than teaching. Guang Han shows his steadfastness and tactfully replies that he wants to stick to teaching because that is what he has been trained for. Not one to miss an opportunity, he turns the suggestion round and asks his wealthy compatriots if they might want to contribute something for the cause of education. As a result, they donated a large sum of money to build a school in the county.

The final paragraph contains an amusing description of Guang Han's habit of nocturnal recitation of his poems when *"…he gets so carried away that he wakes up his [poor] wife to listen to him. He sits there like a schoolmaster, gesticulating with his hands to make his point."* All of us who love to read and to write are guilty of this. Qing Shan is a master of such vivid description that brings the words alive on the page!

The same paragraph also paints a lively scene of Guang Han enjoying the leisure of his retirement. Qing Shan then asks rhetorically, *"…who among them [his wealthy merchant friends] would feel carefree enough to accompany him on his leisurely walk, with pen and ink stone on hand, and honoured with the opportunity to compose this Preface for his Poems and Birthday?"* Qing Shan hastens to answer the call himself, *"This is a privilege I would not dare decline, nor would I allow myself to."*

The Title

A word of explanation here, for the reader who is curious about the Chinese title of this Chapter. The literal meaning of the Chinese title is "Anthology of 'Ocean-House' Poems" 海屋唱酬集. The strange term "Ocean-House Poems" merely means "Birthday Poems". It is derived from a story told by the Song poet Su Dongpo 苏东坡. Three old men came together to discuss their age. One of them said, "I don't really know how old I am. Whenever the ocean (沧海) is transformed into mulberry fields (桑田), I place a bamboo chip in the house (to register time). The bamboo chips now fill ten houses 海水变桑田时，吾辄下一筹，尔来吾筹已满十间屋." The expression "Ocean-House" is a "compression" of this whole account by the old man. It combines the first word "Ocean 海" with the last word "House 屋". The transformation from ocean to mulberry fields (land) is a metaphor for great changes and connotes a long period of time. Hence the term "Ocean-House" 海屋 is used to denote "longevity" or "birthday".

Chapter 63

诗话七则

(一)

征诗难,编次尤不易。先后之间,自不能漫无秩序。琳琅满目,一例珠玑,不可妄分甲乙,一难也;艺术之宫,又非朝廷乡党,序爵序齿,均非所宜,二难也。

曩为寿内乞诗,承各方友好,邮筒相寄。既得佳章四十有四,作者十八人,又适符十八学士之数,私心窃喜,方以为幸。付印之日,对于编次,具煞费踌躇。最后决定,先之以马来亚国外来稿,劳远人也;殿之以王氏,因其亲也;中间诸子,白丘李沈,林周洪杨,欧戴及韩,皆以笔画为序,自谓稍得体例。质诸高明,以为当否?妥否?

My Seven Principles of Poetry

Paragraph 1

It is difficult enough to solicit for poems; to arrange them specially for publication is not a simple task either. The order of appearance cannot be haphazard, without some system. A collection of literary gems are all indescribably beautiful and we cannot begin to grade them—that is the first difficulty. Neither is the realm of the Arts like a gathering of village elders nor the imperial court where custom and protocol dictate the order according to seniority of age or rank of office. Neither age nor rank is appropriate as a criterion: that is the second difficulty. In soliciting for birthday poems recently for my wife, I corresponded by post with my good friends from many parts of the region and received 44 poems from 18 persons. What a remarkable coincidence! The number 18 corresponds with the famous 18 scholars assembled by Emperor Tang Tai Zong (唐太宗). I was personally very happy with this fortunate good response. On the day the draft had to go to press, I was compelled to wrack my brains on how to arrange the order of the poems and I finally decided that the first group to appear should be those from other parts of Malaya and from overseas, as the respondents have taken much trouble. The last group to appear should be the two brothers of the Wang family, as they are relatives. Sandwiched between these two groups are the various gentlemen whose surnames are: *Bai-Qiu-Li-Shen* 白

（二）

拙作《寿内三章》，虽曾油印若干份，分发知交，但亦非望门投止，漫无所择。当时自划范围：一、非平昔相知者不投；二、虽十载知交，对于旧诗不感兴趣者不投；三、多产作家、有求必应者不投。持此三不主义，盖不欲讨人厌，亦不欲强所难。至于应酬之作，不足以寿世传家者，更非所望也。既而各方来稿，果皆如愿以偿。始信条件之苛，不无益处。

（三）

寿内三章，或问何不更作一章，凑成偶焉？盖以三为奇数，不宜于祝寿。此言虽非无据，然勉强充数，亦殊不易。况三之为数，未必匪祯。嵩岳三呼，华封三祝，用于上寿，古已有之。三百篇中，类此者尤多。《关雎》、《葛覃》、《樛木》、《螽斯》、《桃丘李沈, *Lin-Zhou-Hong-Yang* 林周洪杨, *Ou-Dai* 欧戴 and *Han* 韩. I arrange them according to the number of strokes of how their surnames are written. Thus have I ordered the poems with the help of these simple rules. I am now confident enough to ask the learned friends whether they think it appropriate.

Paragraph 2

As for my humble composition of three verses for my wife, although I sent out several stenciled copies to my close friends, I did not do so out of desperation, i.e., sending them out to all and sundry. I had my own criteria for drawing the boundary. Firstly, avoid sending them to those who are not friends of long standing. Secondly, avoid sending them to those who have no interest in classical poetry, even if they are long standing friends. Thirdly, avoid sending them to those prolific writers who write "on demand" whenever and whoever asks of them. Working on this "Three Avoids", I myself avoid being a nuisance to others and do not impose an awkward obligation on them. As for compositions undertaken out of obligation, they are no gift to the world and fall short of being worthy to pass on to our children and grandchildren. These are not what I am looking for. Now that I have seen the actual responses of all and they are indeed what I had wished, it is even more apparent that the strict conditions that had been set are not without benefit.

Paragraph 3

Again, on the three birthday verses for my wife, some might ask why not one more verse to add up to an even number? Three is an odd number and is not appropriate for birthday poems. Although this concern is not without foundation, to force yourself to write one more to make up the number is also no easy task. Moreover, the number "three" is not necessarily inauspicious. For example, there is the three shouts of

夭》、《茉莒》、《麟趾》、《采蘩》，何一非三？而又皆言妇德。自以有例可援，因不复作。

（四）

拙稿发出后，远近知交，纷纷投报，惟太平白仰峰先生后至。初疑三不主义，或犯其一。曾戏作一诗以催之：

闻君慷慨乐输将，安得吟囊似义囊？
雁使北来频问讯，鸡林何日复通商？
居奇莫遣骚坛寂，有美休教韫椟藏。
诗市岂同胶市看，欲求善价始装箱？

仰峰为霹雳胶商钜子，又素以疏财仗义闻，故予诗并及之。诗去不久，即得偿宿欠，并承和一律：

献丑吾诗出故将，因君追急始倾囊。
早知此笔是良友，应悔斯人转学商！

longevity *"Wan sui* 万岁*"* for the emperor; then there are the three wishes of the people of *Huafeng* for Emperor Yao, viz., for longevity, wealth and progeny. All these have been practiced since ancient times. In classical text, we have the three hundred poems in the *Book of Poetry* in which a large number of poems are in three verses, for example, *Guan Ju* 关雎, *Ge Tan* 葛覃, *Ju Mu* 樛木, *Zhong Si* 螽斯, *Tao Yao* 桃夭, *Fou Yi* 芣苢, *Lin Zhi* 麟趾, *Cai Fan* 采蘩. There is not one among them that does not have three verses. Moreover, they all extol the virtues of a wife. There is enough precedence for this and I therefore did not write the additional verse.

Paragraph 4

After I sent out the draft of my poem, friends from far and near all began to respond except for Mr Bai Yang Feng of Taiping. At first, I thought one of my criteria of "Three Avoids" had gone awry. I then playfully wrote a poem to provoke him, saying:

> A generous donation I hear is your great pleasure.
> Why not a donation from your literary treasure?
> I ask the postal courier coming from the north,
> "When will the poetry market reopen thenceforth?"
> Poems are not commercial merchandise to hoard.
> Beautiful things should not be hid for greater reward.
> How could Poetry and the Rubber market be the same,
> Waiting for a price rise before they're boxed, its aim?

Yang Feng is a well-known personality in the Perak rubber trade and is generous with his wealth in giving to charity. Hence my poem to him. Not long after this, I was rewarded with the receipt of a poem from him in response to my birthday poem for my wife. In addition, he wrote a poem in response to the poem I had sent him.

I am embarrassed to offer my poem even as a "donation".

甚爱由来须大费,　厚亡隐患在多藏。
善生不过三餐足,　何计千箱与万箱?

中引老子甚爱大费,多藏厚亡之说,似已悟道。又附书云:"与笔墨不相往来者久,连字都写不成。"其然?岂其然乎!仰峰诗虽不多见,但闻成根云,渠早岁即负诗名;禄宽亦极称其诗。成根与同里、同学,禄宽论诗颇严,不轻相许,是皆可信者。岂搏虎健儿,卒未善士欤?然则今之攘臂下车,未始非得力于激将一诗矣。

(五)

心在自台北寄赠一律,颈联"盈门桃李儒家X"句末一字阙文。余与禄宽、成根、光国、亭又,各拟一字以补,若猜诗谜然。一面空邮寄台询心在,拜媵以一诗云:

诗城坐拥久称王,乍降纶音喜欲狂。
衮职偶然差一着,顿教补阙拾遗忙。

Your urgent importunities spur me into undoing my bag.
If only I had known the pen to be my "true love"!
I now regret having turned away from pen to trade.
A great love begets a great loss;
The greater your possession the greater the loss.
Three meals a day is all we need to live,
Why bother whether it's a thousand
or ten thousand boxes we have.

This is an allusion from Laozi's proposition, "Great love, great loss and the greater the possession the greater the loss". He seems to have grasped the essence of Laozi. Yang Feng also attached a note which says, *"I have not been in contact with pen and ink for so long that I have difficulty even just to write at all."* That may well be, but is it really so? Although I have not seen many of Yang Feng's poems, I have heard from Cheng Gen that Yang Feng had been well known for his poetry even from a very young age; Lu Kuan also had high praises for his poems. Cheng Gen and Yang Feng were classmates and came from the same village. Lu Kuan has strict standards on the subject of poetry and does not easily make allowances. The testimonies of Cheng Gen and Lu Kuan are both credible—it is not likely that two valiant poetry "warriors" like them could suddenly become easy-going. How could Yang Feng be like the proverbial "tiger-killer" Feng-fu (冯妇) who failed to become an eminent scholar? That Yang Feng should finally succumb to rolling up his sleeves and setting to work on a poem is not because of anything else but the result of my strenuous effort in applying the "strategy of provocation".

Paragraph 5

Xin Zai from Taipei sent a poem of eight lines. The third "couplet" of his poem appears to have the last word missing from the line: "Past disciples are everywhere, the Teacher is ___"

未几得回信，乃为一"乐"字，盖取孟子三乐之义。予等所猜，竟无一是，乃知古史阙文，非无故也。来书亦附和韵一首：

旧日槟城无冕王，　一时诗酒少年狂。
而今酒减诗才拙，　却累诸家补缀忙。

心在南游时，曾主槟城《光华日报》笔政，故云。

（六）

远堂为予总角之好，少余一岁，与游德馨女士婚四十年矣。子女成群，皆已知名。去岁丙申三月廿九日，曾以羊毛婚纪念合照寄赠，并附一诗，系之以序："予以民国丁巳年三月廿九日结婚，今年是日，适为羊毛婚纪念之日，因与在家诸人合拍一照，书示内子。"诗云：

唱随轮指卅年才，　纪念婚龄又一回。
夫子信诚吾岂敢，　母亲模范汝何猜。

(盈门桃李儒家__). Each of us from among Lu Kuan, Cheng Gen, Guang Guo and Ting You and myself, chose a replacement word for the missing one. It was like trying to solve a word riddle. We sent our "replacement" words by airmail to Xin Zai in Taipei with an accompanying poem:

> In the City of Poets, long has ruled the King.
> Joyously we hear the royal edict announcing
> The King's inadvertent error of omission.
> Busily engaged we are on this royal commission.

> 诗城坐拥久称王，
> 乍降纶音喜欲狂。
> 衮职偶然差一着，
> 顿教补阙拾遗忙。

Not long after, I received a reply to say the missing word is the word "Happiness" (乐), taken from Meng Zi's principle of "A Gentleman's Three Happiness" (君子三乐). This was not among any of the words we had chosen as replacement. We now know that when there is a missing or defective word in ancient texts, it is not without reason. Xin Zai's reply came with a poem with rhymes matching the poem sent to him:

> In former days, the uncrowned King of Penang was I.
> A wild excess of youth in poetry and wine, I cannot deny.
> A lower intake of wine, lowers the quality of poetry.
> Troubling you all to patch up my work, I am sorry.

> 旧日槟城无冕王，一时诗酒少年狂，
> 而今酒少诗才拙，却累诸家补缀忙。

During Xin Zai's sojourn in Nanyang, he had been the Chief Editorial Writer of the Penang newspaper *Guanghua Ri Bao* which explains why he had written thus.

生儿十九不豚犬，在学寻常俱斗魁。
但觉糟糠情味好，未妨重醉合欢杯。

伉俪之情，活现纸上。予曾作七律二首以贺之。其一云：

欧化东渐遍九州，纵非名士亦风流。
七年之病悲黄脸，几个相随到白头？
垂老方知伉俪笃，平生不识别离愁。
羊毛出在羊身上，多福由来只自求。

"七年之病"原作"七年之痒"，嫌过于俚，后易之。羊毛一句，则因远堂以乙未生，其肖为羊，双关意皆切。然全以俚语入诗，近于打油矣。其二云：

四十年来话短长，故园北望几沧桑。
风云一世今安在？贫贱之交尚不忘。
回忆童年如昨日，相看儿辈各成行。
当君花烛辉煌夜，我向天南正放洋。

Paragraph 6

Yuan Tang and I are childhood friends; he is one year younger. He has been married to Ms You De Xin for forty years and they brought up several children who are all accomplished. Last year, on the 29th day of the third month of Bing Shen 丙申 year (9 May 1956), he sent me a photo that had been taken to commemorate their "Wool Wedding Anniversary" together with a colophon which says, "We were married during the Nationalist Republican era on the 29th day of the third month of Ding Si (丁巳) year (19 May 1917). That anniversary date [1956], happened to be the 'Wool Anniversary' of our wedding. Since we are now having a photo taken with the whole family, I thus write this poem for my wife." His poem for his wife reads:

(Paraphrase)

> "On our reckoning, we've been husband and wife for forty years.
> The time to commemorate our Wedding Anniversary has come around once again.
> You praise me as an honest and sincere person, but I am not truly worthy.
> An exemplary mother you truly are, and there can be no doubt of that.
> Of our children you've brought up, nine out of ten are accomplished,
> Often topping their class in school.
> Although we lived a spartan life of adversity, yet our life together is sweet.
> Indeed, let's drink once more to that and be joyful."

The tender feelings between husband and wife come to life even on paper. I once composed for him two verses of a seven-word regulated poem. The first verse of my poem reads,

回忆远堂婚日,予将去国,适在七洲洋舟中,匆匆四十年矣,抚今追昔,不胜感慨系之!

(七)

投稿诸友好,多有虚怀若谷,自觉一字未安,不惜再三商讨;且有援一般刊物征稿之例,授权改正者,实则皆可不必。白居易云:

天下无正声,悦耳即为娱。

人间无正色,悦目即为姝。

此真诗人语也。应征诸作,皆余耳边之韶頀,眼里之西施,间尝取而诵之,琅琅上口。吾妻在旁倾听,亦觉其悦耳可娱,声发于心,不同应制。本无所谓正,又乌从而正之?

Verse 1

West to East, its wind pervades our land.
It's easy to be Bohemian for any man.
For many, divorces follow the "seven-year itch".
To grow old together is beyond their reach.
How stable a marriage, in old age we'd know.
You have never had a day of parting sorrow.
Sheep's wool grows on the body of a sheep;
Your blessings come, they are what you seek.

Verse 2

We've said all can be said in the past forty years.
The old country has had her upheavals and tears.
The famed men of ancient times, are they still here?
Friendship of humble folks is still held dear.
Our childhood of yesteryears seems like yesterday.
Our numerous children form two long queues today.
While the candles shone on your wedding night,
I was at sea heading south, no more in sight.

    I recall the day of Yuan Tang's wedding; I had left the country and was in a ship sailing on the high seas. These forty years have just gone past in a flash. As I think of his wedding anniversary today—alas, all the memories of yesteryears come flooding back to me.

Paragraph 7

The good friends who accepted my invitation to respond to my poem, mostly have broad and open minds. If they see a word that might not be appropriate, there are even among them those who are prepared to be engaged in an open discussion. Moreover, as is the custom with writing for a publication, they even accord the editor the right to amend their compositions.

香山之诗，老妪都解。毁之者方以此病其俗，誉之者即以此奉为正宗。孰是孰非，安有定论！亦在听者之悦耳与否尔。夫诗，天籁也，庄子所谓"吹万不同"者，其可齐乎？断鹤续凫，徒贼其天而已。予既悦其声而编之，刊之，行且精装成帙，贮以锦函，藏诸芸笥，遗之后嗣，永作家珍。子孙即不能读，视为周鼎商彝，古色古香，亦自至宝。正统派诗人，倘于拙作三章，及吾友诸作而感不满者，当以此言谢之。

It is really not necessary to make any amendment to their poems, as Bai Juyi once said, *"There is no such thing as the right cadence and rhyme. Whatever that pleases the ears is music enough; whatever that pleases the eyes is beautiful".* These are the words of a true poet. The poems of those who responded are like perfect classical music beside my ears and like the beauty of Xi Shi before my eyes. As I recite them aloud, the words resonate in my mouth. My wife who is listening by my side too enjoys the music of the poetry, with every sound coming straight from the heart, unlike the stilted forms of compositions for formal examinations. Since there is no such thing as "correct" poetry, how could anyone have cause to amend any of these poems? The poems of Bai Juyi can be understood even by the old woman of the village. His critics point out this fact as the defect of his poems; his protagonists, on the other hand, single out this very same fact as the hallmark of true poetry. Who is right and who is wrong is yet to be settled! It all depends on whether the listener finds it pleasant or not to his ears. Poetry is the sound of nature; as Zhuangzi said, "When the wind blows, the result is a myriad of different sounds." How can everything be the same? If we should think that the neck of the crane is too long and try to shorten it, or if we think the legs of the duck are too short and try to lengthen them, both will come to grief. To do so would be to offend against what nature has ordained. Delighted as I am with the music of the poems, I shall compile them, publish them and bind them exquisitely, place them in brocade-lined boxes and store them with fragrant scent, to leave behind for my descendants as a family treasure for all time. My children and grandchildren may not know how to read them, but they can look upon them as Zhou and Shang bronze ware of antiquity to be revered and treasured all the same. To the "orthodox" poets who may not be satisfied with my three verses or the compositions of my friends, I thank them with this and offer the foregoing argument as my answer to them.

Background

Written in 1957, this passage was composed as an epilogue to a collection of 44 poems by 15 of Father's poetry friends, our two uncles and Father himself, making a total of 18. The special occasion was Mother's 60th birthday and concurrently, the celebration of the 10th anniversary of the founding of Mother's tailoring school post-World War II.

The first remarkable thing about this passage is where it appeared. It was published in a tailoring school's magazine under the section titled, "Poetry Forum" (吟坛). In this section, Father wrote this delightful epilogue, "My Seven Principles of Poetry 诗话七则". The poetry section takes up four out of 50 pages of the entire magazine published to commemorate the twin events of Mother's 60th birthday and the school's 10th anniversary. This very "learned" composition, written in formal classical language, and the 44 poems in classical form would be more at home in some journal of an academic institution or a poets' society. Instead, they appear in the commemorative magazine of a women's tailoring school, with strange bedfellows like the 20 pages of advertisements of motor spare part shops, a quail farm, restaurants, a Chinese medicine shop, photo studios. We often chuckle when we imagine a 20-year-old student of the tailoring school or even an older alumnus staring incomprehensibly at these four pages of pure and exquisite classical prose and poetry.

It is not unusual for poets to invite their friends to send in poems and have them published on some special occasion like birthdays. Our uncle Wang Guang Han had his friends' birthday poems for him published in 1950 on his 60th birthday. Father wrote the preface for him (Chapter 62) and composed two poems (Chapters 17 and 18). Father's own 60th birthday in 1954 passed without any fanfare or celebration. He was always reluctant to celebrate his own birthday. He loved poetry and could not pass up an occasion for this passion. Mother's 60th birthday and her tailoring school's 10th anniversary were

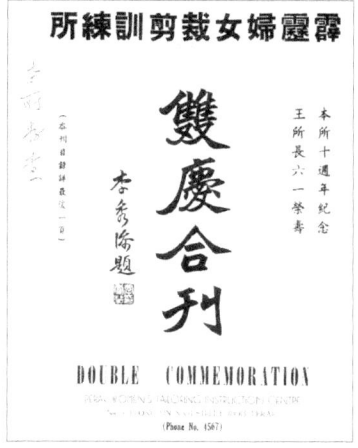

The cover page of Yi Song's tailoring school, Double Commemoration magazine, published in 1957. The twin celebration was for the school's Tenth Anniversary of its founding and the Sixtieth Birthday of its Principal and Founder Yi Song (Qing Shan's wife). The birthday poems for Yi Song and Qing Shan's composition in this chapter appeared at the end of the magazine.

In the closing lines of his composition, "My Seven Principles of Poetry" (詩話七則), Qing Shan expressed his deep feelings for the classical poems for his wife's birthday: "*I shall place them in brocade-lined boxes and store them with fragrant scent for my descendants as a family treasure. They may not know how to read them but can look upon them as Zhou and Shang bronze ware of antiquity to be revered and treasured all the same.*"

a perfect reason for it. Besides, he would have all those "commercials" to help defray the cost of printing!

For Father to borrow the "vehicle" of Mother's tailoring school magazine for poetry is not entirely without justification. Mother's career as the principal and instructor of a tailoring school started even before the Second World War. Father had been responsible for getting Mother to attend formal training school in tailoring and cutting, and was also the "brains" behind the tailoring school venture. He was the school's *de facto* but unpaid administrator. He was responsible for drawing up schedules for classes, examinations, advertising, public relations, and arranging speaking engagements for Mother. We even remember the evenings when he had to personally write by hand the names of the graduands on the school's graduation diplomas.

As Father had made a major contribution towards the success of the school, these four pages of a little indulgence in poetry are perfectly justified. Besides, Mother was the founding principal of the school and her 60th birthday and the school's 10th anniversary are significant events for congratulation.

Appreciation

The three classical prose passages in this book are all associated with poetry. Two of them are prologues. This is the only epilogue and one that shows up like a polished mirror which reflects Qing Shan's pure joy when indulging in poetry. The whole passage consists of seven paragraphs. The first two set the scene and explain the order of appearance of the poems and his criteria for inviting his friends. The third explains why the poem he wrote for Mother has three verses and not some other number. The fourth to the sixth paragraphs takes the reader through each of the three entertaining and lively exchanges he had with his poetry friends when they sent in their poems to him. The final paragraph is a short essay on the hallmark of good poetry as expounded by Bai Juyi. The highlight is probably the few beautiful lines at the end that can only be savoured and enjoyed by actually reading them.

No Protocol in the Arts

The passage is rich in both imagery and thought. In speaking of the poems of his friends he uses the metaphor "literary gems" (琳琅满目) which he says are all beautiful and not capable of being ranked according to merit. He therefore cleverly gets away without having to express the relative merit of the poems. He also declines the idea of arranging the poems in order of age or rank of the composers, quite properly saying, *"Neither is the realm of the arts like a gathering of village elders nor the imperial court where custom and protocol dictate the order according to seniority of age or rank of office."* His use of the imagery of the staid and stilted *"gathering of village elders (or) the imperial court"* very effectively contrasts with the more liberal ambience of the world of arts. He also takes great delight in observing the coincidence of 18 contributors of the birthday poems with the famous 18 scholars assembled by Emperor Tang Tai Zong (唐太宗) during the Tang dynasty. The assembling of talent in one place as a "think tank" is not such a new idea after all.

The Principle of "Three Avoids"

He next explains his three criteria for choosing whom to invite for a poem. In fact, he defines his criteria by saying whom he avoids inviting, thus the "Three Avoids". In order to ensure that his friends feel valued when they receive his invitation, he says, *"I did not do so out of desperation, sending them (the invitations) out to all and sundry."* His third "Avoid" is interesting because he knows there are those who would compose a poem merely as a courtesy and these works are not done with true feelings. Even respectable poets, painters and calligraphers sometimes have to produce a "courtesy" piece of work. Qing Shan only wants to approach someone whom he knows well enough and who has sufficient rapport with him to be able to compose a poem with genuine feelings. Another interesting point to note here is the practice among poets when they invite their friends to respond. The person making the invitation will first compose a poem with a particular rhyming scheme and send it out to his friends. They are invited to respond with their poems that must match his rhyming scheme. This is the sort of challenge the poet friends throw at one another and the "games" they play.

Poetry Not Written to Fill Quota

In explaining why he had only written three verses in his poem for his wife's birthday, he first brushes aside the belief that "three" being an odd number may not be auspicious. The important point he makes is that good poetry cannot be created by command just to fill a quota or satisfy some desired number. Good poetry is written from inspiration. If the inspiration should stop at "three", that is it. He then quotes examples where the number "three" is traditionally used and associated with birthday congratulations. He also quotes as "precedence" eight poems from the three hundred poems in the classic *Book of Poetry*. All eight poems have three verses each and they all extol the virtues of a wife. Why not his three verses for his wife's birthday? Qing Shan is obviously having fun going through all these and saying them almost tongue in cheek.

Qing Shan's Only Difficult "Customer"

All his friends respond to his request in good time, except one Mr Bai Yang Feng, a wealthy rubber merchant in Taiping, about 50 miles north of Ipoh. Yang Feng is a wealthy but generous man who gives regularly to charity. He is also an accomplished poet and a good friend. There is no excuse for him not to respond. Qing Shan decides to have a bit of fun and writes him a provocative poem to tease him out. Praising him first with, "If you're so generous to others with your money," Qing Shan then jabs him with, "why can't you be generous to me with a poem of yours?" He goes on to pull his leg by telling him that poems are not like commercial merchandise which he can hoard until the prices go up. (See Chapter 34 for a fuller treatment this poem.) Yang Feng, the rubber merchant poet, must have been a very busy man, but is finally provoked into action. He sends in a birthday poem but also writes a reply in the form of a poem as an answer to Qing Shan's cheeky "attack". He makes the usual protestations about how unworthy his poems are and that he has not written for a long time. Yang Feng is actually a very learned man as can be seen from his answer to Qing Shan's mock "accusation" that he is being miserly with his poems. He answers Qing Shan by saying why should anyone be miserly with anything at all. He uses an allusion from Laozi's proposition, "Great love, great loss and the greater the possession the greater the loss". And he concludes philosophically that all we can consume is only three meals a day. Ultimately, what difference does it make how much our worldly possessions amount to. Qing Shan must have thoroughly enjoyed this exchange with Yang Feng as can be seen from the exuberance with which he writes.

The Emperor's Critic

The next exchange is with Mr Zhuang Xin Zai of Taipei. Xin Zai has composed a poem for Qing Shan's wife but there is a word inadvertently left out from one of the lines. Qing Shan and his small cohort of poetry friends take it on as a challenge and obviously have great fun trying to speculate what the missing word is. He then sends their guesses to Xin Zai with a poem teasing him. Prior to returning to Taipei, Xin Zai had been the Chief Editorial Writer of a major newspaper in Penang, well respected in the literary circle of Penang which was known by its sobriquet "City of Poets". Qing Shan refers to Xin Zai as the (literary) "King" in Penang; and refers to his own cohort of poetry friends as "court officials" who become wild with joy when this "royal command" comes unexpectedly commissioning them to look for the missing word. The Chinese expression Qing Shan uses for "royal command" (纶音 *lún yīn*) is interesting and colourful. The two words literally mean "silken voice", referring not to the velvety voice of the King but to his edicts and commands traditionally written on silk. Continuing with the analogy of Xin Zai as the King who has inadvertently committed an error of omission by leaving out a word, Qing Shan uses the expression 衮职 *gǔn zhí* to mean the "King". It is another expression rich in literary connotation. The first word 衮 literally means "royal robe" and 职 means "office" or "post" and the two words together 衮职 *gǔn zhí* means either an official post in the King's court or the King himself. This is an allusion from the *Book of Poetry* which tells the story of the upright and capable Premier Shan Fu (山甫) who was a close and trusted confidante of the King. He was the only one honest and courageous enough to point out any of the King's error or omission: "衮职有阙，维仲山甫补之" meaning, "The King commits an error, only Shan Fu dares help him correct it." The use of this allusion also connotes the close relationship between Qing Shan and his friend Xin Zai, a relationship that allows one to point out a mistake of the other. Xin Zai's reply is equally clever. He refers to himself as the "uncrowned" King since it is only Qing Shan who "crowns" him with the title. He then explains that with his current diminished intake of wine, the quality of his poems has similarly been diminished and hence his error of omission. He closes his poem with a mock apology to Qing Shan's cohort of self-appointed "court officials": "I apologise for having troubled you gentlemen to patch up my work."

Sheep's Wool Grows Only on a Sheep

The final exchange is between Qing Shan and his childhood friend Lin Yuan Tang who has also composed a poem for the birthday of Qing Shan's wife. He and Yuan Tang grew up together and Yuan Tang had been married for 40 years. Although Qing Shan was a year older than Yuan Tang, Qing Shan has only been married for 32 years compared with Yuan Tang's 40. Yuan Tang had a photo taken with his wife to commemorate their wool wedding anniversary (in 1924). In 1956, Yuan Tang sent Qing Shan this photo and another more current photo taken with all his family to commemorate their 40th wedding anniversary. Yuan Tang sent these photos to Qing Shan together with a poem he had written for his wife. Qing Shan is touched by the deep bond and love between husband and wife which comes clearly through in the poem. He replies with a poem praising him and his wife for the blessing of 40 years they have enjoyed together (see Chapter 31). Qing Shan's poem contains a number of interesting metaphors and puns. It is interesting to see him use the metaphor "seven-year itch" which, out of decorum, he changes to "seven-year disease". Qing Shan obviously knows this expression and notion comes from the West when he says, *"The European culture has gradually pervaded the entire land of the East. One no longer has to be a famous talented scholar in order to be 'Bohemian'."* The metaphor "seven-year itch" became even more in vogue after the 1955 movie of the same name starring Marilyn Monroe. Qing Shan seems pleased with his pun on a popular Chinese saying, *"Sheep's wool grows only on the body of a sheep"*, and the fact that Yuan Tang was born in the year of the sheep. What triggers off the pun on the word "wool" is the photograph taken on his wool wedding anniversary given to Qing Shan. The Chinese saying means that Yuan Tang's blessing of 40 years with his wife has not been merely fortuitous; their happiness comes only because they seek it and work on it. The final part of the poem brings back a flood of memories to Qing Shan. On Yuan Tang's wedding night 40 years before, Qing Shan was himself in some old ship sailing south towards Nanyang on his first trip away from his native land in China.

Zhou and Shang Bronze Ware of Antiquity

This lengthy seven-paragraph epilogue closes with one of the most beautiful thoughts written by Qing Shan. This final paragraph opens with a quote from Bai Juyi who disdains being constrained by some rigid model of what constitutes good poetry, saying, *"There is no such thing as the right cadence and rhyme. Whatever that pleases the ears is music enough; whatever that pleases the eyes is beautiful".* Despite all that has been said, the poems received for his wife's birthday must have been of discernibly different standards. Qing Shan is saying it does not really matter so long as it sounds good to him and he seems to have enjoyed the poems when he says, "As I recite them aloud, the words resonate in my mouth. My wife who is listening by my side too enjoys the music of the poetry, with every sound coming straight from the heart". The spontaneity, sincerity and the "music" of the poems are more important than any rigid rule for their composition. The highlight of this epilogue is his concluding lines:

> "Delighted as I am with the music of the poems, I shall compile them, publish them and bind them exquisitely, place them in brocade-lined boxes and store them with fragrant scent, to leave behind for my descendants as a family treasure for all time. My children and grandchildren may not know how to read them, but they can look upon them as Zhou and Shang bronze ware of antiquity to be revered and treasured all the same."

His metaphor of "Zhou and Shang bronze ware of antiquity" to describe his classical poems is most appropriate. True, the ordinary person does not understand what these objects of antiquity are all about, but they revere and treasure them nevertheless. Qing Shan's love and passion for classical poems come out touchingly through these words. He does not expect his descendants will be able to read or understand them, but if they can at least revere and treasure them—that will be enough!

Index of Allusions Used in the Poems

- There are 400 entries in this Index. The first two columns displayed are: "Pinyin" pronunciation and the "Chinese text" of the allusions that are found in the original poem, appearing in both the English and Chinese editions *A Scholar's Path* and 《晴山古道》 respectively.
- The third column "Reference" shows the chapter number (with the note number in brackets), in which an explanation of the allusion can be found in Chinese in the Chinese edition 《晴山古道》. The asterisk* against the chapter number indicates that the allusion is also explained in English in *A Scholar's Path* (mostly in the Appreciation section).
- Where more than one chapter number appear against an entry, it means the allusion appears in more than one poem or Chapter.
- Readers who are familiar with the Chinese language are invited to cross-refer to the companion Chinese edition.

Pinyin Pronunciation	Chinese Text	Reference
B		
bā rén (xia li bā rén)	巴人（下里巴人）	43(6)
bái bì zhī xiá	白璧之瑕	29(13)
bǎi huā qí fàng	百花齐放	41*(3)
bǎi shì fēi	百事非	25*(3)
bǎi wú yì jiù (bǎi wú yì yòng)	百无一就（百无一用）	10(2)

bào biàn (jūn zi bào biàn)	豹变（君子豹变）	62(2)
běi táng (běi táng xuān)	北堂（北堂萱）	38*(2)
bēi zhōng wù	杯中物	46(6)
bì luó (bì lì、nǚ luó)	薜萝（薜荔、女萝）	16(2)
bì qiú (jīn jìn qiú bì)	蔽裘（金尽裘蔽）	61*(6)
bō lǐ (bō lǐ xī)	百里（百里奚）	49*(10)
bó shān (bó shān lú)	博山（博山炉）	6*(8)
bǔ què	补阙	35(3)
bú zàn yì cí	不赞一词	29(6)

C

cài gēn	菜根	19(8)
cǎi yī (cǎi yī yú qīn)	彩衣（彩衣娱亲）	18(4)、49(2)
cāng sāng	沧桑	31*(5)、47(2)
cāng shēng yǔ	苍生雨	32*(2)
cè zhàng	策杖	42(5)
cháng ān	长安	23*(6)
cháng hóng (qì guàn cháng hóng)	长虹（气贯长虹）	59(4)
chàng suí	唱随	63(26)
cháng xiù (cháng xiù shàn wǔ)	长袖（长袖善舞）	61*(6)
chēng shāng (chēng shāng shàng shòu)	称觞（称觞上寿）	13(1)、18(5)
chǐ qì	侈气	29(10)
chǔ cái jìn yòng	楚材晋用	51*(10)
chú gǒu	刍狗	43(8)
chuán bǐ	椽笔	18(1)、44(8)
chuī máo qiú cī	吹毛求疵	29(12)
chuí qīng (qīng chuí)	垂青（青垂）	48(15)
chuí shēn	垂绅	32*(5)
chuī wàn bù tóng	吹万不同	63(37)
chūn cán	春蚕	52(11)
chūn jiǔ	春酒	21*(2)
cóng xīn suǒ yù	从心所欲	49(4)
cuī yǔ shī	催雨诗	58*(4)
cuī zhuāng gǎo (cuī zhuāng shī)	催妆稿（催妆诗）	24*(1)
cuō tuó jiāng shòu bǔ	蹉跎将寿补	25*(7)

D

dà jiàng	大匠	39(4)
dà jīng	大鲸	45(1)
dà kuài duǒ yí	大快朵颐	9(8)

dà kuài wén zhāng	大块文章	46(1)
dà qiān shì jiè	大千世界	37*(2)
dá rén	达人	52*(14)
dà rén hǔ biàn	大人虎变	62(2)
dà zhì dà nián	大智大年	42*(1)
dài yuè	带月	8(1)
dān qīng	丹青	45(2)
dāng lú	当炉	8*(6)
dé yú wàng quán	得鱼忘筌	43*(11)
dì huá (táng dì zhī huá)	棣华（棠棣之华）	21(4)
dí miàn	觌面	51(4)
dì xiāng	帝乡	15(13)
diào dǐng nai	调鼎鼐	59*(6)
dīng nián	丁年	62(9)
dōng fāng shuò	东方朔	9*(9)
dōng lí	东篱	46*(3)
dòu mǐ	斗米	55*(2)
duàn hè xù fú	断鹤续凫	63(38)
dūn dūn	墩墩	52*(20)
duō cáng hòu wáng	多藏厚亡	63(16)
duǒ yí (dà kuài duǒ yí)	朵颐（大快朵颐）	9(8)

E

èr máo	二毛	12(8)
èr shù (èr shù wèi nüè)	二竖（二竖为虐）	50(9)
èr yǒu (shū tōng èr yǒu)	二酉（书通二酉）	43(4)

F

fā bù	发菩	43(19)
fàn hòu bīng láng	饭后槟榔	18*(11)
fǎn rì lǔ gē (lǔ yáng huī gē)	反日鲁戈（鲁阳挥戈）	36*(3)
fēi qióng	飞琼	44(4)
fēi yàn	飞燕	9*(4)
fēng chén sān xiá	风尘三侠	48*(2)
fú píng	浮萍	19(2)
fú shēng rú mèng (fú shēng ruò mèng)	浮生如梦（浮生若梦）	37(3)
fù sì	腹笥	15*(11)
fù yán	妇言	30(3)
fú yú	扶余	48(3)
fū zi	夫子	63(27)

Index of Allusions Used in the Poems

G

gān zhǐ	甘旨	15(4)
gāo huāng (bìng rù gāo huāng)	膏肓（病入膏肓）	50(9)
gāo huǒ zī	膏火资	15*(3)
gēng cí	赓词	4*(5)
gōu qú (wěi gōu qú)	沟渠（委沟渠）	50(5)
gòu zhōng	彀中	59*(2)
gǔ pén gē	鼓盆歌	52*(19)
gū shān	孤山	55*(4)
gǔ xī	古稀	49*(5)
gù yǐng zì lián	顾影自怜	20(5)、37(5)
guǎn chéng (guǎn chéng zi)	管城（管城子）	60(1)
guǎn zhòng jī	管仲姬	47*(10)
guǎng shà	广厦	56*(4)
gǔn zhí	衮职	35*(2)
guó sè (guó sè tiān xiāng)	国色（国色天香）	39*(2)
guò xì jū guāng (bái jū guò xì)	过隙驹光（白驹过隙）	20*(2)
guò yǎn yān	过眼烟	20*(2)

H

hǎi jīng	海鲸	45(1)
hán bǔ (hán bǔ gǔ fù)	含哺（含哺鼓腹）	16*(5)
hán méi (yǔ lǐng hán méi)	寒梅（庾岭寒梅）	30*(5)
hán xiào jǔ huá (hán yīng jǔ huá)	含笑咀华（含英咀华）	15(10)
hé hūn pǔ	合婚谱	24*(3)
hé jìng (lín hé jìng)	和靖（林和靖）	55(3)
hé yùn	和韵	25*(1)
hóng chén	红尘	50(10)
hóng yǐng (xuě ní hóng zhǎo)	鸿影（雪泥鸿爪）	20(4)
hǔ biàn (dà rén hǔ biàn)	虎变（大人虎变）	62(2)
hú gōng	壶公	56*(2)
hú hǎi qì	湖海气	30*(1)
hú shān	湖山	48*(12)
hù xī	瓠犀	6*(2)
hù yǒu	户牖	43*(14)
huá fēng sān zhù	华封三祝	63(12)
huā jiǎ	花甲	18*(7)
huà méi	画眉	5*(7)、6*(9)、24*(4)、26*(1)、47*(7)
huáng dào chén	黄道辰	50(6)
huáng liǎn (huáng liǎn pó)	黄脸（黄脸婆）	31*(3)

huí tiān (huí tiān fá shù)	回天（回天乏术）	46(7)
hùn dùn	混沌	52(16)
huò lín (huò lín xī shòu)	获麟（获麟西狩）	59*(8)

J

jí jiù (jí jiù zhāng)	急就（急就章）	4*(3)
jī jué	剞劂	61(10)
jī lín (jī lín jiǎ)	鸡林（鸡林贾）	19(9)、34*(3)、44*(10)、57(6)
jí mén (jí mén dì zǐ)	及门（及门弟子）	27*(4)
jì shēn (rén shēng rú jì)	寄身（人生如寄）	37(1)
jì zhì	萋制	12*(6)
jià yī shang	嫁衣裳	47*(5)、48(11)
jiāng bǐ (jiāng yān bǐ)	江笔（江淹笔）	36(2)
jiàng wéi	绛帷	62(13)
jiàng zhì rǔ shēn	降志辱身	51*(9)
jié huī	劫灰	52(16)
jié xí	结习	5(5)
jīn jìn qiú bì	金尽裘蔽	61*(6)
jīn shēng zhì de	金声掷地	54(5)、58(7)
jīn shí yán (jīn shí liáng yán)	金石言（金石良言）	52(9)
jīn wū (jīn wū cáng jiāo)	金屋（金屋藏娇）	23*(4)
jǐn yī yè xíng	锦衣夜行	17*(3)
jìng luán	镜鸾	50(13)
jìng yóu xīn zào	境由心造	56(3)
jiǔ tiān	九天	8(2)
jiǔ zhōu	九州	42*(7)
jǔ àn (jǔ àn qí méi)	举案（举案齐眉）	12(2)、15*(9)、47*(13)
jū jī	居积	61(4)
jù làng pái kōng	巨浪排空	46(4)
jū qí (qí huò kě jū)	居奇（奇货可居）	9(3)、34*(4)
jù qín měi xīn	剧秦美新	41*(4)
jù wú bà	巨毋霸	56(6)
jūn zi bào biàn	君子豹变	62(2)

K

kǎo jì	考绩	29(3)
kē jiù	窠臼	43*(15)
kǒu chén zhǐ huà	口陈指画	62(12)
kuài zhì	脍炙	15*(5)
kuí yì zú (yì kuí)	夔一足（一夔）	49*(9)

L

lán gān	阑干	50(1)
lán tíng yǎ jí	兰亭雅集	58*(1)
láng dāng	琅珰	53*(3)
lǎo lái (lǎo lái zi)	老莱（老莱子）	52(6)
láo yàn	劳燕	25*(2)
lí gē	骊歌	27*(6)
lí huò	藜藿	13(1)、19(7)
lí qún suǒ jū	离群索居	41(1)
lì wǎn kuáng lán	力挽狂澜	46(5)
lǐ zàn	礼赞	6(1)
lián lǐ (lián lǐ zhī)	连理（连理枝）	47*(9)
lián yín (lián jù)	联吟（联句）	27*(1)
liǎng suō	两梭	36*(1)
liáng yào kǔ kǒu	良药苦口	52(10)
liáo dōng mào (zào mào)	辽东帽（皂帽）	51(8)
lín hé jìng	林和靖	55*(3)
lín qí	临歧	29(4)
lín qióng	临邛	8*(7)
líng yún	凌云	41*(5)
lù bù	露布	26(2)
lù jū (lù jū gòng wǎn)	鹿车（鹿车共挽）	48(5)、49(11)、56*(14)
lǔ gē (lǔ yáng huī gē)	鲁戈（鲁阳挥戈）	36*(3)
lǔ lián (lǔ zhòng lián)	鲁连（鲁仲连）	44*(6)、57*(2)
lún xū	沦胥	54(1)
lún yīn (lún yán)	纶音（纶言）	35*(1)
lún zhǐ	轮指	63(26)
luò mò	落寞	7(15)

M

mǎ chǐ	马齿	43(21)
mǎ zhàng	马帐	8*(3)
mài guā hòu	卖瓜侯	42*(8)
mǎi shān	买山	56(10)
mán yān zhàng yǔ	蛮烟瘴雨	50*(4)
mào lín (mào lín xiū zhú)	茂林（茂林修竹）	58*(13)
méi hè (méi qī hè zi)	梅鹤（梅妻鹤子）	55(3)
měi xīn	美新	41*(4)、57*(7)
mèng guāng	孟光	13*(2)、47(13)、48(10)

mǐ jiā chuán	米家船	44*(11)
mí wú	蘼芜	12*(5)、38(1)
miàn yú (miàn yú bèi huǐ)	面谀（面谀背毁）	61(3)
miǎo gōng	藐躬	52(4)
miào táng	庙堂	16(3)
míng shān yè	名山业	57(5)
míng shì fēng liú	名士风流	31*(2)
mò chóu	莫愁	38*(4)
mó suō	摩挲	7(2)、14(2)
mù guāng rú jù	目光如炬	44(8)
mù xu (pán zhōng mù xu)	苜蓿（盘中苜蓿）	18*(10)

N

nán shān (shòu bǐ nán shān)	南山（寿比南山）	43(7)
ní lí	泥犁	5*(6)
nì lǚ	逆旅	52(17)
niú yī (niú yī duì qì)	牛衣（牛衣对泣）	8*(4)
nǚ luó	女萝	16(2)

P

pán zhōng mù xu	盘中苜蓿	18(10)
páo rén (páo dīng)	庖人（庖丁）	29*(8)
pāo zhuān yǐn yù	抛砖引玉	13*(3)
péng mén	蓬门	22(3)
péng shāng	彭殇	52(18)
piān piān qún jī	翩翩裙屐	17(1)
piān zhōu	扁舟	55(1)
pín wú lì zhuī	贫无立锥	12(3)
pǒ luó	叵罗	16(1)

Q

qí gǒu	耆耉	43(16)
qì guàn cháng hóng	气贯长虹	59(4)
qí huò (qí huò kě jū)	奇货（奇货可居）	9(3)、34*(4)
qǐ luó xiāng	绮罗香	22(3)
qí méi	齐眉	12(2)、15(9)、47(13)
qī qī	戚戚	61(9)
qǐ qiǎo zhēn	乞巧针	10*(4)
qǐ yǔ	绮语	5*(5)
qián jù hòu gōng	前倨后恭	62(4)
qián lóu (qián lóu qī)	黔娄（黔娄妻）	12*(1)、52*(3)

Index of Allusions Used in the Poems 591

qiè zhǒu	挈肘	29(11)
qín jiā	秦嘉	52*(2)
qín sè yǒu	琴瑟友	42(3)
qīng chuí (chuí qīng)	青垂（垂青）	48(15)
qīng niǎo	青鸟	1*(1)、26*(4)、50*(3)
qīng zhān (qīng zhān gù wù)	青毡（青毡故物）	18(12)
qiú qí	蝤蛴	6*(4)
qiú shàn jià (qiú shàn jiǎ)	求善价（求善贾）	34(6)
qiū shuǐ chūn shān	秋水春山	37*(4)
qiú tián wèn shě	求田问舍	42*(2)、56(9)
qū qū (qū qū zhī xīn)	区区（区区之心）	29(15)
qū shuǐ liú shāng	曲水流觞	58(12)
què shàn shī	却扇诗	24*(2)

R

rǎn zhǐ	染指	15(8)
rǎng bì	攘臂	63(17)
rě cǎo zhān huā (zhān huā rě cǎo)	惹草沾花（沾花惹草）	6*(7)
rèn lán	纫兰	12(6)
róng xī (róng xī zhī ān)	容膝（容膝之安）	56*(5)
ròu shí kě bǐ	肉食可鄙	15(6)
róu yí	柔荑	5*(2)
rú guān wù	儒冠误	10*(1)
rù zhǔ chū nú	入主出奴	62(5)

S

sān hù	三户	42*(6)
sān hū	三呼	63(11)
sān jué	三绝	44(3)
sān rì (shì bié sān rì)	三日（士别三日）	22(4)
sān zhù	三祝	63(12)
shàn shì	善士	63(17)
shān yīn dào	山阴道	58(14)
shàng lùn	尚论	51(2)
sháo hù (sháo hù)	韶護（韶濩）	63(34)
shèn ài dà fèi	甚爱大费	63(15)
shēn wú cháng wù	身无长物	54(3)、61(5)
shēng huā bǐ (shēng huā miào bǐ)	生花笔（生花妙笔）	10*(3)、36*(2)
shèng mǔ	胜母	23*(5)
shì bié sān rì	士别三日	22(4)
shī jīn jié lí (shī jīn jié lí)	施巾结褵（施衿结褵）	11(2)

shí nián shù mù	十年树木	47*(11)
shī piáo	诗瓢	13(2)
shí sān xíng	十三行	4*(4)
shí shì zhuāng	时世妆	47*(3)
shì xìng	适性	15(12)
shí yàn	石焰	58*(6)
shí yàng mán jiān	十样蛮笺	48(7)
shí yí	拾遗	35(3)
shī zi hǒu	狮子吼	43(18)
shòu bǐ nán shān	寿比南山	43(7)
shòu shì	寿世	18(1)、63(9)
shù jī	数奇	52(1)
shū jiāng	输将	34(1)
shū tōng èr yǒu	书通二酉	43(4)
shuāng shòu	双寿	49(1)
shuò guǒ jǐn cún	硕果仅存	41(2)
sōng yuè sān hū	嵩岳三呼	63(11)
sù é	素娥	3(1)
sù gēn	宿根	5*(3)

T

tài qīng	太清	44(4)
táng ào	堂奥	43(13)
tāo huì	韬晦	49(8)
táo lǐ (táo lǐ bù yán)	桃李（桃李不言）	12*(9)、48(9)
táo lín fàng niú	桃林放牛	42*(10)
táo yuán (táo huā yuán)	桃源（桃花源）	44*(5)、49(12)、56*(11)
tiān hé	天和	16*(5)
tiān mǎ xíng kōng	天马行空	59(3)
tiān xiāng (guó sè tiān xiāng)	天香（国色天香）	39*(3)
tóu bǐ	投笔	8(5)
tóu xiá (tóu xiá liú bīn)	投辖（投辖留宾）	27*(5)

W

wǎ fǔ léi míng	瓦釜雷鸣	45(3)
wǎn kuáng lán	挽狂澜	46(5)
wán shí dī shǒu (wán shí diǎn tóu)	顽石低首（顽石点头）	5*(4)
wàng jī (lè yǐ wàng jī)	忘饥（乐以忘饥）	25*(5)
wáng yáng	亡羊	27*(2)
wàng yáng (wàng yáng xīng tàn)	望洋（望洋兴叹）	48*(13)

wēi chén	微尘	37*(2)
wéi nuò	唯诺	7(19)
wèi yáng	渭阳	19*(12)
wén jūn (zhuó wén jūn)	文君（卓文君）	8*(6)
wèn shě qiú tián	问舍求田	42*(2)
wèn zì (zǎi jiǔ wèn zì)	问字（载酒问字）	27*(4)
wō lú	蜗庐	56*(12)
wú bà (jù wú bà)	毋霸（巨毋霸）	56(6)
wǔ cǎi (cǎi yī yú qīn)	舞彩（彩衣娱亲）	18(4)
wú cháng wù (shēn wú cháng wù)	无长物（身无长物）	54(3)、61(5)
wǔ dū	五都	43*(3)
wǔ gǔ (wǔ gǔ pí)	五羖（五羖皮）	49*(10)
wǔ hú	五湖	55(1)
wǔ shí wú wén	五十无闻	21*(1)
wǔ yī	五噫	47*(8)
wū zuò	兀坐	61(2)

X

xì jūn	细君	9*(9)、15(9)
xī shī	西施	9*(4)、63(35)
xī shòu (xī shòu huò lín)	西狩（西狩获麟）	59*(8)
xī xia	膝下	28(4)
xia li bā rén	下里巴人	43(6)
xiān xiào hòu hào	先笑后号	62(3)
xiǎo gū dú chù	小姑独处	50*(2)
xié yǐn	偕隐	52(6)
xīn cóng suǒ yù (cóng xīn suǒ yù)	心从所欲（从心所欲）	49(4)
xīn fēi shí (xīn fěi shí)	心非石（心匪石）	38*(3)
xìn líng (xìn líng jūn)	信陵（信陵君）	60*(3)
xíng kōng (tiān mǎ xíng kōng)	行空（天马行空）	59(3)
xíng lù nán	行路难	23(2)
xíng rén	行人	50*(15)
xiū mù	休沐	61(1)
xiū xì	修禊	58*(5)
xù chǐ (xù chǐ)	序齿（叙齿）	15(1)、45(4)
xǔ fēi qióng	许飞琼	44(4)
xū huái ruò gǔ	虚怀若谷	63(32)
xuān cǎo	萱草	38*(2)
xuǎn shèng (xuǎn shèng zhēng gē)	选胜（选胜征歌）	17(2)

Y

yǎ jí (lán tíng yǎ jí)	雅集（兰亭雅集）	58*(1)
yán fāng	炎方	42(4)
yán rú yù	颜如玉	14(3)
yàn shǐ	雁使	34*(2)
yáng zǎo	羊枣	15*(5)
yè gōng hào lóng	叶公好龙	59*(1)
yè xíng hái xiāng	夜行还乡	17*(3)
yī bō (yī bō xiāng chuán)	衣钵（衣钵相传）	12(7)、44(2)
yī jǐn hái xiāng	衣锦还乡	22(5)
yì kuí (kuí yì zú)	一夔（夔一足）	49*(9)
yì niǎn (yì niǎn hóng)	一捻（一捻红）	39*(1)
yīn yōu	殷忧	52(7)
yìng zhì	应制	63(36)
yōng dé	庸德	29(16)
yǒng xù (yǒng xù cái)	咏絮（咏絮才）	50(12)
yōng yán	庸言	29(16)
yòu chéng	右丞	44(1)
yòu fù (yòu fù cí)	幼妇（幼妇辞）	13(4)
yòu jūn	右军	44(1)
yǒu xíng	有行	23*(1)
yóu yán chái mǐ	油盐柴米	4*(1)
yù bǎn	玉版	48(14)
yù chǐ	玉尺	18(13)
yù fēng	御风	23(3)
yù hé	遇合	29(1)
yù huán	玉环	9*(4)
yú jì	逾纪	19(5)
yùn dú ér cáng	韫椟而藏	34(5)
yún jiān	云笺	4*(2)
yún ní	云泥	29(2)
yún sì	芸笥	63(40)

Z

zǎi jiǔ wèn zì	载酒问字	27*(4)
zān yīng	簪缨	44(2)
zǎng kuài	驵侩	59(5)
zǎo jìng	藻镜	48(15)
zāo kāng	糟糠	63(29)
zào mào (liáo dōng mào)	皂帽（辽东帽）	51*(8)

zào shì	造士	29(7)
zé nà	则那	16(7)
zhān huā rě cǎo (rě cǎo zhān huā)	沾花惹草（惹草沾花）	6*(7)
zhān ní xù	沾泥絮	6*(6)
zhàng cháo	杖朝	43*(17)
zhàng guó	杖国	49*(6)
zhàng lí	杖藜	51*(8)
zhàng xiāng	杖乡	49*(6)
zhāo qín mù chǔ	朝秦暮楚	62(6)
zhèn lóng (zhèn lóng fā kuì)	振聋（振聋发聩）	58(7)
zhēng gē	征歌	17(2)
zhèng yǒu	诤友	29(14)
zhí huái	植槐	47*(12)
zhī mìng	知命	20*(3)
zhǐ shàng tán bīng	纸上谈兵	60*(2)
zhòng jī	仲姬	47*(10)
zhǒu hòu (zhǒu hòu fāng)	肘后（肘后方）	18(2)
zhú gǒu	竹笱	43(12)
zhū jī	珠玑	63(2)
zhù yán	驻颜	20(4)
zhǔ zì liáo jī	煮字疗饥	15*(7)
zǐ jiàng lún yú	梓匠轮舆	29*(9)
zi xū (zi xū wū yǒu)	子虚（子虚乌有）	41*(5)
zi yún tíng	子云亭	56*(15)
zǒng jiǎo	总角	63(21)
zòu jì	奏记	26(3)、47(6)
zǔ lóng	祖龙	54*(6)、58*(8)
zǔ niǔ	诅忸	43(20)
zuǒ fēn	左芬	18*(14)
zuò jiǎn (zuò jiǎn zì fù)	作茧（作茧自缚）	52(12)
zuò rén	作人	29(7)
zuò yòu míng	座右铭	52(21)

Acknowledgements

We are greatly indebted to many in the writing of this book comprising the English edition *A Scholar's Path* and its companion Chinese edition 《晴山古道》.

We are especially grateful to:

President S R Nathan, President of the Republic of Singapore;
Dr Ng Eng Hen, Minister for Education and Second Minister for Defence, Singapore;
Professor Dr Wang Gungwu, Chairman of the East Asian Institute, National University of Singapore,

for the kind words in their Preface.

Associate Professor Dr Chan Chiu Ming (陈照明) of National Institute of Education, Singapore, for initially providing advice on the interpretation of the poems and later undertaking to singlehandedly write the Chinese edition of the book 《晴山古道》.

Dr Lee Ting Hui (李庭辉) for providing similar scholarly advice to us in the initial years.

Our thanks also go to:

Mr Peh Long Lim (Bai Ling Lang 白玲琅) of Taiping, for the photo and biographical material of his father Bai Yang Feng (白仰峯).

Madam Bai Rui Xue (白瑞雪) of Ipoh and Madam Bai Rui Can (白瑞璨) of Kuala Lumpur for the material on the biography of their father Bai Cheng Gen (白成根).

Madam Jiang Bao Qin (江宝琴) of Kuala Lumpur, an outstanding graduate and later tutor of Mother's tailoring school, for providing many photos of the school's graduation classes.

The late Lin Jing Xin 林井心 of Putian for providing us with the text of Father's poem in Chapter 51.

Professor Dr Wang Gungwu (王赓武) for providing us with material from "A Memorial Collection of Poems, Essays and Calligraphy" of his father Wang Fu Wen (王宓文).

Mr Lin Qi Xian (林启贤) of Putian, Fujian, son of Father's childhood friend Lin Yuan Tang (林远堂), for photos and material from his father's autobiography.

Madam Lu Jing Bin (卢静滨) of Ipoh for her biographical material and photos of herself and the two poems composed and written for her.

Madam Hong Cui Lan (洪翠兰) of Ipoh, daughter of Hong Lu Kuan (洪禄宽), for the material on the biography of her father.

The late Madam Peng Shi Lin (彭士驎) of Ipoh for providing us (before she passed away in 2004), with much of her biographical material and material about Father.

Our cousin Madam Wang Xia Xian (王霞仙) for giving us the manuscripts and papers of her father (our maternal uncle Wang Guang Guo 王光国).

Madam Lin Ai Yu (林爱毓), daughter-in-law of Wang Guang Guo for lending us her graduation class magazine of 1959.

Ms Gertrude Guok (郭玉英) for use of photos and biographical material on her father, the Reverend Canon Guok Koh Muo who was like a brother to Mother in her adoptive family.

Our cousin the late Mr Lin Zhao Lin (林兆麟) of Putian and to our cousin Mr Li Dang Chun (李当春) also of Putian, for helping us trace material concerning Father's stay during his brief return there in the early to mid-1930s.

Our cousins Dr Wang Xing Zhong (王兴中), Madam Wang Shao Li (王少莉), Madam Wang Shao Hua (王少华) of Wuhu, Anhui, for providing many of the biographical anecdotes regarding their father, our maternal uncle Wang Guang Po (王光坡).

Mr Wang Xian Zhi (王先智) of Ipoh for the biographical material on his father Wang Guang Di (王光地) of Mother's Wang clan in Fuqing.

Our elder sisters who enthusiastically joined us in the search for background stories to the poems and provided us with their recollection of our family circumstances.

The National Palace Museum, Taiwan, Republic of China (國立故宮博物院), for permission to use the picture of the late Shang early Zhou ding (商末周初 獸面紋鬲鼎), illustrated on the cover.

Mr Chong Yin Chat (Zhang Ying Jie 张英傑), Chairman of Perak Cave Temple for his kind permission to use material from "The Wonders of Perak Cave Temple" ("霹雳洞大观").

Mr Lee Chin Seng (李金生), former Head of the Chinese Library of National University of Singapore for his ready help in the search for the material and information needed by us.

Mr David Tan Sing Hwa (陈新华) for his uncanny ability in transforming old photos into new for us.

Dr K K Phua (潘国驹), Chairman of World Scientific Publishing Company for his continued interest in the promotion of bilingual publications and to the staff who worked on the book: in particular to the Editor Ms Ho Wei Ling (何玮琳); to Mr Jimmy Low (刘济琛) who designed the beautiful front and back covers of the book.

Ms Ming Bong (杨明群) for her meticulous proof reading of the entire English edition, sparing no effort in her careful poring over the manuscript, tolerating but few transgressions in the use of the language.

www.ingramcontent.com/pod-product-compliance
Lightning Source LLC
Chambersburg PA
CBHW050522300426
44113CB00012B/1924